THEORETICAL

AND

PRACTICAL

PHONETICS

HENRY ROGERS
University of Toronto

Copp Clark Pitman Ltd.
A Longman Company
Toronto

ISBN 0-7730-5038-8

Executive editor: Brian Henderson
Editor: Brenda Clews
Design and Cover: Joanne Slauenwhite

Canadian Cataloging in Publication Data

Rogers, Henry E. (Henry Edwin), 1940-
  Theoretical and practical phonetics

Includes bibliographical references and index.
ISBN 0-7730-5038-8

1. Phonetics. 2. English language - Phonetics
I. Title.

P221.R63 1991   414   C91-093609-9

An honest attempt has been made to secure permission for all material used, and if there are errors or omissions, these are wholly unintentional and the Publisher will be grateful to learn of them.

Copp Clark Pitman Ltd.
2775 Matheson Blvd. East
Mississauga, Ontario,, L4W 4P7

Associated companies:
  Longman Group Ltd., London
  Longman Inc., New York
  Longman Cheshire Pty., Melbourne
  Longman Paul Pty., Auckland

Printed and bound in Canada
  3 4 5   5038–8   95

Διονυσίῳ

CONTENTS

A INTRODUCTION

1 Introduction	1
2 The Basic Sounds of English	15
3 English Consonants	33
4 English Vowels	55
5 English Suprasegmentals	72
6 English Dialect Differences	88
7 The Sounds of French	107

B ACOUSTIC PHONETICS AND DISTINCTIVE FEATURES

8 Sound Waves, Spectra, and Resonance	124
9 The Acoustics of English Sounds	139
10 Features	164

C GENERAL PHONETICS

11 Vowels and Semivowels	178
12 Place of Articulation	199
13 Manner of Articulation	222
14 Phonation	238
15 Airstream Mechanisms	256
16 Syllables and Suprasegmentals	270
17 Hearing and Perception	294

D APPENDICES

A English Consonantal Allophones	306
B Glossary	312
C Calligraphy	335
D Chomsky–Halle Features	354
E Phonetic Charts	359

BIBLIOGRAPHY	366
INDEX	374

PREFACE

Most people have little idea about phonetics. Commonly it is confused with phonics, a system for teaching children to read. In buying this book, obviously you have some interest in the subject. So what are you in for?

Phonetics is the scientific study of sounds used in language. Since you must be familiar with English to use this book at all, we begin our study with English. As this book is aimed at the Canadian reader, we refer to Canadian English. In particular, we are interested in how the sounds of English are made. What do we do with our bodies to produce each different sound? After examining the sounds of Canadian English in Chapters 1–5, we look at various other dialects of English from around the world in Chapter 6. To round out our Canadian view, Chapter 7 examines French, particularly Canadian French.

In Chapters 8 and 9, we turn to how sound can be studied in the laboratory. We will look at acoustic notions such as sound waves and spectrograms. Chapter 10 introduces us to phonetic features and to feature geometry, an important area of the neighbouring discipline of phonology.

With a good grip on English and on acoustics, we then broaden our scope to include any language (Chapters 11–16). Obviously, we cannot examine all the 5000 or so languages in the world, but we will be looking at a wide variety of languages from all parts of the globe. Chapter 17 concludes our study with an examination of how we hear and perceive sound.

The components of phonetics are interconnected. By looking at English and French first, we get a general overview of the field of phonetics. Then, when we look at other languages, we have a framework to place new information and ideas.

Phonetics uses a large number of technical terms. When these occur, they are in **bold face**. Each chapter has a list of technical terms at the end, and they are all collected and defined in the Glossary (Appendix B). The pronunciation of each term is given as it is introduced and in the glossary.

Appendix C on Calligraphy shows you how to write symbols in a way that others can recognise.

The International Phonetic Alphabet (IPA) is used in this book and is widely used by phoneticians, linguists, and speech pathologists around the world. The latest version (1989) is included in Appendix E.

Appendix A on consonant allophones and Appendix D on Chomsky–Halle features relate to Chapters 3 and 10 respectively.

An important feature of this book is the importance it lays on developing the practical skills of learning to produce various sounds. Every chapter contains extensive exercises at the end. These are divided into two parts: basic and advanced. The basic exercises help you learn to produce the sounds just covered in the chapter. The advanced exercises are cumulative, developing your ability to produce new sounds in combination with ones you already know, and they are more difficult, pushing you towards ever greater lingual dexterity.

The exercises of Chapter 1 give some general advice on how to practise making sounds. Throughout the book, hints and tips are given that have helped others learn to pronounce the various sounds. No book can really teach you practical phonetics. Only close listening and practice can do that. This book will, however, help you do the things necessary for improving your phonetic ability.

Phonetics is for many people a fascinating subject in its own right. Most people who study phonetics, however, do so for its theoretical and practical value. Students of linguistics have to understand how language is spoken, and they have to be reasonably proficient at producing a wide variety of sounds. In speech pathology and audiology, phonetics is crucial. Before a person with a speech problem can be helped, we have to be able to pinpoint what exactly is going wrong in that person's pronunciation and what steps can be taken for improvement. These tasks are clearly phonetic ones.

The usefulness of phonetics in studying another language is obvious. In my experience, people with a background in phonetics have a clear advantage over others in language classes. For example, if you read that 'in Chinese, retroflex approximants are unrounded', you can translate this to 'smile when you say an /r/' and accordingly sound better than your fellow students. Phonetics is also useful for actors, who need to be able to reproduce various accents. They will find Chapter 6 which examines English of various accents useful, as well as the exercises that give examples of how English was spoken in the past — by Chaucer, Shakespeare, and Sir Walter Scott.

The title of this book *Theoretical and Practical Phonetics* emphasises its dual goal: that you acquire a thorough grounding in the theory of phonetics, and that you develop the practical ability to use that theoretical knowledge. I hope that you will find the study of phonetics as enjoyable as I do and as useful as my students have found it over the years.

A great many people have helped me in writing this book. I am very grateful to them all: to Jack Chambers, Brenda Clews, Michael Dobrovolsky, Dennis Helm, and an anonymous reviewer who all read various earlier versions of the manuscript; to Ed Burstynsky, Marshall Chasin, Pierre Léon, Keren Rice, and Yves Roberge who read various chapters; to Laura Labonté-Smith who made many of the spectrograms; to Mike McClean, Peter Reich, Christine Rickards, and Paula Square-Storer who were generous with the use of equipment and facilities; to Brian Henderson for his initial encouragement and continuing support; and to my students for their patience and inspiration. I am grateful to the International Phonetic Association for permission to reprint the chart of the International Phonetic Alphabet found in Appendix E.

Linguists are sometimes a bit awkward socially. After listening to someone's learned dinner-table disquisition on current and eternal verities, we are apt, quite innocently, to say 'What an interesting vowel you have there!' I would not wish to create social difficulties for anyone, but I do hope that this book conveys some of the charm, fun, and intellectual intrigue that are to be found in listening to how we humans talk.

CHAPTER ONE
INTRODUCTION

Every day we hear many types of sounds: bells ringing, machinery clunking, dogs barking, leaves rustling, people talking. The science of **acoustics** /əˈkustɪks/ studies sounds in general, and **phonetics** /fəˈnɛtɪks/ studies the sounds used in human language. Phonetics is part of the wider field of **linguistics** /ˌlɪŋˈgwɪstɪks/ which studies language as a whole.

Phonetics is concerned with the sounds we make in speech: how we produce them, how these sounds are transferred from the speaker to the hearer as sound waves, and how we hear and perceive them. Several thousand languages are spoken in the world; obviously we cannot look at the sounds of each one of them. We will examine English in detail first because it is the language that you are all familiar with; this will be followed by a look at French. Then we will survey the kinds of sounds found in languages all over the world.

In this chapter you will learn about:
- the basic fields of phonetics
- the anatomy of the parts of the body used in making sounds
- how to determine where in your mouth a sound is made.

The chapters in this book end with exercises which will enable you to practise the material covered. The basic portion of the exercises allows you to practise the sounds which have just been presented in that chapter. The advanced exercises include more difficult material, and they are cumulative, reviewing sounds already studied and incorporating the new material.

Phonetics involves a large number of technical terms. As new terms are discussed, they are shown in **bold-face type**. At the end of each chapter is a list of technical terms, and Appendix B presents a complete glossary of technical terms. These terms are essential to being able to talk about phonetics. Later work will go much more easily if you make a point now of learning each term as it occurs; it is helpful, as well, to learn related terms as part of a set. The pronunciation of unfamiliar terms is given between slant lines, *e.g.,* /fə'nɛtɪks/. At the moment, you may not understand these transcriptions, but don't worry; they will be explained in Chapter 2.

THE STUDY OF PHONETICS

BRANCHES OF PHONETICS

ARTICULATORY PHONETICS   The branch of phonetics dealing with the production of sounds is called **articulatory phonetics** /ˌɑɹ'tɪkjələˌtoɹi/. In speech, air passes through a complex passageway consisting of the lungs, the windpipe, the vocal cords, the throat, the mouth, and the nose. In order to describe how sounds are made, we must become familiar with the various parts of our anatomy which are involved in speech production. We will also learn how we change the shape of the vocal organs to make different sounds.

ACOUSTIC PHONETICS   From physics, we know that sound is trans-mitted by vibrations in the air. **Acoustic phonetics** /ə'kustɪk/ studies the vi-brations of speech sounds. With instruments in the laboratory, we can observe and measure various aspects of sound. In Chapters 8 and 9, we will learn how these measurements and observations can be used to widen our understanding of human speech.

AUDITORY PHONETICS   **Auditory phonetics** /'ɑdɪˌtoɹi/ is the study of how sounds are heard and perceived. This area is not so well understood as the other branches of phonetics. Nevertheless, in Chapter 17, we will look at what is presently known about the process of converting vibrations in the air into something which we perceive as speech.

ARTICULATORY PHONETICS

We now begin our study of articulatory phonetics with an examination of the **vocal organs,** the parts of the body used in producing speech. The lungs start the process of speech production by pushing air upwards. The vocal cords, which are located in the neck behind the adam's apple, may vibrate, causing the air that flows between them to vibrate as well. The vibrating airstream is then modified according to the shape of the **vocal tract**—the throat, mouth, and nasal cavity. By moving our tongue and lips, we can produce a large number of modifications on the vibrating air stream, and thus, a wide variety of sounds.

A bicycle horn provides a simple model of how speech sounds are produced. In the bicycle horn, air is pushed out when the bulb is squeezed. The reed located just past the bulb sets the air in vibration as the air passes across the reed. Finally, the air passes through through the flared tube, the 'horn' proper, which gives a particular quality to the sound. In our body, the lungs are the bulb, pushing the air

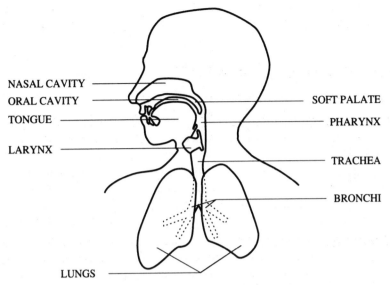

NASAL CAVITY
ORAL CAVITY
TONGUE
LARYNX

SOFT PALATE
PHARYNX

TRACHEA

BRONCHI

LUNGS

Figure 1.1 The primary vocal organs

out. The vocal cords are the reed, setting the air in vibration. The vocal tract is the 'horn' giving speech its particular quality. One important difference is that the bicycle horn can produce only one sound. The human vocal tract can be altered in hundreds of ways to produce a large variety of sounds.

We will now look at the various parts of the vocal organs. In a number of cases, the Latin or Greek name is normally used in phonetics. These terms are given as they are needed. You should become familiar with the anatomy and terminology of the vocal mechanism. This is basic information which will be used throughout the book. Figure 1.1 shows the position of the primary vocal organs.

LUNGS

The **lungs** are cone-shaped structures in the chest composed of spongy, elastic material. The lungs consist of small air sacs, or **alveoli** /ˌælˈviəli/ (sg. **alveolus** /ˌælˈviələs/), where oxygen from the fresh air is exchanged for carbon dioxide in the blood. When the lungs are expanded, air is drawn in; and when they are compressed, air is expelled. Certain muscles enlarge the chest cavity causing air to flow in; other muscles make the chest cavity smaller causing air to flow out. We have a considerable amount of control over the rate of breathing. When speaking, we breathe in fairly quickly and then expel the air more slowly. In English, all speech is made as the air flows out of the body; that is, English speakers do not ordinarily talk while breathing in.

TRACHEA

The small tubes of the lungs repeatedly merge with each other forming larger tubes until they form two large tubes called **bronchi** /ˈbɹɑŋki/, (sg. **bronchus** /ˈbɹɑŋkəs/), one leading out of the left lung and one bronchus out of the right lung. The two bronchi merge into a single vertical tube called the **trachea** /ˈtɹejkiə/, or windpipe. The top of the trachea is just behind the notch at the top of your breastbone. In speech, the bronchi and trachea function simply as tubes to carry the air in and out of the lungs.

LARYNX

The **larynx** /ˈleɹɪŋks/ is a structure made of several cartilages held together by ligaments and supporting several muscles; it is roughly cylindrical in shape and rests on top of the trachea. The front part of your larynx, known as the **adam's apple** sticks out in front. The **vocal cords** (note the spelling, not *chords)* lie inside the larynx, just behind the point of the adam's apple. They are two horizontal bands of ligament and muscle, lying across the air passage; they can open and close, acting as a valve for air coming from the lungs. The opening between the vocal cords is called the **glottis** /ˈglɑtɪs/; the word **glottal** /ˈglɑtəl/ is used to describe activities of the vocal cords. (The adjective for larynx is **laryngeal** /ləˈɹɪndʒəl/.) The portion below the vocal cords is called **subglottal** /ˈsʌbˌglɑtəl/; the portion above the larynx is called **supralaryngeal** /ˌsupɹələˈɹɪndʒəl/

The vocal cords can be adjusted in various ways to give different acoustic effects. When you hold your breath with your mouth open, you close your vocal cords, thus preventing air from leaving or entering the lungs. In phonetics, this act is called a **glottal stop**.

Many sounds in speech are made with the vocal cords separated. As air passes through the opening between the separated vocal cords, a slight friction-like noise is heard. If you make a long /h/— /hhhhhhhhhhh/—, you will hear this noise. This glottal adjustment is called voiceless. Many sounds in English are made with the vocal cords in the voiceless position.

Another adjustment of the vocal cords is also quite common. Try saying a vowel sound such as *ah.* Say it out loud; don't whisper. Your vocal cords are close enough that the air passing between them causes vibrations. While you are making the vowel, place your fingers lightly on your adam's apple. You will feel a vibration. The vibration you feel is known as **voicing**. Try saying the vowel again, but this time with both of your hands over your ears. Now you will hear the voicing as a buzzing sound. When you said the vowel, your vocal cords were vibrating. In English, all vowels and a large number of consonants are made with voicing; sounds made with voicing are called **voiced**. Try saying a long /sssssss/ and then a long /zzzzzzz/. Put you hands over your ears while you do this; you can hear that the /zzzzzzz/ has the buzz of voicing; the /ssssss/ does not have this buzz and is voiceless. Try the same experiment with /vvvvvvv/ and /fffffff/; determine which is voiced and which is voiceless.

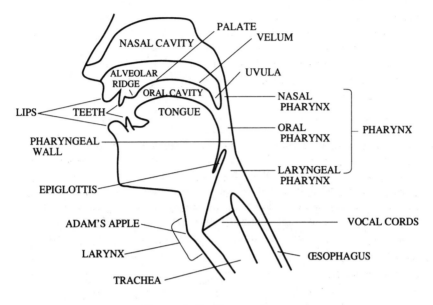

Figure 1.2 The vocal tract

PHARYNX

The **pharynx** /ˈfeɹɪŋks/ is the technical name for the throat, a vertical tube leading up from the larynx. From Figure 1.2, you can see that the pharynx goes up from the larynx past the mouth to the nasal cavity. If you look in the mirror, lower your tongue and say *ah,* you can see the back of your throat or **pharyngeal wall** /fəˈɹɪndʒəl/. The pharynx serves primarily as a tube connecting the larynx with the oral and nasal cavities. It can be divided into three parts as shown in Figure 1.2: the **oral pharynx**, at the back of the mouth, the **nasal pharynx**, leading into the nasal cavity, and the **laryngeal pharynx**, just above the vocal cords.

ORAL CAVITY

The **mouth**, or **oral cavity**, is extremely important in the production of speech sounds. By altering the shape of the mouth, we can produce a large number of different sounds. The various points in the oral cavity are referred to as **articulators** /ɑɹˈtɪkjəˌlejtəɹ/. The **upper articulators** are the upper lip, upper teeth, the upper surface of the mouth, and the pharyngeal wall. The **lower articulators** are the lower lip, lower teeth, and tongue. When we speak, a lower articulator **articulates** with an upper articulator when it is positioned so as to form an obstruction to the air passage.

Figure 1.3 Bilabial.   **Figure 1.4** Labio-dental.

LIPS The outermost articulators are the **lips**. They commonly articulate with each other to form **bilabial** /ˌbajˈlejbiəl/ sounds (Figure 1.3). Another common articulation occurs when the lower lip articulates with the upper teeth to form **labio-dental** /ˌlejbiˌiˈoˈdɛntəl/ sounds (Figure 1.4). In English, the initial sounds in *pea, bee,* and *me* are bilabial consonants; the initial sounds in *fee* and *vow* are labio-dental consonants.

TEETH Sounds made with the forward part of the tongue articulating with the upper teeth are called **dental** (Figure 1.5). (The upper teeth also articulate with the lower lip, as mentioned above, to form labio-dental sounds.) In English, *thin* and *then* begin with dental consonants.

ALVEOLAR RIDGE Just behind the upper teeth, there is a bumpy area known as the **alveolar ridge** /ˌælˈviələɹ/. Put the tip of your tongue against your upper teeth and pull it slowly back. You will likely feel the alveolar ridge between the teeth and the hard palate, although a few people do not have a noticeable ridge. Sounds made here are called **alveolar** (Figure 1.6). In English, *doe, toe, no, so, zoo,* and *low* begin with alveolar consonants.

Other sounds in this area are possible. **Palato-alveolar** /ˌpæləˌtoˌælˈviələɹ/ sounds (Figure 1.7) are made with the blade of the tongue articulating at the back of the

Figure 1.5 Dental.   **Figure 1.6** Alveolar.

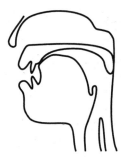

Figure 1.7 Palato-alveolar.

Figure 1.8 Retroflex.

alveolar ridge and the front of the tongue raised towards the palate. (These parts of the tongue are shown in detail in Figure 1.12.) In English, *she, cheese,* and *judge,* begin with palato-alveolar consonants; also, the middle sound in *pleasure* is palato-alveolar. **Retroflex** /ˈɹɛtɹəˌflɛks/ (Figure 1.8) sounds are made with the tip of the tongue curled back to articulate with the area at the back of the alveolar ridge; in English, *red* begins with a retroflex consonant for many speakers.

PALATE The hard palate is a thinly covered bony structure forming the forward part of the roof of the mouth. In phonetics, the hard palate is normally referred to simply as the **palate** /ˈpælɪt/. It extends from the alveolar ridge to the soft palate (velum). Sounds made in this area with the front of the tongue are called **palatal** /ˈpælətəl/ (Figure 1.9). In English, *yes* begins with a palatal sound.

VELUM The soft palate is the rear portion of the roof of the mouth unsupported by bone. If your move your tongue along the hard palate towards the back of your mouth, the texture suddenly becomes soft and flaccid; this soft area is the soft palate. In phonetics it is normally referred to as the **velum** /ˈviləm/. This is short for the longer Latin phrase *velum palati* 'the veil of the palate'. Sounds using the lower surface of the velum as the upper articulator are called **velar** /ˈviləɹ/ (Figure 1.10). In English, *luck, lug,* and *lung* all end in velar consonants.

Figure 1.9 Palatal

Figure 1.10 Velar.

Figure 1.11   Uvular.

UVULA   At the rear of the mouth, the velum narrows to a long, thin pointed structure known as the **uvula** /ˈjuvjələ/. If you look in a mirror and open your mouth wide, you can see the uvula hanging down from the velum. Try snoring; you will feel the uvula flapping against the pharyngeal wall. Sounds made with the uvula are called **uvular** /ˈjuvjələɹ/ (Figure 1.11). English does not have uvular sounds.

TONGUE   The **tongue** is a large, muscular organ which is involved in almost every sound we make. The surface of the tongue is, of course, continuous, but phoneticians find it convenient to divide it into five parts (Figure 1.12).

Tip   The **tip**, or **apex** /ˈejˌpɛks/, of the tongue is its foremost part. Sounds made with the tip of the tongue are called **apical** /ˈæpɪkəl/. **Apico-dentals** /ˌæpɪˌkoˈdɛntəlz/ are made with the tip articulating with the upper teeth, as in *thin, then*. **Apico-alveolars** /ˌæpɪˌkoˌælˈviələɹz/ are made with the tip of the tongue articulating with the alveolar ridge. In English, apico-alveolars are common, as in *toe, dead, nun*.

Blade   Lying just behind the tip of the tongue is a small surface called the **blade**, or **lamina** /ˈlæmɪnə/. Sounds made with the blade are called **laminal** /ˈlæmɪnəl/. Like the tip, the blade commonly articulates with the teeth or with the alveolar ridge. These sounds are called **lamino-dentals** /ˌlæmɪˌnoˈdɛntəlz/ and **lamino-alveolars** /ˌlæmɪˌnoˌælˈviələɹz/. In English, the initial sounds in *ship* and *shoe* are usually **palato-alveolar** /ˌpæləˌtoˌælˈviələɹ/, the blade of the tongue being near the back of the alveolar ridge.

Front   The **front** of the tongue has a most misleading name. It is not at the front of the tongue, but behind the tip and the blade. Fortunately, we do not need to refer to it that often. The front of the tongue articulates against the palate; such sounds are simply called **palatal**. The initial sounds in English of *yes* is made with the front of the tongue raised towards the palate.

Back   The hindmost part of the horizontal surface of the tongue is called the **back** or **dorsum** /ˈdoɹsəm/ (the adjective being **dorsal** /ˈdoɹsəl/). It articulates

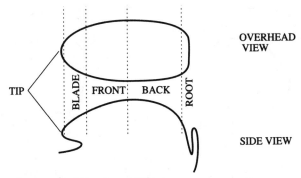

Figure 1.12 Parts of the tongue.

against the velum or uvula to form **dorso-velar** /ˌdoɹˌˌsoˈviləɹ/ and **dorso-uvular** /ˌdorˌˌsoˈjuvjələɹ/ sounds. Be careful not to confuse the *back* of the tongue with the *root*. In English, the final sound in the words *tick, dog,* and *sang* is a dorso-velar.

Root The **root** of the tongue is the vertical surface of the tongue at the rear facing the pharyngeal wall. The root is not used in English, and we will not need to talk about it until Chapter 11. The Latin noun and adjective are **radix** /ˈɹejˌdɪks/ and **radical** /ˈɹædɪkəl/.

EPIGLOTTIS

The **epiglottis** /ˌɛpɪˈglatɪs/ is a leaf-shaped cartilage which sticks up and back from the larynx. The epiglottis is like the appendix: no one is absolutely sure why we have one. It may have some function in preventing food from going into the larynx, but this is disputed. For phoneticians, its position is a nuisance in that it hangs over the larynx, making the larynx difficult to observe. Recent research has shown that the epiglottis may be of some importance in a very few languages (see Chapter 12).

NASAL CAVITY

The pharynx opens upwards into the **nasal cavity**. We have no control over the shape of this cavity; however, the velum can be raised and lowered to open and close the opening from the pharynx to the nasal cavity. When the velum is lowered, air can escape out the nose. If the velum is raised, air cannot escape through the nose. The upper surface of the velum is called the **velic** surface /ˈvilɪk/. Thus we can refer to **velic opening** and **velic closure**. Sounds made with velic opening are called **nasal** or **nasalised**; sounds made with velic closure are called **oral** (Figure 1.13). Note that *velic* refers to the upper surface of the velum which moves against the pharyngeal wall, whereas *velar* refers to the lower surface of the velum which articulates with the back of the tongue. The words *ram, ran, rang* all end in a nasal consonant.

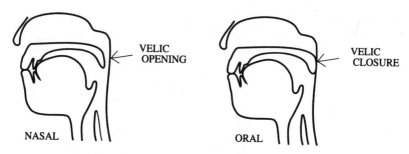

Figure 1.13.

A bilabial nasal is shown on the left with a velic opening allowing air to pass out through the nose. On the right, the same bilabial sound is shown, but with a velic closure preventing air from passing out through the nose.

If you are familiar with French, you know that a word like *on* 'one' has a nasalised vowel, but a word like *eau* 'water' has an oral vowel. Practise saying these two words to feel the velum going up and down. It should go down for *on* and up for *eau.*

SUMMARY OF PLACES OF ARTICULATION

	lip	*teeth*	*alveolar ridge*	*back of alveolar ridge*	*palate*	*velum*
lip	bilabial	labio-dental				
tip		apico-dental	apico-alveolar	retroflex		
blade		lamino-dental	lamino-alveolar	palato-alveolar		
front					palatal	
back						dorso-velar

The upper articulators are shown across the top of the chart. The lower articulators are shown down the left. Each cell contains the name of the sound produced by the combination of lower and upper articulators.

TECHNICAL TERMS

The following technical terms have been introduced in this chapter. Although the list is fairly long, many of the terms are familiar ones. Use this list and the others found at the end of each chapter as a checklist to make sure that you are familiar with each before going on.

acoustic phonetics
   acoustics
adam's apple
alveolar

alveolar ridge
alveoli
apex
   apico-alveolars

apico-dental
articulate
articulatory
articulatory phonetics

articulator
  lower articulator
  upper articulator
auditory phonetics
back
bilabial
blade
bronchus, bronchi
dental
dorsum
  dorsal
  dorso-velar
  dorso-uvular
epiglottis
front
glottis
  glottal
  glottal stop
labio-dental
lamina
  laminal
lamino-alveolars
lamino-dentals

larynx
  laryngeal
linguistics
lips
lungs
mouth
nasal
  nasal cavity
  nasalised
  non-nasal
œsophagus
oral
  oral cavity
palate
  palatal
  palato-alveolar
pharynx
  laryngeal pharynx
  nasal pharynx
  oral pharynx
  pharyngeal wall
phonetics
retroflex

root
  radix
  radical
subglottal
supralaryngeal
teeth
tip
tongue
trachea
uvula
  uvular
velum
  velar
velic
  velic closure
  velic opening
vocal cords
vocal organs
vocal tract
voicing
  voiced
  voiceless

EXERCISES

BASIC

No book can really teach you practical phonetics. Only close listening and practice can do that. However, by following the suggestions presented in the exercise portions of each chapter, you will be able to make significant improvements in your ability to make a large variety of speech sounds.

  1. The following exercises will help you become familiar with the parts of your body used in producing sounds. We will be taking a short tour of the vocal organs. The important point here is to transfer your knowledge of anatomy from a chart to your own body. A few anatomical features not mentioned in the main part of the chapter are presented here. You may be interested in learning these, but they are not essential for understanding this part of the book.

  a. Your adam's apple is the point jutting out below your chin. With your thumb and forefinger, feel the V-shaped plates which come together to form the point of the adam's apple; the plates are made of cartilage forming the front of the larynx. Immediately behind the adam's apple lie the vocal cords.

  b. Now, let's examine the mouth. Your upper and lower lips are easy to see. With the tip of your tongue, feel the rear surface of your upper teeth. Now pull your tongue slowly back until you feel the bumpy ridge lying behind the

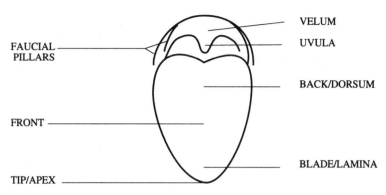

Figure 1.14 The oral cavity.

teeth; this is the **alveolar ridge**. Look at Figure 1.2, and relate the position of the alveolar ridge on the drawing to what you feel with your tongue. For some people, the alveolar ridge is not very prominent.

From the alveolar ridge, move your tongue back across the hard **palate**, a hard slightly curved surface. Most people can reach the back edge of the hard palate with their tongue tip and can just feel the forward part of the soft palate or **velum**. Relate what you feel to the corresponding part of Figure 1.2.

c. Now with a mirror, look straight into your mouth. A small flashlight may help. Compare what you see with Figure 1.14. Stick out your tongue, and identify the **tip**, **blade**, **front**, and **back** of your tongue.

Looking at the roof of your mouth, identify the **palate**, the **velum**, and the **uvula**. Between your uvula and your tongue, you can see a portion of the rear **pharyngeal** wall. There are two vertical folds at the sides, called the **faucial pillars** /ˈfɑʃəl/. At the base of these, you may find your **tonsils**, if they have not been extracted.

2. Figure 1.15 is for you to fill in the names of the important parts of the vocal organs. You may want to make several photocopies of this page for practice work.

ADVANCED

3. The following sentences are intended to help you develop a feel for various types of sounds. As you say each one over a few times, try to feel which articulators are forming most of the sounds.

bilabial:	Peter Brown picked a bushel of Burpee's peppers.
labio-dental:	Verna found five very fine vines.
dental:	Ethel thinks that this other thin thing is their thread.
alveolar:	Ed edited it, didn't he — or did Ted do it?
dorso-velar:	King Carl quickly kissed the Greek queen.

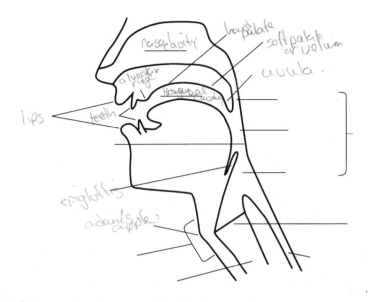

Figure 1.15 Label each of the vocal organs.

4. Fill in the missing terms:

a. Brenda, a tiny enzyme who lives inside Charlotte's mouth, is taking notes on Charlotte's pronunciation as part of a class project on phonetics that Brenda is doing. Charlotte is saying *pigs*. Brenda has an excellent vantage point on Charlotte's lower left premolar. She watches the big lips closing in front of her, plunging the mouth into darkness as Charlotte makes a _____ sound. Just after the lips open again, a loud rumble comes up from below as the _____ begin to vibrate while Charlotte makes the vowel. During the vowel, the middle part of the tongue swoops upwards. At the end of the vowel, Brenda turns around just in time to see the _____ of the tongue move up to touch the _____ for a dorso-velar sound. At least this time the lights stayed on for Brenda. Then, the tip of the tongue flashes past Brenda's ear to move near the _____ for the _____ fricative.

b. This time Brenda is hanging by her toes from the back of one of Charlotte's upper incisors while Charlotte is saying *thing*. The _____ of Charlotte's tongue moves up near the _____ for the _____ sound. Unfortunately, Brenda is knocked briefly unconscious by the force of the airstream and wakes up to discover that she is now on a lower right wisdom tooth. Charlotte is finishing the vowel of *thing*. The _____ of Charlotte's tongue is moving to the _____ . Brenda can hear the air going out of the nose as Charlotte makes a _____ nasal.

5a. Circle all the words below that have a nasal as their final sound:

    pin   tab   tame   sings   sign   lamb

b. Circle all the words below that begin with an alveolar sound:

    fin   sin   dumb   great   thought   just

    lest   church   ten   nest

c. Circle all the words below than have a velar sound:

    care   lick   sing   that   boss   jug

    ridge   mice

6a. Say the word *helps,* and feel how each sound is made. Try to complete the chart below for each of the consonants [l p s] at the end of the word.

	l	*p*	*s*
upper articulator			
lower articulator			
voiced or voiceless			
oral or nasal			

b. Make a similar chart, and fill in the blanks for the [n d] of *sand.*

CHAPTER TWO
THE BASIC SOUNDS OF ENGLISH

Phoneticians divide sounds into two basic categories: **segments** and **supraseg-mentals** /ˌsupɹəˌsɛɡˈmɛntəl/. Segments comprise **vowels** and **consonants.** Vowels include things like the sounds in the words *oh, eye, ooh, ah;* they are made with no major obstruction in the vocal tract so that air passes through the mouth fairly easily. Consonants, on the other hand, involve some type of obstruction in the vocal tract. When you make a /p/, for example, your lips are closed, thereby completely preventing air from leaving through the mouth.

Suprasegmentals involve sound components other than consonants and vowels. These include a variety of things such as stress, pitch, intonation, and length. You will have a clearer idea about these when we can discuss them in detail later in this chapter.

In this chapter you will learn about:
• the basic sounds of English
• symbols for the basic sounds.

TRANSCRIPTION

The ordinary **orthography** /oɹˈθɑɡɹəfi/, or spelling, of English is often quite different from a phonetic transcription. Frequently, words that sound quite different are written similarly; compare the pronunciation and spelling of the words – *tough, though, trough, through, thorough.* All of these words have the letters *ough;* yet, each of them is pronounced differently. On the other hand, words that sound just alike are sometimes written differently; compare *sew, sow, so; to, two, too; led, lead; do, due, dew; you, ewe, U, yew.* Clearly, for phonetic purposes, we want a way of writing things down that avoids this sort of ambiguity.

Phonetic **transcription** is the use of phonetic **symbols** to write down an **utterance** (a stretch of speech). One obvious goal of phonetics is to be able to **transcribe** accurately any utterance in a given language. Achieving this goal is in fact rather more complex than you might think at first. To get started, we will investigate only English. Each sound that we discuss in this chapter will be given a symbol. Appendix C shows how to write phonetic symbols. It is important that you spend some time now becoming proficient at transcribing English. In many ways, transcription is like typing. At first for typing, you have to look up every key; gradually, however, the actions become automatic. At first, for transcriptions, you will have to look up the phonetic symbols; soon, however, they will become quite familiar.

The symbols used in this book follow the usage recommended by the **International Phonetic Association**. This system, popularly known as the **IPA** /ˌaj ˌpi ˈej/, is the most widely used set of symbols.

Quite apart from the choice of symbols is the way in which they are used to form a transcription system for a particular language. Actually, there are quite a number of systems which have been used for transcribing English. I should make it quite clear at the outset that, although I believe the transcription system presented here is a good one, suitable to our purposes, it is by no means universally used. In other books on phonetics or linguistics, you may well encounter other systems.

Although we usually think of speech consisting of a string of sounds, one after the other, phoneticians have discovered that **segmentation**, or the division of a stretch of speech into a string of discrete consonants and vowels, is not a straightforward task. You can easily observe that in most utterances, the tongue is constantly in motion. In a word like *add,* the tongue rises from the vowel to the alveolar ridge, but it is difficult to know exactly at what precise point the vowel ends and the consonant begins. We will continue to represent speech as a series of segments, but it is important to keep in mind that speech is produced by a complexly sequenced interaction of several moving organs.

CONSONANTS

Consonants are sounds that involve a major obstruction or constriction of the vocal tract; **vowels** are made with a very open vocal tract. If you say the vowel *ee* as in *bee,* you can feel that the air flows out of the mouth fairly freely. Now say a long /z/: /zzzzzzz/. Now start with the vowel *ee,* and move to an /z/, as in the word *ease.* You will feel your tongue move closer to the alveolar ridge for the /z/, making a partial closure causing the hissing noise which characterises /z/. On the other hand, if you go from an /z/ to an *ee* sound, as in the American pronunciation of the letter *z,* you can feel your tongue pulling away a bit, with the air passing out more freely. From this simple experiment, you can understand the basic difference between a consonant and a vowel.

Consonants are usually classified along at least three dimensions: voicing, place of articulation, and manner of articulation. In Chapter 1, we learned that a voiceless sound, like /f s/, is made with the vocal cords apart, whereas with voiced sounds, like /v z/, are made with the vocal cords closer and vibrating. For each consonant that we discuss, we will simply note whether it is voiced or voiceless.

The place of articulation describes where the obstruction of the consonant is made, and the manner of articulation describes the nature of the obstruction. Each of the points and manners of articulation has a technical name; you will find phonetics much easier if you spend the time now to become familiar with these terms. These are described in detail below for English sounds.

PLACE OF ARTICULATION

The **place of articulation** is the description of where the obstruction occurs in the vocal tract. To describe the place of articulation of a consonant, we need to describe which of the lower articulators articulates with which of the upper articulators; *e.g.,* for a /d/, the tip of the tongue is against the alveolar ridge, but for a /g/, the back of the tongue is against the velum. We have already discussed places of articulation generally in Chapter 1; now the symbols for English sounds are introduced. Appendix C, at the back of the book, shows you how to write any unfamiliar symbols. Refer to the drawings in Chapter 1 to see how the vocal tract is shaped for each place of articualtion.

BILABIAL   The **bilabial** /ˌbajˈlejbiəl/ sounds of English include /p b m/, as in the initial sounds of the words *pea, bee, me.* The lower lip articulates against the upper lip. The sounds /p b m/ are made by completely closing the lips. The sound /p/ is voiceless; /b m/ are voiced. The sound /w/, as in *we,* also involves a bilabial articulation; it is discussed below under *labial-velar.*

/p/	*pea, creepy, loop*
/b/	*bee, lobby, rub*
/m/	*moo, summer, loam*

LABIO-DENTAL   We have two **labio-dental** /ˌlejbiˌoˈdɛntəl/ sounds in English: /f v/, as in the initial sounds of the words *feel, veal.* When you make these, you will notice that your lower lip articulates against your upper teeth; /f/ is voiceless, and /v/ is voiced.

/f/	*fun, daffy, laugh*
/v/	*veal, movie, glove*

DENTAL   Two **dental** sounds occur in English; both are normally written with the letters *th.* Say the words *thin* and *then* while you feel your adam's apple. You will feel the vocal cords vibrating for *then,* but not for *thin.* The initial sound of *thin* is voiceless [θ], but the corresponding one of *then* is voiced [ð].

The sounds /θ/ and /ð/ are usually **apico-dental** /ˌæpɪˌkoˈdɛntəl/; that is, the tip of the tongue is near or just barely touching the rear surface of the teeth. Air passes out with a soft hissing noise. Some people use the blade instead of the tip of the tongue; such sounds would be called **lamino-dentals** /ˌlæmiˌnoˈdɛntəl/, rather than apico-dental. The word **dental** can be used to include both kinds. In either case, the blade is usually more involved with dental articulations than with alveolar ones. In making dentals in English, some people put their tongue between the upper and lower teeth; such dental sounds can be called **interdentals** /ˌɪntəɹˈdɛntəl/. I, myself, normally have apico-dentals, but I often make interdentals when speaking emphatically, such as when I am making a point in a lecture. Try to find out how you make dentals.

/θ/	(called *theta* /ˈθejtə/)	*thin, ether, health*
/ð/	(called *eth* /ɛð/)	*then, either, loathe*

ALVEOLAR

The **alveolars** /ˌælˈviəlɑɹ/ include more consonants in English than any other place of articulation: /t d s z n l/. If you say the sentence *Ed edited the news nightly,* you will feel the tip of your tongue repeatedly hitting the alveolar ridge. Most English speakers have **apico-alveolars**, but some speakers have **lamino-alveolars**.

/t/	*top, return, missed*	/z/	*zap, lousy, please*
/d/	*done, sudden, mad*	/n/	*gnaw, any, done*
/s/	*see, messy, police*	/l/	*loaf, relief, dull*

PALATO-ALVEOLAR

Palato-alveolar /ˌpælə‖toˌælˈviələr/ refers to the area between the alveolar ridge and the palate. The tongue is arched with the blade near the palato-alveolar area. English has four sounds in this area; /ʃ/ is the initial sound in the word *shoe,* usually spelled *sh.* The voiced variety of this sound is found in the middle of the word *measure;* it is symbolised as /ʒ/. Traditional English orthography has no standard way of writing this sound. Try making these two sounds. Different people make them in slightly different ways, but generally there is an obstruction in the palato-alveolar region. Two other sounds are palato-alveolar: the initial sounds in the word *church,* transcribed /tʃ/, and the initial sound in *gem,* transcribed /dʒ/.

/ʃ/	(called *esh* /ɛʃ/)	*shelf, tissue, mesh*
/ʒ/	(called *ezh* /ɛʒ/)	*treasure, garage, rouge*
/tʃ/		*chin, etching, roach*
/dʒ/		*jam, edgy, ridge*

Instead of IPA symbols, some authors use [š ž č j] for [ʃ ʒ tʃ dʒ], respectively.

RETROFLEX

Retroflex /ˈɹɛtɹəˌflɛks/ sounds are made by curling the tip of the tongue up and back towards the rear edge of the alveolar ridge. The only retroflex sound in English is /ɹ/. This is the sound in the English word *red.* In making this sound the tip of the tongue does not actually touch the back of the alveolar ridge, but approaches it. Many people make the sound /ɹ/ in a quite different manner (Delattre and Freeman, 1968). They bunch the tongue, keeping the tip of the tongue down, sometimes pulling it into the body of the tongue; the articulation is between the rear portion of the blade and the alveolar ridge.

Whichever kind of /ɹ/ you normally make, try to make the other kind. The upside-down *r* is the IPA symbol for the English sound. Later on, we will find a use for the right-side up symbol /r/, which represents a trill.

/ɹ/   *run, airy, war*

PALATAL   Palatals /ˈpælətəl/ are made with the front of the tongue articulating against the palate. In practising palatal sounds, you will find it helpful to anchor the tip of your tongue against the lower teeth. This is not necessary to make palatals, but it helps prevent mistakes.

    The only palatal in English is the sound /j/, the initial sound in *yes*. It is often written *y*, but it is also found in words such as *eunuch, use, few, and ewe*. To avoid any confusion between /j/ and the letter *j* /dʒej/, I would recommend calling the phonetic symbol /j/ by the name *yod* /jɑd/.

/j/   (called *yod* /jɑd/) *yell, onion, fuse*

VELAR   Velar /ˈviləɹ/ sounds are **dorso-velar** /ˌdoɹˌˌsoˈviləɹ/, with the back of the tongue articulating against the velum. In English the velars are /k g ŋ/. These are the final consonants in the words *sick, egg,* and *sing*.

/k/   *kiss, locker, sock*
/g/   *gun, rugger, sag*
/ŋ/   (called *ing* /ɪŋ/)   *singer, bang*

Most people do not have a well-developed **kinæsthetic** /ˌkɪnəsˈθɛtɪk/ feel for velars. **Kinæsthesia** /ˌkɪnəsˈθiʒə/ is the ability to perceive the muscle movements of one's own body. It is important to be able to relate a sound to the position of the organs of the vocal tract which produce the sound. The exercises at the end of this chapter provide material to help you develop this ability.

GLOTTAL   The **glottal** /ˈglɑtəl/ place of articulation is somewhat different from the ones we have discussed so far. Up to now, all the points of articulation have been in the mouth. The glottal stop /ʔ/ is made by holding the vocal cords tightly together so that no air escapes. If you hold your breath with your mouth open, you will make a glottal stop. Try this a few times to get a kinæsthetic feeling for a glottal stop. Many English speakers use a glottal stop in saying *uh-oh:* [ʔʌʔow]. Glottal stops are not ordinary sounds in English, but they occur optionally at the beginning of words which would otherwise begin with a vowel, *e.g.,* /ʔɑl~ɑl/ *all*.

LABIAL-VELAR   The sound /w/ has a double place of articulation **labial-velar**, being both labial and velar. You can easily observe that the lips are rounded when making a /w/; this lip-rounding makes it labial. At the same time, with a little experimenting, you can feel that the back of the tongue is raised up towards the velum; thus, it is velar as well.

/w/   *wet, win, towel*

MANNER OF ARTICULATION

The **manner of articulation** is the degree and kind of constriction in the vocal tract. For example, in making a /t/, the tongue is raised to the alveolar ridge and momentarily seals off the vocal tract so that no air passes out. The manner of articulation for this consonant is called a **stop**. By contrast, during an /s/, we leave a gap between the articulators so that air continues to pass out. This manner of articulation is called a **continuant** /kən'tɪnjuənt/. Notice that you can make a long, continuous /sssss/, but not a long /tttttt/.

STOPS   A **stop** involves a complete closure such that no air passes out of the mouth. In English /p t k b d g / are stops. In making each of these, a complete closure is made, at the lips, the alveolar ridge, or the velum, such that no air can escape through the mouth. The nasal stops /m n ŋ/ are a special kind of stop considered below.

FRICATIVES   Fricatives /'fɹɪkətɪv/ are sounds made with a small opening, allowing the air to escape with some friction. The escaping air is turbulent and produces a noisy effect. The fricatives in English are /f v θ ð s z ʃ ʒ/. For /f v/, the lower lip partially touches the upper teeth, but not so tightly that air cannot escape, creating a soft friction-like noise. The other fricatives /θ ð s z ʃ ʒ/ are all made with the tongue near an upper articulator, perhaps partially touching it, but not completely obstructing the air-flow. The essential element of a fricative is partial air-flow with a friction-like noise.

APPROXIMANTS   Approximants /ə'pɹɑksɪmənt/ are consonants with a greater opening in the vocal tract than for fricatives. Friction-like noise is absent with approximants. In English, this category comprises /l ɹ w j/. These are the initial sounds in *loot, rule, wood,* and *use.* All approximants in English are voiced. Both fricatives and approximants are **continuants**.

The approximant /ɹ/ has already been described as a retroflex consonant. The approximant /l/ is an alveolar lateral. **Laterals** are sounds that are made with only the central part of the articulators touching. Try making a long /l/: /llllllllllllll/. You will be able to feel the tip of your tongue touching the alveolar ridge. Both sides of the tongue, however, are pulled down slightly from the roof of the mouth so that air escapes around the sides of the tongue. A sound which is not lateral is **central**.

The **semivowels** or **glides** /w j/ are considered approximants as well. Although glides function as consonants, phonetically they are moving vowels — hence the name *semivowel.* They are discussed more fully with the vowels later in this chapter.

AFFRICATES   Affricates /'æfɹɪkət/ are sequences of stop plus fricative. The English sounds /tʃ dʒ/ are palato-alveolar affricates. These are the sounds in *church* and *judge,* both at the beginning and the end of the words. In the initial part of /tʃ dʒ/, the tip of the tongue is at the rear of the alveolar ridge, somewhat back of its position in words like *did*. In the second part of the affricate, the tongue pulls away slightly from the roof of the mouth to form a fricative. The affricate /tʃ/ is regularly spelled *ch* or *tch* as in words like *church, child,* and *hitch* ; /dʒ/ is usually spelled *j, g,* or *dg* as in *joke, gem,* and *trudge*. Make sure that you do not write /j/ when you mean /dʒ/ or /c/ when you mean /tʃ/. Note that although affricates are phonetic sequences, they function as a single unit in English. This distinction will be clarified further in Chapter 3.

NASALS The sounds /m n ŋ/ are called **nasals** or **nasal stops**. For these three sounds, there is a velic opening, allowing air to pass out through the nose. Usually the term **nasal** is sufficient, but if we need to be explicit, we can call /m n ŋ/ **nasal stops** and /p t k b d g/ **oral stops**. For a nasal sound, the velum is lowered, allowing air to pass out through the nasal passage. Note that nasals are stops in that no air passes out of the mouth; there is a complete closure in the oral cavity. For nasal stops, air escapes through the nose, but not through the mouth; for oral stops, on the other hand, no air escapes through the nose or through the mouth.

OTHER TERMS The term **obstruent** /ˈɑbˌstɹuənt/ includes oral stops, fricatives, and affricates. Non-obstruents are called **sonorants** /ˈsownəɹənt/; they include nasal stops, approximants, glides, and vowels.

The sounds /s/ and /z/ are often referred to as **sibilants** /ˈsɪbɪlənt/. Sibilants may include /ʃ/ and /ʒ/ as well.

Liquids comprise laterals and r-like sounds. In English, these are /l ɹ/. This grouping is useful because of the acoustic similarity of these sounds.

The glottal stop [ʔ] is optional in English. Although the sound [h] functions as a consonant, its production is more easily discussed with the vowels later in this chapter.

SUMMARY OF ENGLISH CONSONANTS

	bilabial	labio-dental	dental	alveolar	palato-alveolar	retroflex	palatal	velar	labial-velar
stop	p b			t d				k g	
fricative		f v	θ ð	s z	ʃ ʒ				
affricate					tʃ dʒ				
nasal	m			n				ŋ	
approximant				l		ɹ	j		w

VOWELS

English is spoken as a native language by millions of people. We are all aware that there are many different dialects of English. Anyone listening to radio and television is bound to be exposed not just to Canadian dialects, but to varieties of

American and British dialects also, and likely to West Indian, Australian, Scottish, Irish, Indian, and South African dialects as well. Dialect differences which involve pronunciation are termed differences of **accent**. (*Accent* has other meanings; see the Glossary — Appendix B.) Surprisingly enough, we find that the consonants of English are pronounced pretty much the same throughout all English-speaking areas. Vowels, on the other hand, vary considerably in different regions. Generally, to talk about accent differences in English is to talk about vowel differences.

This variation presents me now with a problem. No matter what accent or dialect area I choose to describe, readers of this book from other areas will have accents which will not match my description exactly. My solution is to choose the dialect of central and western Canada. This accent is spoken without a great deal of variation from Kingston west to the Pacific, in Canada and in the adjacent parts of the United States. In general, it is the descendant of the Upper Canadian dialect of the Empire Loyalists, and other early settlers, whose progeny gradually settled the land to the west. The Maritimes have certain differences from the dialect of central and western Canada. Quebec English also has certain special features of its own. The very distinct settlement of Newfoundland has left it with a dialect showing clear differences from that of the rest of Canada.

For the moment, thus, I will restrict my observations to the dialect of central and western Canada. This accent is what I will mean by the term *English*. Chapter 6, on the other hand, will deal specifically with the accents of other English-speaking areas.

HOW VOWELS ARE MADE

In making vowels, the vocal tract is more open than it is for consonants. Two elements are primarily involved in making different vowels: the shape of the lips and the shape and position of the tongue in the mouth. To get started, we will look at some of the vowels of English.

Try making the vowel in *he*. You can feel that the front of the tongue is fairly close to the forward part of the palate. (The *front*, recall, is the part of the tongue behind the tip and the blade.) This vowel is described as a high front vowel, transcribed /i/. Now, try making the vowel in *ah*, the one you make for the doctor to see your throat. This is described as a low back vowel, transcribed /ɑ/. Go back and forth between these two vowels (/i/ and /ɑ/), feeling the difference between high front and low back vowels.

We see then that the shape of the tongue is a primary factor in determining the quality of a vowel. Because of the difficulty of describing the shape of the entire tongue, phoneticians have usually described vowels by the location of the highest point of the tongue as shown in Figure 2.1.

Figure 2.2 shows a type of chart used to plot vowel positions, in this case, the same vowels [i] and [ɑ], as in Figure 2.1. In such a chart, we plot the position of the

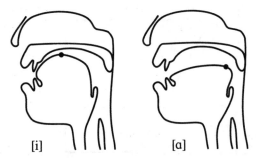

Figure 2.1 The shape of the tongue for English vowels [i] and [a].
The dot shows the highest point of the tongue for each vowel.

highest point of the tongue; we always put front vowels on the left and back vowels on the right. Every vowel that we can make can be plotted either inside the vowel chart or on its edge. The two internal horizontal lines are present simply for reference purposes.

In studying vowels, consult a chart, such as Figure 2.3, which shows where the highest point of the tongue is, make the vowel, and try to feel how your own tongue is shaped. In this way, you will develop a kinæsthetic feeling for making vowels.

The following are the simple vowels of English.

i	peat	u	boot
ɪ	pit	ʊ	put
ɛ	pet	ʌ	putt
æ	pat	ɑ	pot

There are other vowels, involving glides, which are discussed later. For now, we will use these eight simple vowels to examine the three basic articulatory qualities of vowels : **height**, **backness**, and **rounding**.

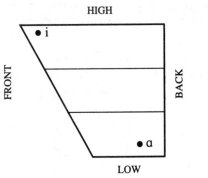

FIGURE 2.2 Vowel chart for [i] and [a].

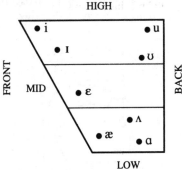

FIGURE 2.3 Simple vowels of English.

23

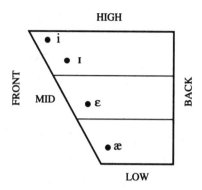

FIGURE 2.4 Front vowels.

HEIGHT Try saying the words *peat, pit, pet, pat.* You will probably notice that your jaw moves down as you go through the list; with each vowel, your mouth is a little bit more open, and the highest point of the tongue is a little bit lower. This variation is what we mean by vowel height. X-ray pictures taken of English speakers uttering these vowels show that the tongue is quite high for /i/, lower for /ɪ/, lower still for /ɛ/, and lowest of all for /æ/.

We say that /i/ is a **high** vowel; that /æ/ is a **low** vowel; that /ɪ/ is higher than /ɛ/; or that /æ/ is lower than /ɛ/. The vowels in the middle range between high and low, such as /ɛ/, are called **mid** vowels.

BACKNESS Try saying the vowels in *pat* and *pot.* These are /æ/ and /ɑ/. Try to say them alone without any consonants: /æ æ æ æ ɑ ɑ ɑ ɑ ɑ/. Although both of these vowels are low vowels, you will feel your tongue changing shape. The high point of the tongue for /æ/ is in the front of the mouth, and the high point for /ɑ/ is in the back of the mouth. Just as we can make high and low vowels, so we also can make **front** and **back** vowels.

ROUNDING Height and backness are not the only dimensions for vowels. Try saying /i/ and /u/ — the vowels for *key* and *coo.* You will note that your lips

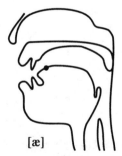

FIGURE 2.5 Tongue position for [æ] and [ɑ].

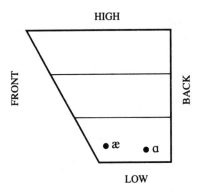

FIGURE 2.6 Low vowels.

are **rounded** for /u/, but not for /i/. Of the eight vowels shown in Figure 2.3, only /u/ and /ʊ/ are rounded; all the other vowels shown there are unrounded. We will encounter other rounded vowels soon. Speakers of some dialects may differ as to which vowels are rounded; in particular, many dialects pronounce words like *pot* with a rounded vowel (see Chapter 6).

For vowels like those found in words like *shoe, push,* and *row,* the lips are rounded. Try saying these words while observing your lips in a mirror. They will be more rounded than they are in words like *heat, miss, say.* We will divide vowels into rounded and unrounded vowels.

GLIDES **Glides** or **semivowels** are moving vowels. Glides move rapidly from one vowel position to another; vowels, on the other hand, have a relatively steady articulation. Although phonetically similar to vowels, glides function either as consonants before a vowel or as the final portion of a syllable nucleus after a vowel.

The glide /j/ moves to or from a high front unrounded position. In a word like *yell* /jɛl/, the tongue starts at a high front unrounded position – approximately the

FIGURE 2.7 Tongue position for [ʊ].

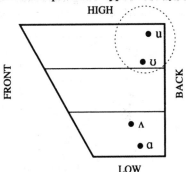

FIGURE 2.8 Back vowels. Vowels inside the dotted circle are rounded; those outside are unrounded.

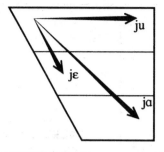

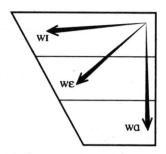

FIGURE 2.9 The semivowel [j].　　**FIGURE 2.10** The semivowel [w].

position for /i/ – and then moves to the lower /ɛ/ position. The glide /w/ is similar, except that it moves either to or from a high, back rounded position; a word like *well*, starts at a high, back rounded position – like the position for /u/ – and moves to an /ɛ/ position. In *yell* and *wet*, the glides precede the vowel; glides can also follow vowels. Such glides will be illustrated in the section below on diphthongs.

/j/　　　*yell, you, yawn*
/w/　　　*well, wit, whoa*

In Figures 2.9 and 2.10, arrows show the directions of movements. A thicker line shows slower speed of tongue movement and thus greater prominence.

DIPHTHONGS　　A **diphthong** /ˈdɪfˌθɑŋ/ can be defined for the time being as a sequence of a vowel and a glide. (Note especially the pronunciation of *diphthong* /ˈdɪfˌθɑŋ/; there is no /p/ sound.) Try saying the word *eye* slowly. If you listen carefully, you will hear that there are two parts to this sound. It starts off with a vowel somewhat like /æ/, as in /pæt/; then it moves upwards to a vowel sound something like an /i/. The first portion is between /ɑ/ and /æ/; we will transcribe it as /a/ (a different symbol from /ɑ/). The second portion moves and is therefore a glide. It moves to a high front unrounded position like /i/, and we can symbolise it as /j/. Thus, the word *eye* is transcribed /aj/. Figure 2.11 shows the diphthong /aj/.

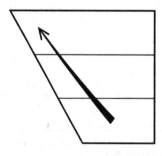

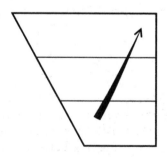

FIGURE 2.11　The English diphthong /aj/.　　**FIGURE 2.12**　The English diphthong /aw/.

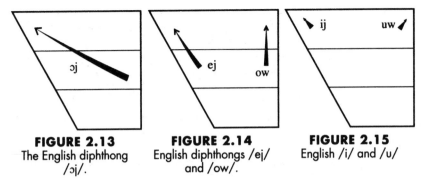

FIGURE 2.13
The English diphthong
/ɔj/.

FIGURE 2.14
English diphthongs /ej/
and /ow/.

FIGURE 2.15
English /i/ and /u/

/aj/   *my, sigh, write, I*

Now in the same way, try saying the word *how* slowly. It starts with a low front vowel very near the /a/ in *eye*, but the diphthong moves to a high back position like the vowel /u/. We can transcribe this diphthong as /aw/. It is shown in Figure 2.12.

/aw/   *cow, mouth, ouch, renown*

A third diphthong is found in the word *boy*. The glide portion of it is /j/. If you try saying *boy* slowly you can feel that your tongue is drawn back and down at the beginning of the diphthong. You will also note that your lips are slightly rounded. We will write this diphthong as /ɔj/. The sound /ɔ/ is a lower mid back rounded vowel shown in Figure 2.13.

/ɔj/   *joy, noise, employ, foist*

There are two further diphthongs in English, written /ej/ and /ow/. You can see from Figure 2.14 that the glides for these diphthongs do not move so far as those of /aj, aw, ɔj/. English speakers generally do not perceive their diphthongal nature so readily as for the other diphthongs. Say the word *oh* slowly; it begins with a mid back rounded vowel and moves upwards to a high position. Watch your lips in a mirror while you say *oh*. You can easily see that your lips become more rounded at the end of the sound. This rounding correlates with the movement of the tongue upwards towards a /u/ position. With practice, you will hear the diphthongal nature of /ow/ more clearly.

The diphthong /ej/, as in *hay*, is also shown in Figure 2.14. It starts out as a mid front unrounded vowel and moves upwards to a high front position.

/ow/   *no, doe, low, roast, bone*
/ej/   *day, laid, rate, age*

The vowels /i/ and /u/, as in *me* and *moo*, are also usually slightly diphthongal as shown in Figure 2.15; however, the glide is very short.

SCHWA   Our last vowel is a mid central unrounded vowel with the special name **schwa** /ʃwɑ/, and written /ə/. The description **mid** shows that is its between high and low, and **central** shows that it is between front and back. Schwa occurs in two environments: before /ɹ/ and in unstressed syllables. Listen to the second vowel in *sofa*. This is a schwa; you may find it hard to hear because it is so short. If you slow down your pronunciation of *sofa* in an attempt to focus on

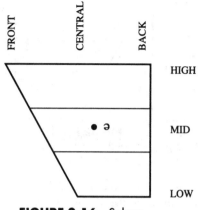

FIGURE 2.16 Schwa.

the schwa more clearly, you are likely to distort its pronunciation. Be patient. The exercises at the end of the chapter will help you recognise and produce schwa.

/ə/   *ago, open, enough, receive, naval*
             fir, fur, fern, occur, server

Because our spelling system has no unique way of writing schwa, many people are unaware of this vowel; however, it is actually the most frequently occurring vowel sound in any sentence or discourse of spoken English. Its high frequency is the result of its function in the sound system or phonology of English. This point will be explained in greater detail in Chapter 4.

/h/   Phonetically, /h/ is ordinarily realised as a voiceless vowel—just like the following vowel, except that the vocal cords are in a voiceless position. Although /h/ is a voiceless vowel in terms of its production, it functions as a consonant, occurring only at the beginning of a syllable.

STRESS

Say the words *sofa, appear, lady,* and *recover* one after the other. Now, hum them, saying something like *hmm* for each syllable. You will notice that some syllables seem more prominent than others; we will say that the prominent syllables have a **primary stress** and that the other syllables are **unstressed**. The first syllables of *sofa* and *lady* have primary stress; whereas the second syllables of *appear* and *recover* have primary stress. Primary stress is shown by a superscript vertical mark placed before the stressed syllable: /ˈsowfə, əˈpiɹ, ˈlejdi, ɹɪˈkʌvəɹ/. The other syllables are unstressed with no special mark.

Stress in English is due to a combination of three elements: greater loudness, higher pitch, and longer duration. Stress is an extremely important element in English. Consider the word *survey,* as a noun and as a verb.

*To build the road, we'll need a new **survey**.*   /ˈsəɹvej/
*This is the site we need to **survey**.*   /səɹˈvej/

Notice that in the noun the first syllable /səɹ/ has primary stress, whereas in the verb the second syllable /vej/ has primary stress. This pattern, although subtle, is fairly common in English. Consider the words: *produce, invite, subject, convert, convict.* Most native speakers of English will pronounce these differently as nouns and as verbs.

Now try saying the words *operator, elevator, phonograph.* These words have primary stress on the first syllable. However, the third syllable in all of them seems to have a degree of stress as well. Say the words again to test this. We, thus, need a third level of stress, intermediate between primary stress and unstressed, which we can call **secondary stress**, marking it with a subscript vertical line before the appropriate syllable.

/ˈɑpəˌɹejtəɹ/	operator
/ˈɛləˌvejtəɹ/	elevator
/ˈfownəˌgɹæf/	phonograph

Secondary stress, by the way, is not limited to the third syllable. It also falls on other syllables, as the following examples show.

/əˌsosiˈjejʃən/	association
/ˌfænˈtæstɪk/	fantastic
/ˌoˈpejk/	opaque

Marking the levels of stress accurately requires some practice. The exercises at the end of this chapter will get you started. We will look at stress in greater detail in Chapter 5.

TECHNICAL TERMS

accent
affricate
alveolar
apico-alveolar
   apico-dental
approximant
back
   backness
bilabial
central
consonant
continuant
dental
diphthong
dorso-velar
fricative
front
glide
glottal
height
high
interdental

International Phonetic
   Association
IPA
labial velar
kinæsthesia
   kinæsthetic
labio-dental
lamino-alveolar
   lamino-dental
lateral
liquid
low
manner of articulation
mid
nasal
   nasal stop
obstruent
oral stop
orthography
palatal
   palato-alveolar
place of articulation

primary stress
retroflex
rounded
schwa
secondary stress
segment
   segmentation
semivowel
sibilant
   shibilant
sonorant
stop
suprasegmental
symbol
transcription
   transcribe
unstressed
utterance
velar
vowel

SYMBOLS

The following list gives the names for the phonetic symbols that we have used which are not ordinary letters of the alphabet.

[ɪ]	small cap i		[ð]	eth	/ɛð/
[ɛ]	epsilon	/ˈɛpsɪˌlɑn/	[ʃ]	esh	/ɛʃ/
[æ]	ash	/æʃ/	[ʒ]	ezh	/ɛʒ/
[a]	front a		[ʔ]	glottal stop	
[ɑ]	back a		[j]	yod	/jɑd/
[ɔ]	open o		[ɹ]	upside-down r	
[ʊ]	small cap u		[ŋ]	ing	/ɪŋ/
[ə]	schwa	/ʃwɑ/	[ˈ]	primary stress	
[θ]	theta	/ˈθejtə/	[ˌ]	secondary stress	

EXERCISES

BASIC

1. Read the following:

    ðɛɹ ˈwɑz ə jʌŋ ˈlejdi nejmd ˈpəɹkɪnz
    hu wəz ɪkˈstɹimli ˈfɑnd əv gɹin ˈgəɹkɪnz
    wʌn ˈdej ət əɹ ˈti
    ʃi ˈejt twɛnti ˈθɹi
    ən ˈpɪkəld əɹ ˈɪntəɹnəl ˈwəɹkɪŋz

2. The following words all have the vowel /ɑ/. Be careful to write it as /ɑ/, not as /a/. Transcribe these words, paying attention to the consonants. Remember to listen to the sounds. English spelling can be quite misleading.

    mop   sod   cot   sock   knot   box
    doll   psalm

3. The following words also have the vowel /ɑ/, but some of the consonant sounds have special symbols: /ŋ/, as in *song;* /ɹ/, as in *are;* and /ʃ/, as in *wash.* Note that /ŋ/ is a single sound, although usually written with two letters —*ng*.

    song   raw   shop   slosh   rod   wrong
    knocks   grog

4. Practise transcribing the following words with /ɑ i u/:

    rot   seed   rude   law   me   moo
    heat   through   moon   soothe   sue   peas
    do   saw   lose   loose

5. Now try a few short vowels: /ɪ/, as in *pit; /ɛ/, as in *pet; /æ/, as in *pat:*

    lip   set   gnat   sick   sham   bad
    debt   ring   his   hiss   bang   fret

6. Practise transcribing these words which have /ʊ/, as in *put;* or /ʌ/, as in *putt:*

   book   nut   foot   lug   buck   good
   mud   should

7. Transcribe these words, which have various short vowels:

   love   push   dumb   zinc   mash   send
   splat   nick   look   said

8. Pronounce:

   sæg   pʌg   zɛn   pʊt   mɛt   mɪl
   wæg   læs   wʌn   væt   kʌd   kʊd

9. Note the difference in voicing between the initial consonants of *thin* /θ/, and *then* /ð/. Transcribe the following words:

   that   thus   myth   three   thee   thumb
   tenth   thwart   thought   though

10. Transcribe the affricates /tʃ/ and /dʒ/ in the following words. Be sure not to confuse them with /ʃ/ and /ʒ/:

    hutch   butch   gem   jump   witch   Scotch
    botch   judge   chump   Jew   gee   jaw

11. Each of the following items is the transcription for more than one word. How many different words can you find for each item?

    e.g.:   /dow/ *dough, doe*
    blu   si   dajɪŋ   pæst   tu   flu
    wejst   pɹej   huz   lɛd   sajt   plejn

12. Correct these transcriptions:

glue	/glju/		gouge	/gawz/
knight	/knajt/		wealth	/wɛlð/
reef	/ɹɪf/		bloom	/blʊm/
shoot	/sut/		done	/down/
chew	/cu/		quite	/kwɑjt/
yes	/yɛs/		says	/sez/
jump	/jʌmp/		lamb	/læmb/

13. Transcribe the following words using the diphthongs /ej ow/:

    note   coat   code   daze   days   posed
    don't   waste

14. Try the following words with the diphthongs /aj aw ɔj/. Note that the first two use the symbol /a/, not /ɑ/:

    ride   boys   loud   dies   lines   soiled
    spine   rouse

15. Transcribe the following words which have various diphthongs:

    sliced   raced   down   joist   loafed   loaves
    coins   signs

16. Schwa /ə/ is used in unstressed syllables, and before syllable-final /ɹ/ (with or without stress). Transcribe the following words; in words with more than one syllable, be sure to mark primary stress: *e.g., whisper* /ˈwɪspəɹ/, *event* /əˈvɛnt/.

her	sir	fern	fur	upon	deeper
fathom	blurt	afire	wallaby	enough	surprise

17. The following words show some dialect variation; that is, they are pronounced differently by people from different places. Transcribe these the way you ordinarily say them. Then compare your transcription with friends, particularly with someone from a different part of the English-speaking world.

with	either	hearth	hover	fast	aunt
pen	schism	brooch	figure	garage	due

ADVANCED

18. We have now covered all the basic sounds of English. The following exercises present material of increasing difficulty. Be sure to pay attention to what you say, not to spelling. With words of more than one syllable, show stress.

a.
have	halve	eggs	voiced	what	why
jazz	cloths	clothes	breath	breathe	foiled
sense	cents	wash	squash		

b.
machine	ocean	seizure	anxious	finger	wringer
longer	danger	sudden	courage	sadness	ginger
pleasure	either	ether	fissure	ensign	resource
colonel	fossils	victuals	marquis	valet	helm
tough	though	through	thorough		

c.
scours	heart	mirth	tired	roar	spark
spearing	chair				

d.
jealous	spank	south	southern	pooch	poach
idea	wow	boiler	higher	English	French

e. In the following words indicate both primary and secondary stress.

tranquility	epilepsy	sassafras	logarithm	chesterfield
ineptitude	architecture	loquacious	salacious	

19. Some people have the diphthong /uj/ in a few words. Try the following examples to see how you pronounce them. You may say these with two syllables. Try pronouncing each with two syllables, and then with only one syllable.

ruin	bruin	cruet

CHAPTER THREE
ENGLISH CONSONANTS

In Chapter 2 we listed all the segments of English. In this chapter, we will look at the various consonants in more detail. We will discover that a consonant may be pronounced differently in different positions.

Put your hand about three inches in front of your mouth. In a normal speaking voice, say the English words *pie* and *spy*. You will feel a puff of air with the /p/ of *pie*, but not with the /p/ of *spy*. This puff of air is called **aspiration** /ˌæspɪˈɹejʃən/. Try the same thing with *tie* and *sty;* and again with *cool* and *school.*

This experiment confirms the point just made that a consonant may be pronounced differently in different positions. In each case when a voiceless stop [p t k] is at the very beginning of the word as in *pie, tie,* and *cool,* the stop is aspirated. When the stop is preceded by [s], there is no aspiration, as in *spy, sty,* and *school.* We will transcribe aspiration with a small raised *h;* the consonants of *pie, tie, cool* can thus be transcribed as [pʰ tʰ kʰ]. An addition to a symbol such as the small raised *h* used to transcribe aspiration is called a **diacritic** /ˌdajəˈkɹɪtɪk/. Unaspirated consonants will be transcribed without a diacritic.

In this chapter you will learn about:

- allophones and phonemes
- broad and narrow transcription
- variations in English consonants.

ALLOPHONIC VARIATION

ALLOPHONES AND PHONEMES

The experiment in the previous section presents us with a theoretical dilemma. On the one hand, English has a single /p/. Ask someone on the street how many /p/-sounds there are in English. To the layperson, the question does not quite make sense because the answer is so obviously 'one'. Despite this general perception, however, we have just seen that English indeed does have two /p/-sounds.

Linguists deal with this problem by positing two different levels for representing sounds. At one level, there is one /p/; at the other level, there are two — [p] and [pʰ]. The level of the single /p/ is called **phonemic** /fəˈnimɪk/. The level of the two [p]-sounds is called **phonetic** or **allophonic** /ˌæləˈfɑnɪk/. **Phonology** /fəˈnɑlədʒi/ is the area of linguistics that deals with this sort of issue extensively. We will concern ourselves here only with the basic notions of these two levels. Note that from now on, phonemic transcriptions are enclosed in **slant lines**, called **solidi** /ˈsɑlɪdi/; whereas, allophonic transcriptions are enclosed in **square brackets**. This convention is simply to keep the reader informed as to which level is being described. Units at the phonemic level are called **phonemes** /ˈfowˌnimz/. Units at the allophonic level are called **allophones** /ˈæləˌfonz/. Appendix A contains an extensive survey of the consonantal allophones in English.

level   unit

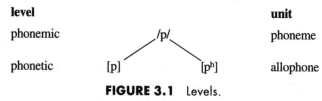

FIGURE 3.1   Levels.

Phonemes **contrast** with each other; that is, if we substitute one phoneme for another, we get another word. For example, if we substitute the phoneme /v/ for /f/ in *fat* /fæt/, we get a different word — *vat* /væt/. Allophones of the same phoneme, such as [p pʰ], do not contrast with each other; that is, if we exchange them, we do not get different words: *e.g.,* [spʰɪt] [pɪt]. These pronunciations just sound odd; the exchange does not form new words.

The **environment** of a sound is the phonetic context in which the sound occurs, *i.e.,* the adjacent sounds. The environment of [m] in *camp* is 'after initial [kʰæ] and before final [p]'. We can symbolise this environment as [kʰæ—p], where the dash shows the position of the sound in question. Allophones which occur in the same environment and create different words are said to contrast and to belong to different phonemes. Thus, in English, the allophones [pʰ] and [kʰ] belong to the different phonemes /p/ and /k/ because both occur in the same enviroment [—ɪt], as in the two words *pit* and *kit*. We say that *pit* and *kit,* form a **minimal pair** in that they differ in only one sound. A minimal pair always shows that two allophones contrast. We can also note that the allophones [p] and [pʰ] do not contrast as they do not occur in the same enviroment creating different words; we can never find a minimal pair with [p] and [pʰ] as the differing sounds.

Occasionally two sounds occur in the same environment without causing a difference in meaing. Such sounds are not considered contrastive but are said to be in **free variation**. In English, both [p] and [pʰ] occur in word-final position. The word *sip* may be heard as [sɪp] or as [sɪpʰ]. This alternation does not create different words and is not contrastive; rather, [p] and [pʰ] are in free variation and are allophones of the same phoneme /p/.

In Chapter 2, we said that the English affricates [tʃ] and [dʒ] are both sequences and single units. We can now see that at the phonetic level, they are sequences of a stop and a fricative. At the phonological level, however, they are single units, contrasting with other single consonants: *chill, Jill, pill, bill, dill, kill, mill.*

BROAD AND NARROW TRANSCRIPTION

Transcriptions may be described along a broad–narrow continuum. A **broad** transcription uses fewer symbols to represent the utterance, showing little phonetic detail. A **narrow** transcription shows more non-contrastive, phonetic detail. Since it is possible to show a little detail, or a lot, it is possible to have transcriptions which are more or less broad or narrow. The sentence *Small birds fly quickly* is transcribed below in broad transcription and then in two degrees of narrow transcription.

broad:	/ˈsmɑl ˌbɚdz flaj ˈkwɪkli/
somewhat narrower:	[ˈsmaɫ ˌbɚdz flaj ˈkʰwɪkli]
narrower still:	[ˈsmaˑɫ ˌbɚ·dz fla·j ˈkʰwɪkli]

A completely broad transcription is a phonemic transcription using the minimum number of symbols, one for each phoneme; such transcriptions are very useful. A completely narrow transcription would show all phonetic detail. This is practically impossible and such a transcription would probably be useless; we would be smothered in detail.

Transcriptions in this book are usually rather broad although we often use narrow transcriptions to illustrate a particular point. In doing so, the relevant parts of the form may be in narrow transcription, but the remainder of the form may be transcribed more broadly. This makes it easier to focus on the question at hand. For example, if we were discussing aspiration, we might transcribe [pʰɪt], rather than [pʰɪtˑ], not showing length with the [t], which would be irrelevant to our concern at the moment. A chart at the end of Chapter 4 gives practical suggestions for the amount of detail to show in broad and narrow transcriptions for English.

MORPHOLOGY

Phonemes are meaningless units of language. The individual phonemes /b/, /ʊ/, /k/, and /s/ have no meaning as such by themselves although in combination /bʊks/ does have a meaning In fact, the word *books* /bʊks/ can be divided into two parts, each with meaning: /bʊk/ is a 'bound piece of writing', and /s/ indicates 'plural'. These meaningful parts are called **morphemes** /ˈmoɹˌfim/. (Note that in our example, /s/ happens to be both a meaningless phoneme and a meaningful morpheme.) We will occasionally use these terms although **morphology** /ˌmoɹˈfalədʒi/ is a separate field of linguistics.

GENERAL

VOICING

Although we usually classify English consonants as voiced and voiceless, we find that the voiced obstruents, the stops and fricatives, are at least partially voiceless when they occur at the beginning or end of a word. In the transcriptions below, a subscript circle [̥] indicates voicelessness. Thus, [b̥b] means that the sound is voiceless at the beginning, but becomes voiced; the transcription [bb̥] indicates that the voiced sound becomes voiceless at the end. In these examples, the voiceless part is much shorter than the voiced part.

e.g.:	bee	[b̥bi]
	dead	[d̥dɛd̥]
	love	[lʌv̥]

We are not ordinarily aware of this short bit of voicelessness; however, if you listen carefully to a word such as *buy,* spoken in a slow, but casual style, you may be able to notice that voicing does not begin until a bit after the lips close to form the stop. Be wary of careful speech; one characteristic of careful speech for many people is to exaggerate various aspects, such as the amount of voicing. We will have more to say about voicing under *aspiration* later in this chapter.

LENGTH

Length refers simply to the duration of a sound. In English, neither consonants nor vowels are distinguished from each other by length. There is, however, a considerable amount of allophonic variation of length for both consonants and vowels.

Obviously, if you are speaking very quickly, you will make shorter sounds than if you are talking slowly. We are not interested in the absolute length of sounds, but in the length of sounds relative to each other. For example, we are interested in knowing whether the initial [k] and final [k] in *kick* have the same length or not.

Most of the variations in consonant length are so short that we require instruments which can measure differences in **milliseconds** (1/1000 of a second). Without trying to approach such accuracy, I will use a raised triangular dot [·] to show slight lengthening, and two dots [:] to show greater lengthening. Remember that the observations about length generally describe tendencies, not absolutes; also, our observations are about English, and are not necessarily true for other languages (Crystal & House, 1988a).

- Consonants at the end of a word are longer than at the beginning: *bib* [bɪb·], *lull* [lʌl·], *known* [nown·].
- Final consonants are longer after the vowels [ɪ ɛ æ ʊ ʌ] than after [i u ɑ] or

the diphthongs: *leap* [lip] — *lip* [lɪp·], *date* [dejt] — *debt* [dɛt·], *pool* [pul] — *pull* [pʊl·]. In Chapter 4, we will call [ɪ ɛ æ ʊ ʌ] the *lax* vowels, and the others *tense*.

- Voiceless consonants are longer at the end of a word than are voiced consonants: *nip* [nɪp·] — *nib* [nɪb], *rate* [ɹejt·] — *raid* [ɹejd], *hiss* [hɪs·] — *his* [hɪz].
- Postvocalically (occurring after vowels), [l n m] are longer before a voiced consonant than before a voiceless consonant: *help* [hɛlp] — *Elbe* [ɛl·b], *sent* [sɛnt] — *send* [sɛn·d], *wince* [wɪns] — *wins* [wɪn·z].

PLACE OF ARTICULATION

All sounds are affected by their environment to some extent. A common tendency, for example, is for a sound to become more like its neighbouring sounds. Some sounds seem susceptible to greater variation of this sort than others. Similarly, some sounds seem to exert greater influence upon their neighbours than do other sounds.

DENTALS AND ALVEOLARS When an alveolar sounds precedes a dental /θ ð/, the alveolar usually becomes dental as well. Say the word *ten;* feel where the tip of your tongue is during the /n/. It is on the alveolar ridge. Now try saying the word *tenth,* and feel where the tip of your tongue is for the /n/. You will find it against the teeth instead of its usual position at the alveolar ridge. The /n/ of *tenth* is a dental [n̪]. Rather than make an alveolar /n/ and then move the tongue forward to make a dental /θ/, we anticipate the dental articulation of the /θ/ and make the /n/ dental as well.

Instead of creating totally new symbols for dentals, we write the alveolar symbol with a diacritic [͜] beneath it: *e.g.,* [t̪ d̪ n̪ l̪], as in *width* [wɪt̪θ] or [wɪd̪θ], *tenth* [tɛn̪θ], *filth* [fɪl̪θ]. Some people may also assimilate a retroflex [ɹ] to a dental [ɹ] in this environment: *worthy* ['wəɹ̪ði].

We can say that in *tenth,* the alveolar [n] **assimilates** to the dental place of articulation of the the following [θ]. **Assimilation** /ə,sɪmɪ'lejʃən/ is the **process** by which one sound becomes more like another sound. Assimilation is a very common phonological process.

Note that this particular assimilation often occurs across word boundaries:

at three	[ˌæt̪ 'θɹi]	*in the book*	[ɪn̪ ðə 'bʊk]
read these	[ˌɹid̪ 'ðiz]	*Will this do?*	[ˌwɪl̪ 'ðɪs 'du]

A different example of assimilation is that after /ɹ/, an alveolar assimilates slightly to the retroflexed position of the /ɹ/. **Retroflexion** is indicated by a subscript dot [̣]: [ṭ ḍ ṇ].

hurt	[həɹṭ]	*bird*	[bəɹḍ]	*barn*	[baɹṇ]

VELARS The velar stops /k g/ are particularly sensitive to the nature of the vowels following them in the same syllable. If the following vowel is a front vowel, the closure for /k/ or /g/ is made quite far forward on the velar surface,

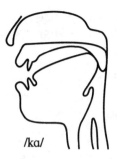

/ki/   /ka/

FIGURE 3.2   Tongue positions of velar stops before [i] and [ɑ].

almost into the palatal area. On the other hand, if the vowel is a back vowel — particularly a low one — the closure is made much farther back.

Try saying *key* /ki/ and *caw* /kɑ/. You can easily feel that, before /i/, the stop is made much farther forward than the stop of *caw* (Figure 3.2). With intermediate vowels, the closure is accordingly made at an intermediate point on the velar surface. Although there are as many /k/'s as there are vowel articulations, we usually note only a basic front–back difference in transcription. We can transcribe the fronted variety with a diacritic [‹], a small arrow pointing to the left [k‹]; this diacritic means that the sound is articulated a bit more forward than usual (always think of the head facing left). Thus, [k‹] is appropriate for a narrow transcription of /k/ before /i ɪ/ : *key* [k‹i], *kid* [k‹ɪd]. For the other types of /k/ made farther back, we will use the diacritic [›]: *coon* [k›un], *caught* [k›ɑt]. For *cave,* both [k‹ejv] or [k‹ejv] occur. Listen to see what you say.

The consonant /g/ has the same variations as /k/: *geese* [g‹is], *gill* [g‹ɪl]. The back variety is found before the other vowels: *good* [g›ʊd], *got* [g›ɑt], *go* [g›ow], *gut* [g›ʌt]; and *gay* varies: [g‹ej] and [g›ej].

HOMORGANIC NASALS   As we learned with *tenth* above, nasals preceding a consonant, particularly in the same syllable, commonly assimilate to the place of articulation as the following consonant. Not only does /n/ become [n̪] in *tenth,* but we also find [m] before /b p/, [n] before /t d/, and [ŋ] before /k g/. Such a nasal is called **homorganic** /ˌhomoɹˈgænɪk/, *i.e.,* made with the same organs; thus two adjacent consonants which have the same place of articulation are said to be homorganic consonants. Examples of a homorganic nasal before a stop are: *limp* [lɪmp], *rumble* [ˈɹʌmbəl], *dent* [dɛnt], *boned* [bownd], *jingle* [ˈdʒɪŋgəl], *rank* [ɹæŋk].

Nasals also generally assimilate to the place of articulation of a following labio-dental or dental fricative: *symphony* [ˈsɪɱfəni], *lymph* [lɪɱf], *circumvent* [ˌsəɹkəɱˈvɛnt]; *tenth* [tɛn̪θ], *enthusiastic* [ən̪ˌθuziˈæstɪk]. The symbol [ɱ] is used for a labio-dental nasal.

Assimilations of this nature are common within a word, particularly within the same syllable. It is not unusual, however, particularly in casual speech, for /n/ to assimilate to the following consonant over a word boundary: *in five* [ˌɪɱ ˈfajv], *ten pieces* [ˌtɛm ˈpisɪz], *on board* [ˌɑm ˈboɹd], *and that* [ˌæn̪ ˈðæt], *in case* [ˌɪŋ ˈkejs], *in gear* [ˌɪŋ ˈgiɹ].

STOPS

ASPIRATION

Voiceless stops are aspirated at the beginning of a stressed syllable: *pull* [ˈpʰʊl], *talk* [ˈtʰɑk], *candle* [ˈkʰændəl], *impel* [ɪmˈpʰɛl], *retard* [ɹɪˈtʰɑɹd], *incur* [ɪŋˈkʰəɹ]. After a syllable-initial /s/ and at the beginning of an unstressed syllable, voiceless stops are not aspirated: *spy* [ˈspaj], *stare* [ˈsteɹ], *skipper* [ˈskɪpəɹ], *super* [ˈsupəɹ], *lucky* [ˈlʌki].

Aspiration involves a delay in the onset of voicing; that is, in the segment following the aspirated stop voicing does not begin immediately, but is delayed slightly. During voicelessness, the vocal cords are more open than they are in voicing; air continues to pass through the glottis during the closure for the stop made higher in the vocal tract. This greater air flow is responsible for the 'puff of air' heard as the stop is released. Aspiration is usually symbolised by the diacritic [ʰ]. An alternative notation would be to show the delay in voicing by placing a symbol for a voiceless vowel before the main vowel to indicate that in aspiration the vowel begins voiceless and then becomes voiced. The ring [̥] below a sound indicates that it is voiceless.

top	[tʰɑp]	*or*	[tɑ̥ɑp]
plum	[pʰlʌm]	*or*	[pl̥ʌm]
queen	[kʰwin]	*or*	[kw̥in]

Figure 3.3 shows the timing of voicing for an initial voiced stop, voiceless stop, and voiceless aspirated stop. In Figure 3.3, time proceeds from left to right. The top two lines show the tongue position and glottal state for a voiced [d]. At the beginning of the [d], the alveolar opening closes to become a stop; this is shown by the merger of the two lines into a single line. At the beginning to the stop, the vocal cords are in a voiceless position. Part way through the stop, the vocal cords begin to vibrate in voicing.

In the voiceless unaspirated stop [t], the onset of voicing is simultaneous with the release of the stop. Thus, the stop is completely voiceless, and the vowel is completely voiced. (Note that [d̥] and [t] are equivalent notations.)

The bottom portion of Figure 3.3 shows an aspirated stop [tʰ]. Here the voicelessness of the stop continues part way into the vowel after the stop is released.

AFFRICATION

The sequences /t # j/ and /d # j/, where /#/ indicates a word boundary, are often realised as [tʃj] and [dʒj]: *I'll hit you* [ˌajl ˈhɪtʃju], *She fed you* [ˌʃi ˈfɛdʒju]. The /j/ in these forms may be lost: [ˌajl ˈhɪtʃu], [ˌʃi ˈfɛdʒu].

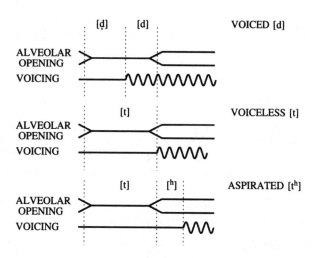

Figure 3.3

The timing of the alveolar closure in relation to voicing is shown for voiced, voiceless, and voiceless aspirated stops. For the position of the tongue, a single line shows closure and a divided line shows opening. In the line for voicing, a straight line shows voicelessness, and a wiggly line shows voicing.

Before /ɹ/, /t/ and /d/ are sometime retroflexed with a retroflexed palato-alveolar fricative component: *tree* [tʃʷɹi], *trap* [tʃʷɹæp], *dream* [dʒʷɹim], *drew* [dʒʷɹu]. The rounding can be explained as due to the inherent rounding of the [ɹʷ]. This type of affrication is quite variable. Different speakers vary considerably, even among their own pronunciations. It seems commonest before /i/, as in *tree, sentry*.

RELEASE

Phonemic voiced stops are usually phonetically somewhat voiceless at the end of a word or phrase, and may on occasion be almost entirely voiceless: [bɛdd̥], [kæbb̥], [dʌgg̊]. It may seem odd to say that *voiced* sounds are *voiceless*, but remember that we are dealing with different levels; stops which are considered voiced at the phonemic level may be voiceless at the phonetic level. The transcriptions [dd̥], etc., are used to show partial voicelessness and not necessarily greater length of the stop.

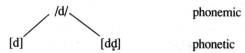

Stops at the end of a phrase may be released immediately or held for some time so that the release is **inaudible**. The raised corner [˺] is used to show stops with inaudible release: *lab* [læb] ~ [læb˺], *rid* [ɹid] ~ [ɹid˺], *beg* [bɛg] ~ [bɛg˺]. The two allophones of /b/ — [b b˺] — are thus in free variation with each other; *i.e.*, a final stop may be released audibly or not with no difference in meaning.

Phonemically voiceless stops at the end of a word or phrase are also phonetically voiceless. They may be plain, aspirated, or inaudibly released. Like the final allophones of the voiced stops, these three allophones are also in free variation: *hip* [hɪp] ~ [hɪpʰ] ~ [hɪp˺], *put* [pʰʊt] ~ [pʰʊtʰ] ~ [pʰʊt˺], *sock* [sɑk]~[sɑkʰ]~[sɑk˺].

In ordinary speech, when two stops with the same place of articulation occur in a row, the cluster is heard as one long stop, with no release at all after the first stop. In phrases like *black coal* and *black gold,* there is no release after the first /k/. We can use [k˺] to symbolise either no release, or inaudible release: [ˌblæk˺ˈkol], [ˌblæk˺ˈgold]. The release of consonants in clusters with different places of articulation is discussed in the following section.

OVERLAPPING

Although we say that in a word such as *peck* the sounds occur in the sequence /p – ε – k/, in fact the tongue moves to a position for /ɛ/ before the lips part at the end of the [p]. Likewise, the back of the tongue is moving upwards getting ready for the /k/ before the end of the /ɛ/. **Overlapping** refers to the fact that the gestures of one sound are not completely discrete as to timing from those of its neighbours.

Many allophonic variations can be explained by overlapping. Most consonants are rounded to some degree before a rounded vowel: *e.g., tulip* [ˈtʷuləp], *knows* [nʷowz]. This is explained as due to the fact that the lips assume a rounded position in advance of the vowel itself. Lip rounding is shown by a diacritic [ʷ].

A particular type of overlapping is shown in words such as *apt*. Phonemically, the word is /æpt/ with a simple sequence of /p/ followed by /t/. Phonetically, however, the /t/ is formed before the /p/ is released (Figure 3.4). Try saying *apt*; now, say it again, but stop half-way through, at the /p/. You will probably feel the tip of your tongue already at the alveolar ridge before the /p/ is released. There is a short period when a simultaneous [p͡t] is made. We do not hear the release of the /p/ when the lips part because the tongue has already made a closure for the /t/. For this reason, we say that in a sequence of two overlapping stops, the first is released silently (Henderson & Rupp, 1982); in a narrow transcription, we can show this as [æp͡t]. We do not hear the release of the /p/ or the onset of the /t/. (The superscript arch [͡] indicates that the sounds are pronounced simultaneously.)

TAPS

In most North American dialects of English, the /t/ in a word like *city* is pronounced quite differently from the /t/ of *top*. Say these words aloud: *city, butter, matter, lettuce.* If you listen carefully, you can feel that the /t/-sound in these words is voiced (feel your vocal cords); you can also note that this sound is made very quickly. This sound is a voiced, alveolar **tap**. Try saying the pair: *city — settee.* In *settee*, with an ordinary [t], the tongue movement seems much more

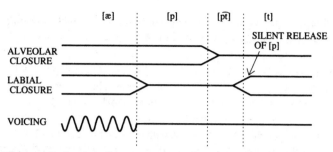

Figure 3.4 Overlapping in *apt*. The timing of the labial closure is shown in relation to the alveolar closure.

deliberate; in *city*, the feeling is that everything is made ready for the /t/, and then — the tongue strikes against the alveolar ridge only momentarily. Taps are faster than stops; compare *latter — ladder, matter — madder*.

The difference between stops and taps can be compared to that between guided and ballistic missiles. Guided missiles are under the command of the control centre from start to finish. Their course can be altered in mid-flight. With ballistic missiles, such as a rifle bullet, the course cannot be altered once the missile has been fired. Stops are like guided missiles. The course of the action of the articulators is the control of the nervous system throughout the production of the stop. Taps, on the other hand, are like ballistic missiles in that once the action starts, they are no longer controlled.

The voiced alveolar tap which occurs in English can be transcribed with the symbol [ɾ]. It occurs as an allophone of /t/ at the beginning of a non-initial unstressed syllable: ['sɪɾi] 'city', ['bɛɾi] 'Betty', ['lɛɾəɹ] 'letter', ['ɛɾɪkət] 'etiquette'. Dialects of English vary in the use of taps.

Many speakers also have a nasal tap in words such as *winter* ['wɪɾ̃əɹ]. Here, the velum is down allowing air to flow out the nose. The diacritic, a *tilde* /'tɪldə/, indicates nasality. In such a word, the consonants form a sequence /nt/ at the phonemic level, but a single segment [ɾ̃] at the phonetic level.

FRICATIVES

The labio-dentals /f/ and /v/ do not exhibit major allophonic variations. The adjacent vocalic articulation overlaps with the labio-dental articulation. The sound /f/ is voiceless and [v] is usually partially voiceless (like the voiced stops described above).

The dental fricatives exhibit some individual variation as to whether the tip or the blade of the tongue is used. The variation in sound is very slight; however, with a little practice, you should be able to make both varieties. We can label these **apico-dentals** and **lamino-dentals**.

Dentals also vary with individuals as to whether the tongue is behind the teeth or partly protrudes between the teeth. The latter are often referred to as **interdentals**. I use these occasionally when speaking in a loud or very careful manner.

Before /s z/, dental fricatives are frequently lost in casual speech: compare *cloths* [klɑ(θ)s] — *clothes* [klow(ð)z]. Would you ordinarily distinguish *booze* from *booths?* For some speakers, although the dental fricative itself is lost, the time span it occupies may be preserved by lengthening the final consonant: [klɑs·] *cloths,* [klowz·] *clothes.*

There is a certain amount of variation in the way /s/ or /z/ is produced. Various tongue positions produce the same sound. Typically, the tip of the tongue is near the alveolar ridge with only a very narrow opening. Air passes through this gap, striking the rear surface of the teeth, and makes a hissing noise. Some speakers make the gap more with the blade of the tongue, with the tip pointing down. The latter can be called **lamino-alveolar**, as opposed to the more common **apico-alveolar**. A common speech problem is the substitution of [θ ð] for [s z]. This is known as a **lisp**.

The palato-alveolar fricatives [ʃ ʒ] are made with a broader surface of the tongue than are the alveolar fricatives. Individuals show considerable variation in producing palato-alveolars. There may be an arching of the tongue so that the laminal surface articulates with the alveolar ridge and the forward part of the palate. Alternatively, the tip of the tongue may be raised or even curled back as for retroflex sounds, but with less hollowing of the tongue body. In English the palato-alveolar fricatives [ʃ] and [ʒ] regularly show rounding, even when not next to rounded vowels: *ship* [ʃʷɪp], *fission* [ˈfɪʃʷən], *measure* [ˈmɛʒʷəɹ]. Rounding is indicated by the diacritic [ʷ].

Like /t # j/ and /d # j/, the sequences /s # j/ and /z # j/ are often realised as [ʃj] and [ʒj]: *I'll miss you* [ˌajl ˈmɪʃju], *I'll buzz you* [ˌajl ˈbʌʒju]. The /j/ in these forms may be lost: [ˌajl ˈmɪʃu], [ˌajl ˈbʌʒu].

At the beginning of a word, [h] is somewhat anomalous. Phonetically, it is not really a consonant, but a voiceless vowel. The mouth is shaped exactly as it would be for the following vowel, but the sound produced is voiceless: *hit* [ɪ̥ɪt], *hoot* [u̥ut], *home* [o̥owm]. The small circle under a sound is a diacritic indicating voiceless-ness. To prove the nature of [h] to yourself, say a vowel, make it voiceless, and you will hear an [h]. Ordinarily we will transcribe this sound as [h], rather than as [ɪ̥ e̥ ɑ̥], etc.

In the middle of a word, such as in *ahoy* or *ahead,* the /h/ is neither voiced nor voiceless. It is made with another adjustment of the vocal cords, called **murmur** /ˈmɚmɚ/. We will discuss murmur more fully in Chapter 14. For the time being, use [ɦ] to transcribe /h/ in the middle of words: [əˈɦɔj əˈɦɛd]. Murmured [ɦ] also occurs in a stressed syllable at the beginning of a word if the preceding sound is an unstressed vowel.

a head	[ə ˈɦɛd]
the high one	[ðə ˈɦaj ˌwʌn]

The initial cluster /hj/ is found in words like *hew, huge, human*. We treat this phonemically as a cluster /hj/ although phonetically it is a single segment — a voiceless palatal glide [j̥]: [j̥u j̥udʒ ˈj̥umən] *hew, huge, human.*

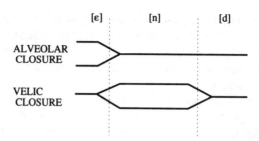

Figure 3.5 Nasal onset in *send*. The timing relationship of the closure for the stop and the closure of the nasal passage are shown.

NASALS

The allophonic alternation of homorganic nasals has already been noted above. The sound /n/ is regularly dental [n̪] before [θ ð]: *anther* ['æn̪θəɹ], *win them* ['wɪn̪ ðəm]. The velar nasal /ŋ/ occurs only **postvocalically** /ˌpowstˌvoˈkælɪkli/ (after a vowel) in a syllable: *singing* ['sɪŋɪŋ]. Velar /y/ is common before /g/ or /k/; otherwise, it is found only at the end of a morpheme; the only exception I know is *hangar* ['hæŋəɹ]. In transcribing /ŋ/, note that the spelling *ng* sometimes includes a [g]-sound, and sometimes not: *finger* ['fɪŋgəɹ], *wringer* ['ɹɪŋəɹ].

NASAL ONSET AND RELEASE

When a nasal occurs next to a homorganic stop, *i.e.*, one with the same place of articulation, the transition between nasal and stop is marked by the minimum articulatory change. For example, consider the consonants after the vowel in *send* [sɛnd]. During the [n], the vocal cords are vibrating, the nasal passage is open allowing air to escape through the nose, and the tip of the tongue is touching the alveolar ridge stopping air from escaping through the mouth. The only difference between an [n] and a [d] is that the velum is lowered for the [n]. Thus, the transition from [n] to [d] is marked only by raising the velum. Taking the stop as

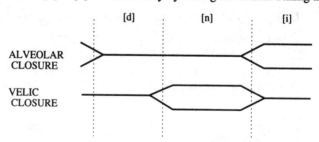

Figure 3.6 Nasal release in *Rodney*. The timing relationship of the closure for the stop and the opening of the nasal passage is shown.

primary, we say that it has a **nasal onset**. Figure 3.5 shows the relative timing for the alveolar closure and the velic closure in nasal onset in the word *send.*

In a word like *Rodney* [ˈɹɑdni] (Figure 3.6), the same transition between stop and nasal occurs except in the reverse order. Here the stop has **nasal release** marked by a lowering of the velum allowing air to escape through the nose.

A word such as *kindness* [ˈkajndnɪs] exhibits both nasal onset and nasal release.

GLOTTALISATION

Many speakers make a simultaneous glottal stop during a /t/ which precedes a syllabic [n̩] or which follows an /n/ at the end of a word. The raised arch [⌐] is used over two symbols, as in [ʔt͡], to indicate that they are pronounced simultaneously.

button	[ˈbʌʔt͡n̩]	*cut*	[kʌʔt͡]
kitten	[ˈkɪʔt͡n̩]	*don't*	[downʔt͡]

Some speakers may have only a glottal stop for a /t/ in these positions: [kʌʔ] 'cut', [ˈbʌʔn̩] 'button'. Such pronunciations are quite common in many British accents.

APPROXIMANTS

LATERAL APPROXIMANT

The lateral approximant /l/ reflects the quality of the following vowel. Try saying just the /l/ of the following words: *leap, lit, late, let, lad, log, luck, lope, look, loom.* The /l/ of each of these has a slightly different **vowel colour** or quality; however, we generally need to distinguish only two kinds of vowel colour with /l/. **Clear /l/** occurs before front vowels; it is simply transcribed as [l]: [lip lɪt lejt lɛt læd] *lip, lit, late, let, lad.* The **dark /l/** is transcribed [ɫ]; it occurs before the back vowels: [ɫʌk ɫowp ɫʊk ɫum] *luck, lope, look, loom.* Dark /l/ also occurs at the end of a syllable *bell* [bɛɫ], *built* [bɪɫt], *ladle* [ˈlejdɫ]; it is particularly noticeable when syllabic (p. 46).

LATERAL ONSET AND RELEASE   Lateral onset and release are par-
allel to nasal onset and release. The transition is from a lateral articulation to a central one, or vice-versa. In going between /d/ and /l/, the only change is that the sides of the tongue rise or fall.

Lateral onset occurs in *build.* During the /l/, the sides of the tongue are down allowing air to pass out laterally, but the tip of the tongue is touching the alveolar ridge. At the beginning of the /d/, the sides of the tongue come up to form a complete closure, thus producing a /d/. In lateral release, as in *fiddler,* the events occur in the reverse order. Lateral onset is shown in Figure 3.8 where the narrowing of the lines indicates the partial closure for the /l/, followed by a complete closure for the /d/.

Figure 3.7 Clear and dark /l/.

SYLLABIC CONSONANTS

Ordinarily every syllable contains a vowel as its central part. Sometimes, however, a syllable contains a sonorant nasal or liquid instead of a vowel. Pronounce the word *sudden* at an ordinary rate. You will notice that the tip of your tongue does not move away from the alveolar ridge between the /d/ and the /n/. Since it stays at the alveolar ridge, there can be no intervening vowel. The /n/ itself forms a syllable; we call it a **syllabic** nasal, transcribed [n̩], with a short subscript stroke as the diacritic to indicate **syllabicity** /ˌsɪləˈbɪsɪti/.

In like manner, you can observe that the final sonorants in *ladle* and *bottom* can be pronounced with syllabic consonants: [ˈlejdl̩], [ˈbaɾm̩]. These words, like *sudden*, can alternatively be pronounced with a vowel: [ˈsʌdən], [ˈlejdəl], [ˈbaɾəm]. However, the pronunciations with the vowel are typical of very careful, slow speech and may sound somewhat stilted and artificial; the pronunciations with the syllabic consonant are much commoner. Syllabic consonants also occur occasionally after fricatives: *prison* [ˈpɹɪzn̩], *prism* [ˈpɹɪzm̩], *rhythm* [ˈɹɪðm̩].

In rapid speech, further combinations occur:

> *bacon* [ˈbejkŋ̩]   *bump 'em* [ˈbʌmpm̩]   *ribbon* [ˈɹɪbm̩]

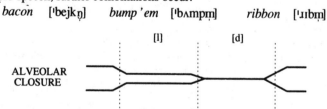

Figure 3.8 Lateral onset in *build*. The timing relationship of the lateral and the alveolar stop is shown.

RHOTIC APPROXIMANT

Initially, /ɹ/ may be pronounced in one of two ways: with the tongue tip up, or with the tip pointing down and the tongue bunched. In either case, initial /ɹ/ in English is usually rounded [ɹʷ]. Speakers who ordinarily make /ɹ/ with the tongue tip up may find that they use a 'bunched /ɹ/' after velars: *crate, green.* Conversely, speakers with a 'bunched /ɹ/' may keep the tongue tip up after alveolar stops: *tree, drain.*

In the phonemic sequence /əɹ/, the **rhotacisation** /ˌɹotəsɪˈzejʃən/, or retroflexion, of the /ɹ/ is commonly simultaneous with the schwa, *i.e.,* the schwa is retroflexed or **rhotic** /ˈɹowtɪk/. Thus, a two-segment phonemic sequence /əɹ/ is realised as a single phonetic segment. This rhotic schwa has a special symbol [ɚ]. The body of the tongue is in position for a [ə], and the tip of the tongue is retroflexed back to the palato-alveolar region. To some degree all vowels preceding /ɹ/ are rhotic; *e.g., beer, care, far, door, cure.* However, the temporal overlapping is much more complete in the case of /ə/.

We have called this sound a rhotic schwa and transcribed it as [ɚ]. We could just as well have called it a syllabic /ɹ/ and transcribed it as [ɹ̩]. The first way conceptualises it as the vowel /ə/ with rhotic properties; the second way thinks of it as the consonant /ɹ/ with syllabic properties. There is no difference in the sound produced, no matter how we conceptualise it. In making narrow transcriptions, I will use [ɚ], and /əɹ/ in broad transcriptions.

In *furry,* both [ˈfəɹi] and [ˈfɚi] occur as pronunciations; even [fɚ̩i] seems possible, although rare. Try to see which you have. Try as well to produce the other pronunciations. Other words of this sort are *curry, slurring, burrow* and, for many speakers, *stirrup* and *syrup.*

Occasionally, /ɹ/ after initial /θ/ is pronounced as an alveolar tap, as in *three* [θɾi]. This is more common in emphatic speech.

TECHNICAL TERMS

affricated	dark [ɫ]	millisecond
allophone	diacritic	minimal pair
allophonic	environment	morphology
apico-alveolar.	free variation	morpheme
apico-dentals	fricative	murmur
approximant	homorganic	narrow
aspiration	inaudible release	nasal onset
assimilate	interdental	nasal release
assimilation	lamino-alveolar	overlapping
broad	lamino-dentals	phonology
centisecond	lateral onset	phoneme
central	lateral release	phonemic
clear [l]	length	phonetic
contrast	lisp	postvocalic

47

process	solidi	syllabicity
retroflexion	square brackets	tap
rhotic	stops	tilde
slant lines	syllabic	vowel colour

SYMBOLS

Name	Use	Name	Use
[ɱ] **m with tail**	labio-dental nasal	[͟] **subscript bridge**	dental
[ɦ] **hooktop h**	murmured h	[.] **subscript dot**	retroflex
[ɫ]	dark l	[ʰ] **raised h**	aspiration
[ɾ]	tap	[ʷ] **raised w**	rounding
[ː] **colon**	extra length	[ˌ] **subscript stroke**	syllabic
[·] **raised dot**	slight extra length	[ʷ] **raised w**	rounding
[̥] **subscript circle**	voiceless	[⌒] **superscript arch**	simultaneous pronunciation

EXERCISES

BASIC

1. Review.

a. Pronounce the following English words written in a broad transcription:

stɹɪp	θɹɪps	ɹʌŋz	tʃæns	θætʃt	plɪnθ
jɛld	θɪŋ	ðʌs	kædʒ	ʃɹʌgd	θɹɛd

b. Transcribe the following in a broad transcription; remember to mark stress in words with more than one syllable:

thin	lung	gin	then	yen	stretch
shin	chin	death	bait	blind	feed
shoal	don	ground	join	moon	mew
blue	through	sigh	feud	tough	coat
food	though	bleed	flood	sew	shade
stealth	thwack	chugged	push	than	yelp
myths	eggshells	thanks	plunge	fling	rubbed

Florence	Kate	Priscilla	Stuart	Nancy	Ida
Edwin	Basil	Veronica	Ethel	Xavier	Jerome
Aaron	Clarissa	Desmond	Leroy	Euphemia	Quincy
Maria	Randolph	Timothy	Gertrude	Yolanda	Oliver
Heather	Zacharias	Winifred	Theodore	Sean	Augusta
Swithin	Ninian				

2. Say *hat*. Stretch out the [h]: [hhhhhæt]. Now, say just the [h] alone: [hhhhhhhh]. In English, /h/ does not occur at the end of a word. One way of improving you phonetic ability is to learn to say a sound in positions where it

does not occur in English In the following exercises, the [h] is at the end of the word. Start slowly, [mɛhhhhh], stretching out the [h]. Then gradually shorten it to [mɛh].

mɛh	mɪh	lɪh	kɪh	wɪh	nɪh
lɛh	mæh	bʊh			

3. Since /h/ is a voiceless vowel, a word like *hiss* can be transcribed as [ɪ̥ɪs], where the diacritic [̥] indicates voicelessness. The /h/ is always the same quality as the following vowel; *i.e., hope* [o̥owp]. Transcribe the following, showing /h/ as a voiceless vowel of the appropriate quality:

hit	head	hat	hut	hoot	hot
heel	hole	hoof			

4. [ŋ] Transcribe:

bang	lung	gangs	sinks	singing	dunking

The sound [ŋ] does not occur at the beginning of words in English. Try the following hints to learn to say [ŋ] at the beginning of a word.

a. Try saying [ŋŋŋŋŋ], and then shorten it gradually to just [ŋ].

b. If this seems not to work, try saying sing [sɪŋ], then [ɪŋ], then [ɪŋŋŋŋ]. Gradually lengthen the [ŋ] until you can say it without any vowel. Now try saying *sing it*. Start with [sɪŋɪt], then say [ɪŋɪt], then [ŋɪt].

Try these nonsense words to learn to pronounce [ŋ] in initial position:

ŋɪt	ŋæk	ŋed	ŋʌbd	ŋɪks	ŋʊlb

5. Aspiration. This exercise will first help you to become aware of aspiration and then to control it.

a. Put the open palm of your hand close to your mouth and say *pit - spit*. You will notice a stronger puff of air with the [p] of *pit* than with *spit*. The puff of air is related to the phenomenon known as aspiration. The /p/ in *pit* is said to be aspirated, and the /p/ in *spit*, unaspirated. In a narrow transcription, aspiration is transcribed with a small, raised [ʰ] after the stop, *e.g.,* [pʰɪt - spɪt].

b. Try the same experiment with your hand with the words *tool - stool* and *cool - school*. In English voiceless stops /p t k/ are aspirated at the beginning of a stressed syllable, but not when the stop is preceded by /s/.

c. In the following exercise, pronounce the words normally and then try to pronounce aspirated stops after /s/. If you have difficulty, try sounding emphatic.

stop	stɑp	stʰɑp	*spun*	spʌn	spʰʌn
skid	skɪd	skʰɪd	*stool*	stul	stʰul

Try these:

spʰɪfi	stʰʌfi	skʰɪni	spʰlin	stʰɛlθ	skʰwɪd

d. To make an initial unaspirated stop, try the following exercise:
   Start with [stɑp]; lengthen the [s] to [sssssstɑp]. Now make a short pause be-tween the [s] and the [t] without aspirating the [t]. It helps to try to relax your mouth. From [sssss tɑp], try to lengthen the pause, and then do away with the [s] altogether.
   It may help to articulate softly when working on unaspirated stops at first.

e. Some people use a special kind of English when speaking to babies. They delete initial preconsonantal /s/ leaving an unaspirated consonant at the beginning:

   e.g.: spit   [spɪt]   →   [pɪt]
       [pɪɾ ɪɾ awt]   'spit it out'
       [tɑp ɪt]   'stop it'
       [gow ɾə kul]   'go to school'

   If you are familiar with this dialect of English, you already know how to produce initial unaspirated stops. If not, now is the time to learn it.
   Try saying
       [ˌpɪɾ awt ðə ˈpʰɪt]   'spit out the pit'
       [ˌɪts kʰul ɪŋ ˈkul]   'it's cool in school'
       [ˌtɑp ðə ˈtʰɑp]   'stop the top'

f. Now try both aspirated and unaspirated stops at the beginning of a word:

top	tʰɑp	tɑp	*cub*	kʰʌb	kʌb
put	pʰʊt	pʊt	*turn*	tʰɚn	tɚn

6. Practise saying the following, making all the voiceless stops unaspirated:
   Tiny Teddy Tucker tripped his two-toed, timid twin, Tutu.
   Pushy Patty Potter paid the punky, pompous parson for the puny pumpkin pie.
   Queen Catherine kissed her crotchety cousin and complimented her kinky colleague King Carl the Cute.
   Tanned Poppy MacLean paid quite close attention to her customer's pleasant trill.

7. Pronounce the following words using [ʒ] for the sound shown in boldface type:

rouge	liege	loge	garage	refuge	azure
Giles	**Jean**	measure			

8. These words have more than one pronunciation. For each transcribe as many pronunciations as possible.

bow	read	sow	lead	mow

9. The symbol [ɚ] is used for the sound in *fur, brother,* or *dirtier.*

a. Pronounce:

kɚ	tʃɚtʃ	ˈɚmɚ	ɪnˈfɚ	pɚˈvɚt	flɚt

b. Transcribe each of the following phonemically and phonetically:

    ladder   summer   irksome   surfer   murder   murderer

10. In English, alveolar [n t d l] occurring immediately before a dental [θ] are regularly changed to a dental [n̪ t̪ d̪ l̪]. The diacritic [̪] is used to change the symbol for an alveolar sound to that of a dental.

    Pronounce *ten* [tɛn] and *tenth* [tɛn̪θ]. Note that the place of articulation of the nasal of *ten* is alveolar whereas the nasal of *tenth* is dental.

Pronounce the following:

    ejt̪θ   fɪl̪θ   ˈsɛvən̪θ

Transcribe:

    wealthy   tenths   width

Try saying the following first with alveolars and then replace them with dentals.

    Ed edited a tiny titilating trilogy on dental trills.

    Daniel doted on Dotty's tantalising tidbits.

11. Taps. Most North American dialects of English have two quite different alveolar consonants in a word such as *titter*. The first is an aspirated alveolar stop [tʰ]; the second is a voiced alveolar tap [ɾ]. A tap feels quick as opposed to the more careful [t]. In North American English this tap replaces [t] at the beginning of an unstressed syllable.

Pronounce the following words and note the tap:

    city   mutter   writing   latter   water   witty
    weighty   hated

Dialects with [ɾ] generally distinguish it from [d], a voiced alveolar stop; *i.e.* they contrast *latter* [ˈlæɾɚ] and *ladder* [ˈlædɚ]. Some dialects, however, merge the two and pronounce *both* as [ˈlædɚ] or [ˈlæɾɚ].

Pronounce the following words first with [ɾ], then with [d], and then with [t]:

e.g.:   city   [ˈsɪɾi — ˈsɪdi — ˈsɪti]
    Betty   writing   fitted   little   better   metal
    kitty   batted   cut it

The following words normally have [tʰ]; pronounce them with [ɾ]:

e.g.: hotel   [howˈtʰɛl] → [howˈɾɛl]
    eternal   retire   deter

For the *t* of the following words substitute in turn [tʰ t ɾ d]:

e.g.: [ɹɪˈtʰɚn — ɹɪˈtɚn — ɹɪˈɾɚn — ɹɪˈdɚn]
    return   cutter   bat   town

12. Inaudible release. At the end of a word a voiceless stop in English has three alternative forms in free variation with each other: aspirated, unaspirated, or inaudibly released. Thus *lip* can be pronounced [lɪpʰ — lɪp — lɪp̚].

Try the following words with all three types of final voiceless stop:

    gnat   neck   knot   rap   hurt   belt
    nest   lint

13. Overlapping. When consonants having different places of articulation come together in English, the articulation of the second is generally in place before the first ends. With a word like *act* [æk˺t], the tip of the tongue is in place before the [k] is released.

    Pronounce the following:

    ˈæk˺təɹ ˈæp˺t ˈlæk˺ˌtejt ˈɹep˺ˌtajl ˈdɛd˺ˌpæn ˈpɪt˺ˌkeɹn

    Transcribe the following, paying attention to overlapping and also to whether the stops are aspirated, unaspirated, or inaudibly released. Write out alternative transcriptions where more than one type is possible. Practise pronouncing all possibilities.

stopping	stopped	topped	diphthong	nightcall	steak
knife	feckless	misplaced	report	restart	ignite
ripcord					

14. Transcribe the following:

    'The variety of quirks, ailments, and miscellaneous disfigurements that can strike the average supermarket shopping cart is truly amazing,' said she.

    'Odd, isn't it,' mused Mabel, simultaneously perusing the posterior of the gentleman thumping a canteloupe, 'how often tins of mushrooms are dented'.

ADVANCED

15. Read aloud:

    /ˌwɪθ əz ˌlɪtəl ˌɛnəɹˌdʒi ənd əz ˌmʌtʃ ˌfals ˈhowp əz ə ˌlabstəɹ ˌkept əˈlajv ɪn ə ˌɹestəˌɹant ˈwɪndow, ˈpitəɹ ˌɹɪtʃəɹdz əˈwowk ən dɪd hɪz ˌfju ˌsmal ˌmɪnɪŋlɪs ˈɛksəɹˌsajzəz/

16. Practise saying the following words, first with a final consonant, then with a final [h], and then with no consonant at all.

    e.g.: lɪk lɪh lɪ

fɛg	wʌŋ	væm	dæb	lʊd	zʌð
fʊn	kɛs	tɪʒ	mɛl	gʊf	bʌk

17. Syllabic consonants are made without a vowel. Transcribe the following with a syllabic consonant. Practise saying them both with a vowel and with a syllabic consonant.

    e.g.: sodden [ˈsadən] [ˈsadn̩]

sodden	sudden	hidden	laden	leaden	wooden

    In words like *button,* we get a variety of pronunciations: [ˈbʌtn̩ ˈbʌʔn̩ ˈbʌʔ͡tn̩] where [ʔ͡t] represents a simultaneous glottal stop and [t].

    Transcribe your pronunciation of the following:

button	kitten	rotten	batten

    Listen closely and transcribe your pronunciation of the following:

bottom	item	atom	datum

Now say these words first with a vowel—nasal and then with a syllabic nasal:

e.g.: button   [ˈbʌtən]   [ˈbʌtn̩]

   kitten   rotten   satan   tighten

Do you have syllabic nasals in *prison, prism* ?

Transcribe the following, using a syllabic nasal wherever possible:

e.g.: blacken   [ˈblækn̩]

   bacon   Fagan   Hogan   ship 'em   stab 'em   happen

Transcribe the following:

   idle   ripple   trickle   dangle   nickel   saddle

18. Voicing practice. We have a number of sounds which form voiceless-voiced pairs.

Try the following, reading across:

   s s s s s   z z z z z   f f f f f   v v v v
   θ θ θ θ θ   ð ð ð ð   ʃ ʃ ʃ ʃ ʃ   ʒ ʒ ʒ ʒ ʒ

While saying these, place your fingers over your adam's apple and feel the vocal cords vibrate during voicing. Practise alternating between voiced and voiceless until you have a sense of control over voicing.

   s z s z s z s z   f v f v f v f v
   θ ð θ ð θ ð θ ð   ʃ ʒ ʃ ʒ ʃ ʒ ʃ ʒ

The sounds [m n l ɹ] usually occur voiced in English; their voiceless counterparts are written with a diacritic [̥]—[m̥ n̥ l̥ ɹ̥]. Many people have a form to show agreement [ʔm̩ˈʔm̥] with the second syllable voiceless and higher in pitch. Say this and feel the voicelessness of [m̥] at your adam's apple.

Practice:

   m m m m m m̥ m m̥ m m̥   l l l l l l̥ l̥ l̥ l̥ l̥
   n n n n n n̥ n̥ n̥ n̥ n̥   ɹ ɹ ɹ ɹ ɹ ɹ̥ ɹ̥ ɹ̥ ɹ̥ ɹ̥
   l̥ l̥ l̥ l̥ l̥   m m m̥ m m̥
   n n̥ n n̥ n   ɹ ɹ ɹ̥ ɹ ɹ̥

none	m̥ɔmæ	lalu	nan̥ɛ	ɹ̥ʌɹɛ	mɛnɑ
læ̥ɹɑ	noɹ̥ʊ	m̥ʊm	lilo̥	ɹɑɹɪ	ŋum̥o
n̥oɹʊ	m̥ælɔ	ɪnm̥ɛ	ɹ̥ilu		

19. Voiceless sonorants. When an aspirated stop precedes [l ɹ w j] in English, the sonorant is usually voiceless.

Transcribe the following:

   pray   tray   cute   puny   cream   twin
   quince   plump   plough

Pronounce each of the following words listening to the voiceless sonorant. After saying each one, repeat it without the initial stop, but leaving the sonorant voiceless:

e.g.: pray   [pɹ̥ej — ɹ̥ej]

   pray   cram   trip   plough   clay   trump
   puny   cute   quash

20. Tap.
    Practise these forms with intervocalic [ɾ]:
    ɑɾɑ   ˈiɾi   ˈɛɾu   æɾə   ˈɪɾʊ   ˈʌɾə
    Now try pronouncing these forms with initial [ɾ]:
    ˈɾɑɾɑ   ˈɾiɾi   ˈɾɛɾu   ɾəˈɾu   ɾɪˈɾej   ˈɾuɾɪ
    Try the following gradual changes reading down. Don't rush.

ˈdɪɾædu	doˈdedu
ˈdɪɾæɾu	doˈɾedu
ˈɾɪɾæɾu	doˈɾeɾu
ˈɾɪdæɾu	ɾoˈɾeɾu
ˈɾɪdædu	ɾoˈdeɾu

21. In English words such as *winter,* many North Americans have a nasal tap; This can be transcribed as [ɾ̃]: [ˈwɪɾ̃ɹ]. In general, [ɾ̃] represents /nt/. Transcribe the following:
    plenty   resented   Monty   flinty   cantor   scented
    Do you distinguish *winter* and *winner* in careful speech? in colloquial speech? Try replacing the [ɾ̃] of the previous examples with [n]: [ˈpleni], [ɹəˈzɛnɾɪd], etc.

22. Pronounce these nonsense words:

bɪmpʌv	zʊdsæl	fɛpgɪk	nʊlwɪf	vʌntel	mæpwʌg
wʊbkɪm	lʌvkɛz	stɛks	slʊnts	znʌgz	mlɪbd
bdækt	ktɪmpt	dzɛtp	zblɪndg		

23. There is a pattern in language play *mud - shmud* [mʌd - ʃmʌd]; to do this, simply repeat the word with an [ʃ] at the beginning. Try this pattern with the following:
    e.g.: [ˈmʌni]   [ˈʃmʌni]
    money   books   raisins   duchess   nose   painful
    crumbs   tastefully   filigree
    Instead of [ʃ], try [v] in the same way before the same words:
    e.g.: [mʌd]   [vmʌd]
    Now try the consonants [z ð ʒ] in the same way.
    e.g.: [zmʌd]   [ðmʌd]   [ʒmʌd]

CHAPTER FOUR
ENGLISH VOWELS

In Chapter 2, we found that Canadian English has fourteen vowel phonemes, nine simple vowels or **monophthongs** /ˈmɑnəf,θɑŋ/, and five diphthongs. Now we will look at English vowels in greater detail.

In this chapter you will learn about:

- which vowels occur in which environments
- the differences between tense and lax vowels
- the allophonic variation of English vowels.

DISTRIBUTIONAL RESTRICTIONS

Not all vowels occur in all possible environments. For example, /bi/ and /bej/ are possible monosyllabic words in English, whereas /bɪ/ and /bɛ/ are not. The description of the distributional possibilities of sounds is called **phonotactics** /ˌfoˌnoˈtæktɪks/.

TENSE AND LAX

English vowels are commonly divided into two categories: **tense** and **lax**. You must be careful not to read too much into these terms. In English, the tense vowels are longer than the lax ones, usually produced a little higher and a little more to the periphery of the vowel area than the corresponding lax vowels. The muscles of the vocal tract are not necessarily in a state of greater tension during the production of tense vowels. Instead of thinking of the terms **tense** and **lax** as descriptions of the musculature, you should consider them simply as arbitrary names for two categories of vowels. From the charts below, you can see that the tense vowels are either long vowels or diphthongs, whereas the lax vowels are all short. As we will see, schwa is anomalous and does not fit well into the tense-lax classification; we will list it as a special case of the lax vowels.

Tense
　　monophthongs　　　　i u ɑ
　　diphthongs　　　　　ej ow aj aw ɔj

Lax　　　　　　　　　　ɪ ɛ æ ʌ ʊ
　　　　　　　　　　　　　ə

The usefulness of the categories tense and lax is that they divide English vowels into two groups which are distinguished by the environments in which they occur.

OPEN AND CLOSED SYLLABLES　Word-finally, the lax vowels /ɪ ɛ æ ʌ ʊ/ occur only in a **closed syllable**, *i.e.*, one ending in a consonant. We have /pɪt pɛt pæt pʌt pʊt/ *pit, pet, pat, putt, put,* but there are no possible words in English /pɪ pɛ pæ pʌ pʊ/. In other words, we can state the generalisation that in English lax vowels do not occur in word-finally open syllables. An **open syllable** is one which does not end in a consonant.

The tense vowels occur in both open and closed syllables: *pea, peak; pay, paid; boo, boot; saw, sawed; go, ghost; rye, ride; bow, bout; coy, coin.*

The distribution of schwa /ə/ is somewhat different. In stressed syllables, it occurs only before /ɹ/; otherwise, it occurs only in unstressed syllables, where the tense–lax distinction does not exist.

BEFORE /ʃ ŋ/　A second fact about the distribution of tense and lax vowels is that only lax vowels occur before /ʃ/ or /ŋ/; tense vowels do not occur before these consonants.

There are a few exceptions to these general statements. The words *leash, quiche,* and *(micro-)fiche* have a tense vowel /i/ before /ʃ/; *gauche* has the tense diphthong /ow/. These words are all borrowed from French. *Quiche, fiche,* and *gauche* seem to be exceptions to the rule because they have only come into English fairly recently, and their French form has not been adapted to conform to the general tense–lax distribution. *Leash,* on the other hand, although originally borrowed from French, has been around in English for several hundred years; I do not know why it is an exception.

The other exceptions are words like *wash, slosh, long,* and *wrong,* which have /ɑ/ before /ʃ/ or /ŋ/. Historically these vowels had a (low back rounded) lax vowel [ɒ] in earlier times, thus conforming to the general rule of lax vowels before /ʃ/. Subsequently, in our dialect, this vowel became a tense [ɑ], thus creating exceptions to the general rule.

BEFORE /ɹ/　A third fact about tense and lax vowels is that both sets do not occur before /ɹ/. We never have a contrast, for example, between [iɹ] and [ɪɹ] or between [uɹ] and [ʊɹ]. Since /i/ and /u/ are tense vowels, and /ɪ/ and /ʊ/ are lax ones, we can restate this as 'tense and lax vowels do not both occur before /ɹ/'. Which one does occur before /ɹ/? Since the diphthongs do occur before /ɹ/, as in *fire* and *our,* and since the diphthongs are tense, it follows that it is the tense rather than the lax vowels that precede /ɪ/. The vowel /ə/ occurs before /ɪ/ even though it is not labelled tense.

Summary of Vowel Phonotactics

	Closed syllables	Open syllables	— ʃ	— ŋ	— ɹ
Tense vowels					
Monophthongs					
/i/	peat	pea	(leash)	——	fear
/u/	boot	sue	(douche)	——	pure
/ɑ/	pot	paw	(wash)	(long)	car
Diphthongs					
/ej/	bait	pay	——	——	fare
/ow/	boat	dough	(gauche)	——	more
/aj/	bite	buy	——	——	fire
/aw/	pout	cow	——	——	hour
/ɔj/	voice	toy	——	——	coir
Lax vowels					
/ɪ/	pit	——	dish	ring	——
/ɛ/	pet	——	mesh	strength	——
/æ/	pat	——	lash	hang	——
/ʌ/	putt	——	hush	sung	——
/ʊ/	put	——	push	——	——
/ə/	——	——	——	——	purr

ALLOPHONIC VARIATION

Vowels have phonetic variation, just as consonants do. Some variation is inherent; some is conditioned by the environment. The conditioned variation of vowels is usually determined by the shape of the syllable, the neighbouring consonants, or stress.

LENGTH

INHERENT LENGTH   The tense vowels are longer than the lax vowels. This length, which is independent of context, is called **inherent length**. For the diphthongs /ej, ow, ɔj/, this length is explained as due to the presence of the glide. (The diphthongs /aj/ and /aw/ are discussed below under 'Canadian Raising'.) The high vowels /i/ and /u/ have very slight upward glides, as shown in Figure 4.1; in a narrow transcription, they can be phonetically transcribed as [ij] and [uw]. The tense vowel /ɑ/ is longer than the lax vowels, but it is monophthongal

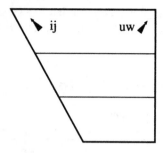

Figure 4.1 [ij] and [uw].

with no glide. We can transcribe it as [ɑː] phonetically, where length is indicated by a colon made of two small triangles [ː]. There is, in addition, some evidence (Crystal & House, 1988b) that low vowels are slightly longer than high vowels.

Tense				**Lax**			
meat	[miːt]	mate	[mejt]	mitt	[mɪt]	put	[pʊt]
moot	[muːt]	moat	[mowt]	met	[mɛt]	mutt	[mʌt]
pot	[pɑːt]	quoit	[kwɔjt]	mat	[mæt]		

CONTEXTUAL LENGTH   Try saying the pairs: *beet — bead, rick — rig, luff — love* . Say them aloud in a relaxed fashion. You will probably be able to notice that the vowel in *bead* is longer than the vowel in *beet*. Similarly, the vowels of *rig* and *love* are longer than those of *rick* and *luff*. The general rule in

ALLOPHONIC VOWEL LENGTH

	Closed Syllable				Open Syllable	
	Before voiceless consonant		***Before voiced consonant***			
Tense	pot	[pɑːt]	pod	[pɑːˑd]	pa	[pɑːˑ]
	beet	[bijt]	bead	[biˑjd]	bee	biˑj
	moot	[muwt]	mood	[muˑwd]	moo	[muˑw]
	wait	[wejt]	wade	[weˑjd]	way	[weˑj]
	wrote	[ɹowt]	rode	[ɹoˑwd]	row	[ɹoˑw]
Lax	rick	[ɹɪk]	rig	[ɹɪˑg]	*(Lax vowels do not occur in open syllables.)*	
	bet	[bɛt]	bed	[beˑd]		
	bat	[bæt]	bad	[bæˑd]		
	mutt	[mʌt]	mud	[mʌˑd]		
	put	[pʊt]	should	[ʃʊˑd]		

English is that vowels are longer before a voiced sound than before a voiceless sound. Now try saying the pair *bee — beat,* and you will be able to hear that the vowel in an open syllable is also longer than before the voiceless consonant. (This length, which is dependent on the phonetic context, is known as **contextual length**). The extra bit of length before the voiced consonants is shown by a raised dot [·]. The raised dot shows length, but not of so great a degree as does the colon. In diphthongs, the vowel portion is lengthened, not the glide. For /ɑ/, the transcription [ɑː·] shows a length somewhat longer than that shown by the colon alone [ː], combining the inherent and the contextual length.

The work of Crystal & House (1988b) agrees with the widespread observation that stressed vowels are longer before voiced stops than before voiceless stops, but it found that the same vowels were shorter before a voiced fricative than before a voiceless one. See also Chapter 9.

/aj aw/ — CANADIAN RAISING

The diphthongs /aj/ and /aw/ both begin with a low front unrounded vowel [a] and then glide up to [j] or [w]. As you can see from Figure 4.2, at the allophonic level, the [a] of /aj/ is a bit farther back that the [a] of /aw/. Both are quite low, even lower than [æ].

The contextual variation for these two diphthongs forms a distinctive feature of Canadian English, commonly known as Canadian raising. If you listen to yourself carefully as you pronounce *loud* and *lout,* you will probably be able to hear certain differences in the vowels. First, the vowel portion of *loud* is longer than that of *lout.* This is the usual contextual variation we expect before a voiced sound. But there is a difference in the quality of the vowels as well: the vowel portion of *lout* is made higher in the mouth than that of *loud;* compare Figure 4.2. We can symbolise this higher vowel as [ʌ]. In dialects with Canadian raising, /aw/ is realised as [ʌw] before voiceless sounds, and as [a·w] elsewhere.

| loud | [la·wd] | how | [ha·w] | noun | [na·wn] |
| lout | [lʌwt] | mouse | [mʌws] | ouch | [ʌwtʃ] |

The diphthong /aj/ has a parallel variation: raising, with [ʌj], before voiceless consonants, and [a·j] elsewhere.

| ride | [ɹa·jd] | sigh | [sa·j] | wives | [wa·jvz] |
| write | [ɹʌjt] | like | [lʌjk] | wife | [wʌjf] |

VOWELS AND STRESS

In Chapter 2, we distinguished three levels of stress: primary, secondary, and unstressed. The vowels we have been describing so far are the ones which occur with primary stress. As we mentioned above, the tense–lax distinction is found only in syllables with primary or secondary stress. With secondary stress, [e o i u] are usually monophthongs. With secondary stress [a] is not lengthened.

| unite | [juˈnʌjt] | pneumatic | [ˌnuˈmærɪk] |
| hobnob | [ˈhɑːbˌnɑb] | opaque | [ˌoˈpʰejk] |

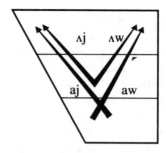

Figure 4.2 The diphthongs of Canadian raising.

A syllable with secondary stress and ending in /ej/ or /ow/ often retains the glide if the followed syllable begins with a vowel. In the same stress pattern, a syllable ending in /i/ or /u/ has a glide before a vowel: [ij] [uw]

| chaotic | [ˌkejˈɑːtɪk] | oasis | [ˌowˈejsɪs] |
| meander | [ˌmijˈæ·ndəɹ] | Lou-Ann | [ˌluwˈæ·n] |

Occasionally, the syllable boundaries shift, particularly with very deliberate pronunciation:

| chaotic | [ˌkeˈjɑːtɪk] | oasis | [ˌoˈwejsɪs] |
| meander | [ˌmiˈjæ·ndəɹ] | Lou-Ann | [ˌluˈwæ·n] |

In unstressed syllables, the only common vowels are /ə ɪ/:

| about | [əˈbʌwt] | effect | [əˈfɛkt] |
| goodness | [ˈɡʊdnɪs] | village | [ˈvɪlɪdʒ] |

To some degree, /ə/ and /ɪ/ are in free variation in unstressed syllables. Different speakers may use different vowels: *e.g., goodness* /ˈɡʊdnəs/ or /ˈɡʊdnɪs/. Individual speakers may in fact use one vowel sometimes and the other at other times. Unstressed syllables are usually quite short.

At the end of a word, an unstressed [i] occurs, as in *company* [ˈkʌmpəni], *milky* [ˈmɪlki], *lady* [ˈlejdi]. This [i] is a variant of /ɪ/ found in word-final position. It is usually a bit longer than other unstressed vowels.

Crystal & House (1988b) report that in connected speech tense vowels are about 1.5 times as long when stressed as when unstressed, and that lax vowels are about two times as long when stressed as when unstressed. Also, they found stressed vowels to be shorter before velars than before labials or alveolars.

Stress is discussed at greater length in Chapter 5.

VOWELS BEFORE /ɹ/ AND /l/

BEFORE /ɹ/ It is useful to consider the special case of vowels occurring before /ɹ/, as in *beer* /biɹ/ (See also Chapter 3). The chart below shows the vowels which occur before /ɹ/.

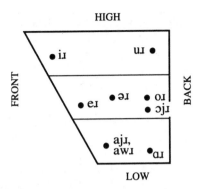

Figure 4.3 Vowels before /ɹ/.

beer	[bi·ɹ]		boor	[bu·ɹ]
bare	[be·ɹ]	burr [bə·ɹ]	bore	[bo·ɹ]]
			bar	[bɑ·ɹ]
fire	[fa·jɹ]		coir	[kɔ·jr]
our	[a·wɹ]			

Since /ɹ/ is voiced, all preceding stressed vowels are somewhat lengthened, as shown by the [·]. Our dialect has no examples of /æɹ/ or /ʌɹ/. The sequence /əɹ/ is the only place where schwa /ə/ occurs in a stressed syllable. *Coir* is a kind of fibre for ropes; it is the only word I know having /ɔjɹ/.

The postvocalic /ɹ/ requires a retroflex pronunciation. We mentioned in Chapter 3 that this can be accomplished in two ways: with the tip curled back and the under surface of the tongue near the back of the alveolar ridge, or bunched with the tongue tip pointing down. Whichever kind of /ɹ/ is produced, the tongue is flexible enough that the body of the tongue is free to adopt a variety of vowel shapes. Thus, we simultaneously produce a vowel and an [ɹ]. Such a vowel is said to be **rhotic** or retroflexed. All vowels in English before syllable-final /ɹ/ are somewhat rhotic, although the quality is most noticeable with /ə/. With the high vowels [iɹ] and [uɹ], the [ɹ] is less simultaneous with the vowel, and there is a noticeable movement from the vowel to the [ɹ]-position.

Note that before /ɹ/, /ej ow/ lose their glide to become [e o]. As we pointed out before, members of the vowel pairs /i ɪ/, /ej ɛ/, and /u ʊ/ do not contrast before /ɹ/ as they do before other consonants. Phonetically, the vowel sound of *beer* lies between our usual values for [i] and [ɪ]. I have transcribed these vowels as tense, /iɹ eɹ uɹ/, to be consistent with the general observation that only tense vowels occur before /ɹ/.

Many speakers of Canadian English have a fairly low /eɹ/ which can be transcribed [ɛɹ] in a narrow transcription. There is as well a good deal of dialect variation in words like *marry, merry, Mary*. We will discuss this further in Chapter 6, but you may want to sample the pronunciation of a few people from different regions to see how they pronounce these three words.

BEFORE /l/   The entire repertoire of vowel phonemes occurs before /l/:

peel	[pi·əl]	pool	[pu·əl]	pile	[pa·jl]
pill	[pɪ·l]	pull	[pʊ·l]	owl	[a·wl]
pail	[pe·əl]	poll	[po·l]	toil	[tɔ·jl]
bell	[bɛ·l]	dull	[dʌ·l]		
pal	[pæ·l]	doll	[dɒ·l]		

Before [l], /ɑ/ becomes rounded to [ɒ]. To make [ɒ], the tongue is in the same position as for [ɑ]; the lips, however, are rounded. Try saying the following list of words, all of which have [ɒ] before [l]: *all, call, ball, doll, moll, dollar, collar, holler.* Some speakers also have rounding when /ɑ/ follows /l/. Pronounce *cause* — *calls* — *claws* to see if you have this rounding; watch your lips in a mirror. Since [l] is voiced, all preceding vowels are somewhat lengthened, as shown by the [·].

The diphthongs /ej/ and /ow/ often lose their glide before /l/; however, like /il/ and /ul/, /el/ sometimes becomes a diphthong with a schwa glide: [iə uə eə]. Less commonly, /ow/ becomes [oə]. The symbol [ə] indicates a glide to a [ə] position. There is some tendency for words with [a·wl] like *owl* to break into two syllables: ['a·w – əl].

Figure 4.4 shows the glides to a [ə]-position before /l/. This glide is more noticeable in slow, deliberate speech and may not be present in rapid speech.

Nasalised Vowels   Vowels occurring next to a nasal consonant /m n ŋ/ are frequently nasalised. In articulatory terms, this means that the velum is lowered during the first part of the vowel allowing air to pass out through the nose. In a word like *me* [mĩj], the velum is down for the /m/. The vowel following the /m/ is **nasalised**, that is, the velum stays down for at least a portion of the vowel. **Nasalisation** is shown by a **tilde** [˜] /'tɪldə/ above the vowel.

A vowel preceding a nasal consonant is also often nasalised. In a word like *ran* [ɹæ̃·n], the velum is lowered during the vowel in anticipation of the following nasal consonant. In *man* [mæ̃·n], where the vowel is both preceded and followed by nasal consonant, the nasalisation may be somewhat stronger. Note that the vowel and the nasal must be in the same syllable for the vowel to become

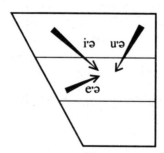

Figure 4.4   Glides before /l/.

nasalised; in *doughnut* [ˈdowˌnʌt], for example, the [ow] is not nasalised because the nasal is in the following syllable.

Nasalised vowels in English are noncontrastive. English dialects and individual speakers vary considerably in their use of nasalised vowels and in the degree of nasalisation that they employ. Some speakers, however, report a curious contrast. For them, the word *united* (particularly in *United States* and *United Nations*) has a nasalised second vowel [ˌjuˈnãˑjɾɪd]; on the other hand, the corresponding vowel is not nasalised in *you knighted (him)* [juˈnaˑjɾɪd]. How do you pronounce these items?

PRACTICAL TRANSCRIPTION

In Chapter 3, we distinguished broad and narrow transcriptions: broad having less detail, and narrow having more. From now on, I will generally transcribe English in a fairly broad fashion. The following chart shows the detail which will be included and that which will be omitted in a broad transcription. Obviously, for a particular purpose, we may want to include more or less detail.

Broad Transcription

Included	*Omitted*
[ɾ]	aspiration
Canadian raising	dental assimilation
loss of glides with secondary stress	dark [ɫ]
loss of glides before /ɹ/ and /l/	length
syllabic consonants	devoicing at ends of words

Note: the transcription of technical terms and names of languages is given in a very broad transcription omitting even the detail just given for a broad transcription.

TECHNICAL TERMS

closed syllable	monophthong	phonotactics
contextual length	nasalised	tense
inherent length	nasalisation	tilde
lax	open syllable	

SYMBOLS

:	**colon**	length	**ɒ** **turned back a**	low back rounded
·	**raised dot**	half length		vowel
˛		glide to schwa position	**˜** **tilde** /ˈtɪldə/	nasalisation

63

EXERCISES

BASIC

1. Read the following broad transcriptions:

/fud/	/dʌn/	/bejk/	/kiʃ/	/mɪks/	/ɹowst/
/najf/	/bɹɛd/	/dow/	/fɹaj/	/mɔjst/	/pɑt/
/kʊk/	/lin/	/mæʃ/	/bɹawn/	/najvz/	/ti/

2. Transcribe the following words broadly:

web	dig	melt	gnat	puff	bins
come	soot	dull	pull	dipped	wealth
loop	knead	loud	toyed	tied	psalm
wipe	rogue	nude	waist	combed	louse

3. Transcribe, using a narrow transcription for the consonants:

lift	dread	splat	tuft	could	tank
wing	stunk	plugs	clam	woods	tap
cud	stab	scum	twitch		

4. Tense and lax. For each of the following words, identify whether the vowel is tense or lax.

sound	air	out	this	can	say
said	drink	sung	cod	put	move
write	foist	fish	rang	clove	wipe
fudge	bathes				

5. Add stress to the following transcriptions by placing a vertical stroke [ˈ] at the beginning of the stressed syllable:

   e.g.: /hæmpəɹ/ → /ˈhæmpəɹ/

/owpən/	/əkəɹ/	/ʌpəɹ/	/iɔkʌmbənt/
/mɛlədi/	/əpɑn/	/kənvej/	/səpoɹt/
/həɹtfəl/	/ɹɪlæks/	/æləɹdʒi/	/glædli/

6. For the following words, make a broad transcription marking stress:

loading	conveyor	resident	ginger	retire
elegy	resistance	hospital	coffin	business

7. With the following words, practise short, medium, and long vowels. Be careful to keep your tongue steady so as not to produce a diphthong.

   e.g.: mass [mæs mæ·s mæːs]

bed	bit	foot	lad
cup	dot	suck	look

   The following words have diphthongs. Pronounce each making the vowel portion of the diphthong first short, then long:

e.g.: so [sow so·w].

pay	load	loud	do	sigh
bee	died	teak	wave	coy
coy	doe	fine	joys	rhyme

8. This exercise is to increase your repertoire of low back vowels. Most Canadians have only one phonemic /ɑ/ vowel, and two phonetic [ɑ ɒ] vowels in the low back area. Pronounce the following lists of words, paying attention to the difference in vowel quality:

[ɑ]   ah, raw, palm, sock, dawn, gnaw, calm
[ɒ]   all, doll, fall, call, moll, ball,

First say [ɑ] as in *father*. Now saying [ɑ], slowly round your lips without changing the position of your tongue. If nothing else changes you should be saying [ɒ]. Many Canadians say this regularly as the vowel in *doll, fall, collar.*

The following strategy also works for learning a new sound, particularly a vowel.

Try to find a context where you can already make the vowel.

Exaggerate the vowel by stretching it out. Gradually remove the context without changing the vowel.

Practise saying the new vowel in alternation with similar ones that you already know.

Now try applying this strategy to learning to say [ɒ]. Say *all*, stretching it out to [ɒɒɒɒl]. Now remove the [l] without changing the vowel quality to produce [ɒɒɒɒ]. Now, unround the lips and you will produce [ɑɑɑɑ]. Without rushing, go back and forth between [ɑ] and [ɒ]: [ɑɑɑ ɒɒɒ ɑɑɑ ɒɒɒ ɑɑɑ ɒɒɒ]. The difference should be the rounding of the lips. Practise the following combinations with [ɑ] and [ɒ]:

ɑ	ɒ		o	ɒ
mamɒ	momɒ		sɒsa	sɒso
lado	nafɒ		dɒso	gɒna
mamɒma	dɒdodɒ		kɒmɒda	lomɒvo
pɒmado	pomadɒ		pamɒda	pomɒda

You already say [ɔ] as part of the diphthong [ɔj] as in *boy*. Say *boy* a few times paying attention to the vowel portion. Stretch out the vowel [bɔɔɔɔj]. Now try for a steady [ɔɔɔɔɔɔ]. Do the same thing, but start with *coin*: [kɔjn] → [kɔɔɔɔɔjn] → [ɔɔɔɔɔ]. Now practise this vowel in alternation with [ɑ].

ɑ	ɔ		ɑ	ɔ
ma	mɔ		mama	mɔmɔ
mamɔ	mɔma		lɔla	lalɔ
sɔna	sanɔ		dɔga	paznɔ

9. The vowels in *bay* and *go* are diphthongs [bej] and [gow] (I am ignoring length here). Many languages have similar monophthongal vowels: [e o]. It is useful to learn to make these without any glide.

a. First, exaggerate the diphthongal quality of *bay* by stretching it out: [beeeeeejjj].

b. Now, focus on stretching out the vowel portion: [eeeeeej]

c. Try again, keeping your mouth and tongue quite steady during the [e] portion.

d. Start over. Say a long [eeeeeej], but before you get to the glide, abruptly put in a glottal stop [ʔ] (*i.e.*, hold your breath): [eeeeeeʔ]

e. Now try saying [eeeeee] without the glottal stop and without any glide.

f. If you have difficulty with the preceding steps, try saying *Graham* [ˈgɹe – əm]. The [e] here often has very little glide. Hold the first vowel steady and drop the second syllable, ending up with [gɹeeee].

g. Try the same procedures to say [o]. Start with [oooooow], then cut off the glide with a glottal stop [ooooooʔ], then just [oooooo].

For [o] it is useful to practise in front of a mirror. The [o] has moderate lip rounding, but the [w] glide has considerably more lip rounding; thus to get rid of [w], make sure that you are not changing the lip rounding.

h. English as spoken in Scotland and northern England has monophthongs [e:] and [o:] rather than [ej] and [ow]. Saying [e] and [o] without glides will make you sound like a Scot; saying [eʔ] and [oʔ] will make you sound like a startled Scot.

Practise the following. First exaggerate the glides and use glottal stops to get rid of them. Then speed up slightly, and try to omit the glottal stop.

ejkej	ejkeʔ	eʔkeʔ	ekeʔ	eke
owfow	owfoʔ	oʔfoʔ	ofoʔ	ofo
nejsow	nejsoʔ	neʔsoʔ	nesoʔ	neso
gowlej	gowleʔ	goʔleʔ	goleʔ	gole
owkow	owkoʔ	oʔkoʔ	okoʔ	oko
ejmow	ejmoʔ	eʔmoʔ	emoʔ	emo

Try the following, first with the diphthongs [ej ow], and then with monophthongs [e o].

The rain in Spain stays mainly in the plain.

Joe's folks hoped that most of the old blokes would go home.

10. Canadian Raising. Pronounce the following lists of words aloud. The words in each list should have the same vowel sound. Most Canadians will have the diphthong [aw] for the words in list a., and [ʌw] for the words in list b.

a. [a·w]: how, loud, gown, gouge, foul, thou, browse, plough, round

b. [ʌw]   out, pouch, south, mouse, oust, lout, couch

Refer to Figure 4.2 to see where the vowel portion of these diphthongs is made. Try to identify the way your tongue feels with the position of the vowel on the chart. The words in lists c. and d. are parallel to those in lists a. and b., except that the vowels are [aj] and [ʌj]. Note that the conditioning environments are the same.

c. [aˑj]:   high, died, line, tribe, aisle, eye, rise, kind, writhe, knives

d. [ʌj]:   sight, rice, knife, Christ, ripe, like, rite, type, iced

Transcribe the following words, paying attention to the diphthongs.

site	side	light	lied
rout	sound	house (n)	house (v)
pride	nigh	night	tyke
cowl	grouse (n)	cows	louse

Try saying the following pairs, pronouncing both words with the vowel of the first word. When you are through, pronounce them both with the vowel of the second word.

e.g.: ride — right   [ɹaˑjd — ɹaˑjt]   [ɹʌˑjd — ɹʌjt]

lout — loud	couch — gouge	side — sight
dice — dies	doubt — now	wife — wives
crowd — gout	high — height	

Do you have raising in the following words?

microscope	microscopy	titanic	icon	iconic	titan
nitrate	night rate	bicycle			

Try these:

a. Use [ʌw] and say   'How now brown cow?'

b. Use [aj] and say   'A quite bright nightlight'.

c. Use [aw] and say   'I doubt that our house has a couch'.

d. Use [ʌj] and say   'My tie lies awry, but thine is fine'.

11. Vowels before /ɹ/. Make a narrow transcription of the following:

nurse	care	bar	war	cork	fear
sport	dare	fire	sour	roar	cure
fir	fur	fern	mere	sure	bear
hearth	lure	sore	sire	north	lurch

12. Vowels before /l/. Make a narrow transcription of the following:

dill	sole	sell	aisles	doll	cull
real	cowl	full	fool	nails	Al
oil	ruled	kneel	foul	ghoul	dial
awl	gulls				

13. Make a narrow transcription of the following, showing stress.

It was a dark and stormy night; the rain fell in torrents — except at occasional intervals, when it was checked by a violent gust of wind which swept up the streets (for it is in London that our scene lies), rattling along the housetops, and fiercely agitating the scanty flame of the lamps that struggled against the darkness.

ADVANCED

14. Pronounce:

pʰɪk	kʰʊf	mæb	tʰɪŋ	vʌtʰ	nɛ dɛv
gæ	zæn	wɪl	ŋæm	kʰæn	stʊ
splændz	twɛŋks	plʊmb	sklʌps	tlɛŋz	klʌŋgz
dlɪmbz	tʌd	stʰɛn	skʰʌŋ	spʰlɪŋ	pædɪ
kɛgz	ŋʌfs	tʊpf			

15. Practise saying the following words in Swahili (/ˌswɑˈhili/, a language spoken widely in eastern Africa); pay attention to aspiration:

pɑ	*roof*	pʰɑ	*gazelle*
tando	*fungus*	tʰando	*swarm*
tʃuŋgu	*cooking pot*	tʃʰuŋgu	*black ant*
pʰembe	*horn*	pembe	*big horn*
tʰundu	*hole*	tundu	*big hole*
tʃʰupa	*bottle*	tʃupa	*demijohn*
kʰuta	*walls*	kuta	*large walls*

16. Say the word *my* [maj]. Now make the diphthong long: [maaaaaj]. Try to remove the [j] without changing the vowel [maaaaa]. Practise the same steps with these words:

lie	die	cry	sigh
ride	guide	sign	lime

17. Try the same technique with *how* [haw]. Lengthen the diphthong to [haaaaaw], and then try to remove the glide: [haaaaa]. Practise with the following words.

cow	now	sow	row
loud	town	house (v.)	gouge

18. Practise the following low back vowels:

dɑ	dɒ	sɔ	sɒ	gɔ	gɒ
ɑnɔ	ɒnɒ	ɑnɒ	bɔbɑ	bɒbɑ	bɒbɔ
gɔbɑ	zɒvɑ	lɔpɒ	ɹɒdɒ	mɒg	sɔk
dɒl	dɔl	mɑŋ	wɒŋ	θwɔd	glɒp

19. In Exercise 9, you learned to make the simple vowel [o] without a glide. Practise alternating [ɔ o].

ɔ	o	ɔ	o
nɔ	no	nonɔ	nɔno
kɔko	lolo	fɔfo	tɔtɔ

20. The glottal stop [ʔ] is found in English in casual forms:
    e.g., [ˈʔm̩ʔm̩] *no* [ˈʔʌˌʔow] *uh-oh* .

    Hints:

    1. Take a breath, keep your mouth open, say [ɑ], and suddenly hold your breath.
       The slight catch is a glottal stop.

    2. Pretend to hiccough. The catch at the end is a glottal stop, but with inhaled air.
       Try for the same sound with exhaled air.

    3. Try saying [ʔɑʔ], then [ʔɑʔɑ], then [ʔɑʔɑʔɑʔɑʔɑ].

    4. Now try to distinguish [sɑ - sɑʔ].
       Practise:

fɑ	fɑʔ	li	liʔ	du	duʔ
mɛ	mɛʔ	dʒæ	dʒæʔ	θʌ	θʌʔ

    Try to distinguish a vowel with and without a glottal stop at the beginning:

ɑ	ʔɑ	ɑʔ	ʔɛ	ɛ	ɛʔ	ʔi	i	iʔ
i	ʔi	iʔ	ʔi	ʔiʔi	iʔ	uʔ	u	ʔu

    Try these:

ko	koʔ	ʔok	bik	bi	biʔ	lʊʔ	lʊ	lʊʔ
ne	neʔ	neʔɑ	eʔ	eʔe	ʔeʔ	keʔ	ʔek	ke
ajˈdiə	ʔajˈdiə	ʔajˈdiʔə						
ʔajˈdiə	ajˈdiə	ajˈdiəʔ						

21. Nasal vowels. The English sound of surprise, written *huh,* is usually spoken
    with a nasal vowel [hʌ̃ʔ]. Say this a few times to get the feel of a nasal vowel.
    Now say a long [ʌ̃ʌ̃ʌ̃ʌ̃]. You may find that it helps to get quite relaxed, let
    your head drop, and just let the air flow out as though you were dead tired.

    Try saying [ãããã]; this sounds something like a tugboat horn. Try the
    other vowels: [ĩj ẽj ɛ̃ æ̃ ʌ̃ ɔ̃ ɑ̃ː õw ʊ̃ w ũ w ãj ãw̃ ɔ̃j].

    Say the following sentences, making all the vowels nasalised; you should
    try to sound obnoxiously whiny.

    > The rain in Spain stays mainly in the plain.
    > All my old clothes are already outside on the line.
    > My maid Mame mends minute moth holes.

    Now try the same sentences with as little nasalisation as you can.

22. Buildup:

['pi tɛ 'lɑ nɔ 'fi ʃu]

To do this, the first time say   ['pi];

the second time say   ['pi tɛ];

the third time say   ['pi tɛ 'lɑ];

the fourth time say   ['pi tɛ 'lɑ nɔ]; etc.

When you can pronounce the whole sequence, practise until you can say it comfortably three times without looking.

Now try some others:

['kɑ wi 'ɹɒ bɪ 'ŋæ mʊ]

[jʌ 'tʃɔ gɪ 'θu fʌ 'væ]

['ɪɒ nʊ ɲi 'ðɛ ʒu hɛ]

Did you pay attention to stress?

23. Every dictionary contains a guide or key to explain the symbols that it uses to describe pronunciation. One dictionary that I use has a key that begins as shown below. Each symbol used is followed by an example.

ā	mate	ē	mete	i	mite
ō	mote	ū	mute	ōō	moot
a	mat	e	met	i	mitt
u	good	ä	palm	oj	joy

Although the system used in this dictionary is quite different from the one used in this book, a conversion key can easily be made to go from the dictionary's transcription system to the one in this book.

Dictionary	Here	Example	Dictionary	Here	Example
a	æ	mat	ā	ej	mate
e	ɛ	met	ē	i	mete
i	ɪ	mitt	ī	aj	mite
u	ʊ	good	ō	ow	mote
ä	ɑ	palm	ū	ju	mute
oi	oj	joy	ōō	u	moot

In your own dictionary, find the section which explains the pronunciation symbols, and make a conversion key to the symbols used in this book. Very likely, you will find a fair bit of difference for the vowels and rather little for the consonants.

Transcribe the following words according to the method used in this book. Then, with your conversion key, convert the transcription to that used in your dictionary. When you have done this, look them up and compare your transcriptions to those of the dictionary. Can you explain any discrepancies?

take	know	thine	butter
wealth	sour	toot	foot
calm	pot	soil	ruin
fuse	neat	thirst	lid

24. Words in the following list are known to have different pronunciations in various dialect areas of English. Transcribe them according to your own pronunciation, and then be on the look-out for people who pronounce them differently. Check what pronunciation(s) your dictionary gives.

either	lever	khaki	data	with
schedule	lieutenant	ration	shone	figure
apricot	pecan	suggest	thirteen	hover
progress	hearth	missile	leisure	envelope
status	economic	arctic	often	Newfoundland
path	resources	garage	programme	anti–war

25. Try reading the following nonsense words aloud:

ˈbiʃʌ	tʊˈwej	ˈŋɑɹdʒu
ˈlæŋu	ˈjajðɛ	ˈvɔjθawgɛ
ˈɹowdɛ	ʒæˈtʃaw	hæˈʃejlu
ˈhɪpɛpu	noˈlɛsa	ʒiˈdamʌ
ˈsɔfiŋe	wedoˈki	aloˈŋu
fʊˈmoɹɪ	æˈgɹomʌ	ˈzɔðulæ
θanˈdʊfle	ˈskoefɔ	ɛlʒbɪnˈdʌ

CHAPTER FIVE
ENGLISH SUPRASEGMENTALS

Speech consists not merely of a string of consonants and vowels pronounced one after the other. Rather, there are several levels of organisation. The study of **suprasegmentals** /ˌsupɹəˌsɛɡˈmɛntəl/ involves two different aspects. One is how segments are organised to form larger units, in particular, syllables. The other aspect is the study of phonetic entities which apply to syllables or longer stretches of speech.

In this chapter you will learn about:
- syllables and their structure
- phonotactics
- stress
- intonation
- rhythm.

CONNECTED SPEECH

We are familiar with concepts such as syllable, word, phrase, and sentence. These form a hierarchical structure with sentence at the top and segments at the bottom, as shown in Figure 5.1.

The lowest level, segment, is the familiar one of consonants and vowels. English speakers are generally aware of syllables, which exist at the next higher level. Every word consists of one or more syllables. Stress occurs on syllables.

A **phonetic word** is the smallest unit that can be pronounced ordinarily in a language. Thus, /bɪɡ/ is a word, but /ɡ/ or /ɡʌ/, in English, are not words because they cannot be pronounced alone. The same is true of /kæ/, /lɪkʌ/, or /ŋəɹ/. At the same time, /ˈðeɹɪzəbʊk/ is not a word because it can be broken into smaller units which can be pronounced separately: /ˈðeɹ ɪz ə bʊk/ *there is a book*.

A **phonetic phrase** is a group of words pronounced together without a break. We easily see that a group of words such as *in my book* is ordinarily pronounced together /ɪnˌmajˈbʊk/. Of course, it is possible to pronounce this as three separate phrases: /ˈɪn/ /ˈmaj/ /ˈbʊk/; here each word is also a phonetic phrase.

Figure 5.1
Hierarchical structure of linguistic units.

In linguistics, the definition of the terms *word* and *phrase* poses some difficulties. I have used 'phonetic' in the definitions above to make it clear that we are thinking of these as phonetic and not as grammatical units.

SYLLABLES

Although linguists are in general agreement as to what a **syllable** /ˈsɪləbəl/ is in terms of consonants and vowels, phoneticians have a harder time in describing precisely the articulatory actions that make up a syllable and the actions that divide a string of consonants and vowels into a sequence of syllables. In Chapter 16 we will look more closely at various attempts to define the syllable.

All languages have syllables. Usually they are fairly easy to count. For example, most English speakers can tell us that *intercontinental* has six syllables. On the other hand, it is sometimes difficult to divide a word into syllables. We generally agree that a word such as *drugstore* is to be divided as /ˈdɹʌg – ˌstoɹ/, and the division of *definition*, as /ˌdɛ – fɪ – ˈnɪ – ʃən/ seems acceptable. Speakers of English, however, are less confident whether to divide *very* as /ˈvɛ – ɹi/ or /ˈvɛɹ – i/.

STRUCTURE

The vowel of a syllable, and any following semivowel, is regarded as the **nucleus** /ˈnukliəs/ (plural: **nuclei** /ˈnukliˌaj/) or centre of the syllable. The prenuclear elements are called the **onset**; and the elements after the nucleus are called the **coda** /ˈkowdə/. The nucleus and coda taken together are known as the **rhyme** /ɹajm/. Figure 5.2 shows the internal structure of a simple syllable like *mat* /mæt/.

A syllable with an empty coda is called an **open** syllable; one with a filled coda is called a **closed** syllable. Note that the /j/ or /w/ of a diphthong belongs to the nucleus and does not close a syllable.

open:	/gu / /now/ /ɛ/ /kʌ/ /mej/
closed:	/ʃin/ /ʌk/ /wajp/

PHONOTACTICS

English has a large number of consonant clusters formed of sequences of consonants. Not all sequences of consonants occur. We will examine in this chapter what consonants in English occur with what other consonants. We distinguish two

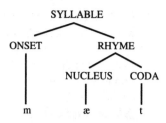

Figure 5.2 Structure of the syllable.

types of forms which do not occur. Some combinations, like /bnɪk/, violate a structural condition of the language; here, /bn/ is not a permitted consonant sequence for the onset. The other type can be illustrated by /gʊt/. I am unaware of any such word in English, although it is clearly a possible word; it is very similar to the words *good* and *foot*. The first type of non-occurrence /bnɪk/ is simply not English; it is a **systematic gap**. The second type of non-occurrence /gʊt/ is a possible, although unknown, form; it is called an **accidental gap**. The study of the possible combinations of sounds in a language is called **phonotactics** /ˌfoˌnoˈtæktɪks/. Note that a systematic gap is language-specific: *i.e.*, although it is true for some language (*e.g.*, English), it is not necessarily true for all languages.

ONSET

All consonants except /ŋ/ occur as the onset of the syllable. The sound /ʒ/ is found initially in very few words, mostly borrowed from French: *Gilles, gigue, genre.* The onset may be empty, as in *ice, on, odd.*

The following list shows clusters with a stop and another consonant in the onset:

stop + approximant

bl	bɹ	bw	bj	*blow, bray, bwana, beauty*
—	dɹ	dw	—	*drive, dwell*
gl	gɹ	gw	gj	*glow, green, Gwen, gules*
pl	pɹ	pw	pj	*plough, pry, pueblo, puny*
—	tɹ	tw	—	*try, twin*
kl	kɹ	kw	kj	*clay, cry, queen, cute*

s + voiceless stop

sp	*spin*
st	*stop*
sk	*skip*

/s/ + voiceless stop + approximant

spl	spɹ	—	spj	*splice, sprint, spume*
—	stɹ	—	—	*straddle*
skl	skɹ	skw	skj	*sclerosis, scrimp, squeamish, skew*

The chart above shows certain systematic gaps (/tl dl stl/), certain accidental gaps (/spw stw/, and certain rarities (/pw gj/). In English, the lateral /l/ occurs after /b p g k/ but not after /t/ or /d/: *i.e.,* there are no words beginning /tl dl stl/. Note that, as part of a consonant cluster, /j/ occurs only before the nucleus /u/: /pju, bju, kju, gju, spju, skju/. For most speakers of our dialect, /j/ does not occur after the alveolars /t d n/. The clusters /pw/ and /bw/ are rare in native words although *bwana, Buenos (Aires), and pueblo* are thoroughly anglicised. Some people pronounce *puerile* /ˈpwerˌajl/ giving another example of /pw/; other speakers, however, have /ˈpjuəɹəl/ or /ˈpjuəˌɹajl/. *Gules* /gjulz/ is a rare word used to describe the colour red in heraldry. This is the only example of word-initial /gj/ that I am aware of, however, /gj/ occurs word internally in words such as *legume* /ləˈgjum/. Although the clusters /spw/ and /stw/ seem possible, I know of no examples. The clusters /stl stj/ do not occur because /tl/ and /tj/ do not occur. Clusters with /skl/ are very rare.

In addition to the clusters above, the following ones occur in the onset:

m + j	mute		s + l w f v	sleep, swim, sforzo, svelte
f + l ɹ j	fly, fry, few		ʃ + ɹ l	shrine, schlemiel
v + j	view		h + j	huge
θ + ɹ w	thrive, thwart			

CODA

All consonants occur singly in the coda except /h/. The coda may be empty in one-syllable words if the nucleus contains a tense vowel. Many clusters occur in the coda; some are described below. Notice that many of the clusters exist only because a suffix (either 'plural' or 'third singular present') in /s/ or /z/ is added. In *digs,* the cluster /gz/ is formed by adding the third singular present morpheme /z/ to the final /g/; I am unaware of any single morpheme ending in /gz/. Similarly, many clusters are formed by the addition of the past tense morpheme in /t/ or /d/.

p	+	t θ s	apt, depth, hops	f	+ t θ s	miffed, fifth, reefs
t	+	θ s	eighth, lets	v	+ d z	moved, leaves
k	+	t s	act, axe	θ	+ t s	unearthed, myths
b	+	d z	rubbed, cobs	ð	+ d z	bathed, wreathes
d	+	z	adze	s	+ p t k	lisp, nest, task
g	+	d z	lagged, digs	z	+ d	buzzed
tʃ	+	t	latched	ʃ	+ t	hushed
dʒ	+	d	judged	ʒ	+ d	rouged
m	+	p f θ d z	damp, lymph, warmth, harmed, roams			
n	+	t tʃ θ s d dʒ z	bent, lunch, tenth, sense, honed, lunge, tons			
ŋ	+	k d z	bank, ringed, songs			
ɹ	+	p t k tʃ f θ s ʃ	harp, sort, dirk, lurch, wharf, earth, parse, kirsch			
		b d g dʒ v z m n l	curb, mired, morgue, purge, carve, beers, harm, corn, furl			

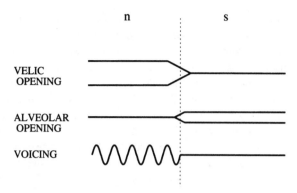

Figure 5.3a Timing of closures for wince /wɪns/.

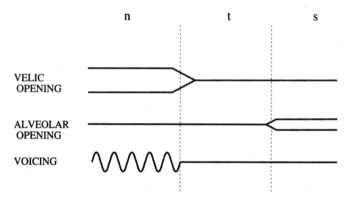

Figure 5.3b Timing of closures for wince /wɪnts/.

English has a number of three consonant final clusters as well, and even a few with four consonants. I give only a few examples here.

sps	lisps	lps	helps	tθs	eighths
sts	lists	kts	acts	lks	milks
ɹbd	absorbed	lvz	shelves	ndz	ends
lfθ	twelfth	lkts	mulcts	ksts	texts

In the nasal–fricative transitions /mf mθ ms nθ ns/, as in *lymph, warmth, glimpse, sense, tenth,* it is often difficult to say with certainty whether the nasal and the fricative follow each other directly or whether an intervening stop occurs, *i.e.,* [lɪmf] (or [lɪɱf]) or [lɪmpf], [sɛns] or [sɛnts]. Some speakers seem to favour one pronunciation, and others favour the other. Some speakers may vary somewhat as well. I have never met a native speaker of English who consistently contrasted words like *cents — sense* with the presence or absence of [t]. The difference is one of timing: in [wɪns] *wince* (Figure 5.3a) the release of the stop is simultaneous with the closure of the nasal passage. With the pronunciation /wɪnts/, (Figure 5.3b) the alveolar opening follows the velic closure and the onset of voicelessness.

STRESS

Stress is a complex auditory impression which the listener perceives as making one syllable more prominent than its neighbours. A number of different things, either individually, or in combination — greater loudness, higher pitch, greater length — contribute to the perception of stress. A stressed syllable in English often has all three of these characteristics. In other languages, stress may be created by combining just two of these (*e.g.,* loudness and pitch, or pitch and length) or even just using one of the characteristics.

LEVELS OF STRESS

A word like photograph /fowrəgɹæf/ has three levels of stress. You can easily hear that the first syllable /fow/ has the strongest stress. The last syllable /gɹæf/ is not so strongly stressed as /fow/, but it has stronger stress than the middle syllable /rə/. We mark the strongest or primary stress with a short raised stroke [ˈ], the middle level or secondary stress with a short lowered stroke [ˌ]. These strokes are placed before the onset of the affected syllable: /ˈfowrəˌgɹæf/. Unstressed syllables are not marked.

Three levels of stress are adequate for a word like *elevator* /ˈɛləˌvejrɹ/. The second syllable /ə/ and the third /rɹ/ are both unstressed. The word *operator* /ˈɑpəˌɹejrɹ/ has a similar stress pattern. By itself, each of these words exhibits three levels of stress. We can, however, combine them into a single compound word *elevator-operator*. Just combining the transcriptions as /ˈɛləˌvejrɹ-ˈɑpəˌɹejrɹ/ is not enough in itself. The ordinary way this compound word is pronounced is with a greater stress on *elevator* than on *operator*. There is a general rule in English that a word has only one primary stress. The effect of this rule is that /ˈɛl/ continues to have a primary stress, but the other stresses are reduced by one level: /ˈɛləˌˌvejrɹ-ˌɑpəˌˌɹejrɹ/. Here, a single lowered stroke /ˌ/ continues to show secondary stress, which is now on /ˌɑp/, and a double lowered stroke /ˌˌ/ shows a new level of stress, **tertiary stress**. Syllables with the weakest level of prominence are called unstressed and are unmarked in the transcription.

We could probably continue this extension of the number of stress levels. In fact, however, it is almost impossible to be certain of the relative level of stress in comparing syllables that are separated by more than a few syllables. Say the sentence *Where did you put the paper I brought home last night?*, and try to decide whether the stress levels of *put* and of *last* are the same or different.

In our transcriptions of English, we will generally mark only three levels of stress: primary, secondary, unstressed. Tertiary stress will occasionally be marked when it is relevant. In rapid speech, syllables with tertiary, and sometimes even secondary, stress are often reduced to unstressed. In extremely slow or careful speech, syllables normally unstressed may acquire tertiary or even secondary stress. Generally, every phonetic phrase contains one and only one primary stress.

English stress has been the subject of extensive research in recent years. This work, known as metrical theory, has generally been phonological, even syntactic, in nature, and has been less concerned with the phonetic nature of the syllable. It has emphasised the point that stress is relational, that a certain syllable has stronger or weaker stress than its neighbours. In Chapter 16, we will look at the stress patterns of various languages, comparing them to that of English.

STRONG AND WEAK FORMS

Read the following sentence aloud emphasising the italicised word:

> *That* is the book that I wanted.

You probably pronounced the first *that* as /ˈðæt/, and the second one as /ˈðət/. Many words in English are pronounced both with and without stress depending on the structure of the sentence. The presence or absence of stress changes the quality of the vowel. With stress, either primary or secondary, we get a full vowel, such as in /ˈðæt/; without stress, we get /ə/ or /ɪ/, as in /ˈðət/. The form with stress is called the **strong form**, and the form without stress is called the **weak form**. Generally, it is the functional words, such as articles, prepositions, conjunctions, and pronouns which have this alternation; verbs, nouns, and adjectives generally do not.

	Strong	**Weak**
and	ˈænd	ənd, ən, n̩
when	ˈwɛn	wən, wɪn
them	ˈðɛm	ðəm, əm
as	ˈæz	əz
the	ˈði	ðə, ðɪ
a	ˈej	ə
of	ˈɑv	əv, ə

You can see from these examples that the weak form of certain words, *e.g., and*, may lose consonants as well.

A characteristic of formal speech is that it is slower than colloquial speech. In slow speech the phrases are smaller, and thus more words are stressed and fewer are left without stress. Thus, an utterance spoken in a formal style has more strong forms than the same utterance spoken in a colloquial style.

Sometimes people think that the weak forms are 'wrong' or 'inferior'. This is not the case. Native speakers of English from all social classes regularly use weak forms. Not to use weak forms when they are appropriate gives English a stilted, artificial sound. If you are not a native speaker of English, you may find it useful to practise the weak forms as they are often not taught sufficiently. Gimson (1980:261–3) has quite an extensive list of weak forms, although with a British accent. See also the exercises at the end of this chapter.

It is interesting to note that for some people, the original strong form has been lost and a new one created. The environments which cause prepositions and

Marge has a new *computer.*   Marge has a new *computer?*

Figure 5.4   Intonation contours of a statement and a question.

articles to be stressed are very rare. We use the weak forms most of the time, rarely needing the strong forms. For some people the strong form of a word such as *of* is so rare that the older strong /ˈav/ has been lost. In the rare cases where a strong form is needed, the /ə/ of the weak form /əv/ is stressed to the most similar vowel sound of /ʌ/ as in /ˈʌv/. As a result, many speakers have /ˈfrʌm/, /ˈðʌ/, and /ˈwʌz/ rather than the older /ˈfrɑm/, /ˈði/, and /ˈwɑz/. Similarly, some Canadians and most Americans do not use the strong form of *been* /ˈbin/, having instead /ˈbɪn/. Note here that /ɪ/ can be a full or a weak vowel. By contrast, most North Americans do not have a weak form for *my;* British speakers, however, frequently use /mɪ/ as the weak form, as in *my books* /mɪ ˈbʊks/.

PITCH AND INTONATION

Pitch is the quality we hear in playing two different notes on the piano. In speech, we control the pitch of an utterance by changing the vibration rate of the vocal cords. The faster they vibrate, the higher the pitch. We will examine this in greater detail in Chapter 14.

Some languages, like Chinese, use pitch to distinguish different words; they are called **tone languages** (see Chapter 14). In such languages a word spoken with a high pitch might be a completely different word from the same segments spoken with a low pitch. English does not work like this; it does, however, distinguish different phrases and sentences with different intonation contours. **Intonation** is the use of pitch in a phonetic phrase.

Say the two sentences in Figure 5.4; each constitutes a single phonetic phrase. They are the same except that one is a statement, and the other is a question. The major stress is on *computer.*

The pitch pattern of each sentence is drawn above the sentence. In each utterance, the pitch pattern has two parts. For both utterances, the pitch gradually falls in the first part; the second part of the pitch pattern, however, differs for the two utterances. In the statement, the pitch starts high and falls; in the question, the pitch starts low and rises. The pitch pattern for an utterance is called the **intonation contour**. The intonation system of English is very complex and not completely understood. We will examine a number of typical contours.

CONTOURS

Try saying the sentence in Figure 5.5 with the major stress on *Thursday.*

You can hear that the pitch starts moderately high and falls slightly. At the stressed syllable of *Thursday,* the first curve stops, and a new contour starts

Nancy bought a new house on *Thursday*.

Figure 5.5 Intonation contour for a statement with stress on *Thursday*.

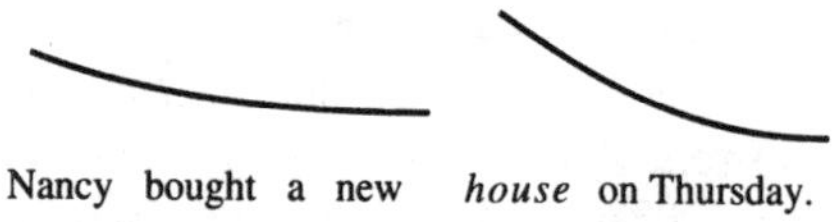

Nancy bought a new *house* on Thursday.

Figure 5.6 Intonation contour for a statement with stress on *house*.

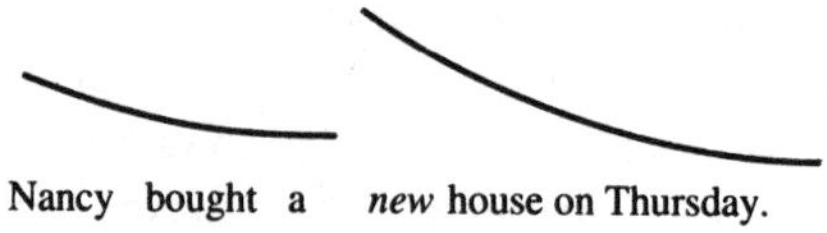

Nancy bought a *new* house on Thursday.

Figure 5.7 Intonation contour for a statement with stress on *new*.

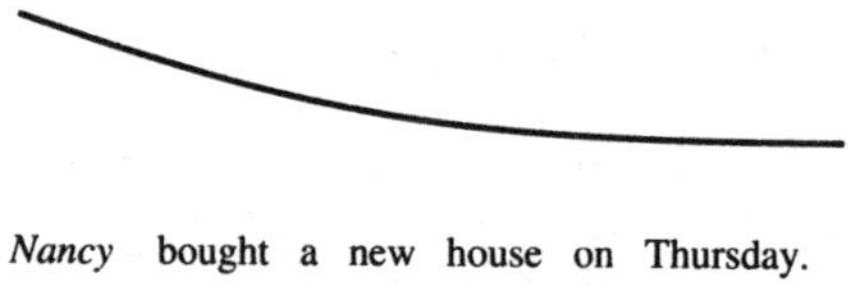

Nancy bought a new house on Thursday.

Figure 5.8 Intonation contour for a statement with stress on first word, *Nancy*.

from a high pitch and once again falls. Now, move the major stress to *house* (Figure 5.6).

We find two falling contours again, except that the second one starts at the stressed syllable of *house*. Try the same sentence once more with the major stress on *new* (Figure 5.7).

Again, we have two contours with the second beginning at the major stressed syllable of the sentence. You can experiment with the intonation when the major stress is on *Nancy, bought,* and even *a* or *on*. The intonation contours shown for these examples are by no means the only ones possible for such sentences; they are, nevertheless, commonly used as neutral contours.

Typically, we find that in a simple statement like the sentence above, the intonation contour has two falling contours with the break between them coming at the beginning of the tonic syllable. The **tonic syllable** is the syllable having primary stress in the word bearing the major stress of the sentence. In the example given in this section the tonic syllable is the syllable in the italicised word with the primary stress.

You might wonder what would happen if the first syllable of the utterance were the tonic syllable. Try saying the sentence again, stressing *Nancy* (Figure 5.8).

Here, the tonic syllable /ˈnæn/ is at the beginning of the second part of the contour, but the first part of the contour is empty and thus does not occur.

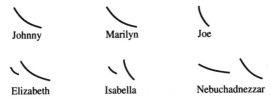

Figure 5.9 Intonation contours for names of varying length.

This same intonation contour used for statements is also used for calling someone. Think of yourself calling for children (Figure 5.9):

The intonation contour is a general shape. We take whatever phonetic material we are given and fit it to the intonation contour, placing the tonic syllable properly. The main break in the contour is determined by the position of the tonic syllable.

So far we have focussed on one intonation contour. There are, however, a large number of them. We will now examine a few others.

English has three basic types of questions as shown in Figure 5.10.

Word order	Answer	Intonation Contour	Example
regular	yes–no	question	*Nancy bought a new computer?*
inverted	yes–no	statement	*Did Nancy buy a new computer?*
inverted	wh-word	statement	*What did Nancy buy?*

Figure 5.10. Types of questions in English.

In questions with regular word order, the verb follows (here *bought*) the subject; with inverted word order, the verb (here *did*) precedes the subject. **Yes-no questions** require an answer of 'yes' or 'no'. **Wh-questions** contain a wh- word such as *what, who, where, when, why,* or *how* and ask the listener to fill in a blank

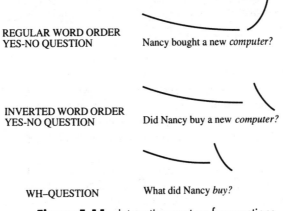

REGULAR WORD ORDER
YES-NO QUESTION   Nancy bought a new *computer?*

INVERTED WORD ORDER
YES-NO QUESTION   Did Nancy buy a new *computer?*

WH–QUESTION   What did Nancy *buy?*

Figure 5.11 Intonation contour for questions.

one, two, three, four   Jane, Wilbur, Winifred, Imelda, and Mrs. Benoit

Figure 5.12   **Figure 5.13** Another intonation contour
Intonation contour for a list.   for a list.

(*e.g., a new computer*)? Where the word order is the same for a statement and a question (*e.g., Nancy bought a computer*), a special intonation contour for questions tells the listener that the utterance is a question, not a statement. In questions with inverted word order, the word order signals the fact that the utterance is a question; as a result, no special intonation contour is required.

There is a special contour for counting or listing things (Figures 5.12 and 5.13). We use a rising intonation for non-final items, and a falling intonation for the final one.

Note that the rising contour shows that the series is not finished. We immediately recognise that the list is over when we hear the falling contour.

Subordinate clauses preceding the main clause typically have a contour with a more level pitch, as in Figure 5.14. The more level pitch on *soon* tells us that the clause is over, but not the sentence.

There is a great variety of intonation contours available in English. Most sentences are capable of being said with several different patterns. The ones shown here are common, but by no means the only intonation contours possible for the sentences illustrated.

RHYTHM

English sentences follow certain patterns of **rhythm** /ˈɹɪðəm/. Say the following sentence aloud at a normal speaking rate:

Which is the train to Guelph, please?

Now, clap your hands together at even time intervals, like a metronome. While you are doing this, say the sentence again, say *which* just as your hands come together. You will likely find that the stressed syllables also fall on the beat of your hands. We can show this using × for the hand-beat.

×	×	×	×
Which is the	train to	Guelph,	please?

The sentence consists of four time units called feet. Each **foot** has one stress, and the stresses come at equal intervals of time. Thus, each foot occupies the same amount of time. The first foot *which is the* has three syllables; the second foot *train to* has two; and the last two feet *Guelph* and *please* have only one foot each.

If he comes soon, we will be able to make the movie.

Figure 5.14 Intonation contour showing a subordinate clause.

In the sentence *Which is the train to Winnipeg, please?*, we can see that the three syllables of *Winnipeg* are spoken more quickly so that they take the same amount of time as the single syllable of *Guelph*.

×	×	×	×
Which is the	train to	Winnipeg,	please?

Note that if a foot has several syllables, the syllables are said faster; however, if a foot has only one syllable, the nucleus is lengthened. This is necessary to equalise the time between stresses.

In the following examples, notice that each phrase constitutes a single foot and takes the same amount of time. As more syllables are added to *speed,* you can hear that the duration of the syllable /spid/ decreases.

× ×	× ×	× ×
speed demon	speedy demon	speedily driven

The equal timing of feet is a tendency rather than an absolute requirement. Poetry is often written to emphasise this quality and often has very evenly timed feet. Prose offers somewhat more variety. Languages in which stresses come at equal intervals, such as English, are called **stressed-timed**. In Chapter 7, we will discover that French is a **syllable-timed** language, with each syllable occurring at equal intervals of time.

TECHNICAL TERMS

accidental gap	phonetic phrase	syllable
closed syllable	phonetic word	syllable-timed
coda	phonotactics	systematic gap
foot	pitch	tertiary stress
intonation	rhyme	tone language
intonation contour	rhythm	tonic syllable
nucleus	stress	weak form
nuclei	stressed-timed	wh-question
onset	strong form	yes-no question
open syllable	suprasegmental	

EXERCISES

BASIC

1. Review
a. Transcribe:

slight	crowd	sigh	dine
sauerkraut	night-time	found out	out of sight

b. Pronounce:

ʌj	ʌw	aw	aj	zʌj	fajt
ɹʌwd	lʌjg	najf	wʌjvz	lawp	sʌwg

2. Transcribe the following with three degrees of stress: /ˈ/ preceding a syllable with strong stress, /ˌ/ before syllables with secondary stress, and unstressed syllables unmarked. Remember that in English almost all unstressed syllables have one of the vowels /ə ɪ ɚ/ or a syllabic consonant.

social	noises	human	whistle	animal	creature
practise	finger	of course	the book	a hundred	the bottom

3. Read the following nonsense words aloud. Some are potential English words and some are not. Can you tell which ones could not be English words? Why not?

stɛks	blɪnd	pluθk	ðɑd	ŋæt	flɔjf
plʊtʃ	tluð	hɪmpks	dwawn	bɹajl	dʒʌnd
pawb	sklʊŋk	lbowg	θɹʌdʒ	vlejmb	knujθs

4. Many phrases and words have two stresses. The secondary stress commonly precedes the strong stress immediately. Note that stressed (primary or secondary) syllables can have any vowel except /ə/; /ɚ/ occurs with stress.

irate	/ˌajˈɹejt/	produce (v.)	/ˌpɹoˈdjus/
verbose	/ˌvɚˈbows/	chaotic	/ˌkejˈɑtɪk/
urbane	/ˌɚˈbejn/		

5. Transcribe the following:

centimetre	laboratory	fundamental
at the school	the darkest one	four o' clock

6. Transcribe the following words, and for each find three others which have exactly the same stress pattern:

Chinese	alone	invoice	husband	understand	quantity
appetite	affiliation	remarkable	rhinocerous	enumerate	tomato

7. Many words vary in pronunciation, having syllables occurring either as a secondary stress with a full vowel or as unstressed with a weak vowel; the unstressed form occurs more often in casual speech, whereas the full vowel occurs in slower, more formal speech.

Transcribe and pronounce the following using both styles:

financial	/ˌfajˈnænʃəl/~/fəˈnænʃəl/

pronounce   umbrella   Sir William   St. George   subsumed   repeat

8. For each of the following words, transcribe how it occurs as a strong form, and then transcribe as many weak forms for each that you can find:

was	them	at	for

9. Transcribe the following, paying particular attention to the vowels in the unstressed syllables:

We watched *Miami Vice* Wednesday evening.

Incandescent lighting changes the appearance of colours.

10. For each syllable in the following, draw a labelled tree showing the *onset, rhyme, nucleus, and coda:*

    not at or can

11. Find two words beginning with each of clusters /pl bl kl gl/.

    e.g.: pl *play, pleonasm*

    What other initial clusters have /l/ as the second element? Give two examples for each cluster you can think of.

    e.g.: fl

12. In each of the following, draw the intonation contour.

    Charlotte brought in the last of the corn.

    Is Harold coming?

    When is Harold coming?

    Alpha, beta, gamma, delta, epsilon.

    The more, the merrier.

13. Say the following poem aloud, clapping your hands at regular intervals. Mark the stressed syllables with an ×. Read it aloud again, timing your reading so that each syllable marked × occurs at the same time as your hands clap.

    Ring around the rosie,

    Pocket full of posey

    Hasha, hasha,

    They all fall down.

14. The following poem has two silent beats; that is, if you clap your hands as in Exercise 13, some beats will have no words. Mark all the rhythmical stresses with an ×. See if you can discover where the silent beats are. Mark them with an × as well. Try repeating the poem without a break

    Row, row, row your boat,

    Gently down the stream,

    Merrily, merrily,

    Merrily, merrily.

    Life is but a dream.

ADVANCED

15. Here are the first sounds we have encountered which do not occur in English at all:

    /φ/: a voiceless bilabial fricative. The symbol is the Greek letter phi /faj/.

    /β/: a voiced bilabial fricative. The symbol is the Greek letter beta /ˈbejtə/.

    Note that /φ β/ are bilabial and /f v/ are labio-dental.

    To make /φ/ form your lips so as to make a /p/. Hold the lips together in a relaxed fashion and blow through them.

    Try saying:

    φi φaj φow φʌm

Now try /β/. It is just like /φ/, except voiced. Try these:

βi	βɪ	βej	βɛ	βæ	φɑ
βɔ	φɪ	βu	φɔj	βow	φʊ
βug	φɪm	βʌl			

Some people seem to make these sounds with a following /w/: /φwɑ/ rather than /φ ɑ/. If this is the case for you, try extending the /φ/: /φφφφφφ/. Practise this a couple of times, and then try opening the lips suddenly to /ɑ/ - sneak up on the /ɑ/. Now try the corresponding trick with /ββββ/.

If you still have trouble with /φ β/, try smiling; pretend to blow out a candle while still smiling.

Be sure to keep /φ β/ separate from /f v/. If you find /φ/ turning into an /f/, extend your lower lip a bit. Ultimately the /φ β/ should have about the same lip position as /p b/, except slightly open.

Practise the following in pairs:

pɑ	fɑ	fɑ	pɑ	pɑ	φɑ	fɑ	φɑ
φɑ	pɑ	φɑ	fɑ	bɑ	βɑ	vɑ	βɑ
βɑ	vɑ	βɑ	bɑ				

16. Ewe (/ˈɛˌvɛ/; Ghana, West Africa) has contrastive bilabial and labio-dental fricatives:

ɛβɛ	*the Ewe language*	ɛvɛ	*two*
eφa	*he polished*	efa	*he was cold*
eβlo	*mushroom*	evlo	*he is evil*
eφle	*he bought*	eflẽ	*he split off*

17. Now try the following nonsense words:

pɑfɑ	φufu	vɛbɛ	pɛφɛ	bɑβɑ	βʌvʌ
fiφi	βɔvɔ	φiβi	pifɑ	φuβʌ	βɑβu
bɔφi	βɔvɛ	fɛvɔ	fɛφɑ	φʊbu	vɒφu
vʌfæ	φivɔ	bʌvæ			

18. Read the following poem aloud.

Peter Piper picked a peck of pickled peppers;
A peck of pickled peppers Peter Piper picked.
If Peter Piper picked a peck of pickled peppers,
Where's the peck of pickled peppers that Peter Piper picked?

a. Now try reading it, substituting [φ] for [p].

b. Now try it with [β].

c. Try it with unaspirated [p].

19. Each of the following words has a strong form and at least one weak form. Transcribe the strong form and as many weak forms as you can find for each.

could   them   at   Saint   have   us

20. *Syntax* is the study of the structure of sentences; it can be transcribed as /ˈsɪnˌtæks/. The tax on alcohol and tobacco could be called a *sin tax*. Try saying *syntax* and *sin tax*. Some people distinguish these two forms by lengthening the first syllable of *sin tax*, but not of *syntax*.

    syntax /ˈsɪnˌtæks/   *sin tax* /ˈsɪnːˌtæks/

Try another example. A *greenhouse* [ˈgɹinˌhʌws] is a 'building for growing plants'. The *Greene house* [gɹinːˌhʌws] is a 'house belonging to the Greene family'. For me at least, this last phrase has a lengthening of the first syllable. Not everyone makes such lengthenings.

Try these examples to see if you have this lengthening:
Long Island is a *long* island. (Constrastive stress on second *long*.)
My suitcase is unpacked. ('I haven't put anything in it yet.')
My suitcase is unpacked. ('I have taken everything out of it.')
In the last pair of sentences, look for lengthening in the syllable *un-*.

21. The following selection is from *Julius Caesar* (adapted from Kökeritz, 1953, by permission) showing how it would have been pronounced in Shakespeare's day. Practise your sixteenth-century acting skills.

Julius Caesar 3.2.79-86

ˈfrɛnz ˈroːmənz ˈkʌntrɪmən
ˈlend mi juɹ ˈiːɹz.

Friends, Romans, countrymen,
lend me your ears;

ʌj ˈkʌm tə ˈberɪ ˈseːzəɹ
ˈnɒt tʊ ˈpreːz ɪm.

I come to bury Cæsar,
not to praise him.

ðɪ ˈiːvɪl ðət ˈmɛn ˈduː
ˈlɪvz ˈæːftəɹ ðəm

The evil that men do
lives after them,

ðə ˈgʊd ɪz ˈɔːft ɪnˈtəːrɪd
wɪð ðəɹ ˈboːnz

The good is oft interred
with their bones;

ˈsoː let ɪt ˈbiː wɪθ ˈseːzəɹ.
ðə ˈnoːbl̩ ˈbruːtəs

So let it be with Cæsar.
The noble Brutus

əθ ˈtoːld ju
ˈseːzəɹ wəz æmˈbɪʃɪəs

hath told you
Cæsar was ambitious;

ɪf ɪt ˈwɛːɹ ˈsoː
ɪt wɔz ə ˈgriːvəs ˈfɔːlt

If it were so,
it was a grievous fault,

ən ˈgriːvəslɪ
əθ ˈseːzəɹ ˈæːnsəɹd ɪt.

And grievously
hath Cæsar answer'd it.

22. Transcribe the passage of *Julius Caesar* as it would be said today in your dialect. What differences do you find between your accent and Shakespeare's?

CHAPTER SIX
ENGLISH DIALECT DIFFERENCES

INTRODUCTION

English is spoken as a native language by some 450 million people around the world. It is spoken on every continent. According to the 1991 census, 16,169,880 Canadians (60%) speak English as their mother tongue. Like all languages, English varies in the way it is spoken from place to place. These varieties are called **dialects**. The term **accent** is often used to refer to the phonetic or phonological aspects of a dialect.

In this chapter you will learn about:
- history of English
- widespread English dialects
- how Canadian English differs from other dialects.

BACKGROUND   Two thousand years ago, Britain was inhabited by Celtic-speaking people known as Britons, the ancestors of the present-day Welsh of Wales and Bretons of France. In 55 B.C., Julius Caesar visited Britain, and from A.D. 43, Roman soldiers colonised and ruled southern Britain until the early part of the fifth century when Rome recalled the soldiers to help with difficulties at home. The political vacuum created by the Romans' departure was filled from around A.D. 450 by sizable settlements of Germanic-speaking people from continental Europe. These people are traditionally known as the Angles, Saxons, and Jutes; in Britain they became known as the English. They established themselves strongly, pushing back the Britons towards the west and also south across the water to Brittany. The English seized and settled all of Britain except for Wales and the north of Scotland. The language spoken at that time is known as Anglo-Saxon or Old English.

All languages change over time. Modern English is very different from Old English. In addition to internal changes, English was influenced slightly by the

Scandinavians who held much of England in the ninth and tenth centuries, and to a much greater extent by the conquest of the French-speaking Normans in 1066.

From the beginning there were dialect differences among the English. Certainly there is considerable variation now in the local dialects between Scotland in the north and the southern coast of England. The rural dialects show the greatest variation, although they seem to be slowly giving way to urban dialects. There is less variation in the various accents of the cities, although generally enough to tell where someone comes from.

About the same time as the Germanic speakers invaded Britain (fifth century A.D.), Gaelic speakers from Ireland conquered much of Scotland. The Anglo-Saxons settled in the lowlands (south and east) of Scotland. Since then, English has gradually pushed Scots Gaelic back to the north and west. The lowland dialects, described below, have many interesting features, such as *twa* /twɑ/ for 'two' and *ane* /en/ for 'one'.

In the highlands (the north and west) of Scotland, English was introduced widely in the nineteenth century by teachers speaking upper-middle class Scottish English. As a result, highland English has standard grammatical features with an urban Scottish accent and few of the features specifically associated with rural lowland speech.

In Wales, English has steadily pushed west over the centuries eroding the territory where Welsh is spoken. Welsh English is thus essentially an extension of the kind of English spoken in the west of England.

Ireland previously spoke Irish Gaelic, a Celtic language. Since the seventeenth century English has been spoken there, first in Dublin, then spreading out from the capital. The north of Ireland was colonised in the early seventeenth century by English speakers, many of whom had Scottish accents. During the nineteenth century almost the entire country adopted English as its native language.

English came to North America with the British settlers in the early seventeenth century. The earliest settlers were from England, but they were soon joined by English speakers from Scotland and Ireland as well. Much of the West Indies became English speaking; however, its linguistic history is a bit more complicated, as we will see when we look at Jamaican English.

The great colonial enterprise of the nineteenth century saw English become established in South Africa, Australia, and New Zealand as English-speaking peoples settled in those areas. English became the predominant second language in other areas such as India, Singapore, Hong Kong, and much of Africa.

GENERAL SCHEME In considering the dialects of English, we are in some danger of being overwhelmed by detail. I will try to avoid this problem by presenting only the major ways that the various dialects differ from Canadian English. There are minor variations in the consonants, but most of the variation is in the vowels. The vowels are presented in two different ways. First, there is the general inventory of the vowel system. For Canadian English, this inventory is given below:

i		u	
ɪ		ʊ	
ej	ə	ow	ɔj
ɛ	ʌ		aj [ʌj]
æ	ɑ		aw [ɑw]

The vowels are roughly in the position they would be on a phonetic chart. The diphthongs /ej ow/ are with the monophthongs; the diphthongs /aj aw ɔj/ are given separately. Certain phonetic variations (here, the ones involved in raising) are given in brackets; the square brackets will remind you that these are allophonic variations.

The second presentation gives a list showing a sample word and the vowel used in that word. In the last three words, *baby, runner,* and *sofa,* it is the second syllable which is of interest, as shown by the boldface print.

beat	i	*boot*	u	*peer*	iɹ
pit	ɪ	*put*	ʊ	*pear*	eɹ
hate	ej	*boat*	ow	*part*	ɑɹ
pet	ɛ	*bought*	ɑ	*hurt*	əɹ
pat	æ	*pot*	ɑ	*cure*	uɹ
path	æ	*soft*	ɑ	*four*	oɹ
but	ʌ	*palm*	ɑ	*baby*	i
bite	aj, ʌj	*out*	aw, ʌw	*runner*	əɹ
		choice	ɔj	*sofa*	ə

This presentation gives you some help in figuring out the pronunciation of other words with a fair degree of accuracy. If you want to know how to pronounce a word in a certain accent, you find a word, on the relevant chart, that has the same vowel in Canadian English. For example, if you want to say *cot* with a West Indian accent, you find that the word *pot* is on the West Indian list with the vowel /a/. From your own knowledge of English, you can guess that *cot* and *pot* have the same vowel. Therefore, you can make a fairly reliable guess that *cot* also has the vowel /a/. For Canadian, American, and British dialects, there are dictionaries readily available giving the respective pronunciations. The type of chart presented here is particularly useful for accents where appropriate dictionaries may not be available. (See Wells, 1982, for many more details on the accents of English and for a full discussion of this type of presentation.)

RECEIVED PRONUNCIATION (Great Britain)

Around 1400, the dialect of the royal court emerged as the prestige dialect of English. This dialect was essentially the speech of upper-class London. The modern-day descendant of this dialect continues as the prestige dialect of England, and to a lesser degree of Scotland and Ireland as well. It is the accent not only of the royal family and the nobility, but of the upper and upper-middle classes generally. It is the accent commonly used by announcers for the BBC. This accent is known to linguists by the name **Received Pronunciation (RP)** (pronounced /ˌaɹ ˈpi/), where the term *received* is used in the nineteenth-century sense of 'correct, proper'. Although RP is spoken by individuals scattered throughout Britain, it has little regional variation. RP is also spoken in Scotland and Ireland by many people on the higher end of the social scale although both Scotland and Ireland have prestige accents of their own.

Britain is a country with a rather rigid social structure mirrored fairly closely in its accents. For social reasons, many people who do not start off life as RP-speakers shift their speech in various degrees towards RP. Wells (1982) has an interesting discussion of acquired RP.

RP is usually the British accent taught to foreigners. Even by people who do not speak it, RP is widely regarded as 'correct'. Linguists, of course, do not describe an accent as 'correct' or not; rather, they say that it is spoken by certain social groups, here by the upper classes and, in addition, by many of the well-educated.

CONSONANTS   The consonants of RP are much the same as those of Canadian English. One large difference is that /ɹ/ as a syllable coda has been lost in RP, so that Canadians say /kaɹ/ *car* whereas RP has /ka/, also /had/ *hard*, /pɔ/ *pour*, /ˈbʌtə/ *butter*.

If a word is written with a final *r*, and the next word begins with a vowel, RP retains the /ɹ/:

/ˈfaðə/	'father'	*but*	/ˈfaðəɹ ən ˈmʌðə/	'father and mother'
/ˈmʌðə/	'mother'	*but*	/ˈmʌðəɹ ən ˈfaðə/	'mother and father'
/ˈhiə waz/	'here was'	*but*	/ˈhiəɹ ɪz/	'here is'

Many RP speakers insert an /ɹ/ between a word ending in a schwa and a word beginning with a vowel:

Emma /ɹ/ is   Korea /ɹ/ and Japan
the idea /ɹ/ of it   put a comma /ɹ/ at the end
even sometimes
I saw /ɹ/ it.   draw/ɹ/ing

The presence or absence of postvocalic /ɹ/ in English dialects is so distinctive a feature that dialects with postvocalic /ɹ/ are called **rhotic** /ˈɹowtɪk/, and those without /ɹ/ are called **nonrhotic**. RP is nonrhotic, and Canadian English is rhotic.

Intervocalic /ɹ/, as in *very*, is frequently pronounced in RP as an alveolar tap [ˈvɛɾi], giving rise to such dialect spellings as *veddy*. Thus, Canadian *Betty* and RP *berry* are pronounced very similarly: Can. [ˈbɛɾi], RP [ˈbɛɾi].

/j/ after alveolars   Canadian English and many other varieties of North American English have generally lost the glide /j/ after the alveolar and dental consonants /t d n θ s z l ɹ/; *e.g.*, /tun, dun, nu, ən'θuzi,æzəm, su, ɹɪ'zum, lut, ɹud/ *tune, dune, new, enthusiasm, sue, resume, lute, rude*. RP has regularly retained /j/ after /t d n/, kept it occasionally after /s l θ/, and lost it after /ɹ/. Interestingly, the dialect of East Anglia (around Norwich) has lost /j/ everwhere before /u/ resulting in forms such as /ˈbutɪ/ *beauty* and /ˈmuzɪk/ *music*.

tjun	*tune*	djun	*dune*
nju	*new*	ənˈθjuziæzəm	*enthusiasm*
sju, su	*sue*	ɹɪˈzjum, ɹɪˈzum	*resume*
ljut, lut	*lute*	ɹud	*rude*

Some Canadian speakers do have a /j/ after alveolars. For some people, the absence of /j/ is socially highly stigmatised. A Toronto newspaper columnist once stated her views on speakers who use /u/ rather than /ju/:

> The minute you hear that mush-mouthed vowel, you picture the beetling forehead, tiny eyes, slack jaw, the flecks of spittle in the corners of the loose mouth. You know that here is a brain but one evolutionary spin away from the cave.
>
> — Michele Landsberg (*Toronto Star,* 26 June 1980)

My own survey at the time showed that neither the Prime Minister nor any of the ten premiers used /j/ after alveolars. Landsberg's comments probably reflect how she thinks things ought to be, rather than any accurate observation of who uses /j/ and who does not. It is curious how exercised we can become over something as inherently trivial as the presence or absence of a high front unrounded glide after alveolars.

VOWELS The main differences between RP and Canadian English lie with the vowels; indeed, the vowels provide the main source of variation for English accents in general. The following chart gives basic RP vowels:.

i		u	i̯ə		
ɪ		ʊ		ʊ̯ə	
ej	ə	əw			
ɛ	ɜ	ɔ	ɛə		ɔj
æ	ʌ	ɑ,ɒ	aj		ɑw

beat	i	*boot*	u	*peer*	i̯ə		
pit	ɪ	*put*	ʊ	*pear*	ɛə		
hate	ej	*boat*	əw	*part*	ɑ		
pet	ɛ	*bought*	ɔ	*hurt*	ɜ		
pat	æ	*pot*	ɒ	*cure*	ʊ̯ə		
path	ɑ	*soft*	ɒ	*four*	ɔ		
but	ʌ	*palm*	ɑ	*baby*	ɪ		
bite	aj	*out*	ɑw	*runner*	ə		
		choice	ɔj	*sofa*	ə		

RP English does not have raising:

out	awt	*loud*	lawd
wife	wajf	*live*	lajv

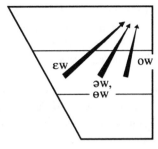

Figure 6.1 Various realisations of /ow/: [əw], [ɵw], and [ɛw] in RP, and [ow] in Canadian English.

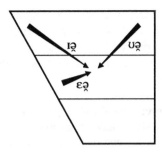

Figure 6.2
Vowels before historic /ɹ/.

/ɑ/   In a number of words, RP has /ɑ/ where Canadian English has /æ/. One subset of these words has a fricative in the coda:

ask   ɑsk   calf   kɑf   path   pɑθ

Another subset has a cluster of /n/ plus obstruent in the coda:

dance   dɑns   can't   kɑnt   branch   bɹɑntʃ

/əw/   Where Canadian English has [ow], RP has [əw] with the diphthong beginning with the tongue in a central position as shown in Figure 6.1. Some speakers may start the diphthong farther front and have [ɛw].

gəw   go   səwp   soap

The diphthong [əw] may have a rounded vowel, symbolised as [ɵ] (smaller than a theta [θ]): [gɵw sɵwp]. The pronunciation of /ow/ as [əw] or [ɵw] is also quite common in southern dialects of the U.S.

Low back vowels   Canadian English /ɑ/ corresponds to three different RP vowels — /ɑ ɔ ɒ/.

1. The vowel /ɑ/ is a tense low back unrounded vowel, a bit farther back than Canadian /ɑ/: *father, palm.* Notice that it also occurs in RP words such as *cart, farther* (which sounds the same as *father*), where Canadian English has /ɑɹ/.

2. The vowel /ɔ/ is a tense lower-mid back rounded vowel. It is commonly found in words spelled with *aw, au, augh,* and *ough* : *law, dawn, gnawed, taut, caught, fought, sword, floor, all, bald.*

3. The vowel /ɒ/ is a lax low back rounded vowel. It is like /ɑ/ except lax and rounded. It is common in words spelled with *o: cot, bother, lost, sorry, was, what, cough, because.*

Vowels before /ɹ/   Postvocalic /ɹ/ often affects the preceding vowel as we have already noticed in Chapter 4. As well, the loss of /ɹ/ after vowels left RP with special results, often a diphthong ending in /ə̯/. Here /ə̯/ represents a glide ending in a mid central vowel; see Figure 6.2.

/ɪə̯/   beer, fear, weird, serious /ˈsɪə̯ɹɪəs/, idea, museum, Ian, real

/ɛə̯/   dare, hair, wear, care, caring /ˈkɛə̯ɹɪŋ/, Mary /ˈmɛə̯ɹɪ/, mayor

/ʊə̯/   cure, poor, during /ˈdjʊə̯ɹɪŋ/, sewer /sjʊə̯/, jewel /dʒʊə̯l/

Younger speakers of RP are tending to replace /ʊə̯/ with /ɔ/. This means that a number of words are indistinguishable in speech: *pour, pore, poor,* and *paw* are all pronounced /pɔ/; also, *moor, more,* and *maw* have merged as /mɔ/.

Canadian English /ɑɹ/ is regularly /ɑ/ in RP: *car* /kɑ/, *sharp* /ʃɑp/, *aardvark* /ˈɑd‚vɑk/.

In stressed syllables, the Canadian sequence /əɹ/ is found in RP as /ɜ/, a central vowel somewhat lower than [ə]: *hurt* /hɜt/, *verb* /vɜb/, *worth* /wɜθ/, *dirk* /dɜk/, *colonel* /ˈkɜnəl/. In unstressed syllables, this sequence in RP is simply /ə/: *letter* /ˈlɛtə/, *centre* /ˈsɛntə/, *liar* /ˈlajə/, *stupor* /ˈstjupə/, *fervour* /ˈfɜvə/.

/æɹ/ The sequence /æɹ/ does not occur word-finally in most dialects of English; however, some dialects, such as RP, have this sequence when followed by vowel. RP distinguishes the words *merry* /ˈmɛɹi/, *marry* /ˈmæɹi/, and *Mary* /ˈmeə̯ɹi/.

berry	ˈbɛɹi	*Barry*	ˈbæɹi	*airy*	ˈɛə̯ɹi
very	ˈvɛɹi	*vary*	ˈvæɹi	*wearing*	ˈweə̯ɹiŋ
Kerry	ˈkɛɹi	*carry*	ˈkæɹi	*caring*	ˈkeə̯ɹiŋ

Canadian dialects differ in treating these words. In eastern Canada, many people distinguish *merry* /ˈmɛɹi/ and *marry* /ˈmæɹi/, and pronounce *Mary* as /ˈmeɹi/. In central Canada and the West, most people merge all three, pronouncing them all as /ˈmɛɹi/.

Final /ɪ/ RP has /ɪ/ as an unstressed final vowel corresponding to Canadian /i/: *lady* /ˈlejdɪ/, *busy* /ˈbɪzɪ/, *curry* /ˈkʌɹɪ/, *lily* /ˈlɪlɪ/.

AMERICAN ENGLISH

The United States is a very large area with considerable dialect variation, although not nearly so much as in Britain. The East of the U.S., having been settled longer, shows greater variation than the central and western areas. Unlike Britain, there is no single prestige dialect for the whole country; rather, each region has a range of social dialects. An important type of American English is Black English which originated with Black people in the South and is now spoken widely throughout the United States. The dialect presented here is spoken by educated people in the central and western areas. It is perhaps most familiar as the accent generally used by radio and television announcers for the national networks. It is very similar to the Canadian accent we have presented in detail. The major differences are presented here.

CONSONANTS Many Americans, particularly in the south and midwest, preserved the distinction of /w/ and /hw/, as in words such as *wear* and *where*. The sequence /hw/ represents a voiceless /w/. Some Americans in other areas, as well as some Canadian speakers, also have this distinction. The sequence /hw/ is discussed further below under Scottish English.

| when | /hwɛn/ | whale | /hwel/ | wheat | /hwit/ | whine | /hwajn/ |

cf. *why (question)* /hwaj/   *why (exclamation)* /waj/

VOWELS

i		u				
ɪ		ʊ				
ej	ə	ow				
ɛ		ɔ				ɔj
æ		ɑ		aj		
				aw		

beat	i		boot	u		peer	iɹ
pit	ɪ		put	ʊ		pear	eɹ
hate	ej		boat	ow		part	ɑɹ
pet	ɛ		bought	ɔ		hurt	əɹ
pat	æ		pot	ɑ		cure	uɹ
path	æ		soft	ɔ		four	oɹ
but	ə		palm	ɑ		baby	i
bite	aj		out	aw		runner	əɹ
			choice	ɔj		sofa	ə

1. This dialect does not have raising:

   | out | awt | *loud* | lawd | *wife* | wajf | *live* | lajv |

2. The vowels of *cot* and *caught,* are generally distinct, but not those of *father* and *bother.*

cot	kɑt		caught	kɔt		calm	kɑm
bother	ˈbɑðəɹ		lawyer	ˈlɔjəɹ		father	ˈfɑðəɹ
chock	tʃɑk		chalk	tʃɔk			
hot	hɑt		dog	dɔg		bra	bɹɑ

   In this respect, American English lies between Canadian English and RP. RP has three distinct vowels: /ɒ ɔ ɑ/; American English has two: /ɔ ɑ/; and Canadian English has only one: /ɑ/. The following chart compares different words in the three dialects; notice that for RP some words in /ɑ/ result from the loss of /ɹ/.

	RP	US	Can
not	nɒt	nɑt	nɑt
naught	nɔt	nɔt	nɑt
rot	ɹɒt	ɹɑt	ɹɑt
wrought	ɹɔt	ɹɔt	ɹɑt
ah!	ɑ	ɑ	ɑ
tart	tɑt	tɑɹt	tɑɹt
taught	tɔt	tɔt	tɑt
tot	tɒt	tɑt	tɑt

The /ɑ/ of the American dialect is generally more forward than the Canadian /ɑ/.

3. A few American speakers, particularly in the South, distinguish *hoarse* /hoɹs/ and *horse* /hɔɹs/.

pork	poɹk	*fork*	fɔɹk	*ore, oar*	oɹ
or	ɔɹ	*four*	foɹ	*for*	fɔɹ
cored	koɹd	*cord*	kɔɹd		

4. The /æ/ of US English is generally higher than Canadian /æ/. In the accents of New York City and other cities in New York, /æ/ is quite high, often misunderstood by Canadians for /ɛ/.

5. In much of American speech, particularly in the south, the words with Canadian /ʌ/ have a higher and more centralised vowel /ə/. This vowel thus occurs both in stressed and unstressed syllables.

NEWFOUNDLAND ENGLISH

Newfoundland certainly has the most distinctive dialect of English in Canada. This is not surprising considering its early settlement, political independence from Canada (until 1949), and large numbers of fairly isolated outport communities. All of these factors have acted to distinguish Newfoundland English from that of its Maritime neighbours (Paddock, 1974).

CONSONANTS   1. The dental fricatives are often pronounced as alveolar stops: [t] and [d]. In some areas dental stops are used: [t̪] and [d̪]. Some speakers substitute [f] and [v] for [θ] and [ð]: [dɪs d̪ɪs vɪs] *this*.

2. Most of the island is rhotic with quite strong retroflexion although certain communities are nonrhotic.

3. Mainland Canadian /hj/ appears simply as /j/, in words like *humour* and *human*. ['jumɚ 'jumən].

4. Many speakers have a clear [l] in postvocalic position [bɛl, hɛlp] *bell, help,* although others have [ɰ], a voiced velar approximant (See Chapter 13), [bɛɰ, hɛɰp].

5. Initial fricatives are sometimes voiced: [zɪŋk] *sink*, [væn] *fan*.

VOWELS   The vowel inventory is:

i		u		
ɪ		ʊ		
ɛː	ə	ʌw	əj	əw
ɛ	ɔ̃			
æ		ɑ		

beat	i	boot	u	peer	ɛɹ
pit	ɪ	put	ʊ	pear	ɛɹ
hate	ɛː	boat	əw	part	æɹ
pet	ɛ	bought	ɑ	hurt	əɹ
pat	æ	pot	ɑ	cure	ɔɹ
path	æ	soft	ɑ	four	ɔɹ
but	ɔ̈	palm	æ	baby	i
bite	əj	out	əw	runner	əɹ
choice	əj	sofa	ə		

The vowel /ɔ̈/ is a central rounded vowel. It lies between [ɔ] and [œ].

WEST INDIAN ENGLISH

English in the West Indies is quite varied, although generally British-oriented in its phonology. Some West Indians speak RP or near-RP; almost all English speakers there are aware of RP and will tend to shift their accent towards RP in formal social situations. In addition to ordinary English, most of the English-speaking islands have languages which linguists call **creoles** /ˈkɹiˌol/. These are full-fledged languages with a very interesting history. (For general information about creoles, see Wardhaugh, 1986; for details of West Indian English, see Roberts, 1988.) We will use the non-creole English spoken in Jamaica as an example of West Indian English.

CONSONANTS   1. The dental fricatives /θ/ and /ð/ are pronounced as alveolar stops /t/ and /d/.

this thing	dɪs tɪŋ
mother	mada

2. Certain consonant clusters are reduced:
   fact /fak/, mask /maːs/, west /wɛs/

3. The consonant /h/ is generally absent; this is also typical of many popular accents of England.
   half /aːf/, hit /ɪt/

4. Post-vocalic /ɹ/ is optional:
   short /ʃɔɹt, ʃɔt/

5. The glide /j/ is sometimes found unexpectedly after initial velar stops:
   garden /ɡja:dn̩/, car /kjaː(ɹ)/, cow /kjɔw/

VOWELS

i			u		
ɪ			ʊ		
e			o		
ɛ	ʌ				ɔw
a, aː			aj		

beat	i	*boot*	u	*peer*	e(ɹ)
pit	ɪ	*put*	ʊ	*pear*	e(ɹ)
hate	e	*boat*	o	*part*	aː(ɹ)
pet	ɛ	*bought*	aː	*hurt*	ʌ(ɹ)
pat	a	*pot*	a	*cure*	o(ɹ)
path	a	*soft*	aː	*four*	o(ɹ)
but	ʌ	*palm*	aː	*baby*	ɪ
bite	aj	*out*	ɔw	*runner*	a
		choice	aj, ɔj	*sofa*	a

The following chart illustrates the major vowels of Jamaican English:

i	*heat, meet, clean*	o	*goat, hope, glow*
ɪ	*bit, hit, kit, happy*	ʊ	*put, foot, good*
e	*face, mate, great*	u	*blue, goose, do*
ɛ	*wet, neck, sweat*	aj	*nice, ride*
a	*cot, rob, nod, sofa*	ɔw	*mouth, loud*
aː	*bath, palm, father, caught*	ɔj, aj	*choice, boil*
ʌ	*nut, hum, blood*		

Note especially the vowels /a/ and /aː/; /a/ corresponds to RP /æ ɒ ə/, and /aː/ corresponds to RP /ɑ ɔ/. The mid vowels /e o/ are monophthongs, not diphthongs.

SCOTTISH ENGLISH

Until 1603, Scotland had a separate monarch, and until 1707, it was a country politically independent from England. It is not surprising, then, that it has its own standard accent different from RP, although some Scots, the Queen Mother, for example, do speak RP. Grammatically, standard Scottish English is quite similar to the standard dialect of England. Lowland Scotland also has a traditional local dialect, known as **Scots** or **Lallans** /ˈlælənz/, which has maintained a literary presence. The accent described here is that of educated speakers of central Scotland.

CONSONANTS   One significant difference among the consonants is the retention of the older distinction between /w/ and /hw/, which has been lost in Canadian and RP English, which have only /w/. Scottish English regularly distinguishes words such as *where* /hweɹ/ and *wear* /weɹ/. This distinction is parallel to the one between /j/ and /hj/ found in most dialects. Some authors use a special symbol /ʍ/ for /hw/; in a narrow transcription, this sound could be represented as [w̥] or [ʍ]. (See the discussion in Chapter 4.) In Scottish English, dark [ɫ] is found in all positions: *list* [ɫɪst], *bill* [bɪɫ].

Scottish speakers also use a voiceless velar fricative /x/ in words such as *loch* /lɔx/, and in many place names —*Tulloch* /ˈtʌlʌx/. (See the advanced exercises at the end of this chapter for help in producing [x]). Scottish English is rhotic, the *r* is usually a tap [ɾ] or even a trill [r]; I transcribe this sound phonemically as /r/.

VOWELS

i	ʉ				
ɪ					
e		o			
ɛ	ʌ	ɔ		ʌw	ɒj
a			aẹ [ʌj]		

beat	i	boot	ʉ	peer	ir
pit	ɪ	put	ʉ	pear	er
hate	e	boat	o	part	ar
pet	ɛ	bought	ɔ	hurt	ər
pat	a	pot	ɔ	cure	ʉr
path	a	soft	ɔ	four	or
but	ʌ	palm	a	baby	e
bite	aẹ, ʌj	out	ʌw	runner	ər
		choice	ɒj	sofa	ʌ

The transcription [aẹ] represents a diphthong starting at [a] with a following glide to a [ə] position.

1. Examples of the simple vowels of Scottish English are shown below:

i	heat, meet, clean	ʉ	put, foot, good, look, Luke, goose
ɪ	bit, hit, kit, happy		
e	face, mate, great	o	goat, hope, glow
ɛ	wet, neck, sweat	ɔ	hot, rob, law, caught
a	bath, hat, palm	ʌ	nut, hum, blood, sofa

In particular, note that words like *bath*, *hat*, and *palm*, which are all distinct in RP, have merged, all of them having a low front vowel (lower than the /æ/ of *hat*). Also, the RP vowels /ʊ/ and /u/ are merged as /ʉ/ (a high central vowel, pronounced more towards the front of the mouth than the RP or Canadian /u/. The mid vowels /e o/ are monophthongs. The unstressed vowel corresponding to schwa is often /ʌ/.

2. Length is quite different in Scottish English from other dialects.

a. At the end of a morpheme, vowels, except /ɪ/ and /ʌ/, are long:

no	no:	*rowed*	ro:d	*road*	rod
me	mi:	*agreed*	ʌ'gri:d	*greed*	grid

In these examples, *rowed* and *agreed* both consist of two morphemes: *row #ed* and *agree # d*, ending in long /o:/ and /i:/, respectively, whereas *road* and *greed* consist of only one morpheme each with short /o/ and /i/.

b. Vowels, except /ɪ/ and /ʌ/ are long before the consonants /v ð z r/:

move /mʉ:v/, *seethe* /si:ð/, *size* /sa:ẹz/, *pour* /po:r/

DIPHTHONGS The alternations described just above apply to diphthongs as well; for the diphthong of *tie*, there is an alternation of quality as well.

tie	ta:ẹ	*tied*	ta:ẹd	*tide*	tʌjd
cow	kʌ:w	*cows*	kʌ:wz	*loud*	lʌwd
joy	dʒɒ:j	*toys*	tɒ:jz	*Lloyd*	lɒjd

Note that *tied, cows,* and *toys* consist of two morphemes each, whereas *tide, loud,* and *Lloyd* consist of only one.

AUSTRALIAN ENGLISH

Australian English is structurally very similar to RP; there are, however, a number of phonetic differences. Within Australia, there is little regional variation, although social variation may be quite marked (Mitchell & Delbridge, 1965).

CONSONANTS   1. Like RP, Australian English is nonrhotic.

   car   /ka/

2. Initial /h/ is frequently lost, as in much of the popular speech of England.

   hat   /æt/

3. Intervocalic /t/ is often voiced:

   city   /sɪdi/

VOWELS

i		u				
ɪ	ɜ	ʊ			ɪə̯	ʊə̯
	ə					
e	ʌ	ʌw		ʌj, ʌw		eə̯
æ	ɔ	æw		ɔj		
a	ɑ, ɒ			ɑj		

The following chart shows the basic pronunciation of Australian vowels:

beat	i	boot	u	peer	ɪə̯
pit	ɪ	put	ʊ	pear	eə̯
hate	ʌj	boat	ʌw	part	a
pet	e	bought	ɔ	hurt	ɜ
pat	æ	pot	ɑ	cure	ə
path	a	soft	ɒ	four	ɔ
but	ʌ	palm	a	baby	i
bite	ɑj	out	æw	runner	ə
		choice	ɔj	sofa	ə

1. Note the vowel /e/ in *pet* which is slightly higher than the /ɛ/ of Canadian English. The vowels /ɪ/ and /æ/ are also somewhat higher than in RP. The vowel of *path* and *palm* is a front /a/, as is the vowel of *part* and *car.*

2. Many of the tense vowels and diphthongs have qualities quite different from those of RP or Canadian English.

	Australia	RP	Canada			Australia	RP	Canada
hate	ʌj	ej	ej		bite	ɑj	aj	ʌj
boat	ʌw	əw	ow		loud	æw	aw	aw
bide	ɑj	aj	aj		lout	æw	aw	ʌw

TECHNICAL TERMS

accent	Lallans	rhotic
creole	Received Pronunciation	nonrhotic
dialect	RP	Scots

EXERCISES

BASIC

1. Some dialects of English replace all final voiceless stops with a glottal stop:

   taʔ 'top'   fɪʔ 'fit'   dʌʔ 'duck'

   Try imitating such a dialect in the following words:

stop	cat	back	wit	tap	rat tack
stack	belt	wart	sent	rest	

   Do the same with this sentence:

   At eight, that bike sat outside in the dirt on top of the mat.

2. Practice:

e i ɑ	e i ʔɑ	e ʔi ʔɑ
ʔe i ɑ	ʔe i ʔɑ	ʔe ʔi ʔɑ
e ʔi ɑ	ʔe i ɑ	e i ʔɑ

3. Many dialects of English distinguish voiced and voiceless [w], particularly before unrounded vowels. See if someone you know distinguishes *which* and *witch* /hwɪtʃ - wɪtʃ/. Try pronouncing the following words in the left column with /w/ and those in the right column with /hw/:

/w/	/hw/	/w/	/hw/
witch	which	we	whee
wet	whet	why (interj.)	why (question)
watt	what	went	when
win	whim	ware	where
		were	whir

4. There is also a distinction of /j - hj/ as in *you - hue*, found in most dialects of English, but in only a few words.

   Transcribe and pronounce the following:

huge	Hubert	Hugh	hew	Houston	Hume

   Pronounce the following nonsense pairs:

jow - hjow	wɑ - hwɑ	ji - hji
je - hje	wo - hwo	jɛ - hjɛ
wu - hwu	jɔ - hjɔ	wʊ - hwʊ
wɛ - hw	jæ - hjæ	jʌ - hjʌ

5. Most English dialects of North America outside the south of the U.S. do not

distinguish *do* and *due*; they are usually both pronounced /du/. In general, these dialects distinguish /u — ju/ after labials and velars, as in *coot* — *cute* and *booty* — *beauty;* after alveolars, however, /ju/ does not occur.

Practise making this distinction with the pairs below. Use /u/ in the words on the left and /ju/ in the words on the right.

/u/	/ju/	/u/	/ju/
do	dew, due	stooge	student
Dooley	duly	noose	news
too	tune	noon	newt

Try pronouncing the following words with /ju/ after the initial consonant: *e.g.:* /ljuɹ/

| lure | ruse | sure | super | lucid | runic |

6. Find a Canadian dictionary (make sure that it is edited in Canada; *e.g.,* by Gage Publishing) and look up the sample words below and write down the dictionary's transcription of the vowel. You now have a conversion key to go back and forth between our transcription system and that of the dictionary's :

beat	i	*boot*	u	*peer*	iɹ	*pit*	ɪ
put	ʊ	*pear*	eɹ	*hate*	ej	*boat*	ow
part	ɑɹ	*pet*	ɛ	*bought*	ɑ	*hurt*	əɹ
pat	æ	*pot*	ɑ	*cure*	uɹ	*path*	æ
soft	ɑ	*four*	oɹ	*but*	ʌ	*palm*	ɑ
baby	i	*bite*	aj, ʌj	*out*	aw, ʌw	*runner*	əɹ
		choice	ɔj	*sofa*	ə		

7. Transcribe the following paragraph into the standard Canadian dialect we have been using:

> After thirty years on the force, your gut tells you more than your brain, and when Pete's calm, blood-shot, hound-dog eyes saw the moist, butchered corpse of the world's nicest dolphin, once the most popular animal star on television and now left for the swimming vultures of the gulf to devour, he knew something both sinister and perverted was about.

The dictionary may help you if you have difficulties, but you will have to use the conversion key. Show raising and [ɾ] where appropriate; dictionaries do not usually show these. Does your own accent differ from this transcription? In which words?

8. British dictionaries give RP pronunciation. Find a British dictionary in the library (one of the Oxford dictionaries, for example), look up the list of sample words below, and transcribe the vowel. This will give you a key for converting between our system for RP and that of the dictionary you found.

beat	i	*boot*	u	*peer*	iə	*pit*	ɪ
put	ʊ	*pear*	ɛə	*hate*	ej	*boat*	əw
part	ɑ	*pet*	ɛ	*bought*	ɔ	*hurt*	ə

pat	æ	*pot*	ɒ	*cure*	ʊə	*path*	ɑ
soft	ɒ	*four*	ɔ	*but*	ʌ	*palm*	ɑ
baby	ɪ	*bite*	aj	*out*	aw	*runner*	ə
		choice	ɔj	*sofa*	ə		

9. Now, transcribe the paragraph of Exercise 7 into RP, using our system of transcription. Use the information in the main part of this chapter. A British dictionary will help you, although you will have to convert it to our system of transcription using the chart you made in Exercise 8 above. Pay particular attention to the vowels written with *o* — *dog, dolphin,* etc.— also to *knew* and to the final vowel in *thirty.*

10. Now repeat exercises 7 and 8 using an American dictionary. First make a conversion key between the dictionary and our system using the list of sample words below:

beat	i	*boot*	u	*peer*	iɹ	*pit*	ɪ
put	ʊ	*pear*	eɹ	*hate*	ej	*boat*	ow
part	ɑɹ	*pet*	ɛ	*bought*	ɔ	*hurt*	əɹ
pat	æ	*pot*	ɑ	*cure*	uɹ	*path*	æ
soft	ɔ	*four*	oɹ	*but*	ə	*palm*	ɑ
baby	i	*bite*	aj	*out*	aw	*runner*	əɹ
		choice	ɔj	*sofa*	ə		

11. Now, transcribe the paragraph of Exercise 7 into General American. The American dictionary may help you, but you will need to convert its transcription to ours. Note especially the vowels spelled with *o* and the consonants in *when.*

12. Look up the following words in the Canadian, American, and British dictionaries and compare the pronunciations. Do you agree with the pronunciations indicated?

	Canadian	American	British
carry			
hairy			
wary			
staff			
gaff			
disaster			
aster			
cloth			
ensign			
resource			
khaki			
garage			
either			

13. The so-called *horse - hoarse* distinction is fairly rare. *Horse* is [hɔɹs], whereas *hoarse* is [hoɹs]. Try making this distinction with the following words:

[ɔɹ]	[oɹ]		[ɔɹ]	[oɹ]
horse	hoarse		for	four
fork	pork		cord	cored
or	oar		aural	oral

ADVANCED

14. Using the information from the main part of the chapter, transcribe the paragraph below into a Newfoundland, West Indian, Scottish, or Australian accent. Try to find a friend with the accent you have chosen. Ask your friend to read the passage in a relaxed fashion. Tape record the passage, if you can, to work on your transcription later. Read the passage aloud as you thought it would be pronounced. Ask your friend to correct where you went wrong. Did you make a mistake or does the person have a different accent from the one described in the book?

> After thirty years on the force, your gut tells you more than your brain, and when Pete's calm, blood-shot, hound-dog eyes saw the moist, butchered corpse of the world's nicest dolphin, once the most popular animal star on television and now left for the swimming vultures of the gulf to devour, he knew something both sinister and perverted was about.

15. Find another friend who speaks English with an accent different from the ones described in this chapter — for example, from the southern U.S., India, Ireland, or Africa. Tape record your friend reading the paragraph in Exercise 14. Make sure to ask him or her to speak in a relaxed fashion as if speaking to friends back home. Transcribe this as narrowly as you can. Transcribe how you expect your friend to pronounce the words below. Try to mimic your friend's accent. Be sure to make it clear that you are learning from your friend and not making fun of his or her accent.

beat	*boot*	*peer*	*pit*	*put*	*pear*
hate	*boat*	*part*	*pet*	*bought*	*hurt*
pat	*pot*	*cure*	*path*	*soft*	*four*
but	*palm*	*baby*	*bite*	*out*	*runner*
choice	*sofa*				

16. The sounds [x] and [ɣ] are two new consonants.

The sound [x] is a voiceless velar fricative; [ɣ] is a voiced velar fricative. The symbol [ɣ] is the Greek letter gamma ['gæmə].

Hints:

a. The sound [x] is in Scottish *loch* [lɒx], and in German *ach* [ɑx] or *Bach* [bɑx].

b. Many people have this sound in an expression of disgust *yeccchhh* [jɛxxx].

c. Try saying [kɑ], then say it again but release the [k] very slowly — [kxxɑ].

d. Children sometimes use [kxxxxx] to imitate the sound of a gun.

e. Say [k], but make it very weak.

Once you have some success with [x], try these combinations.

xɑ	xu	xɔ
xu	xɒ	xʊ
xɔxɑ	xɑxu	xuxʌ
xɑxæ	xɒxɔ	xæxʊ

Try the following, making sure that the back of your tongue stays back and does not slip forwards.

xɑxɛ	xɔxæ	xʊxi
xɑxi	xuxɪ	xɔxɪ
xɒxɛ	xixɛ	xæxɛ

17. Try the following words in German which contrast [k x].

bɑx	*stream*	bux	*book*	tauxt	*dips*
nɑx	*towards*	bawx	*belly*	vɑxən	*wake*
dɔx	*but*	vɑxt	*wakes*	vɔxən	*weeks*
hox	*high*	kɔxt	*cooks*	zuxən	*seek*
brux	*breach*	buxt	*inlet*		

18. The sound [ɣ] is like [x], but voiced.

Hints:

a. Say [x] with voicing. Try [sssssxzzzz] and then [xxxxxɣɣɣɣɣ].

b. Say [ga] and release the [g] very slowly to produce [gɣɣɣɑ].

c. Start with [ɑ], raise the back of your tongue slowly so as to make a [g]. Just before you get to [g], you should be making a [ɣ].

d. Try making the following:

ɣɑ	ɣu	ɣɔ
ɣu	ɣɒ	ɣʊ
ɣɔɣɑ	ɣɑɣu	ɣuɣʌ
ɣɑɣæ	ɣɒɣɔ	ɣæɣʊ

Try the following again making sure that the back of your tongue stays back and does not slip forwards.

ɣɑɣɛ	ɣɔɣæ	ɣʊɣi
ɣɑɣi	ɣuɣɪ	ɣɔɣɪ
ɣɒɣɛ	ɣiɣɛ	ɣæɣɛ

19. Try the following sentences, replacing the velar stops with the corresponding fricative:

Queen Catherine kissed her crotchety cousin and complimented her colleague King Carl the Cantankerous.

Gertie's granny goes gaga over great gooey green gumdrops from Guernsey.

20. The following are names of Georgian (USSR) towns; pay particular attention to the consonant clusters:

tbilisi	batumi	tsxinvali	mtsxeta	kutaisi	bolnisis
soxumi	maxaradze	gori	rustavi	axaltsixe	poti
gagra	duʃeti	telavi	satʃxere		

21. In exercise 21 of Chapter 5, a passage of *Julius Caesar* was given in Shakespeare's own pronunciation of the sixteenth century. Today Shakespeare is usually presented on the stage in an RP accent, even in North America. Using the information in this chapter, transcribe the passage from *Julius Caesar* into RP. A British dictionary might be helpful.

22. Pretend that you are Shakespeare listening to a modern performance of your play with the actors using an RP accent. With the transcription from *Julius Caesar* that you made in exercise 21 just above, note the points in which RP English would sound odd to you (Shakespeare).

   Why do you think that directors and actors would choose RP as the accent for Shakespeare's plays?

CHAPTER SEVEN
THE SOUNDS OF FRENCH

French is a modern form of Latin. The descendants of Latin — French, Spanish, Portuguese, Italian, Rumanian, Catalan, Rhæto-Romansch, etc. — are collectively known as the Romance languages. Latin itself is a descendant of a large family of languages known as Indo-European, which includes most of the languages spoken across the area stretching from Europe to central India.

French is spoken in France, in parts of Belgium and Switzerland, in Luxembourg, and in the various French settlements throughout the world, including, of course, Canada. French was brought to Canada in the early part of the seventeenth century. It is spoken primarily in Québec and by significant numbers of people in New Brunswick, Nova Scotia, Ontario, and Manitoba. The other provinces have relatively small communities of French speakers. In the 1986 census, 6,502,865 or about 24% of all Canadians said they spoke French as their mother tongue. There are approximately 122 million French speakers in the world.

The early French settlers in North America generally came from the northern and western regions of France and brought with them the local dialects of those areas. The subsequent isolation of French Canada from France meant that Canadian French was not strongly influenced by Parisian French which developed as the prestige dialect in France.

Canadian French exhibits a certain amount of geographical variation, Acadian French in New Brunswick being noticeably different from that of Québec. Social dialects within French Canada are, however, generally stronger than geographical ones. At the upper end of the social scale and in formal situations, a dialect which can be called **standard French** is used; in morphology and syntax, this dialect is substantially the same as the standard French of France. Phonologically, it is fairly similar to continental French, although it has a number of features of its own, mostly of a phonetic rather than a phonological nature. The dialect at the other end of the scale is often given the name **joual** /ʒwal/, from the joual pronunciation of the word *cheval* 'horse' (standard /ʃfal/). Speakers may use all or only a portion of the social continuum between standard French and joual. The colloquial speech of educated French Canadians is the dialect which will be presented in this chapter.

INVENTORY OF SOUNDS

The consonants and vowels of French are given below. We will discuss the details in the following sections.

p	t		k	i	y		u
b	d		g	e	ø	ə	o
m	n	ɲ	(ŋ)	ɛ	œ		ɔ
f	s	ʃ		a		ɑ	
v	z	ʒ					
	l		r	ɛ̃	œ̃		ɔ̃
							ɑ̃

CONSONANTS

STOPS French stops are much like the ones in English; /t/ and /d/ are, however, dental, not alveolar. The voiceless stops are unaspirated, and the voiced stops are voiced throughout. In general, the muscular tension during articulation of all sounds is greater in French than in English.

/p/ voiceless bilabial stop
  paix /pɛ/ 'peace', *appel* /apɛl/ 'call', *tape* /tap/ 'tap'

/b/ voiced bilabial stop
  bas /bɑ/ 'low', *èbène* /ebɛn/ 'ebony', *club* /klœb/ 'club'

/t/ voiceless dental stop
  tôt /to/ 'early', *été* /ete/ 'summer', *brut* /bryt/ 'rough'

/d/ voiced dental stop
  dos /do/ 'back', *odeur* /odœr/ 'smell', *sud* /syd/ 'south'

/k/ unaspirated velar stop
  coup /ku/ 'blow', *accord* /akɔr/ 'agreement', *lac* /lak/ 'lake'

/g/ voiced velar stop
  gauche /goʃ/ 'left', *égal* /egal/ 'equal', *zigzag* /zigzag/ 'zigzag'

FRICATIVES The fricatives in French are similar to those in English, except that /s/ and /z/ are dental, not alveolar.

/f/ voiceless labio-dental fricative
  fille /fij/ 'daughter', *effet* /efe/ 'effect', *sauf* /sof/ 'except'

/v/ voiced labio-dental fricative
  ville /vil/ 'town', *éveiller* /eveje/ 'wake up', *rêve* /rɛv/ 'dream'

/s/ voiceless dental fricative
  sot /so/ 'stupid', *ici* /isi/ 'here', *fils* /fis/ 'son'

/z/   voiced dental fricative
      zèle /zɛl/ 'zeal', *aisé* /ɛze/ 'easy', *gaz* /gɑz/ 'gas'
/ʃ/   voiceless palato-alveolar fricative
      chou /ʃu/ 'cabbage', *achat* /aʃa/ 'purchase', *ruche* /ryʃ/ 'bee hive'
/ʒ/   voiced palato-alveolar fricative
      jeu /ʒø/ 'game', *léger* /leʒe/ 'light', *âge* /ɑʒ/ 'age'

NASALS   In addition to the nasals also found in English, French has a palatal nasal /ɲ/.

/m/   bilabial nasal
      mon /mɔ̃/ 'my', *aimer* /ɛme/ 'love', *femme* /fam/ 'woman'
/n/   dental nasal
      nu /ny/ 'naked', *honneur* /ɔnœr/ 'honour', *saine* /sɛn/ 'healthy'
/ɲ/   palatal nasal
      gnole /ɲol/ 'booze', *agneau* /aɲo/ 'lamb', *digne* /diɲ/ 'worthy'
/ŋ/   velar nasal; found only in borrowed words
      camping /kãpiŋ/ 'camping', *smoking* /smokiŋ/ 'tuxedo'

APPROXIMANTS   Several of the French approximants are different from those in English. The lateral /l/ is dental and always clear, not dark as in English. The phoneme /r/ exhibits quite a lot of dialect variation. In addition to the glides /w j/, French has a glide /ɥ/, which is like /j/, except with the lips rounded.

/l/   dental lateral
      lent /lã/ 'slow', *aller* /ale/ 'go', *bal* /bal/ 'ball'
/r/   dental trill or uvular approximant
      rare /rɑr/ 'rare', *pourri* /puri/ 'rotten', *or* /ɔr/ 'gold'
/w/   high back rounded semivowel
      oui /wi/ 'yes', *bois* /bwa/ 'wood', *reçois* /rəswa/ 'receives'
/j/   high front unrounded semivowel
      yeux /jø/ 'eyes', *travailler* /travaje/ 'work', *ail* /aj/ 'garlic'
/ɥ/   high front rounded semivowel
      huit /ɥit/ 'eight', *lui* /lɥi/ 'him/her', *persuader* /pɛrsɥade/ 'persuade'

VOICING

The voiceless stops in French are unaspirated in all positions.

    pas [pɑ] 'step', *plus* [ply] 'more', *jupe* [ʒyp] 'skirt'
    tomber [tɔ̃be] 'fall', *toi* [twa] 'you', *haute* [ot] 'high'
    coup [ku] 'blow', *craindre* [krɛ̃dr] 'believe', *duc* [dzʏk] 'duke'

English speakers should practise making initial /p t k/ voiceless and unaspirated. The voicing of the vowel starts immediately at the end of the consonant; in English, aspiration delays the onset of voicing until after the beginning of the vowel.

    The stops /b d g/ are voiced throughout.

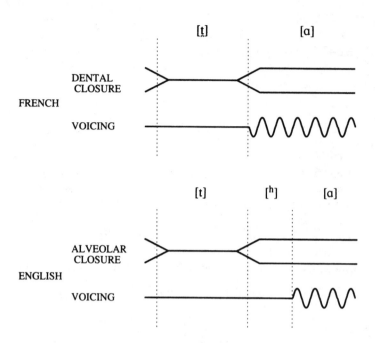

Figure 7.1
The relative timing of the unaspirated voiceless stops of French versus the aspirated voiceless stops of English. For the activity of the tongue, a single line shows closure and a divided line shows opening. A straight line shows voicelessness, and a wiggly line shows voicing.

    bis [bɪs] 'twice', *abeille* [abɛj] 'bee', *robe* [rɔb] 'dress'
    donner [dɔne] 'give', *modèle* [mɔdɛl] 'model', *laide* [lɛd] 'ugly'
    goût [gu] 'taste', *second* [zgɔ̃] 'second', *bague* [bag] 'ring'

In English the stops /b d g/ are voiced only part way through. English speakers learning French can usually improve their pronunciation if they emphasise the voicing, lengthening the stop very slightly.

AFFRICATION   Canadian French pronounces the dental stops /t d/ as affricates [ts dz] before a high front vowel or glide — /i y j ɥ/.

    tigre [tsɪgr] 'tiger', *petit* [ptsi] 'small', *tiens* [tsjɛ̃] 'well!'
    tu [tsy] 'you', *vertu* [vɛrtsy] 'virtue', *tuer* [tsɥe] 'kill'
    dit [dzi] 'said', *indiquer* [ɛ̃dzike] 'point out', *indien* [ɛ̃dzjɛ̃] 'Indian'
    dû [dzy] 'ought', *perdu* [pɛrdzy] 'lost', *duel* [dzɥɛl] 'duel'

DENTALS   The consonants /t d n s z l/ have a dental place of articulation. In a narrow transcription this can be shown by the diacritic [̪]. For [t̪ d̪ n̪ l̪] the tip of the tongue is against the rear surface of the teeth as shown in Figure 7.2. Some speakers produce a lamino-dental by placing the blade of the tongue against the upper teeth with the tip of the tongue touching the lower teeth.

Figure 7.2
The apico-dental place
of articulation of [l].

Figure 7.3
Dark English [ɫ].
Compare the tongue
position of this with the
clear [l] of Figure 2.

Figure 7.4
The uvular place of
articulation.

/l/   The sound /l/ is a clear dental lateral. It is particularly important to note the clarity of the French /l/. The English /l/ is fairly clear at the beginning of a syllable and dark (velarised) elsewhere (cf. Chapter 3). The French /l/ is clear in all positions. Compare the clear French [l] of Figure 7.2 with the dark English [ɫ] of Figure 7.3 to see the different positions of the tongue.

long [lɔ̃] 'long', *col* [kɔl] 'neck', *faible* [fɛbl] 'weak'

/r/   The sound written as *r* is remarkably varied in its phonetic realisation. The earliest form seems to be a dental trill [r̪]. In a dental trill, the tip of the tongue articulates with the upper teeth in such a way that the air passing over the tongue causes it to vibrate rapidly against the teeth. This sound is occasionally heard in Scottish dialects of English. Trills are discussed more in the exercises at the end of this chapter and in Chapter 13. The trill may be fairly short, involving only one or two taps. The dental trill is used regularly in much of the south of France and is sometimes used on the stage.

During the eighteenth century, the apico-dental trill [r̪] was replaced by a dorso-uvular trill [ʀ], first in popular speech and then generally in Parisian French. From there it spread quite widely, particularly through the north of France. More recently, the uvular trill has been replaced by a uvular fricative [ʁ˔] or a uvular approximant [ʁ], which is now generally considered the standard pronunciation of *r* in France.

The uvular place of articulation involves using the uvula as the upper articulator and the rear portion of the dorsum of the tongue as the lower articulator. Uvular trills are made by allowing the uvula to touch the dorsum of the tongue and by then forcing air between them causing the uvula to vibrate against the tongue. In a uvular approximant the same articulators are used, but the back of the tongue does not quite touch the uvula, leaving an opening through which air can pass freely. The position for a uvular approximant is shown in Figure 7.4.

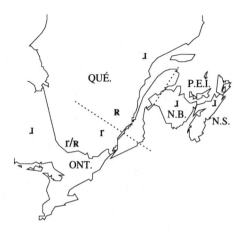

Figure 7.5 The geographical distribution of /r/. Notice the English-type [ɹ] found in Ontario and New Brunswick

In Canada, the apico-dental trill has historically been the most common realisation of *r,* except in Québec City and its surroundings (Vinay, 1950; Dulong and Bergeron, 1980), where the uvular trill is found. At present, the dental [r] is found generally in southwestern Québec and in the Maritimes, and the uvular [ʀ] to the north of Montréal. The map in Figure 7.5 shows the geographical distribution of [ɹ] and [ʀ]. In certain areas, especially in Ontario and New Brunswick, where French is in extensive contact with English, the retroflex [ɹ] of English is found. In this chapter, I use [r] to indicate the r-sound of French without reference to dialectal variants.

In recent years, [r] has been increasingly replaced by the uvular approximant [ʁ]. Santerre (1979, 1982; see also Thomas, 1987) reports that three-quarters of speakers under the age of 35 in Montréal use a uvular rather than a dental *r.*

rapide	[rapɪd]	'rapid'	*arrêt*	[arɛ]	'stop'
faire	[fɛr]	'do'	*brin*	[brɛ̃]	'piece'
ferme	[fɛrm]	'farm'	*dormir*	[dɔrmɪr]	'sleep'

OBSTRUENT-SONORANT CLUSTERS Word-initial consonant clusters are found consisting of obstruents followed by one of the sonorants /j ɥ w l r/. After voiceless obstruents the sonorant is also voiceless.

bien	[bjɛ̃]	'well'	*pièce*	[pj̥ɛs]	'room'
duel	[dɥɛl]	'duel'	*tuer*	[tɥ̥e]	'kill'
moi	[mwa]	'me'	*foie*	[fw̥a]	'liver'
glace	[glas]	'ice'	*clef*	[kl̥e]	'key'
vrai	[vrɛ]	'true'	*tranche*	[tr̥ɑ̃ʃ]	'slice'

The consonants /r l/ occur finally after obstruents. Note carefully that these sounds do not form an additional syllable as in English *butter, little.* After voiceless consonants, the /r/ or /l/ is also voiceless. These final consonants are very frequently

Figure 7.6
The palatal place of articulation.

omitted entirely in casual speech: *e.g.,* [arb] 'tree', [pov] 'poor', [tab] 'table', [sɛrk] 'circle'.

arbre	[arbr]	'tree'	*âpre*	[apr̥]	'harsh'
timbre	[tɛ̃br]	'stamp'	*autre*	[otr̥]	'other'
aigre	[ɛgr]	'sour'	*vaincre*	[vɛ̃kr̥]	'conquer'
pauvre	[povr]	'poor'	*souffre*	[sufr̥]	'sulphur'
table	[tabl]	'table'	*peuple*	[pœpl̥]	'people'
aveugle	[avœgl]	'blind'	*cercle*	[sɛrkl̥]	'circle',
épingle	[epɛ̃gl]	'pin'	*pantoufle*	[pãtufl̥]	'slipper'

The consonant /m/ occurs finally after /s/; in this position it is voiceless.

prisme	[pr̥ɪsm̥]	'prism'
communisme	[kɔmynɪsm̥]	'communism'

/ɲ/   The nasal /ɲ/ has a palatal place of articulation. This is made with the front of the tongue at the palate and the tip pointing down, as in Figure 7.6. Note that French has both /ɲ/ and the sequence /nj/. The first is a single palatal sound; the second is a sequence of dental nasal followed by a glide. English speakers should be careful not to substitute English /nj/, as in English *onion*, for /ɲ/. Initially, /ɲ/ is found only in words belonging to slang and baby-talk.

	agneau	[aɲo]	'lamb'	*oignon*	[ɔɲɔ̃]	'onion'
	digne	[diɲ]	'worthy'	*gnangnan*	[ɲãɲã]	'namby-pamby'
cf.	*nous peignons*	[nu peɲɔ̃]	'we paint'			
	nous peinions	[nu penjɔ̃]	'we were toiling (imperfect)'			

VOWELS

The vowels of French sound different from those of English. In standard French, they are not diphthongal, and the position of the tongue in making the vowels is different from English.

/i/ *île* /il/ 'island', *vie* /vi/ 'life', *type* /tip/ 'type', *pire* /pir/ 'worse'
/e/ *église* /egliz/ 'church', *été* /ete/ 'summer', *donner* /dɔne/ 'give'
/ɛ/ *aider* /ɛde/ 'help', *mais* /mɛ/ 'but', *fête* /fɛt/ 'feast', *fermé* /fɛrme/ 'closed'
/a/ *ma* /ma/ 'my', *patte* /pat/ 'paw', *année* /ane/ 'year', *barre* /bar/ 'bar'

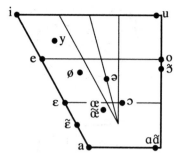

Figure 7.7 The vowels of French.

French has both front and back rounded vowels, in contrast to English, which has only back rounded vowels. The front rounded vowels /y ø œ/ are like the unrounded vowels /i e ɛ/, but with lip rounding.

/y/ *eu* /y/ 'had', *flûte* /flyt/ 'flute', *mûr* /myr/ 'wall', *bureau* /byro/ 'office'

/ø/ *œufs* /ø/ 'eggs', *lieu* /ljø/ 'place', *jeûne* /ʒøn/ 'fast', *heureux* /ørø/ 'happy'

/œ/ *œuf* /œf/ 'egg', *heure* /œr/ 'hour', *jeune* /ʒœn/ 'young', *cueillir* /kœjir/ 'gather'

/u/ *août* /u/ 'August', *trou* /tru/ 'hole', *bouche* /buʃ/ 'mouth' *poule* /pul/ 'hen'

/o/ *eau* /o/ 'water', *dos* /do/ 'back', *fausse* /fos/ 'false', *hauteur* /otœr/ 'height'

/ɔ/ *robe* /rɔb/ 'dress', *corps* /kɔr/ 'body', *bonheur* /bɔnœr/ 'happiness'

/a/ *mât* /ma/ 'mast', *pâte* /pɑt/ 'paste', *passer* /pɑse/ 'pass', *âgé* /ɑʒe/ 'old'

French has nasal vowels contrasting with the oral vowels.

/ɛ̃/ *vin* /vɛ̃/ 'wine', *plaindre* /plɛ̃dr/ 'pity', *impur* /ɛ̃pyr/ 'impure'

/œ̃/ *un* /œ̃/ 'one', *lundi* /lœ̃di/ 'Monday', *humble* /œ̃bl/ 'humble'

/ɔ̃/ *on* /ɔ̃/ 'one', *pont* /pɔ̃/ 'bridge', *nombre* /nɔ̃br/ 'number', *longue* /lɔ̃g/ 'long'

/ɑ̃/ *en* /ɑ̃/ 'in', *blanc* /blɑ̃/ 'white', *centre* /sɑ̃tr/ 'centre', *changeant* /ʃɑ̃ʒɑ̃/ 'changing'

Schwa in French is somewhat like schwa in English in that it occurs only in unstressed syllables. Very often it is lost completely.

/ə/ *le* /lə/ 'the', *dessous* /dəsu/ 'underneath', *crever* /krəve/ 'burst'

Figure 7.7 shows the articulatory position for all the vowels of French. In practical terms, vowels are best learned from a native speaker. A chart like Figure 7.7 will help you get an approximate pronunciation (Chapter 11 describes how such a chart can be used.) Once you have learned the vowels of French, such a chart is helpful in showing the overall vowel pattern.

The vowels of French differ from those of English in a number of ways. French has, for example, front rounded vowels and also nasalised vowels; English does not have front rounded vowels. The nasal vowels of English are allophonic and predictable, not contrastive as they are in French. Note especially that the vowels are monophthongs. The French vowels in *beauté* /bote/ have no glide whatsoever; they sound quite different from the English vowels /ej ow/. English speakers should make a strong attempt to remove the glide in pronouncing French. The exercises at the end of this chapter will help you.

There is considerable variation in the use of /a/ and /ɑ/. In non-final syllables these vowels are widely merged in European French as /a/: e.g., *passer* /pase/ 'pass', *âgé* /aʒe/ 'old'. In final syllables there is considerable variation among speakers (see Tranel, 1987, for details). Canadian French continues to distinguish these vowels, although their distribution is sometimes different from traditional standard usage (Walker, 1984).

FRONT ROUNDED

The vowels /y ø œ/ are front rounded vowels. The simplest way to make them is to round your lips while making a front vowel. To make a [y], for example, round your lips, keep them rounded, and say an [i]. The same procedure will turn an [e] into [ø], and an [ɛ] into [œ].

NASALISED

Nasalised vowels are produced by making a vowel while lowering the velum so that some of the air escapes through the nose. French has four nasalised vowels: /ɛ̃ œ̃ ɔ̃ ɑ̃/. Nasalisation is indicated by a **tilde** /ˈtɪldə/ [~] written above the vowel. Many speakers of European French have merged the nasalised vowels /ɛ̃ œ̃/ as /ɛ̃/; that is, they have lost the lip-rounding in /œ̃/. For those speakers, the words *brun* 'brown' and *brin* 'blade (of grass)' are both pronounced /brɛ̃/. Most Canadian speakers, however, have remained fairly conservative and in this respect maintain the difference, pronouncing these words as /brœ̃/ and /brɛ̃/ respectively. Phonetically, the /ɛ̃/ is quite low; some authors transcribe it as [æ̃].

LENGTH

Although long vowels in French are quite common, for the most part they are predictable and not phonemically distinct. The vowels /ø o ɑ/ and the nasal vowels are always long in closed syllables.

feu	'fire'	[fø]	*feutre*	'felt'	[fø:tr̥]
faux	'false' m.	[fo]	*fausse*	'false' f.	[fo:s]
bas	'low' m.	[bɑ]	*basse*	'low' f.	[bɑ:s]
saint	'holy' m.	[sɛ̃]	*sainte*	'holy' f.	[sɛ̃:t]
défunt	'defunct' m.	[defœ̃]	*défunte*	'defunct' f.	[defœ̃:t]
don	'gift'	[dɔ̃]	*donc*	'then'	[dɔ̃:k]
grand	'large' m.	[grɑ̃]	*grande*	'large' f.	[grɑ̃:d]

All vowels are lengthened in a syllable closed by /v z ʒ j r/ or by the cluster /vr/

vie	'life'	[vi]	*vive*	'alive' f.	[vi:v]	*vif*	'alive' m.	[vɪf]
cas	'case'	[ka]	*case*	'box'	[ka:z]	*calque*	'tracing'	[kalk]
jus	'juice'	[ʒy]	*juge*	'judge'	[ʒy:ʒ]	*juste*	'just'	[ʒʏst]
buffet	'buffet'	[byfɛ]	*bouteille*	'bottle'	[bute:j]	*complète*	'complete'	[kɔ̃plɛt]
fait	'done'	[fɛ]	*faire*	'do'	[fɛ:r]	*veste*	'jacket'	[vɛst]
sou	'penny'	[su]	*s'ouvre*	'is open'	[su:vr]	*souffre*	'suffers'	[sʊfr̥]

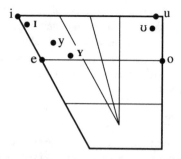

Figure 7.8 The positions of the high vowels.

Canadian French preserves a historic phonemic distinction between long and short /ɛ ɛ:/. This distinction is found in conservative speech of other dialects.

belle	'beautiful'	/bɛl/	*bêle*	'bleats'	/bɛ:l/
bette	'beet'	/bɛt/	*bête*	'beast'	/bɛ:t/
saine	'healthy'	/sɛn/	*scène*	'scene'	/sɛ:n/
faite	'done'	/fɛt/	*fête*	'feast'	/fɛ:t/
lettre	'letter'	/lɛtr/	*l'être*	'the existence'	/lɛ:tr/
mettre	'put'	/mɛtr/	*maître*	'master'	/mɛ:tr/

Walker (1984) reports other vowels which are distinctively long in Canadian French. A few examples of these are given below:

neiger	'snow'	/ne:ʒe/
heureux	'happy'	/ø:rø/
lâcher	'loosen'	/lɑ:ʃe/
côté	'side'	/ko:te/

LAXING   A well-known feature of Canadian French is the laxing, or lowering, of high vowels /i y u/ before a syllable-final consonant. Laxing does not occur before the consonants which lengthen preceding vowels /v z ʒ r/ and /vr/. The lax versions of [i y u] are [ɪ ʏ ʊ]; see Figure 7.8.

Tense			**Lax**		
vie	'life'	[vi]	vif	'alive'	[vɪf]
si	'if'	[si]	site	'site'	[sɪt]
petit	'small' m.	[ptsi]	petite	'small' f.	[ptsɪt]
lu	'read'	[ly]	Luc	'Luke'	[lʏk]
plu	'pleased'	[ply]	plume	'pen'	[plʏm]

GLIDES   The glide /j/ follows a number of vowels. Its pronunciation is tenser than that of the English /j/, with a closer approximation of the tongue to the upper oral surface. As noted just above, final /j/ lengthens the preceding vowel. A certain amount of friction is sometimes heard. In a narrow transcription, the higher position of the tongue can be shown by the diacritic [ˆ].

fille	'daughter'	[fɪːjˆ]
soleil	'sun'	[sɔlɛːjˆ]
travail	'work'	[travaːjˆ]
bataille	'battle'	[bataːjˆ]
feuille	'leaf'	[fœːjˆ]
œil	'eye'	[œːjˆ]
grenouille	'frog'	[grənʊːjˆ]

DIPHTHONGISATION   In Canadian French, stressed vowels, except /a/, frequently occur as diphthongs. Front unrounded vowels acquire a /j/ glide; front rounded glides acquire a /ɥ/ glide; and back vowels acquire a /w/ glide. The following examples illustrate this phenomenon.

/i/	[ij]		/y/	[yɥ]	/u/	[uw]
	vire	'turns'	*pur*	'pure'	*tour*	'turn'
	arrive	'arrives'	*juge*	'judge'	*rouge*	'red'

/e/	[ej]		/ø/	[øɥ]	/o/	[oɥ]
	neige	'snow'	*neutre*	'neuter'	*chaude*	'hot'
	steak	'steak'	*jeûne*	'fast' n.	*côte*	'side'

					/ɑ/	[ɑw]
					pâte	'paste'
					part	'leaves'

/ɛ̃/	[ɛ̃j]		/œ̃/	[œ̃ɥ]	/ɔ̃/	[ɔ̃w]
	crainte	'fear'	*défunte*	'defunct'	*honte*	'shame'
	teinte	'ink'	*emprunte*	'borrows'	*ombre*	'shadow'

LIAISON   Many words in French have two alternate pronunciations: one at the end of an utterance and before consonants, the other before vowels and glides. The details of this phenomenon, known as **liaison** /ˈlieˌzɑn ~ ljeˈzɔ̃/ or **linking**, are quite complex. One common place where liaison occurs is with the plural article *les*. At the end of an utterance and before consonants, the form is /le/; before vowels and glides, the form is /lez/.

attendez-les	/atɑ̃de le/	'look at them'
les femmes	/le fam/	'the women'
les maisons	/le mɛzɔ̃/	'the houses'

les autres	/lez otr/	'the others'
les hommes	/lez ɔm/	'the men'
les oiseaux	/lez wazo/	'the birds'
les yeux	/lez jø/	'the eyes'

ELISION   A number of words, mostly short, common ones, lose their vowel when the next word begins with a vowel.

je + aime	→ j'aime	/ʒɛm/	'I love'
ce + est	→ c'est	/se/	'it is'
le + ami	→ l'ami	/lami/	'the friend'
la + œuvre	→ l'œuvre	/lœvr/	'the work'
quelque + un	→ quelqu'un	/kɛlkœ̃/	'someone'

Very often a /ə/ is lost within a word or within a phrase:

petit	/ptsi/	'small
médecin	/medsɛ̃/	'doctor'
semaine	/smɛn/	'week'
vous revenez	/vurvəne/ *or* /vurəvne/	'you come'
tout le monde	/tulmɔ̃d/	'every one'
trois chemises	/trwaʃmiz/	'three shirts'
il est debout	/ilɛdbu/	'he is standing'

H-ASPIRÉ Certain words in French which phonetically begin with a vowel are written with an initial letter *h*. This *h* is an orthographic peculiarity and is not pronounced. Some of the words behave as expected in liaison and elision; that is, the preceding word treats them as beginning with a vowel (or glide).

les hommes	/lezɔm/	'the men'
les heroïnes	/lezɛrɔin/	'the heroines'
les huiles	/lezɥil/	'the oils'

Other words, however, act as though they began with a consonant: that is, liaison and elision treat them as if they began with a consonant, even though no consonant is heard. The *h* of the words in this latter group is called **h-aspiré** /aʃaspire/ 'aspi-rated-h'. This name is traditional and should not be equated with the way we have used *aspirated* in this book. The words with *h-aspiré* must be learned; dictionaries regularly give this information.

les haricots	/le ariko/	'the beans'
les héros	/le ero/	'the heroes'
les huées	/le ɥe/	'the hoots'

The words *onze* 'eleven' and *onziéme* 'eleventh' behave like the h-aspiré words even though they lack an orthographic *h*.

| *les onzièmes* | /le ɔ̃zjɛm/ | 'the eleventh ones' |

SUPRASEGMENTALS

SYLLABIFICATION Every phrase in French is pronounced so as to maximise the number of syllables having an onset. Consider the phrase, *le petit amiral agile*, 'the small agile admiral'. If we were to transcribe each word separately, showing syllable boundaries with a hyphen, we would get:

| le | petit | amiral | agile |
| [lɛ | ptsɪt | a- mi-ral | a-ʒɪl] |

The syllabification rule stated above, that in a phrase we maximise the number of syllables having an onset, requires that the /t/ from the end of *petit* is made part of the first syllable of *amiral*. Similarly, the final /l/ of *amiral* is moved to the first syllable of *agile*. The phrase, now correctly syllabified, is:

[lə - ptsi - ta - mi - ra - la - ʒil]

The effect is that word boundaries may be completely unmarked in speech. Of three internal word boundaries in this utterance, two occur within the syllable. Speakers of English sometimes have difficulty in mastering this phenomenon in French, particularly in perception. They complain that they 'can't hear the spaces between the words'.

RHYTHM   We saw in Chapter 5 that English is a stress-timed language; *i.e.*, the stresses come at evenly timed intervals. The rhythmic pattern of French is quite different. Every syllable takes the same amount of time. The phrase above, *le petit amiral agile,* has eight syllables, the first seven taking approximately equal amounts of time, with the final syllable being somewhat longer. Languages like French are said to be **syllable-timed**.

×   ×   ×   ×   ×   ×   ×

[lə - ptsi - ta - mi - ra - la - ʒil]

STRESS   Stress in French does not play the important role that it does in English. In general, stress occurs on the last syllable of a phrase. The following cheery aphorism from La Rochefoucauld is divided into phrases with the stress marked.

Si on juge de l'amour	*par la plupart de ses effects,*
siɔ̃ʒyʒdəlaˈmur	parlaplypardəsezɛˈfɛ
il ressemble plus à la haine	*qu'à l'amitié.*
ilrəsɑ̃bləplyzalaˈɛn	kalamiˈtsje

'If one judges love mainly by its effects, it resembles hatred more than friendship.'

TECHNICAL TERMS

h-aspiré	liaison	syllable-timed
joual	nasalised vowel	tilde
laxing	Standard French	

SYMBOLS

ɲ	palatal nasal	y	tense high front rounded vowel
ɥ	high front rounded glide	ʏ	lax high front rounded vowel
R	voiced uvular trill	ø	higher mid rounded vowel
ʁ̝	voiced uvular fricative	œ	lower mid rounded vowel
ʁ	voiced uvular approximant		
ɾ	voiced dental trill		
r	used in this Chapter		
	for any French r-sound		

EXERCISES

BASIC

1. Remember that initial voiceless stops are not aspirated:

pas	pɑ	'step'	*peau*	po	'skin'
tas	tɑ	'heap'	*tout*	tu	'all'
cas	kɑ	'case'	*caisse*	kɛs	'chest'

2. Initial voiced stops [b d g] are voiced more than the corresponding stops in English. Try to start the voicing a little early.

belle	bɛl	'beautiful'	*bout*	bu	'end'
dent	dɑ̃	'tooth'	*doux*	du	'soft'
guerre	gɛːr	'war'	*gauche*	goːʃ	'left'

3. French like many languages uses dental, not alveolar consonants. Try saying the following in French.

> Ton thé a-t-il ôté ta toux?   'Has your tea gotten rid of your cough?'
> [t̪ɔ̃ t̪e a t̪i l̪ ot̪e t̪a t̪u]

Try it again remembering that French has only unaspirated stops.
Practise these:

t̪o	d̪u	n̪i	l̪ɛ	t̪ɪ
t̪e	d̪o	n̪æ	l̪ʌ	t̪u
n̪ɑlʊ	d̪ɔd̪æ	t̪inɛ	d̪ul̪ɑ	ɛn̪æ

4. To make the palatal nasal [ɲ], place the tip of your tongue against your lower teeth (as you get better, this is not necessary, but for the moment, it keeps it from doing things it shouldn't be doing). Then, raise the middle of the tongue to the palate and make a nasal.

agneau	aɲo	'lamb'
peigner	peɲe	'to comb'
oignon	ɔɲɔ̃	'onion'
digne	dɪɲ	'worthy'
montagne	mɔ̃taɲ	'mountain'
gnognote	ɲɔɲɔt	'junk'

5. Practise the following words. Remember that the vowels [e] and [o] are not diphthongised as in English. See the exercises in Chapter 4 for practice in this.

si	si	'if'	*sous*	su	'under'
lit	li	'bed'	*loup*	lu	'wolf'
riz	ri	'rice'	*roux*	ru	'red'
qui	ki	'who'	*cou*	ku	'neck'
et	e	'and'	*eau*	o	'water'
fée	fe	'fairy'	*beau*	bo	'beautiful'
été	ete	'summer'	*auto*	oto	'car'

toujours	tuʒur	'always'	*trop tôt*	troto	'too early'
tout à coup	tutaku	'suddenly'	*beau roseau*	borozo	'beautiful reed'
coucou	kuku	'cuckoo'	*à vau-l'eau*	avolo	'adrift'

6. Try these nasal vowels from French:

le banc	lə bɑ̃	'the bench'	*le bond*	lə bɔ̃	'the jump'
blanc	blɑ̃	'white'	*blond*	blɔ̃	'blond'
les dents	le dɑ̃	'the teeth'	*les dons*	le dɔ̃	'the gifts'
il fend	il fɑ̃	'he splits'	*il fond*	il fɔ̃	'he melts'
le gant	lə gɑ̃	'the glove'	*le gond*	lə gɔ̃	'the hinge'
les gens	le ʒɑ̃	'the people'	*les joncs*	le ʒɔ̃	'the rushes'
lent	lɑ̃	'slow'	*long*	lɔ̃	'long'

7. The French vowels [y ø œ] are front and rounded. To make them make the corresponding unrounded vowel and then reverse the rounding.

   Start by saying [iiiii]. Hold your tongue in the position for [i] and round your lips. This will produce [y] if you haven't changed anything else. Another way is to round your lips and 'say' [i]. The same technique changes [e] to [ø], and [ɛ] to [œ].

   Practise:

i y	i y	y i	y i		e ø	e ø	e ø	e ø
ɛ œ	ɛ œ	ɛ œ	ɛ œ		i e	y ø	e i	ø y
e ɛ	ø œ	e e	œ e		i e ɛ	y ø œ	i ø ɛ	y e œ

   Practise:

futur	fyty:r	'future'
peu à peu	pøapø	'little by little'
cumulus	kymylʏs	'cumulus'
deux œufs creux	døzøkrø	'two hollow eggs'
le seul menteur	ləsœlmɑ̃tœr	'the only liar'
feuillu	føjy	'leafy'
cuit au four	kɥiofur	'baked'
eux ou nous	øunu	'them or us'
tout heureux	tutørø	'happy'
orgueilleux	ɔrgɛjø	'proud'

8. French has three glides. The difficult one for English speakers is the high front rounded glide [ɥ]. To say *lui* 'him' [lɥi], try saying [yyyyy], then [ly – i], first slowly, and then gradually shorten the [y] until you are saying [lɥi].

oui	wi	'yes'	*ouatte*	wat	'wadding'
iode	jɔd	'iodine'	*yeux*	jø	'eyes'
huile	ɥil	'oil'	*huître*	ɥitr	'oyster'
bien	bjɛ̃	'well'	*nuit*	nɥi	'night'
pied	pje	'foot'	*voir*	vwa:r	'see'
deuil	dœ:j	'mourning'	*œil*	œ:j	'eye'
fille	fi:j	'daughter'	*fouille*	fu:j	'digging'
travail	trava:j	'work'	*faille*	fɑ:j	'must (subj)'

miette	mjɛt	'crumbs'	*muette*	mɥɛt	'mute'
mouette	mwɛt	'gull'	*nier*	nje	'deny'
nuée	nɥe	'cloud'	*nouer*	nwe	'knot (v)'
sciait	sjɛ	'sawed'	*suait*	sɥɛ	'sweated'
souhait	swɛ	'wish'			

ADVANCED

9. The following words will help you with [e] and [ɛ]. Make both pure vowels with no diphthongal quality.

dé	de	'thimble'	*dais*	dɛ	'canopy'
épée	epe	'sword'	*épais*	epɛ	'thick'
gai	ɡe	'gay'	*guet*	ɡɛ	'watch'

10. The following words will help you with [o] and [ɔ]. Make both pure vowels with no diphthongal quality.

haute	ot	'high'	*hotte*	ɔt	'basket'
heaume	om	'helmet'	*homme*	ɔm	'man'
l'auge	loʒ	'trough'	*loge*	lɔʒ	'box'
(le) nôtre	notr	'ours'	*notre*	nɔtr	'our'

11. The following words are helpful with [ø] and [œ]:

heureuse	ørøz	'happy'	*chanteur*	ʃɑ̃tœr	'singer'
peuple	pœpl̩	'people'	*neutre*	nøtr̩	'neutral'
veule	vøl	'spineless'	*veulent*	vœl	'want'
beugle	bøɡl	'bellows'	*aveugle*	avœɡl	'blind'

12. French has a front [a] and a back [ɑ].

rat	ra	'rat'	*ras*	rɑ	'short'
tache	taʃ	'stain'	*tâche*	tɑʃ	'task'
patte	pat	'paw'	*pâte*	pɑt	'dough'
(je) bois	bwa	'(I) drink'	*(le) bois*	bwɑ	'(the) wood'

13. Nasal vowels. Pay particular attention to the difference between [ɑ̃] and [ɔ̃].

mais	mɛ	'but'	*main*	mɛ̃	'hand'
sec	sɛk	'dry'	*cinq*	sɛ̃k	'five'
fin	fɛ̃	'end'	*vingt*	vɛ̃	'twenty'
aucun	okœ̃	'none'	*commun*	kɔmœ̃	'common'
champ	ʃɑ̃	'field'	*temps*	tɑ̃	'weather'
bon	bɔ̃	'good'	*plomb*	plɔ̃	'lead'
ponton	pɔ̃tɔ̃	'pontoon'	*pendant*	pɑ̃dɑ̃	'during'
on fond	ɔ̃fɔ̃	'one melts'	*enfant*	ɑ̃fɑ̃	'child'
content	kɔ̃tɑ̃	'happy'	*canton*	kɑ̃tɔ̃	'district'
son sang	sɔ̃sɑ̃	'his blood'	*sans son*	sɑ̃sɔ̃	'without sound'

14. The vowel with the diacritic is voiceless.

Istamboul	ɪstãbʊl	'Istambul'	*université*	ynivɛrsi̥te	'university
piston	pi̥stɔ̃	'piston'	*support*	sypɔr	'support'
réputation	repy̥tasjɔ̃	'reputation'	*député*	depy̥te	'deputy'
écouter	eku̥te	'listen'	*acoustique*	aku̥stsɪk	'acoustic'
coupé	ku̥pe	'cut'			

15. Try the following diphthongs in French:

soleil	sɔlɛj	'sun'	*puis*	pɥi	'then'
fauteuil	fotœj	'chair	*œillet*	œjɛ	'carnation'
fenouil	fənuj	'fennel'	*abeille*	abɛj	'bee'
œil	œj	'eye'	*grenouille*	grənʊj	'frog'
fille	fij	'girl'	*diamant*	djamã	'diamond'
bien	bjɛ̃	'well'	*pied*	pje	'foot'
nuit	nɥi	'night'	*muet*	mɥɛ	'mute'
écuelle	ekɥɛl	'bowl'	*clouer*	klwe	'nail (v)'

16. Cluster practice

roi	rwa	'king'	*loi*	lwa	'law'
trois	trwa	'three'	*cloison*	klwazɔ̃	'partition'
croix	krwa	'cross'	*voile*	vwal	'sail'

17. Practise making the lowered high vowels typical of Canadian French. These occur only in closed syllables.

électrique	elɛktrɪk	'electric'
il s'habille	isabɪj	'he gets dressed'
pipe	pɪp	'pipe'
jupe	ʒʏp	'skirt'
luxe	lʏks	'luxury'
grenouille	grœnʊj	'frog'
ours	ʊrs	'bear'
toute	tʊt	'all'

18. Transcribe the following technical terms in phonetics into French. Check your answer with a French dictionary that gives pronunciations.

uvule	occlusive	langue	racine	lèvre supérieur
larynx	trachée	poumons	palais dur	lèvre inférieure
pharynx	épiglotte	alvéoles	glotte	cordes vocales
latéral	consonne	voyelle	apex	fosses nasales
plosive	fricative	affriqué	dos	cartilages aryténoïdes

CHAPTER EIGHT
SOUND WAVES, SPECTRA, AND RESONANCE

Acoustics is the branch of physics dealing with the properties of sound. **Acoustic phonetics** is the sub-branch which focusses on the sounds used in human language. As we know from physics, the sounds we hear are caused by **vibrations** in the air. These vibrations are conveyed through the air in the form of **waves**, regular alternations of high and low pressure. This chapter examines the basic properties of these sound waves. Chapter 9 will apply this knowledge in an acoustic description of the sounds of English.

In this chapter you will learn about:
- sine waves and complex waves
- how waves are measured
- sound spectra
- resonance.

SOUND WAVES

In this section we will look at two questions: What are the measurable properties of vibrations in the air caused by speech? And how do these vibrations travel through air?

As we speak, we push a stream of air out of our body. This airstream has a constantly varying pressure. The variations are caused by the many individual actions in the vocal tract. They are conveyed through the air to the listener and interpreted as speech. To understand these complex actions, we first need to examine simpler vibrations, such as those produced by a tuning fork.

A tuning fork is a device constructed with two arms which **oscillate** /ˈɑsɪˌlejt/, that is, swing back and forth in a regular fashion, alternately pushing and pulling the neighbouring air. Figure 8.1 shows the effect of the vibrations of the tuning fork on the air. The dot in front of the fork represents a molecule of air. Striking the tuning fork sets the arms of the fork in motion. When the right arm of the fork moves to the right (b), the pressure between the arm and the air molecule is

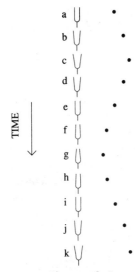

Figure 8.1
Movement of a tuning
fork.

increased and the air molecule is pushed to the right. Eventually, the arm of the tuning fork stops moving to the right (c) and begins to move leftwards (d), reducing the pressure between it and the molecule of air. This motion pulls the molecule of air towards the left. The leftward movement continues until the right tuning fork arm reaches the leftward limit of its range (g). Then the movement starts to the right again (h). We can see that each movement of the tuning fork causes a corresponding movement in the air.

If we were to fix a pen onto the molecule of air and draw a sheet of paper past the pen, the travels of the air molecule would be recorded as shown in Figure 8.2. The horizontal dimension shows time going from left to right, and the vertical dimension shows the displacement of the molecule of air from its resting place, which is indicated by the horizontal line. The resulting shape is a **waveform** which shows the movement of the air over time.

As the tuning fork moves, the air pressure surrounding the air molecule increases and decreases proportionally to the movement. Since it is rather hard to observe the movement of a molecule of air, but relatively easy to measure changes in air pressure in the laboratory, we usually use variation in air pressure in describing a sound.

The pattern of movement in Figure 8.2 produced by a tuning fork is called a **sine** or **sinusoidal wave** /ˈsajn, ˌsajnjəˈsɔjdəl/ because of certain mathematical properties of the wave. Physicists can make a number of measurements of waves. Sound waves of actual speech are usually more complex than a sine wave, but it is easier to understand the basic principles if we start with simple sine waves.

Speech is fairly rapid. We average around seven segments a second. To

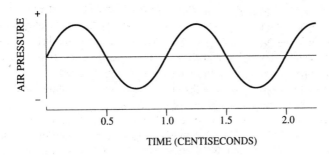

Figure 8.2 Sine wave.

measure such short units, phoneticians use **centiseconds** (csec: 1/100 of a second) or **milliseconds** (msec: 1/1000 second). In Figure 8.2 we see that one complete oscillation takes about 1.0 csec (10 msec).

AMPLITUDE AND INTENSITY

The distance of the molecule of air from its resting position is called its **amplitude**. On a chart of a sine wave, as in Figure 8.3, amplitude is the vertical dimension. Figure 8.3 shows two waves which are the same except that they have different amplitudes. Line a — a' shows the amplitude of wave A at time 0.25 centiseconds. At the same time, the amplitude of wave B is greater, as shown by the longer line b — b'. At time 0.8 csec, the amplitudes of the two waves are negative as shown by the lines c — c' and d — d'. The amplitude of a sine wave as a whole is considered to be its maximum amplitude, *i.e.,* the distance from the base-line to the highest point of the curve. Thus, wave A would be said to have an amplitude of a', and wave B would have an amplitude of b'.

Frequently amplitude is converted into **intensity**, which describes the power transmitted by a wave. In this book, I will often use intensity because it is more closely related to the psychological property of loudness. The unit **decibel** (/ˈdɛsɪbəl/~/ˈdɛsɪˌbɛl/; abbreviated dB) is used to compare the intensities of two sounds. Commonly, we compare the intensity of a particular sound to that of a just audible sound. Note that decibel is a relative, and not an absolute, measurement. The following chart gives you an idea of a few common intensities.

Intensity (dB)	Sound
130	4-engined jet aircraft, 120 ft.
120	Threshold of pain; pneumatic hammer, 3 ft.
110	Rock band
100	Car horn, 15 ft.; orchestra playing loud
90	Pneumatic hammer, 4 ft.
80	Noisy subway train; loud radio music
70	Busy traffic, 70 ft.
60	Conversation, 3 ft.; car 30 ft.
50	Quiet office
40	Residential area, no traffic; subdued conversation
30	Quiet garden; whispered conversation
20	Ticking of watch, at ear; broadcast studio
10	Rustle of leaves
0	Threshold of audibility

Mrs. Hebbard of Richmond, B.C., suffered partial hearing loss as a result of her husband Mark's snoring. His nocturnal noise was measured as 90 dB, slightly higher than the 86 dB of Vancouver's Automated Light Transit System. Mr.

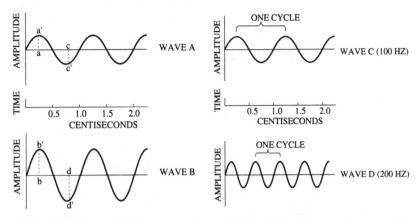

Figure 8.3 Two sine waves with different amplitudes.

Figure 8.4 Two sine waves with different frequencies.

Hebbard's snoring has since been dramatically softened by the surgical removal of his uvula (*Toronto Star,* December, 1988).

FREQUENCY

Consider sine waves like the ones in Figure 8.4. Both have the same intensity but they differ in the frequency of their repetition. One complete repetition of the pattern is called a **cycle.** The **frequency** of a wave is the number of cycles per second. One cycle of wave C, for example, takes 0.01 seconds (1.0 csec); thus, there would be a total of 100 cycles in a second. One **Hertz** (/hɜ.ts/; abbreviated **Hz**) equals one cycle per second; thus, the frequency of this wave is 100 Hz. In wave D, there are two cycles in 0.01 seconds or 200 cycles per second. The frequency of wave D is therefore 200 Hz.

PERCEPTION

We perceive intensity as **loudness** and frequency as **pitch.** The greater the intensity of the wave, the louder it will seem. The higher its frequency, the higher the pitch we hear. Remember that pitch and loudness are psychological, perceptual properties, whereas frequency and intensity are physical properties.

The pitch range that an individual can produce varies considerably. The range of pitch found in speech is about 60 – 500 Hz although we do not usually use the entire range in speaking. Typical average pitches used in speaking are:

Children	265 Hz
Women	225 Hz
Men	120 Hz

We can hear a much wider range of sounds than we use in speech. Our hearing is usually best in our youth when we can hear sounds in the range of about 20 –

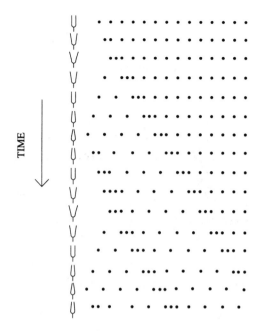

Figure 8.5 The cyclical propagation of waves.

20,000 Hz. A modern piano has a low note of 27.5 Hz and a high note of 3520 Hz. The instruments of an orchestra are tuned so that the A above middle C is 440 Hz.

Pitch and loudness are related in our hearing ability; that is, at some frequencies, the sound must be louder for us to hear it than at other frequencies.

PROPAGATION

So far we have been talking about a single molecule of air vibrating as a result of speech. Sound, however, is **propagated** or transmitted through air. Air comprises some 400 billion billion molecules per cubic inch at ordinary atmospheric pressures. Air molecules tend to maintain a constant pressure between themselves and thus a constant distance from each other. The distance from each other acts in an elastic fashion. If something pushes the molecules of air closer together, they will resist and try to move back to the original position. Likewise, if pulled apart, they will resist and try to return to the original position.

A simple analogy is to think of the molecules of air connected to each other by springs. If one molecule moves towards the next, the spring between them is compressed and will try to push them apart. On the other hand, if the molecules are pulled apart, the spring is stretched and will try to pull them back to their original position.

If we take our tuning fork and molecule of air from Figure 8.1 and add several other molecules of air, we can see how vibration is propagated. The tuning fork causes the molecules of air to move, and the movement of one molecule of air causes a corresponding movement on the next one, and so on. Figure 8.5 shows this. Note that the waves, alternations of high and low pressure, travel away from the source of energy (the tuning fork); however, the individual molecules of air return to their original position.

In our model, the wave would continue for ever. In real life, of course, the tuning fork loses energy and gradually comes to rest. In addition, as the wave spreads out in a circular fashion from the tuning fork, the energy is spread over an increasingly large area, and the wave gradually dissipates.

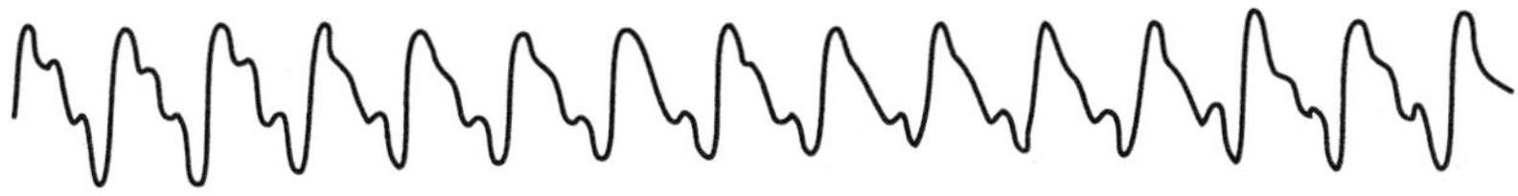

Figure 8.6 A complex repetitive wave.

COMPLEX WAVES A property of tuning forks is that they are constructed so as to produce wave forms that closely approximate sine waves. Most sounds are more complex than sine waves. Figure 8.6 shows the wave of someone producing the vowel [ɛ]. Clearly this is not a sine wave. A wave like this is called a **complex repetitive wave**: complex, because it is more complicated than a simple sine wave, and repetitive, because it has a pattern of repeating cycles.

In this form, complex waves such as in Figure 8.6 are of limited use to phoneticians. Fortunately, a nineteenth-century French mathematician and Egyptologist, Joseph **Fourier** /ˈfuɹiˌe/, formulated an analysis which allows any complex repetitive wave to be analysed into a series of sine waves. The mathematical calculations of Fourier analysis are formidable, but the reverse observation that sine waves can be added together to form a complex wave is also true, and the calculation for this involves only addition.

Consider the two sine waves in Figure 8.7. Wave A has a frequency of 100 Hz; wave B has a frequency of 200 Hz. If we consider these as components of a single complex wave, we can find the complex wave C. At any point in time, the intensity of the complex wave equals the sum of the intensities of the components. Figure 8.7 shows this. At about 0.2 csecs, the intensity of A is measured as (a); then, at the same point in time, the intensity of B is measured as (b). Thus, the

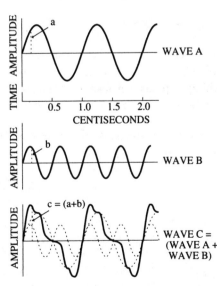

Figure 8.7 The addition of two sine waves to form a complex wave.

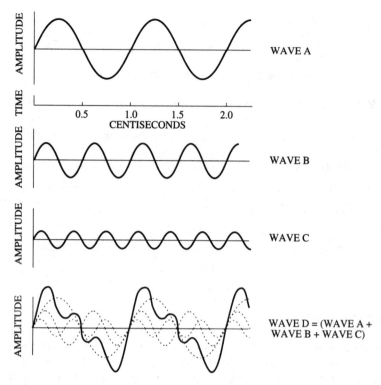

Figure 8.8 The addition of three sine waves to form a complex wave.

intensity for the complex wave C is (c) which equals (a + b). In the lower part of Figure 8.7, waves A and B (dotted lines) are superimposed, and their intensities are added together at every point in time to produce the complex wave C (solid line).

Figure 8.8 shows how three sine waves go together to form a complex wave. For example, at every point, we add the intensity of the 100-Hz wave, the 200-Hz wave, and the 300-Hz wave to get the intensity of the complex wave.

Fourier analysis is the reverse of the addition process illustrated above. It takes the complex wave and analyses it into a series of sine waves, telling us the frequency and amplitude of the individual components.

HARMONICS

The individual components of the complex wave are called **harmonics**. Harmonics are numbered from the lowest upwards: the first harmonic, second harmonic, etc. The first harmonic has the special name of **fundamental (harmonic)**; its frequency is called the **fundamental frequency** (often abbreviated F_0). The frequency of every harmonic is a whole multiple of the frequency of the

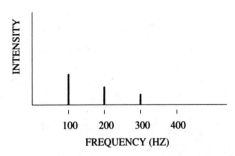

Figure 8.9 Spectrum of the complex wave of Figure 8.8.

fundamental; that is, if the fundamental harmonic has a frequency of 70 Hz, the second harmonic has a frequency of 140 Hz, the third of 210 Hz, etc. Note that the frequency of a complex wave with these harmonics is also 70 Hz. The frequency of the repetitive complex wave is always the same as the frequency of its fundamental. Since the frequencies are always the same, the pitch we perceive from a complex wave can be described as dependent on the frequency of the fundamental or on the frequency of the whole wave.

SPECTRUM

A **spectrum** /ˈspɛktɹəm/ (pl. **spectra** /ˈspɛktɹə/) is a display showing the intensity (or amplitude) and frequency of the harmonic components of a wave. Figure 8.9 shows the spectrum of the wave shown in Figure 8.8. It has three harmonics at 100 Hz, 200 Hz, and 300 Hz. The three harmonics have different intensities.

A sound **spectrogram** /ˈspɛktɹəˌɡɹæm/ is a visual representation of the spectrum of a sound. Phoneticians generally use three dimensions in talking about the harmonic analysis of an utterance: frequency, intensity, and time. In order to put three dimensions on a two-dimensional piece of paper, the axes of the spectrogram are usually frequency (vertical) and time (horizontal); intensity is shown by darkness. For example, Figure 8.10 shows a spectrogram of the phrase *in union* [ɪn ˈjunjən]. The first harmonic is the lowest horizontal line; the second harmonic is the second lowest line; and so on. In this example in the vowel /u/, the first harmonic is at about 300 Hz and the second at 600 Hz. The frequencies of the harmonics can be established by referring to the scale at the right.

In the example in Figure 8.10, the first, second, and generally the third harmonics are continuous throughout the utterance; the higher harmonics are broken. In a spectrogram, time moves from left to right. Thus, in this utterance, we can say that there are three points in time where the higher harmonics are strong, with weaker gaps in between. These darker areas on the spectrogram correspond to greater intensity in the acoustic signal. In this example the areas of greatest intensity correspond to the vowels and glides: from left to right, [ɪ], [ju], [jə].

In Figure 8.11 we see a spectrogram of the vowel [ɑ], spoken with a rising and

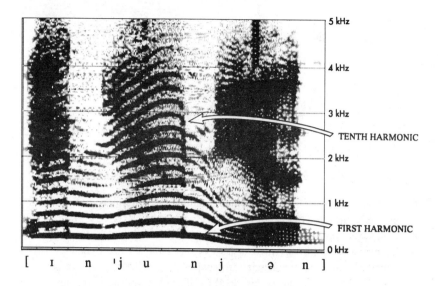

Figure 8.10 [ɪnˈjunjən].

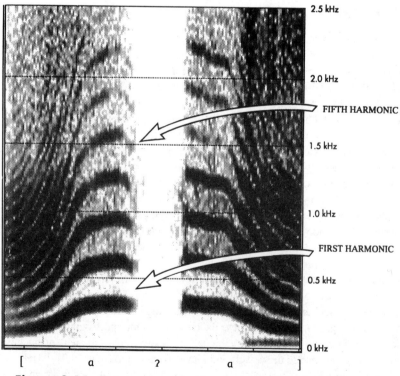

Figure 8.11 Spectrogram of [aʔa] spoken with rising, then falling pitch.

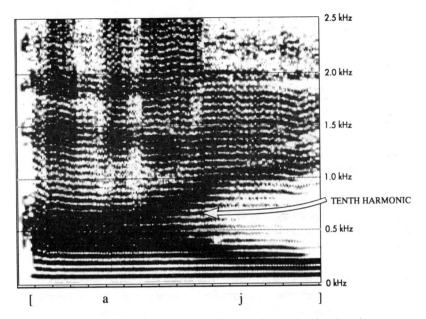

Figure 8.12 Spectrogram of [aj] spoken with a level pitch.

then a falling pitch. The frequency of the harmonics changes corresponding to the changes in pitch first with rising harmonics and then falling. Since harmonics are all multiples of the fundamental, if one harmonic changes, they all change. We perceive this as a sound with a rising pitch. In the later part of Figure 8.11, the harmonics fall; we perceive this as a sound with a falling pitch.

Figure 8.12 shows the diphthong [aj] spoken at a steady pitch. Note that the harmonics stay level, but their intensities change. Level harmonics indicate a steady pitch; changes in their intensity indicate a changing vocalic quality.

We see that in making a vowel, the pitch and the vowel quality are completely independent. We can easily test this by saying the same vowel at different pitches; try singing a tune, saying only the vowel [u]. Conversely, we can say different vowels at the same pitch. Remember, pitch depends on the frequency of the fundamental, controlled by the vibration rate of the vocal cords. Vowel quality depends on the shape of the vocal tract.

RESONANCE

Before we apply what we have learned to speech sounds, we need one more theoretical notion: **resonance**, the natural tendency of a body to vibrate at a certain frequency. You know that if you pluck a string on a violin, it vibrates at a certain frequency. This is because a string has a natural resonating frequency, which depends on its mass, length, and tension. A tube or other cavity also has a resonating frequency. If you blow across the lip of a bottle, the air in the bottle will

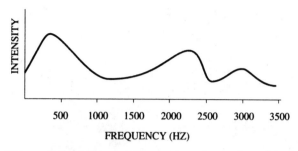

Figure 8.13 Resonance curve (vocal tract shaped for [i]).

vibrate at a certain frequency. If the volume of this cavity is changed, the resonating frequency changes as well. If you drink some of the fluid out of the bottle, the air cavity within is enlarged. Now, when you blow across the lip, the resulting pitch is lower than before. The larger the cavity, the lower its resonating frequency.

A body resonates not just at a single frequency but over a range of frequencies. Figure 8.13 shows the **resonance curve** of a certain complex tube. Such a curve shows how strongly the tube will resonate at various frequencies. The tube in Figure 8.13 will resonate strongly at frequencies around 400, 2300, and 3000 Hz, but less strongly at other frequencies. In fact, our vocal tract has approximately the resonance curve of Figure 8.13 when it is shaped to produce the vowel [i].

Suppose we have two objects: a vibrating string and an open tube. The string, when set into vibration, produces a complex wave with a spectrum like the one in Figure 8.14a. The tube has a resonance curve like that shown in Figure 8.13. Suppose now that we connect the string and the tube in sequence, so that the wave form produced by the string passes through the tube. The resulting spectrum is shown in Figure 8.14b. The frequencies of the fundamental and the harmonics are determined entirely by the vibration of the string. Passing the vibration through the tube changes the intensities of the harmonics produced by the string to agree more closely with its resonance curve.

Our vocal cords are like the string, vibrating so as to produce a glottal wave with a spectrum like that in Figure 8.14a. Our vocal tract is a tube. If it is shaped for the vowel [i], it has a resonance curve like that of Figure 8.13. The output, after the glottal wave has been modified by the vocal tract, is a sound which we hear as that vowel, with a spectrum like that of Figure 8.14b. The peaks of intensity shown in Figure 8.14b at 400, 2300, and 3000 Hz are called **formants** /ˈfoɹmənt/. In the following chapter, we will see that changing the shape of the vocal tract (*i.e.*, the resonating chamber) changes the frequencies of the formants. Formants are crucial in distinguishing different sounds.

We can change the shape and tension of our vocal cords so as to change the fundamental frequency (and thus the frequencies of the harmonics). We can also change the frequencies of the formants by changing the shape of our upper vocal

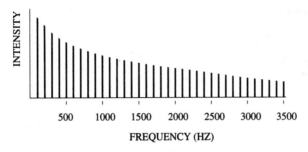

Figure 8.14a Glottal tone

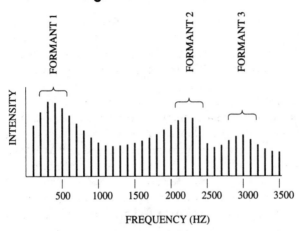

Figure 8.14b Spectrum after passing though the resonating tube (the vocal tract shaped for [i])

tract. By moving our jaw, tongue, lips, etc., we can produce many different shapes, each with its own resonance curve and thus produce a great variety of sounds.

TECHNICAL TERMS

acoustic phonetics	fundamental (harmonic)	resonance
acoustics	fundamental frequency	resonance curve
amplitude	harmonic	sine wave
centisecond	Hertz (Hz)	sinusoidal wave
complex repetitive wave	intensity	spectrogram
cycle	loudness	spectrum
decibel (dB)	millisecond	spectra
F_0	oscillation	vibration
formant	overtone	wave
Fourier analysis	pitch	waveform
frequency	propagation	

EXERCISES

BASIC

1. Determine the frequency of each of the following waves.

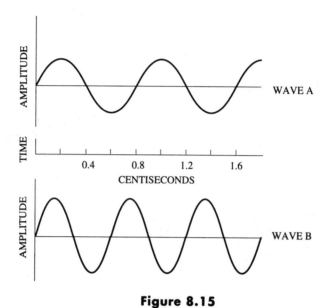

Figure 8.15

2. What is the frequency of the wave (taken as a whole) below?

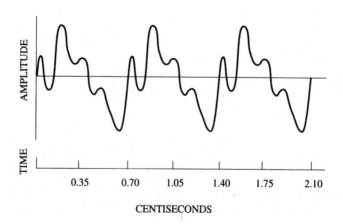

Figure 8.16

3. Two sine waves, A and B, are given. You are to add them together to get the resulting complex wave C. To help you, waves A and B are shown together at the bottom in dotted lines.

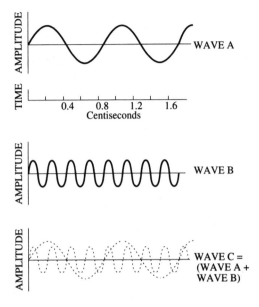

Figure 8.16

ADVANCED

4. The following selection is from *The Canterbury Tales* written in Middle English by Geoffrey Chaucer (adapted from Kökeritz, 1978, by permission). It is a reconstruction of how it would have been pronounced by Chaucer in the fourteenth century. If you are unfamiliar with any of the symbols, cheat and look ahead to find out how to pronounce them.

General Prologue, 1 - 42

hwan ðat ˈa·pril wiθ iz ˈʃu·rəz ˈso·tə
ðə dru·xt əv martʃ aθ pe·rsəd to θə ˈro·tə

an ˈba·ðəd ˈevri væjn in switʃ liˈku·r
əv hwitʃ verˈty· inˈdʒendrəd iz ðə flu·r
hwan ˈzefirus e·k wiθ iz ˈswe·tə brɛ·θ
inˈspi·rəd haθ in ˈevri hɔlt and hɛ·θ
ðə ˈtendrə ˈkrɔpəz an θə ˈjuŋgə ˈsunə
haθ in ðə ram iz ˈhalvə ku·rs iˈrunə
and ˈsma·lə ˈfu·ləz ˈma·kən ˌmeloˈdi·ə
ðat ˈsle·pən al ðə ni·çt wiθ ˈɔ·pən ˌi·ə

Whan that Aprill with his shoures soote
The droghte of March hath perced to the root,
And bathed every veine in swich licour
Of which vertu engendred is the flour;
Whan Zephirus eek with his sweete breeth
Inspired hath in every holt and heeth
The tendre croppes, and the yonge sonne
Hath in the Ram his halve cours yronne,
And smale foweles maken melodie,
That slepen al the night with open ye

sɔ· ˈprikəθ əm na·ˈty·r in ir kuˈra·dʒəz
ðan ˈlɔŋgən fɔlk to gɔ·n ɔn ˌpilgriˈma·dʒəz
and ˈpalmərz fɔr to ˈse·kən ˈstrɑwndʒə
    ˈstrɔndəz
to ˈfernə ˈhalwəz ku·ð in ˈsundri ˈlɔ·ndəz
an ˈspesjali frɔm ˈevri ˈʃi·rəz ˈendə
əv ˈeŋgelɔnd to ˈkɑwntərbri ðæj ˈwendə
ðə ˈhɔ·li ˈblisful ˈmartir fɔr to ˈse·kə
ðat hem haθ ˈhɔlpən hwan ðat
    ðæj wɛ·r ˈse·kə.

So priketh hem nature in hir corages;
Thanne longen folk to goon on pilgrimages,
And palmeres for to seken straunge
    strondes,
To ferne halwes, kowthe in sondry londes;
And specially from every shires ende
Of Engelond to Caunterbury they wende,
The hooly blisful martir for to seke,
That hem hath holpen whan that
    they were seeke.

CHAPTER NINE
THE ACOUSTICS
OF ENGLISH SOUNDS

Phoneticians have known for many years that it would be useful to analyse the spectra of various speech sounds. In the middle of the nineteenth century, Georg Ohm proposed the notion that somehow, our ear and brain act as though they perform a Fourier analysis on incoming sounds (Handel, 1989). Until the 1940's, the process of performing the necessary mathematical calculations for Fourier analysis for a complex wave was so time-consuming that it was seldom attempted. World War II, however, saw the invention of the sound spectrograph which displays the changing spectrum of a short segment of speech. Since the 1950's, a large amount of phonetic research has been done using this machine. In recent years, computers have been used to analyse digitised speech. The spectrograms in this book were made on a Macintosh computer with the MacAdios MacSpeech Lab from GW Instruments.

In this chapter you will learn about:
- spectrograms
- formants
- how English vowels and consonants are analysed acoustically.

THEORY

When the vocal cords are vibrating, the steady flow of air from the lungs is broken up into a series of bursts by the repeated opening and closing of the vocal cords. By this mechanism, a glottal wave is formed; Figure 9.1 shows this wave.

Figure 9.2 shows the spectrum of the glottal wave. Note that the fundamental is strongest in amplitude with gradually decreasing amplitudes as the harmonics get higher in frequency.

The **vocal tract** acts as a resonator for the glottal wave. The vocal tract is an extremely complex tubular system. It is a vertical tube (pharynx) with two horizontal tubes (oral and nasal cavities) leading from it opening to the outside air. Throughout its length, this tube system constantly changes in its shape and cross-sectional area. Further, the walls of the vocal tract vary as to their rigidity; the tongue, for example, is soft and flexible, whereas the palate is hard and rigid. Each of these variations affects the resonating properties of the vocal tract.

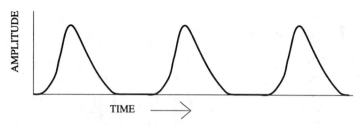

Figure 9.1 The glottal wave.

Under the speaker's control, the vocal tract is capable of assuming a large number of different positions, modifying the source wave from the glottis and thus producing a corresponding number of different sounds. A basic task of the phonetician is to relate the variations in the spectrum to the articulatory actions of the various sounds of language. In this chapter we will try to do this, first for the vowels of English and then for the consonants.

SPECTROGRAMS

Consider now the spectrograms in Figures 9.3 and 9.4. These are two different spectrograms of the exact same utterance 'Peggy tied a bowknot.' The first spectrogram (Figure 9.3) is called a **narrow-band spectrogram**; it is the kind that we saw in the previous chapter. The second spectrogram (Figure 9.4) is called a **broad-band spectrogram.** The two types of spectrograms are made by different adjustments of the machine. The technical details need not bother us. The narrow-band spectrogram gives good resolution for frequency, but blurs time somewhat; the broad-band spectrogram blurs frequency, but has good time resolution. Note that the individual harmonics are clear on the narrow-band spectrograms, but are blurred together on the broad-band spectrogram. On the broad-band spectrogram, we see thick black lines, called **formants.** Formants indicate clusters of harmonics with high intensities, relative to their neighbours. Formants are particularly useful in distinguishing vowels. These are numbered from the one with the lowest frequency: F1, F2, F3, etc. In general, the broad-band spectrogram is more useful in phonetics than the narrow-band spectrogram.

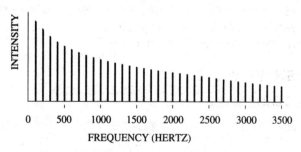

Figure 9.2 Spectrum of the glottal wave.

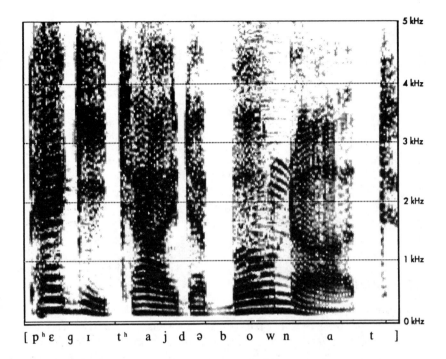

[pʰ ε   g   ɪ   tʰ   a   j   d   ə   b   o   w   n   a   t   ]

Figure 9.3 Narrow-band spectrogram of *Peggy tied a bowknot.*

Let's examine now the broadband spectrogram of *Peggy tied a bowknot* in Figure 9.4, describing it from left to right in some detail. The initial aspirated [pʰ] shows up as a blank followed by a short burst of scattered energy. The vowel [ε] is shown by the presence of very dark vowel formants. There is a gap again for the stop [g], followed by another vowel with dark formants. The stop [tʰ], like the previous [pʰ], has a gap followed by a burst of random energy showing the aspiration. Notice that in the diphthong [aj], vowel formants change frequency quite dramatically; this shows that the vowel quality is changing during the glide. The [d] shows up as a short gap. The vowel [ə] is shorter than other vowels on the spectrogram. The [b] of *bow* makes a fairly long gap, followed by another vowel with formants. During the [n] we see some energy at low frequencies. The vowel in *knot* is fairly light, indicating that the speaker reduced the intensity at the end of the sentence. We see the release of the [t] as a burst of energy.

ENGLISH VOWELS

VOWEL FORMANTS

Let's examine now the short vowels of English [ɪ ε æ ʊ]. The data we need are given below in Figure 9.5, which has spectrograms for the words *pit, pet, pat,* and *put.* We are particularly interested in the frequency of the formants.

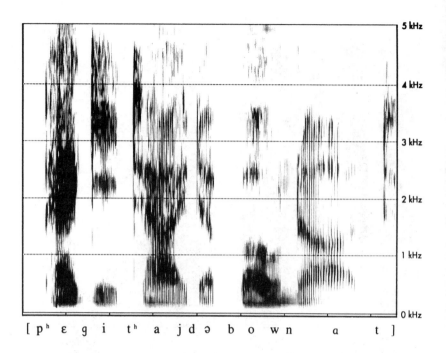

[pʰ ɛ g i tʰ a j d ə b o w n ɑ t]

Figure 9.4 Broad-band spectrogram of *Peggy tied a bowknot.*

In the vowel [ɪ], the first formant (F1) has its highest intensity at approximately 300 Hz; the second formant (F2) falls slightly, but its average frequency is about 2200 Hz. F3 is at 2500 Hz, and F4 at 3200 Hz. The following chart shows the approximate frequency for each of the vowels:

	F1	F2	F3	F4
ɪ	300	2200	2500	3200
ɛ	700	2000	2500	3100
æ	800	1700	2600	3000
ʊ	500	1200	2300	2800

The first three formants vary according to which vowel is being pronounced. Occasionally we can see a fourth formant or higher. Formants F4 and higher vary among speakers, but not much for the same speaker. The higher formants are primarily determined by the shape and size of the individual's head, nasal cavity, sinus cavities, etc., physical characteristics which the individual cannot vary.

Phoneticians focus on the first three formants for linguistic information. We see that F1 is low for [ɪ] and [ʊ], high for [æ], and mid for [ɛ]. This distribution correlates fairly well, in reverse, to the articulatory height of the vowel; *i.e.,* if the tongue is high, the first formant is low, and if the tongue is low, the first formant is high.

Now consider F2. Going through the vowels in the sequence [ɪ ɛ æ ʊ], F2 starts

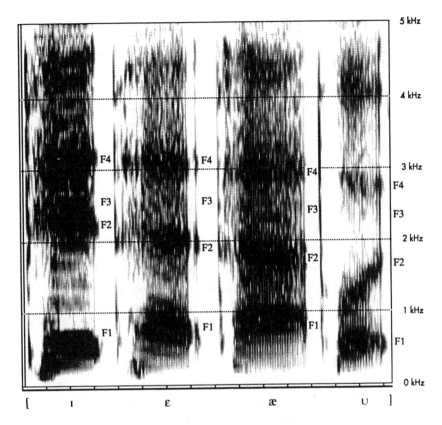

Figure 9.5 The vowels in *pit, pet, pat, put.*

high and becomes progressively lower. The height of F2 correlates roughly with the backness of the vowel, with [ɪ] being the vowel farthest to the front, and [ʊ] farthest to the back.

Let us consider just how the changing shape of the vocal tract causes different formants, *i.e.,* different resonant curves. Think of the highest point of the tongue dividing the vocal tract into a front cavity and a back cavity. From the preceding chapter, we know that the resonating frequency is higher for a small vibrating cavity than for a large one.

Moving from [ɪ] to [æ], the body of the tongue is pulled back making the front cavity larger and the back cavity smaller; thus, the resonating frequency of the back cavity is raised as it becomes smaller, and the resonating frequency of the front cavity is lowered as it becomes larger as we go from [ɪ] to [æ]. If we identify the back cavity with the first formant and the front cavity with the second formant, we can understand the relationship between the shape of the vocal tract and the frequencies of the formants.

Applying the same technique to the back vowels gives moderately satisfactory results. Moving from [æ] to [ʊ], both F1 and F2 become lower. The back

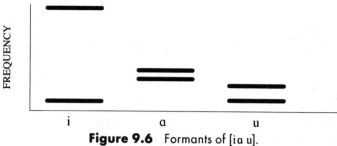

Figure 9.6 Formants of [i ɑ u].

cavity becomes larger as the root of the tongue is drawn up for the high vowel, and the front cavity becomes larger as the high point of the tongue moves farther back.

In a rough way then, we can see that the first two formants tell us which vowel we hear: F1 is related to the cavity behind the highest point of the tongue and F2 to the one in front. This generalisation turns out to be useful, although not completely accurate. In particular, it works better for front vowels than for back ones. The upper vocal tract acts as a single, although complex, resonating system. It is an oversimplification to identify one portion of its spectrum with one portion of its physical shape. Nevertheless, you will find this generalisation helpful in understanding how vowels work. We will look at the relationship between cavity size and formants again in Chapter 11. F3 is not easily identifiable with a specific part of the vocal tract.

A useful way of remembering the formant frequencies relative to each other is to use the following rules of thumb:

1. Line up the vowels progressively in the order:

    high front → low front → low back → high back.
2. The following statements can then be applied to the vowels proceeding from left to right.
a. F1 starts low and rises until the vowel [ɑ], then F1 falls.
b. F2 starts high and falls.
c. F3 is similar to F2, but higher.

To see how this works, consider the vowels [ɑ i u]. First we arrange them according to (1): [i ɑ u]. Figure 9.6 shows the formants of each after the rules of (2) are applied. Note that we can not determine absolute frequencies of the formants from this, but we can have an idea as to the formant pattern.

Figure 9.7 shows the actual formants of these vowels. We can see that the relative pattern of the formants corresponds to our predictions in Figure 9.6.

DIPHTHONGS

Diphthongs consist of a vowel and glide in either order. In Chapter 4 we described [aj] as moving from a low front to a high front position. From Figure 9.8 we can see that the first two formants for [aj] start off fairly close together as we would expect for a low vowel. During the glide, they move apart ending in the position

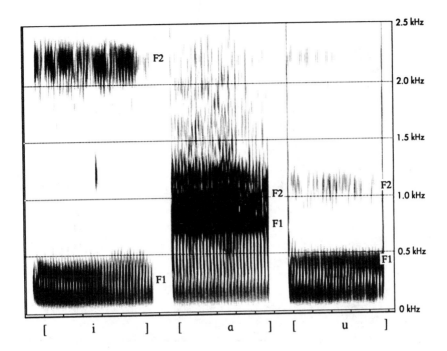

Figure 9.7 Spectrograms of [i ɑ u].

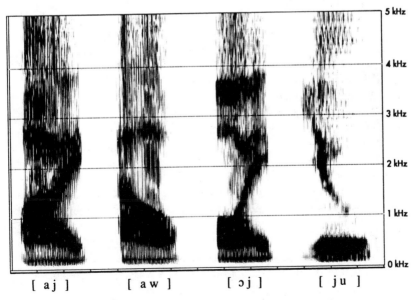

Figure 9.8 Spectrograms for the glides [aj aw ɔj ju].

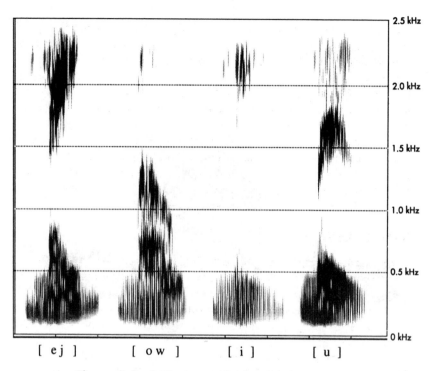

Figure 9.9 Spectrograms for the glides [ejowiu].

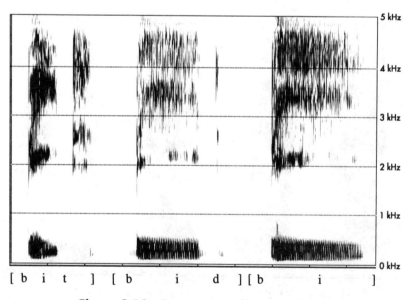

Figure 9.10 Spectrograms of beat, bead, bee.

for [i]. This makes sense since [j] is a glide with an end point roughly of [i]. In the spectrograms for [aw], the first two formants start off in the mid-range and both fall, moving closer together, as we would expect moving to the position of the vowel [u].

Also in Figure 9.8, we can see that for [ju], the glide with its moving formants precedes the vowel with its steadier formants. Can you explain the location and movement of the formants for[ɔj]?

In Figure 9.9, the formants in the diphthongs [ej] and [ow] move somewhat showing the changing vowel quality of these diphthongs, but not so dramatically as with [aj] and [aw]. This is reasonable since the distance of going from [e] to [i] is less than that of [a] to [i]. In Figure 9.9, we also see that [i] and [u] have a very slight diphthongal quality, as we noted in Chapter 4.

VOWEL LENGTH

In Chapter 4, we discussed the allophonic lengthening of vowels in English. On a spectrogram, the length of a vowel can be measured easily. Compare the spectrograms for *beat, bead,* and *bee* in Figure 9.10. You can easily see that the vowels are not of the same length. The vowel before a voiceless consonant is shorter; the vowel before a voiced consonant and in an open syllable are longer. This length is consistent with our statement of vowel length in Chapter 4.

Figure 9.11 also compares the length of [ow] and [æ] in similar environments. The diphthong [ow] appears in the words *goat, goad, go.* The [æ] appears in *fat* and *fad;* recall that, in English, [æ] does not occur word-finally.

STRESS

Consider the words: *table,* and *machine,* shown in Figure 9.12. In the spectrograms for each word, you can see that the syllable with major stress has greater intensity and usually takes longer than those syllables that are unstressed. In *table,* the first syllable has stronger formants than does the second syllable. The first syllable in *machine* is extremely short, with little intensity.

Figure 9.13 shows spectrograms for *quantity* and *excessive.* The stressed syllable in these words is easy to recognise. Note in both words as well that a final unstressed syllable tends to be longer than an unstressed syllable earlier in the word. In this example, the /t/'s of *quantity* can be seen to be stops with some aspiration, rather than taps.

VOICING

In broad-band spectrograms, you notice vertical lines. These **vertical striations** /ˌstɹajˈejʃən/ show voicing. Each of these striations corresponds to the opening and closing of the vocal cords. Striation is typical of voiced sounds generally. You can even tell the pitch of a sound by measuring the distance between two striations and calculating the frequency of the vibration. With the better time resolution of the

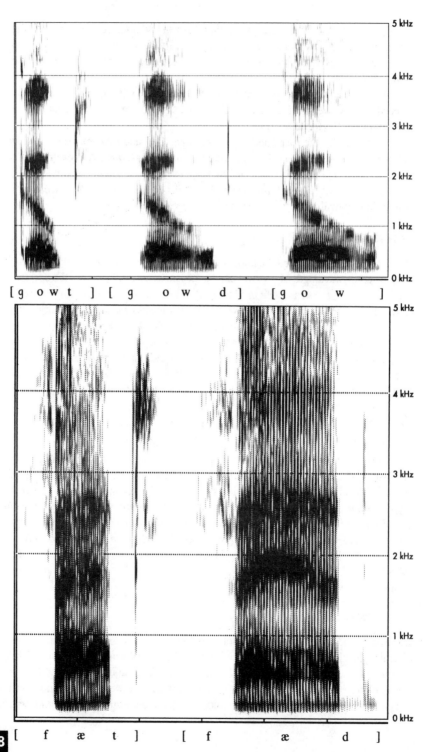

[g o w t] [g o w d] [g o w]

[f æ t] [f æ d]

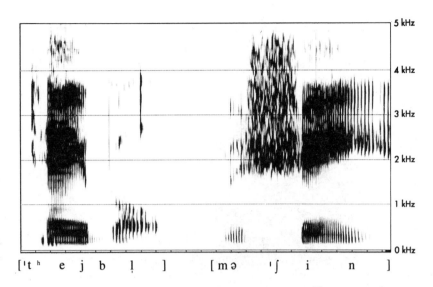

['tʰ   e   j   b   l̩   ]   [m ə   'ʃ   i   n   ]

Figure 9.12   Stress appears as greater intensity and longer vowels:
table, machine.

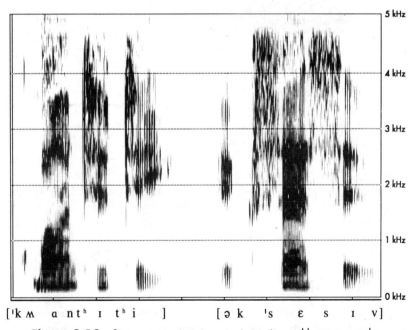

['k ʍ   ɑ nt ʰ ɪ t ʰ i   ]   [ə k   's   ɛ   s   ɪ   v]

Figure 9.13   Stress appears as greater intensity and longer vowels:
quantity, excessive.

Figure 9.11 (facing page)   Allophonic length in [ow] and [æ].

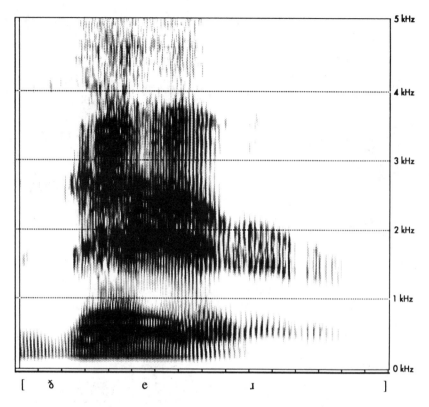

[　　ð　　　　　e　　　　　ɹ　　　　　　　　　]

Figure 9.14 Spectrogram of the coda [eɹ] of *there*.
The vertical striations correspond to individual vibrations of the vocal cords.

broad-band spectrogram these striations show up clearly; on the narrow-band spectrogram with poorer time resolution, they are not visible.

The spectrogram in Figure 9.14 shows the rhyme of the word *there* — [eɹ]; the time display has been stretched to make the time differences more obvious. The word is said with a falling pitch. At the beginning of the vowel, the vertical striations are 0.006 seconds apart, giving a frequency of 166 Hz. At the end, the striations are 0.012 seconds apart, a frequency of 83 Hz. We hear the decrease in frequency as a decrease in pitch. Voicing usually shows up stronger in the lower frequencies.

CONSONANTS

Consider the spectrogram in Figure 9.15 of *I can pass it*. Phonemically, the transcription is /ˌaj kæn ˈpæs ɪt/. A narrow transcription would be something like [ˌaj kŋ ˈpʰæs ɪt]. The vowel portions show strong formant patterns. The diphthong [aj] is at the beginning, the vowel [æ] is just past the middle, and the vowel [ɪ] is near the end. The stop consonants show up as gaps: first, [k] is fairly long, [pʰ] shows

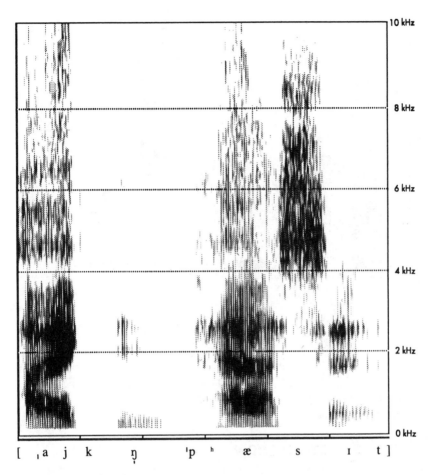

Figure 9.15 Spectrogram of *I can pass it.*

aspiration at its release as scattered bits of energy, and the [t] at the end is a gap. The fricative [s] shows up as random energy, without a formant pattern, with energy particularly in the higher frequencies.

Up to now, most of the sounds we have discussed have had a repetitive cyclical wave form, and thus a fundamental frequency and harmonics. There are, however, in speech sounds which do not have such wave forms. Certain sounds, such as fricatives, exhibit scattered energy called **noise.** In Figure 9.15, the /s/ of *pass* shows this pattern of noise. The aspiration after the /p/ of *pass* also shows some noise.

VOICING

In Chapter 3, we discussed the voicing of consonants. Consonants in English are generally voiceless both at the very beginning and at the very end of a word. Compare the spectrograms in Figure 9.16 for *bit, pit, spit.* You can see that the

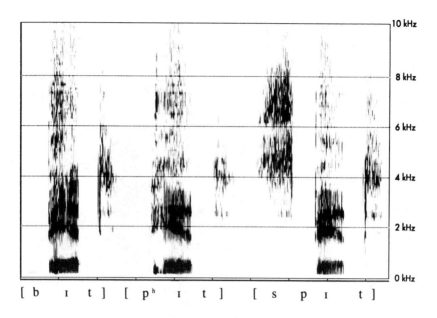

Figure 9.16
Spectrograms of *bit, pit, spit.*

voicing starts part way through the consonant for the [b] in *bit,* at the end of the voiceless unaspirated stop [p] in *spit,* and with the aspirated stop [pʰ] of *pit,* the initial part of the stop is voiceless. We have already said that aspiration is realised as the delay in the onset of voicing.

PLACE OF ARTICULATION

Place of articulation is not so readily determined from a spectrogram. Consider three voiceless stops [p t k]. During these three sounds, nothing is happening to make an acoustic impression. No air is exiting from the body, and the vocal cords are not vibrating. For each of these, the spectrogram shows a blank. How then can we distinguish three blanks, three gaps in the acoustic record? The answer is that we do not distinguish these sounds by themselves, but by the effect they have on their neighbouring sounds. Consider the sequences [pɛ tɛ kɛ]. The mouth, in moving from the [p] to the [ɛ], changes shape in a particular fashion. In moving from [t] to [ɛ], it changes shape in a different fashion, and from [k] to [ɛ], in a still different fashion. This means that the initial edge of the [ɛ] is slightly different for each of the three syllables [pɛ tɛ kɛ]. The edge of the vowel next to the consonant is called the **transition,** the time period when the mouth is changing shape between vowel and consonant.

The important spectrographic feature distinguishing the various consonant-

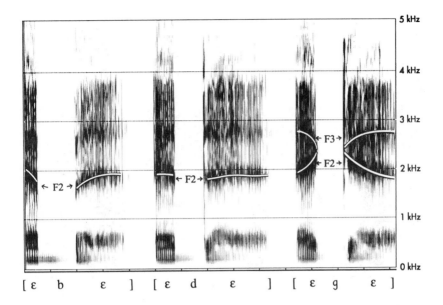

[ɛ   b   ɛ   ]   [ɛ   d   ɛ   ]   [ɛ   g   ɛ   ]

Figure 9.17   Spectrograms of [ɛbɛ ɛdɛ ɛgɛ] showing different places of articulation.

vowel transitions is the second formant. If you examine the transitions in Figure 9.17, you will see that in [ɛbɛ], the edges of the second formant point down slightly; in [ɛdɛ], the transitions are fairly level; and in [ɛgɛ], the transitions point up. The velar transitions (release) are further marked by a noticeable coming together of the second and third formants. Stops are generally characterised by fairly abrupt onset and release. The release is often marked by a strong vertical **spike**. Aspirated stops have a bit of noise before the vowel formants begin.

MANNER

The manner of articulation can usually be determined from a spectrogram. During stops, no air passes out, and the spectrogram shows a gap. Fricatives are characterised by random noise. Affricates can be recognised by a gap for the stop portion followed by noise for the fricative portion. We have already seen that vowels show formant patterns with strong intensity. Laterals and nasals generally have formant patterns, but weaker than those for vowels.

FRICATIVES   Fricatives are not easy to distinguish from each other. Figure 9.18 shows spectrograms of the English fricatives. Often [f v θ ð] are so weak that they barely show up at all. The fricatives [s z ʃ ʒ] are usually easier to detect; they appear in spectrograms with energy in the higher frequencies. The alveolar

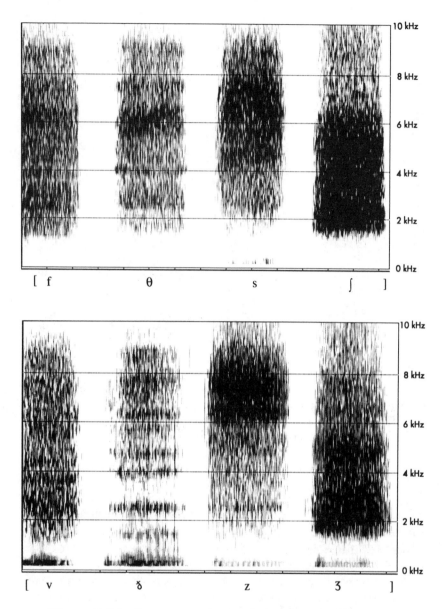

[f   θ   s   ʃ   ]

[v   ð   z   ʒ   ]

Figure 9.18 Spectrograms showing the noise pattern of fricatives.

fricatives [s z] have energy concentrated in the high frequencies, in the range 4000–8000 Hz. The palato-alveolar fricatives [ʃ ʒ] are somewhat lower, in the range 2000–6000 Hz. The voiced fricatives are similar to their voiceless counterparts; they often show a **voice bar**, or a formant-like band of energy at very low frequencies.

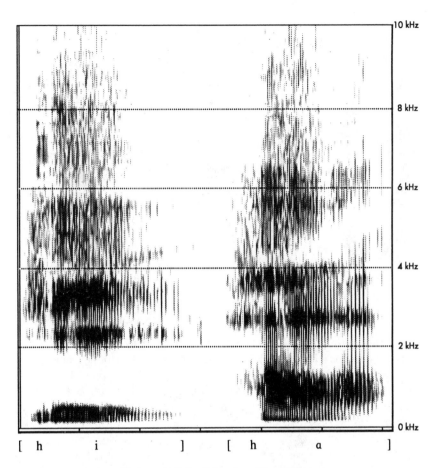

[h   i   ]   [h   ɑ   ]

Figure 9.19   [h] before [i] and [ɑ].

[h]   We have described [h] as a voiceless vowel. Accordingly, it shows up as a weak bit of noise but with a concentration of energy at the frequency level of the formants of the following vowel, as in Figure 9.19.

NASALS   Nasals are voiced stops. The vocal cords are vibrating; there is a complete obstruction in the oral tract, and air is exiting only through the nose. As you can see from Figure 9.20, nasals have a weak formant-like pattern. They typically have energy at a low frequency around 250–500 Hz and weaker energy at higher levels. Note the abrupt loss of overall energy during the nasal. The nose is less efficient than the mouth in radiating energy to the outside, and this loss of energy is quite apparent in the spectrogram. The place of articulation for the nasals shows up as for the oral stops: *e.g.,* for [m], the bilabial nasal, the second formant has a transition pointing down; for [n] the alveolar nasal, the second formant has a level transition; and the transition with a velar points up, merging with the third formant.

155

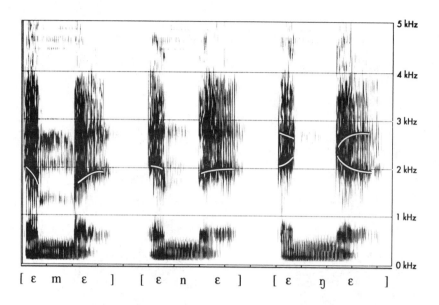

[ɛ   m   ɛ   ]   [ɛ   n   ɛ   ]   [ɛ   ŋ   ɛ   ]

Figure 9.20   Spectrograms showing the nasals [m n ŋ].

[ɹ]   The approximant [ɹ] lowers the third formant of the surrounding vowels. With postvocalic [ɹ], as in [hɚɹ], the lowering may be present through most of the vowel. Figure 9.21 shows *head, hair, red, rare*. You can see [ɛ] with no rhotic element in *head*. Compare this with the initial [ɹ] in *red* and with the final [ɹ] in *hair*. *Rare* has an [ɹ] both initially and finally.

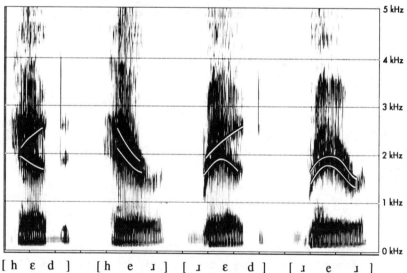

[h   ɛ   d]   [h   e   ɹ]   [ɹ   ɛ   d]   [ɹ   e   ɹ]

Figure 9.21   Spectrograms showing a lower mid vowel with and without [ɹ]: *head, hair, red, rare*.

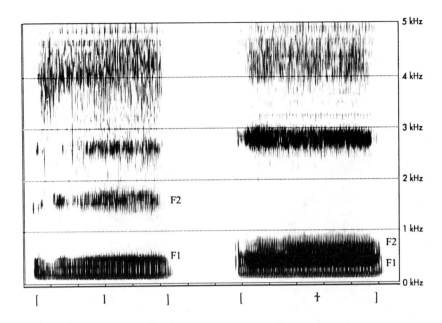

Figure 9.22 Clear and dark /l/.

LATERALS   The English lateral, /l/ has a formant-like pattern. The difference between the clear and dark l-sounds [l ɫ] may be seen in Figure 9.22. These have respectively the timbre of a high front vowel and of a high back vowel. With clear [l], F1 and F2 are farther apart as we would expect for a high front vowel and closer and lower for the dark [ɫ], like a high back vowel.

TAPS   Figure 9.23 shows *latter* and *ladder*. Note the much shorter gap for the tap [ɾ] than for the stop [d].

TECHNICAL TERMS

broad-band spectrogram   noise   vertical striation
formant   spike   voice bar
narrow-band spectrogram   transition

EXERCISES
BASIC

'Reading' spectrograms requires patience and practice. Even experienced pho-neticians cannot just sit down and see immediately what a spectrogram 'says'. In working with spectrograms, it is helpful to try to identify first the obvious features, and then to work on the more difficult parts. There is no need to start at the left and work steadily to the right; jumping around may be more helpful. Use your knowledge of the language to help you. Pay attention to the frequency and time scales.

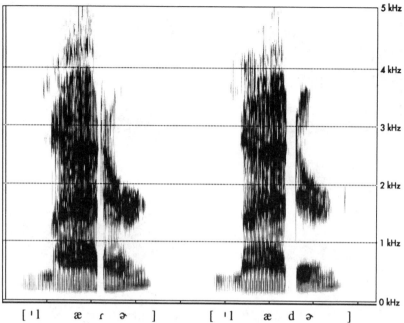

[ˈl   æ   ɾ   ɚ   ]   [ˈl   æ   d   ɚ   ]

Figure 9.23 Spectrogram constrasting an alveolar tap and stop.

1. The spectrogram below shows the vowels [ɪ ej ɑ ɔj]. Identify each vowel on the spectrogram with the correct symbol.

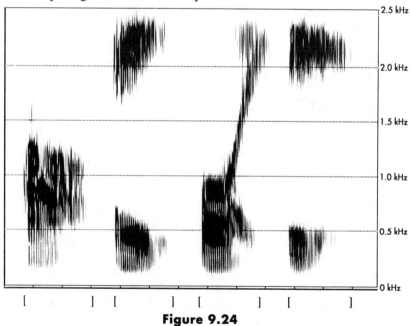

[   ] [   ] [   ] [   ]

Figure 9.24

2. The spectrogram below shows the words *kin, list,* and *rasp.* Identify each word correctly and divide it into segments.

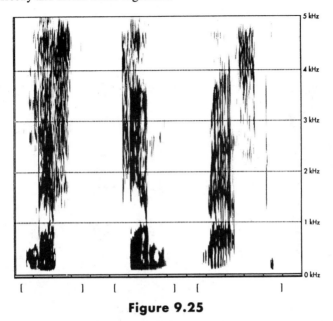

[   ]   [   ]   [   ]

Figure 9.25

3. Below is a spectrogram of the sentence *Does Cathy play tennis?* Transcribe the sentence, and then label the segments by placing the symbol below the appropriate portion of the spectrogram.

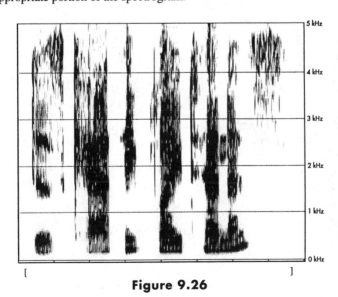

[   ]

Figure 9.26

4. The spectrogram below is of the sentence *I stayed in Saskatchewan.*
   Transcribe the sentence, and label the segments by placing the symbol below
   the appropriate portion of the spectrogram.

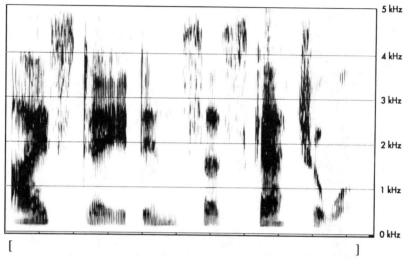

[   ]

Figure 9.27

5. The spectrogram below is of the sentence *I stayed in* ———. The blank represents a province different from the one in exercise 4.
   What is it? Explain your answer.

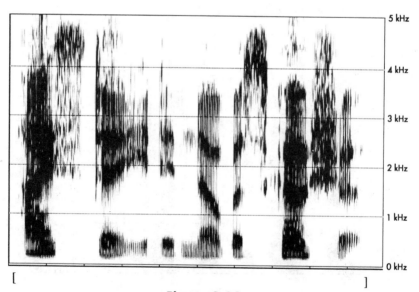

[   ]

Figure 9.28

6. The following spectrograms show two different pronunciations of a word. For each, identify which pronunciation goes with which transcription. Then, transcribe both words by placing the symbols under the appropriate portion of the spectrogram.

a. schedule   [ˈskɛˈdʒul] — [ˈʃɛˈdʒul]   b. either   [ˈiðəɹ] — [ˈajðəɹ]

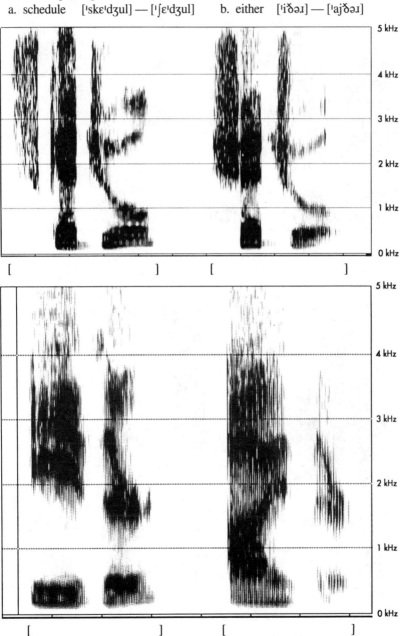

ADVANCED

7. Can you figure out what the two spectrograms below represent?

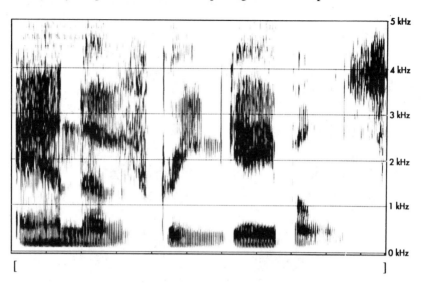

[   ]

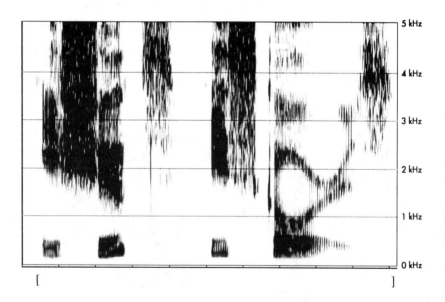

[   ]

8. Learn this passage by heart to impress your high school English teacher on visits home (adapted from Kökeritz, 1953, by permission) :

HAMLET 3.i.56-68

tə ˈbiˑ əɹ ˈnɒt tə ˈbiˑ,
  ˈðæt ɪz ðə ˈkwestʃn̩
	To be, or not to be,
	  that is the question:

ˈhwɛðəɹ tɪz ˈnoˑbləɹ
  ɪn ðə ˈmʌjnd tə ˈsʌfəɹ
	Whether 'tis nobler
	  in the mind to suffer

ðə ˈslɪŋz ən ˈæroz
  əv ʌwtˈreˑdʒəs fɔˑɹtɪn
	The slings and arrows
	  of outrageous fortune,

ɔˑɹ tə ˈteˑk ˈaˑɹmz
  əˈgenst ə ˈseˑ əv ˈtrʌblz̩
	Or to take arms
	  against a sea of troubles

ən bʌj əˈpoˑzn̩ ˈend əm.
  tə ˈdʌj, tə ˈsliˑp,
	And by opposing end them.
	  To die — to sleep,

noˑ ˈmoˑɹ, ən bʌj ə ˈsliˑp
  tə ˈseˑ wi ˈend
	No more; and by a sleep
	  to say we end

ðə ˈhaˑɹteˑk ən ðə
  ˈθʌwzn̩ ˈnætrəl ˈʃɒks
	The heartache and the
	  thousand natural shocks

ðət ˈfleʃ ɪz ˈɛˑɹ tuˑ,
  ˈtɪz ə ˌkɒnsəˈmeˑʃn̩
	That flesh is heir to:
	  'tis a consummation

dɪˈvʌwtlɪ tə bɪ ˈwɪʃt.
  tə ˈdʌj, tə ˈsliˑp,
	Devoutly to be wish'd.
	  To die, to sleep;

tə sliˑp, pəɹˈtʃæˑns tə ˈdreˑm,
  ˈʌj ˈðɛˑɹz ðə ˈrʌb
	To sleep, perchance to dream
	  —ay, there's the rub:

fɔˑɹ ɪn ðæt ˈsliˑp əv ˈdeˑθ,
  hwat ˈdreˑmz meˑ ˈkʌm
	For in that sleep of death
	  what dreams may come,

hwen wi əv ˈʃʌfld̩ ˌɔˑf
  ðɪs ˈmɔˑɹtəl ˈkʌjl,
	When we have shuffled off
	  this mortal coil,

ˈmʌst gɪv əs ˈpɔˑz.	*Must give us pause.*

CHAPTER TEN
FEATURES

Up to now, we have represented utterances as a sequence of **segments** — consonants and vowels. We have, however, frequently described aspects of a segment, such as voiceless, nasal, labial or rounded. Such aspects are called **features**. In this chapter we will develop a theory of features for describing the sounds of English. In later chapters, we will expand this theory so that it can be used for any language.

In this chapter you will learn about:
- why features are useful
- phonological oppositions
- which features are necessary for English
- the basics of feature geometry.

REASONS FOR FEATURES

CONTRAST

We saw in Chapter 2 that sounds may **contrast** with each other; for example, [t] and [d] contrast in English. If we substitute one for the other, we get different words: [hɪt] — [hɪd]. Linguists have found that overall the phonological system of a language is best described in terms of features rather than in terms of segments. In English, for example, /t/ and /d/ are identical except that /t/ is voiceless and /d/ is voiced. In distinguishing /t/ and /d/, we do not need to contrast the entire segments with each other; rather, the difference can be explained as simply a difference in voicing. Furthermore, the same difference can be used to account for the same contrast in other pairs: /p b/, /s z/, and /k g/.

NATURALNESS

We have seen that voiceless stops in English are aspirated under certain conditions. A grammar of English must be able to predict this occurrence of aspiration. If we use segments, we need three separate rules:

a. /p/ → [pʰ] / at the beginning of a stressed syllable
b. /t/ → [tʰ] / at the beginning of a stressed syllable
c. /k/ → [kʰ] / at the beginning of a stressed syllable.

Using segments, we miss the generalisation that there is a **class** of sounds, voiceless stops, which is aspirated in this environment. Such a class can easily be described with a rule using features:

$$\begin{bmatrix} \text{voiceless} \\ \text{stop} \end{bmatrix} \rightarrow \text{[aspirated]} \ / \ \text{at the beginning of a stressed syllable.}$$

Linguists have noted that there are processes such as aspiration, assimilation, and intervocalic voicing (see Chapter 17) which occur in many languages. These have been termed **natural processes**. We want our theory to allow us to state natural processes easily. A basic way of meeting such a goal is to recognise **natural classes** of sounds. With English aspiration, we see that the term 'voiceless stop' defines a natural class of sounds, the members of which are all subject to the same process. We want our set of features to allow us to define natural classes easily, *e.g.*, all voiced fricatives or all nasal vowels.

So far in our presentation, we have often used features in describing sounds, but our transcriptions have been in terms of segments. Even though we will continue to use segments in transcribing sounds, we now will view a segmental symbol not as representing the sound directly, but as an abbreviation for the set of features which themselves represent the sound. Note that features are written within square brackets: *e.g.*, [nasal], [lateral].

OPPOSITIONS

Linguistic sounds are **discrete**; they do not blend into each other. For example, if we hear an English word clearly, we can assert definitely that the first phoneme of that word is a /t/, or it is not a /t/. We do not say, for example, that 'the first phoneme was sort of /t/-ish, but tending a little towards an /f/'. This discreteness in language means that sounds **contrast** with one another: /p/ is in opposition to /b/, and /d/ is in opposition to /n/, etc. Features describe these oppositions; *e.g.*, the feature [voiceless] distinguishes /p/ from /b/, and [nasal] describes the opposition between /d/ and /n/.

Considerable controversy has existed over the nature of oppositions. A simple position is that all oppositions are **binary** /ˈbajnəɹi/; *i.e.*, each feature has two values, shown by a plus or a minus sign. For example, [+nasal] describes nasal sounds, and [−nasal] describes all non-nasal sounds. Chomsky and Halle took this position (except for certain features, such as stress and tone) in their important book *The Sound Pattern of English* (1968), and most subsequent work followed their lead until the early 1980's.

Recent thinking on oppositions has taken notions from earlier studies on oppositions (Troubetzkoy, 1939) and allows three kinds of oppositions: unary, binary, and multivalued. **Unary** /ˈjunəɹi/ features have only one value: they are either present or not. For example, we could use a unary feature [nasal] to distinguish the nasals from non-nasal sounds. For nasals, the feature is present; for non-nasals, it is not. The difference between binary and unary features is not great;

note, however, that we can use the binary feature [–nasal] to refer to the class of non-nasal sounds, whereas with the unary feature [nasal], we can refer to the class of sounds which contain [nasal], but we have no way of referring directly to the class of non-nasal sounds. In phonetics, where we are primarily concerned in distinguishing contrastive sounds from each other, the difference between unary and binary features is not so important as it is in phonology, where phonological rules must refer to classes of sounds.

The third kind of feature, **multivalued**, has more than two values. For example, we can characterise vowel height by means of an multivalued feature [height] with three values [1height], [2height], and [3height].

Now let's compare how these three types of features would be used in English to distinguish the lax front vowels [ɪ ɛ æ] from each other, and how they would be used to distinguish [t] from [d].

Unary

ɪ	ɛ	æ	t	d
[high]	[mid]	[low]	[voiceless]	——

Binary

ɪ	ɛ	æ	t	d
$\begin{bmatrix} \text{+high} \\ \text{–low} \end{bmatrix}$	$\begin{bmatrix} \text{–high} \\ \text{–low} \end{bmatrix}$	$\begin{bmatrix} \text{–high} \\ \text{+low} \end{bmatrix}$	[–voice]	[+voice]

Multivalued

ɪ	ɛ	æ	t	d
[1height]	[2height]	[3height]	[1voice]	[2voice]

With unary features, each vowel has its own feature. With the stops, we understand that [voiced] is the default value; thus, we leave [d] unspecified and specify [voiceless] for [t], an exception to the default value.

With binary features, each feature has a [+] or [–] value. To distinguish the three vowels height, we need only two features: [high] and [low]. Combinations of these two features allow us to distinguish the three vowel heights. The use of [voice] to distinguish /t/ and /d/ is straightforward.

With multivalued features, we number the values. There is only one features [height], but it has three values. Where there are only two values, as with [voice] for /t/ and /d/, the multivalued and the binary descriptions are equivalent.

FEATURES FOR ENGLISH

In stating reasons for features earlier, we said that they must be adequate to distinguish the contrastive segments of a language and that they should make natural classes easy to describe. The second criterion is primarily a concern of phonology. We will first develop a set of features adequate for distinguishing the contrastive sounds of English. Then, we will organise them in a framework called feature geometry.

The choice of features is not a cut and dried matter. Different people use different feature systems. For example, I have generally chosen to use unary features. Although this choice is, I believe, a reasonable one, you will certainly find different systems of features in other works on phonetics and phonology.

MAJOR CLASS FEATURES

First, we must divide segments into consonants and vowels. With consonants, we need as well a way of distinguishing obstruents from sonorants. We will use two **major class features**, **[consonantal]** and **[sonorant]**, to distinguish these three categories.

Obstruents	Liquids, Nasals	Vowels, Glides
[consonantal]	$\begin{bmatrix} \text{consonantal} \\ \text{sonorant} \end{bmatrix}$	[sonorant]

[consonantal]: sounds with a constriction as great as that of an approximant, or greater.
Stops, fricatives, affricates, liquids, nasals.

[sonorant]: sounds with a relatively open vocal tract and with a high level of acoustic energy.
Vowels, approximants, nasals.

Note that all features are unary unless otherwise specified. The requirement for a sound to be consonantal depends on the degree of closure. Note that [consonantal] refers to oral constriction; air may or may not flow out the nasal passage. On the other hand, [sonorant] is concerned with over-all air flow, whether through the oral or the nasal passage. Thus a nasal stop is both [consonantal] and [sonorant]; there is an oral obstruction, but the vocal tract is fairly open with air flowing out the nasal passage.

PLACE OF ARTICULATION

For English we need three basic places of articulation: [labial], [coronal], and [dorsal]. These describe where an obstruction occurs in the vocal tract.

[labial]: sounds made with an obstruction involving the lips.
Bilabial, labio-dental.
[coronal]: sounds made with the tip or blade of the tongue.
Dental, alveolar, palato-alveolar, retroflex.
[dorsal]: sounds make with the front or back of the tongue.
Palatal, velar.

Note that each of the terms is a cover term including more than one specific place of articulation. We will use additional features to distinguish contrasting sounds within these categories. The feature [labial] includes both bilabials and labio-dentals. The feature [dorsal] is used somewhat differently from our earlier use of the term; as a feature, it includes sounds made with both the front and the dorsum of the tongue. The term [coronal] /ˈkoɹənəl -kəˈɹownəl/ is new; it includes both the apex and lamina of the tongue.

The glides /j/ and /w/ are both considered [dorsal]. With [j], the front of the tongue is raised, and with [w], the back of the tongue is raised. For the moment, we will omit the affricates [tʃ dʒ], returning to them later in the discussion of feature geometry. Note that [h] is made with an obstruction at the glottis; thus it is not covered by any of these features. We will return to it later.

MANNER

To distinguish stops from fricatives, we need a feature [continuant]:

[continuant]:   sounds made with air flowing out the mouth.
                 Fricatives, approximants, vowels.

Note that nasal stops are not [continuant] since no air flows out the mouth. If we use the place features and [continuant], we can divide the consonants into groups as shown in the chart below:

	[labial]	[coronal]	[dorsal]
——————	p b m	t d n	k g ŋ
[continuant]	f v	θ ð s z ʃ ʒ l ɹ	j w

The feature [nasal] distinguishes [m n ŋ] from the other stops.

[nasal]:   sounds with air passing out the nose.
         Nasals.

We will use three features which apply only to [coronal] sounds. In Chapter 2, we pointed out the the blade of the tongue is more involved with dentals than with alveolars; accordingly, we use the feature [laminal] to distinguish laminal [θ ð] from apical [s z].

[laminal]:   [coronal] sounds made with a laminal articulation.
           Lamino-dentals.

In the same manner, we use [posterior] (following Avery and Rice, 1989) to distinguish palato-alveolars [ʃ ʒ] from alveolar [s z].

[posterior]:   [coronal] sounds made with the place of articulation farther back.
              Palato-alveolars.

The feature [lateral] distinguishes [l] from [ɹ].

[lateral]:   [coronal] sounds made with air prevented from escaping at the middle of the tongue, but allowed to escape at one or both sides of the tongue.
Laterals.

With the features we have developed so far, we can now distinguish the consonants of English, as shown in Figure 10.1.

	[labial]	[coronal]	[dorsal]
	p b	t d	k g
[nasal]	m	n	ŋ
[continuant]	f v	s z	j w
		[laminal] θ ð	
		[posterior] ʃ ʒ	
[lateral]		l	
		ɹ	

Figure 10.1 Features for English consonants.

We need a feature [voiceless] to distinguish the several voiced-voiceless pairs of sounds. The choice of [voiceless] over [voiced] is made because all types of sounds in languages are found voiced whereas only obstruents are commonly voiceless. This implies that [voiced] is the default condition, and therefore [voiceless] must be specified (see also Browman and Goldstein, 1985, 1989).

[voiceless]:   sounds made with the vocal cords in the voiceless position.

We have left the affricates [tʃ dʒ] and the fricative [h] for later discussion. The glides [j w] are similar to the vowels and will be distinguished by the features we develop for vowels. With these exception, we have a sufficient set of features to distinguish all the contrasting consonants of English.

VOWEL

Vowels require a specification of height, backness, rounding, and tense. The feature **[height]** is a three-valued feature for high, mid, and low vowels. For convenience' sake, I use **[high]**, **[mid]**, and **[low]** as equivalent to [1height], [2height], and [3height], with the understanding that only one of these can occur for a single segment and that they are the values of a multivalued feature.

Front vowels are specified **[front]**; back vowels lack this specification. Phonetically central vowels, such as [ə] are considered back. Rounding is specified by a feature **[round]**. Tense vowels are specified **[tense]**. This feature is quite controversial in phonetics as we will see in Chapter 11.

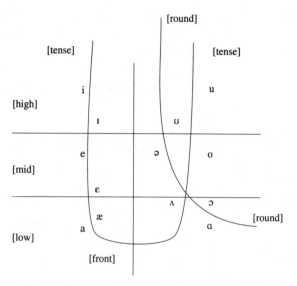

Figure 10.2 Features for English vowels.

[height]: a multivalued feature distinguishing vowels by the position of the highest point of the tongue.

Values: [high], [mid], [low].

[front]: sounds made with the tongue in the front part of the vowel area.

[round]: sounds made with rounded lips.

[tense]: certain vowels in a language.

In English, the vowels [i u ɑ] and all diphthongs are [tense].

The use of these features in specifying vowels is shown in Figure 10.2. The semivowels /j/ and /w/ have the same feature specification as their corresponding vowels /i/ and /u/. Semivowels and vowels are distinguished by their position in the syllable, rather than by features.

Stress and intonation are important aspects of English. Current thinking is that they are not best analysed as features. Chapter 16 discusses these aspects of language in greater detail.

FEATURE GEOMETRY

Features have always been an important part of phonetic work. During this century, they have assumed an increasingly important role in phonology as well. From an incidental aspect of a phonological description, they have become the core.

HISTORY In *Preliminaries to Speech Analysis* (1952), Jakobson, Fant, and Halle proposed some 13 features to account for all contrasts in all languages. These features had both articulatory and acoustic definitions and were all binary.

Later research (for example, Ladefoged, 1964, in particular) showed that this small number of features was quite inadequate.

Building on the work of Jakobson, Fant, and Halle, Chomsky and Halle set out in *The Sound Pattern of English* (1968) a theory of features which formed the standard framework during the 1970's. For example,

$$[\text{b}] \text{ in English is} \begin{bmatrix} -\text{ continuant} \\ +\text{voiced} \\ -\text{nasal} \end{bmatrix}$$

The specification [–continuant] distinguishes [b] from [v]; the specification [+voiced] distinguishes [b] from [p]; and the specification [–nasal] distinguishes [b] from [m]. A full feature specification of [b] would include many other features; Chomsky and Halle discuss about 30 features. This example, however, gives a notion of how their features can be used. Note that features belonging to the same segment are enclosed in the same pair of brackets. The order of the features in the Chomsky–Halle theory is irrelevant:

$$\begin{bmatrix} +\text{ voiced} \\ -\text{nasal} \end{bmatrix} = \begin{bmatrix} -\text{ nasal} \\ +\text{ voiced} \end{bmatrix}.$$

Chomsky-Halle features are defined only in articulatory terms. All features are binary except for stress and tone, which can be multivalued. Because of the enormous amount of phonetic and phonological literature in existence which uses the Chomsky–Halle features, they are presented in Appendix D to help you when you encounter them in other reading.

RECENT THEORY   In the past few years, a number of proposals usually known as **feature geometry** have been put forward which differ substantially from the Chomsky-Halle theory set out in 1968. At the moment, there is no consensus as to the exact form this new theory should take (Clements, 1985; McCarthy, 1988).

Although feature geometry incorporates many of the insights of its predecessors, it differs from the Chomsky-Halle theory in that a segment has an internal structure, with some features more closely related to each other than to other features. A segment is not simply an unordered group of features as in the Chomsky–Halle theory. Also, in feature geometry, features are not necessarily binary. Feature geometry allows unary and multivalued features as well.

In this chapter, we will examine how feature geometry can be applied to the sounds of English. As we study non-English sounds in later chapters, the appropriate features will be introduced there.

In presenting features in this book, I have attempted to give you one possibility of how a theory of feature geometry might be structured. Much of the rationale for adopting one position or another depends on phonological rather than phonetic evidence and thus is beyond the scope of this book. As well, current theoretical

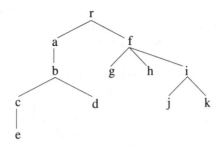

Figure 10.3 Tree with nodes.

thinking on feature geometry is very much in flux, and I fully expect that you may disagree with some of my choices.

HIERARCHICAL STRUCTURE We consider each segment to be represented by a hierarchical structure known as a **tree**. Each point on the tree is called a **node**. The top node is called the **root node**. All other nodes depend from (are connected to) a higher node. A single node may have more than one dependent nodes, but no node is directly connected to more than one higher node. In Figure 10.3, *r* is the root node; *a* and *f* are daughter nodes of *r* ; *c* has only one daughter node *e*.

GENERAL STRUCTURE OF ENGLISH FEATURE TREES The features we have developed can be arranged as a tree shown in Figure 10.4. Note that some nodes are features: [voiceless], [coronal], [consonantal]. Other nodes, shown in italics, are categories: *laryngeal, place*. The root node itself consists of the major class features [consonantal] and [sonorant]. The features [continuant], [nasal], and [lateral] are dependent directly from the root node.

The feature [round] is dependent from the feature [labial]; the implication of this is that a segment that is specified for [round] must also be specified for

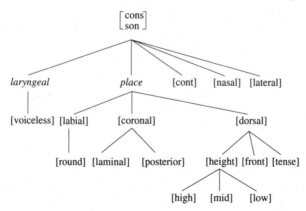

Figure 10.4 Feature tree for English.

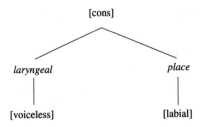

Figure 10.5 Feature specification of /p/.

[labial]. The features [laminal] and [posterior] apply only to [coronal] and are thus dependent from that feature.

The features for vowels are dependent from the feature [dorsal]. The most forward vowel we can make is [i] in the palatal area; the most retracted vowel is [ɑ] with the dorsum low. The feature [dorsal] includes all articulations within the palatal and dorso-velar areas; thus, vowels fall under the feature [dorsal]. Recall that [height] is a multivalued feature; a vowel is either [high], [mid], or [low]. Tense is a very controversial feature as we shall see in Chapter 11; it is placed under [dorsal] since it applies only to vowels.

ENGLISH SEGMENTS IN FEATURES

We have seen how the overall feature tree for English works; we will now look at trees appropriate for specific segments. Consider the segment [p]; its tree is shown as Figure 10.5. The root node consists of [consonantal]. Since it is voiceless, we must specify both *laryngeal* and [voiceless]. The place of articulation is specified as [labial].

The tree for /p/ is very simple. Note that we do not specify irrelevant features. Since /p/ is neither [continuant] nor [nasal], those features are omitted. The large number of items under [coronal] and [dorsal] only apply when those features are chosen.

Figure 10.6 shows the specification of /b/. It is even simpler than that of /p/ since *laryngeal* and [voiceless] are omitted.

```
[cons]
  |
  |
place
  |
[labial]
```

Figure 10.6
Feature specification
of /b/.

Figures 10.7–15 show the configuration for other consonants.

Note the specification of /h/ shown in Figure 10.15. This segment is simply specified as [voiceless] and [continuant] with no place of articulation specified.

The affricates [tʃ] and [dʒ] are complicated. In one sense, they are a single segment; in another sense, they are two segments, a stop followed by a fricative. One possible way to account for this complexity is to allow the feature hierarchy to branch into two subnodes. The

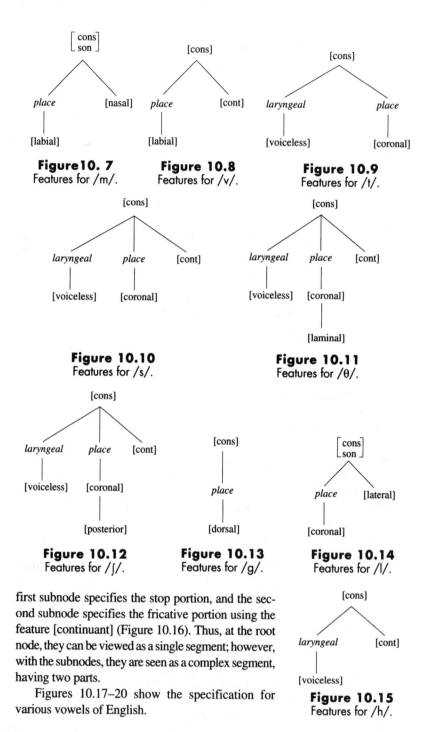

Figure 10. 7
Features for /m/.

Figure 10.8
Features for /v/.

Figure 10.9
Features for /t/.

Figure 10.10
Features for /s/.

Figure 10.11
Features for /θ/.

Figure 10.12
Features for /ʃ/.

Figure 10.13
Features for /g/.

Figure 10.14
Features for /l/.

first subnode specifies the stop portion, and the second subnode specifies the fricative portion using the feature [continuant] (Figure 10.16). Thus, at the root node, they can be viewed as a single segment; however, with the subnodes, they are seen as a complex segment, having two parts.

Figures 10.17–20 show the specification for various vowels of English.

Figure 10.15
Features for /h/.

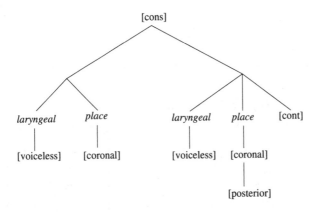

Figure 10.16 The feature specification of the affricate /tʃ/.

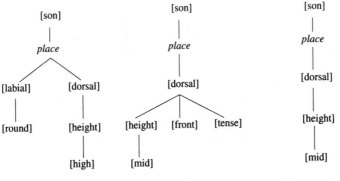

Figure 10.17
Features for /ʊ/.

Figure 10.18
Features for /e/.

Figure 10.19
Features for /ə/.

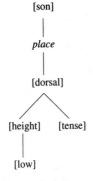

Figure 10.20
Features for /a/.

THE FEATURE SPECIFICATION OF A WORD

We will illustrate how a word is specified in features with the word *fin* [fɪn]. The root nodes of each segment are aligned in a row. This row is known as the the **root tier**. Each slot on the root tier is known as the **root node**. In Figure 10.21, the root nodes are represented as solid circles, and the root tier as a horizontal line.

The specification for each segment of *fin* then is shown as a plane hanging from its root node (Figure 10.22).

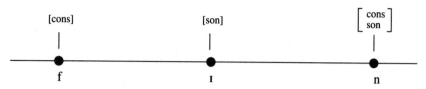

Figure 10.21 The root tier for fin.

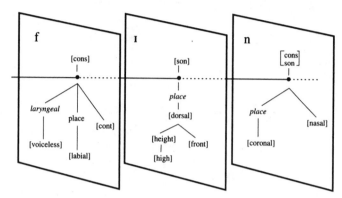

Figure 10.22 The features for fin.

TECHNICAL TERMS

binary
contrast
discrete
feature
feature geometry
frication

major class features
multivalued
natural class
natural process
node

opposition
root node
root tier
segment
unary

FEATURES

consonantal
continuant
coronal
dependent
dorsal
front

height [high mid low]
labial
laminal
lateral
nasal

posterior
round
sonorant
tense
voiceless

EXERCISES

BASIC

1. Draw feature trees for the following English segments:
   /d k f ð z ʒ ɹ n ŋ dʒ/ (Consider /ɹ/ to be the approximant equivalent of /ʒ/.)
   /ɪ æ a u o ʌ ɔ/ Remember that /a o ɔ/ only occur in diphthongs.

2. Draw the appropriate structure to show the features in the word *flaps.*
3. Draw trees for the vowels in French. Review Chapter 7 if you need to. (Hint: consider the lower-mid vowels /ɛ ɔ œ ɛ̃ œ̃ ɔ̃ ə/ as non-tense).

ADVANCED

4. Practise the following:
   Try these slowly at first. Pay attention to the stresses.
   ˈsɪpɛˌŋowʌgæ
   kʌˈθɪtuˌnihɑ
   ˌmɛlʊˈʃobɛˌvi
   ɹiˌjekɔˈʒæbʊ
   ˌfudɑˌŋeɹʊˈðæ

5. Transcribe the following:
   It was a stark and dormy night; the streakers ran from hall to hall (for it is on a university campus that our scene lies), except at occasional intervals when they were checked by security officers who were rattled and fiercely agitated by the inflaming sight of the rain-streaked, flashing white, yellow, and black bodies, the last-named seen only in the scant, intermittent alabaster illumination by the now-and-then bursts of lightning.

CHAPTER ELEVEN
VOWELS AND SEMIVOWELS

IN CHAPTERS 1–7 of this book, we examined the sounds of English from an articulatory point of view. In Chapters 8–10, we added acoustic analysis and distinctive features to our descriptive repertoire. In this section, we start over and examine the entire range of sounds found in human language, looking at them in both articulatory and acoustic terms.

Acoustic research is considerably less well developed than articulatory work, particularly for the less common phenomena. Sometimes in the following chapters, I have not been able to say much about the acoustic aspects of certain phenomena because of a lack of unambiguous evidence.

In this chapter you will learn about:
- cardinal vowels
- problems in vowel description
- additional vowel qualities
- glides and diphthongs.

VOWELS

Vowels are traditionally described along three dimensions: **height, backness**, and **rounding**. Height and backness are used to describe the shape of the tongue, usually by indicating the highest point of the tongue. As we have seen for English, the tongue may be bunched so that its highest point is near the palate, for a vowel [i], or drawn back and down so that the highest point is low and back, as for [ɑ]. Vowels lying between **front** and **back** are called **central** vowels; those lying between **high** and **low** are called **mid**. A vowel right in the centre of the vowel area is thus a **mid central** vowel. We can use **higher high, lower high, higher mid, lower mid, higher low, lower low** if we need to distinguish more than three heights.

Rounding is the third dimension of vowel production; it refers to the shape of the lips. We have seen that in English, the vowels [u ʊ o ɔ] are rounded and that all other vowels are unrounded. In Chapter 7, we learned that French has both

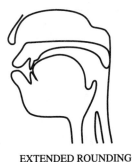 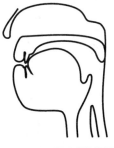

EXTENDED ROUNDING   RETRACTED ROUNDING

Figure 11.1 Lip rounding. Extended rounding is found with back vowels and retracted rounding with front vowels.

rounded and unrounded front vowels. In fact, any vowel can have the lips rounded or unrounded; languages, however, tend to prefer low unrounded vowels, and for the non-low vowels, front unrounded and back rounded.

If you say [u ʊ o] while looking at your lips in a mirror, you will see that there is more rounding for the higher vowels and less as the vowels get lower. The English diphthong [ow] glides from mid to high, and the rounding increases accordingly. Languages differ as to the degree of rounding, but in a particular language, high vowels are generally more rounded than the lower ones.

Ordinarily, the lower jaw is lowered as we go from the higher to the lower vowels. You can, however, verify that jaw opening is not essential for producing different vowels. If you clench a pencil between your teeth, you will find that you are still able to produce a fairly good series of vowels — [i e ɛ æ ɑ ɔ o u]. You can see that tongue and jaw movement are independent of each other. The tongue can compensate if the jaw is immobilised.

Languages with both front and back rounded vowels often make the rounding slightly differently for the two types (Figure 11.1). In back rounded vowels, e.g., [u o ɔ], the lips are extended and the sides drawn in to form a short tube. With front rounded vowels, e.g., [y ø œ], the lips are rolled slightly inwards, leaving a narrow opening in the middle.

CARDINAL VOWELS

The most precise system used by phoneticians for describing vowels is the **cardinal vowel system**, elaborated by Daniel Jones and adopted by the **International Phonetic Association (IPA)**. This system arbitrarily picks certain vowels as basic or **cardinal** and describes all other vowels in terms of their relationship to these cardinal vowels.

The illustration in Figure 11.2 defines the extreme limits of vowel production. The black dots show the tongue position of the highest point of the tongue for Cardinal Vowel [i], the highest and farthest front vowel that you can

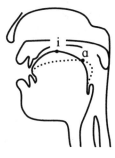 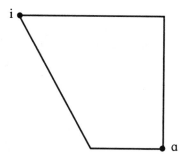

Figure 11.2 The extreme limits of vowel production.

Figure 11.3 The Cardinal Vowel quadilateral.

make and the highest point of the tongue for Cardinal Vowel [ɑ], the lowest and farthest back vowel that you can make.

This figure is usually altered to the stylised quadrilateral shown in Figure 11.3 The black dots again show the positions of Cardinal Vowel [i] and Cardinal Vowel [ɑ].

Figure 11.4 shows the vowel quadilateral divided equally from high to low. At each level, a vowel is shown at the extreme front and extreme back. The vowels [i] and [ɑ] define two extreme corners of the vowel continuum; the six other vowels are placed on the periphery of the chart. These eight vowels constitute the primary cardinal vowels; they are numbered from one to eight. Note that the front vowels are all equidistant from each other and that the back vowels are also all equidistant from each other. These eight cardinal vowels are not necessarily the vowels of any particular language; they are arbitrarily fixed. The interior lines of the quadrilateral are merely to facilitate the accurate placement of points within the vowel space.

We can use the cardinal vowel chart to locate any vowel. If we want to describe a particular vowel of a particular language, for example, the vowel of Canadian *hat,* someone familiar with this system listens to the sound, and relates it to the fixed cardinal vowels. The process goes something like this: 'It is a little

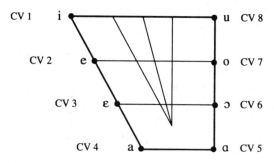

Figure 11.4 The primary cardinal vowels.

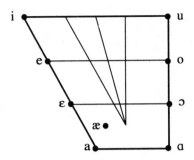

Figure 11.5 The vowel [æ].

higher than cardinal vowel [a], and a little farther back'. A dot for English [æ] can now be placed on the cardinal vowel chart as in Figure 11.5. The advantage of this system is that one person can learn and record a vowel on a chart, and another person, seeing this chart with no further information, can reproduce it quite accurately. Experiments have shown a high degree of accuracy in using this system (Ladefoged, 1967).

Although the pronunciation of the cardinal vowels is best learned from someone already familiar with them, you can make a fairly close approximation by noting the following observations. Several of the French vowels are very close to cardinal vowel positions: in particular [i e ɛ a ɑ] (*vie, thé, mettre, patte, pâte*). RP speakers have a vowel close to cardinal [ɔ] in *law*. Cardinal [o u] are similar to the French vowels in *beau, tout,* but farther back. The French vowel qualities intended here are monophthongs, not the diphthongs found in some Canadian accents.

The cardinal vowel system terms the vowels [i e ɛ a ɑ ɔ o u] **primary** (Figure 11.4) and the vowels [y ø œ ɶ ɒ ʌ ɤ ɯ] **secondary** (Figure 11.6). The secondary vowels have the reverse rounding from the primary ones. The primary vowels are common in languages, the secondary vowels less so.

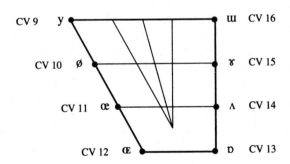

Figure 11.6 The secondary cardinal vowels.

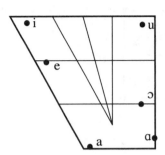

Figure 11.7 A hypothetical language with six vowels .

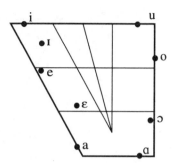

Figure 11.8 Hypothetical language with nine vowels.

Unrounded		Rounded	
Primary	Secondary	Primary	Secondary
i	ɯ	u	y
e	ɤ	o	ø
ɛ	ʌ	ɔ	œ
a			Œ
ɑ			ɒ

The English names of letters and the sounds they represent in phonetics sometimes lead to confusion. If, for example, I say [i], I may mean the sound [i], or I may mean the letter *e*. To avoid this sort of confusion, users of the cardinal vowel system often refer to the cardinal vowels by number. The vowel [ɛ] is thus 'cardinal vowel 3,' and [ʌ] is 'cardinal vowel 14'.

Cardinal vowel symbols are used in two slightly different ways. They can be used to symbolise the cardinal vowels themselves. Other vowels can be located on the chart in relation to the cardinal vowels. Alternatively, the symbols can be used in a non-cardinal sense. Suppose that we plot the vowels of some language on a cardinal vowel chart. We now want symbols for these vowels. We can attach the cardinal vowel symbols to the vowels of this language, fitting them as appropriately as possible.

If we have a six vowel system as shown in Figure 11.7, we would likely give these vowels the names as shown there. The symbols must be used so as to suggest an approximately accurate sound to the reader. We pick [e] rather than [ɛ] as the symbol for the front mid vowel because the vowel in our hypothetical language is closer to cardinal vowel [e] than to cardinal vowel [ɛ]. Similarly, we pick [ɔ], not [o].

Consider now a language with nine vowels as shown in Figure 11.8. If we assign the closest cardinal symbols to these as we did in Figure 11.7, we discover a problem. This language simply has more vowels than we have appropriate cardinal symbols. We have used [i] and also [e], but we need a symbol for a vowel between these. This situation is not uncommon in the languages of the world, and consequently, we sometimes have to resort to extra symbols. Note that these extra symbols do not represent cardinal vowels; they are usable in a general area of the vowel space, but they do not have a fixed definition as does a cardinal vowel. They are extra symbols to be used in addition to the cardinal symbols when describing a particular language. They are not to be used if an appropriate cardinal vowel symbol is available. We can now solve our problem in the language with nine vowels by symbolising the extra vowel as [ɪ].

Extra symbols with the areas where they are to be used:

[ɪ]   lower high front unrounded, between [i] and [e]
[ʏ]   lower high front rounded, between [y] and [ø]
[æ]   higher low front unrounded, between [ɛ] and [a]
[ɨ]   high central unrounded, between [i] and [ɯ]
[ʉ]   high central rounded, between [y] and [u]
[ə]   mid central unrounded
[ɵ]   mid central rounded
[ɜ]   mid central unrounded, in addition to [ə]
[ɐ]   higher low central unrounded vowel
[ʊ]   lower high back rounded, between [u] and [o]

Distinctive Features   We have discussed in Chapter 10 how the features [high, mid, low] are used for vowels.

	front	——
high	i	u
mid	e	o
low	a	ɑ

Acoustic Features   We have discussed the acoustic properties of English vowels in Chapter 10. Essentially, the first three formants indicate the quality of the vowel. F1 correlates inversely to the height of the vowel. F2 and F3 generally fall as we go from high front to low vowels and on to high back vowels. Figure 11.9 shows average frequencies of the first two formants for the cardinal vowels spoken by a male (Catford, 1988).

Unrounded	F1	F2	Rounded	F1	F2
i	240	2400	y	235	2100
e	390	2300	ø	370	1900
ɛ	610	1900	œ	585	1710
a	850	1610	ɶ	820	1530
ɑ	750	940	ɒ	700	760
ʌ	600	1170	ɔ	500	700
ɤ	460	1310	o	360	640
ɯ	300	1390	u	250	595

Figure 11.9.
Formant frequencies of the cardinal vowel.

By comparing the frequencies in Figure 11.9 for unrounded and rounded vowels, you can see that rounding has little effect on the frequency of the first formant. However, rounding quite clearly lowers the frequency of the second formant, particularly with the back vowels. This seems plausible if we recall that the front cavity generally corresponds to the second formant. Rounding, and particularly the kind of rounding used with back vowels, extends the lips, thus enlarging the front cavity and lowering the frequency of the second formant.

PROBLEMS IN THE DESCRIPTION OF VOWELS

In several publications Ladefoged (1964, 1967, 1971, 1982) has pointed out problems in the way we describe vowels. Essentially, the articulatory, acoustic, and cardinal vowel descriptions do not completely agree with each other. He has demonstrated this with the vowels of Ngwe, an African language. Ladefoged says that the Ngwe vowels are fairly close to the cardinal vowel positions. Thus, what we find out about the phonetic quality of Ngwe vowels should apply to cardinal vowels as well. X–rays were taken of a Ngwe speaker producing the vowels; tracings of these are shown in Figure 11.10. From these tracings, the highest point of the tongue can be determined. Figure 11.11 shows the acoustic pattern with the first and second formants plotted so as to arrange the vowel in a pattern similar to that of the highest point of the tongue. Since the Ngwe vowels are auditorially close to the cardinal vowels, they appear at each of the cardinal points in Figure 11.12.

We can see that neither the articulatory description (from X-rays, Figure 11.10), nor the acoustic description (formants, Figure 11.11), nor the cardinal

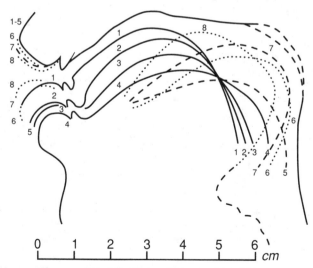

Figure 11.10   X-rays of the vowels of Ngwe.
(Ladefoged, 1964; by permission)

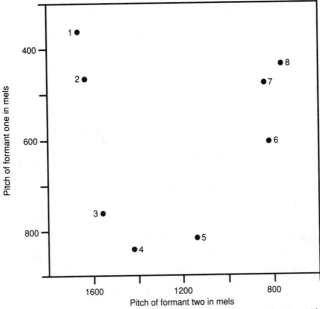

Figure 11.11   Ngwe vowels. F1 plotted against F2 in mels. See Chapter 17 for an explanation of mels. (Ladefoged, 1964; by permission)

vowel chart (Figure 11.12) totally agrees with any of the others. From the X-rays, the front vowels are generally in a line and fairly evenly spaced, but the acoustic analysis shows a large distance between [e] and [ɛ]. The back vowels are worse; they are not in a row, not evenly spaced, and the highest point of the tongue for [u] is considerably farther to the front in the X-ray than on the acoustic display.

It is possible that phoneticians using the cardinal vowel system do not use it in an articulatory fashion, but in an acoustic fashion. That is, they learn the formants of the cardinal vowels and compare any other vowel to those formants. Lieberman and Blumstein (1988) have argued that fundamentally we have an auditory image of a vowel and that we do what is necessary with our vocal tract to produce such a sound. Our previous experiment which showed that we can produce reasonable vowels with a pencil clenched in our teeth is evidence supporting their argument. Normally, we move the jaw in making vowels; such motion has an effect on positioning the tongue. If that motion is impossible, we use our auditory image of what a vowel should sound like to guide the positioning of our tongue so as to produce as similar a sound as possible.

Users of the cardinal vowel system have, however, maintained that they are making articulatory comparisons. Whatever the truth may be, the traditional cardinal vowel chart is a kind of representation which does work psychologically to allow phoneticians to place a vowel in a visual space.

At the moment, we have no explanation which satisfactorily resolves the discrepancies between our articulatory, acoustic, and auditory observations.

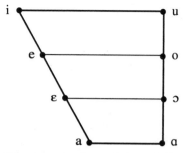

Figure 11.12   A cardinal vowel chart of the Ngwe vowels.

ADDITIONAL VOWEL QUALITIES

In addition to the main dimensions of height, backness, and rounding, vowels may have additional qualities.

NASALISATION   In producing a **nasalised** vowel, the velum is lowered, and air passes out through the nose. Nasalisation is shown by a **tilde** /ˈtɪldə/ [˜]. We have encountered nasalised vowels already in French (Chapter 7). Yoruba (/ˈjɔɹəbə/; Nigeria, West Africa) also has nasalised vowels.

fi	use	ijafĩ	wife	ijɛ̃	that
ɔbɔ	monkey	ibɔ	gun	w̃ɔ̃	they
su	scatter seed	sũ	push	mɛrĩ	four

Yoruba

Chinantec /ˈtʃɪnɑnˌtɛk/, a language of South America, is reported as having three degrees of nasal vowels: oral, slightly nasal, and strongly nasal (Merrifield, 1963; Ladefoged, 1971).

| ha | *so, such* | hã | *spreads open* | hã̃ | *foam, froth* |

The Chinantec examples are interesting in two ways. First, they provide empirical data about an unusual way in which languages operate. Second, they present a theoretical problem. Our present feature system is inadequate to account for two degrees of nasality. We have no feature which can distinguish these sounds in a straightforward manner. Chinantec, however, is the only language known to have two contrastive degrees of nasality. Our dilemma is: Do we tinker with our feature system to account for a unique phenomenon, or do we consider it an anomaly and overlook it? This is one kind of problem which theoretical phoneticians grapple with. As for us, we will have to be content with noting the problem and continuing on without being able to use features to account for the nasals of Chinantec.

Distinctive Features   Nasalised vowels are specified [nasal].

RHOTACISATION   In English, **rhotacisation** /ˌɹotəsɪˈzejʃən/ is formed by curling the tip of the tongue to the back of the alveolar ridge (some people retract the tip into the body of the tongue and move the front of the tongue towards the back of the alveolar ridge). English /əɹ/ is a **rhotacised** /ˈɹowtəˌsajzd/ or **rhotic**

/ˈɹowtɪk/ vowel. Phonetically, this is a single segment [ɚ], although we have analysed it phonemically as a sequence /əɹ/.

Any vowel can be rhotacised although it is slightly more difficult to curl the tongue tip with high front vowels. In rhotacised vowels, there is often a hollowing of the body of the tongue which is not present with non-rhotacised vowels. Rhotacised vowels can be symbolised with a postposed diacritic, *e.g.,* [ɑ˞, o˞, u˞, ɚ]. You can hear for yourself that this sound is a single segment because it can be sustained in its articulation: [ɚɚɚɚɚɚɚɚɚ]. It does not require a sequence [əəəəɹɹɹɹ].

Distinctive features   There is no distinctive vowel feature for rhotacisation since it can always be analysed phonemically as a sequence: vowel + /ɹ/.

Acoustic features   As shown in Figure 11.13, the presence of rhotacisation causes a lowering of the third formant.

EXPANDED   In many languages of West Africa, the vowels are divided into two sets. In Akan (/əˈkɑn/, Ghana; Lindau, 1978), for example, Set A consists of [i e o u], and Set B consists of [ɪ ɛ ɔ ʊ]. These vowels sets contrast: [fí] 'leave' and [fɪ] 'vomit'. Akan also shows vowel harmony in that any particular word will have only vowels of Set A or only vowels of set B. Thus, we find [òfí] 'he leaves', but [ɔ̀fɪ] 'he vomits', where the third singular prefix [ò ~ ɔ̀] harmonises with the following vowel; similarly, [mìfí] 'I leave' and [mɪ̀fɪ] 'I vomit'. There is also a low vowel [a] which does not harmonise but occurs in words with both vowel sets.

X-rays taken of speakers of Akan (Painter, 1973) have shown that the pharynx

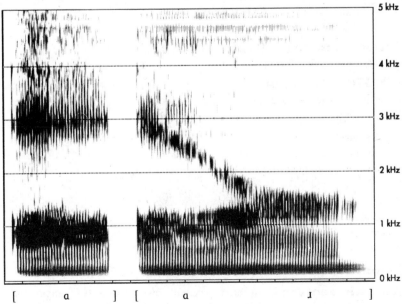

Figure 11.13   Plain and rhotacised /ɑ/.

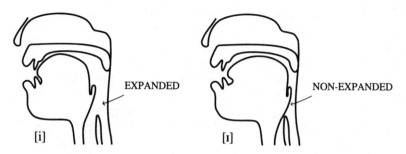

Figure 11.14 Expanded and non-expanded vowels in Akan.

is expanded for the production of the vowels of set A by moving the tongue root forward and by lowering the larynx (Figure 11.14).

Distinctive features Vowels of Set A are said to be [**expanded**] and those of Set B are not [expanded]. The term [advanced tongue root] has been suggested for this feature. I prefer Lindau's (1978) term [expanded] as it includes the lowering of the larynx.

Some phoneticians (Halle and Stevens, 1969) have suggested that such a feature be used for vowels to replace [tense] since no language requires both [tense] and [expanded] for vowels. Lindau's review of the research points out two differences between English and Akan. Unlike Akan, English speakers do not consistently lower the larynx for [tense] vowels, and further, only some speakers use tongue root movement to distinguish the two classes of vowels in English. I follow Lindau and use [expanded] for the distinction found in languages such as Akan and continue to use [tense] for the distinction found in English.

Acoustic features The larger pharyngeal cavity with [expanded] vowels gives a lowered first formant.

LENGTH Many languages have long and short varieties of the same vowel. **Length** is shown by [ː]; a single raised dot [·] can be used to indicate an intermediate degree of length. The IPA dots are really small triangles.

[ˈsapadʒ]	'fight'	[ˈsaːpadʒ]	'Sabbath'
sabaid		*sàbaid*	
[ˈahið̃]	'father'	[ˈmaːhið̃]	'mother'
athair		*màthair*	
[ənˈtul]	'the flood'	[ənˈtuːl]	'the eye'
an tuil		*an t-sùil*	

Scots Gaelic

Distinctive Features Long vowels can be specified [long].

Acoustic Features In languages with distinctive vowel length, long vowels are typically some 1.5 to 3 times longer than their short counterparts (Catford 1977).

TENSE-LAX This distinction is extremely controversial. Phonologists have frequently divided English vowels into tense–lax as we did in Chapter 4. Phoneticians however, have been unable to identify any articulatory or acoustic trait which consistently corresponds to this distinction. Generally, tense and lax have been used in two ways with vowels: of a pair of similar contrastive vowels, the higher and more peripheral one has been called tense, or, of a pair of vowels contrasting in length, the longer one has been called tense. You will recall that in Chapter 4 we justified the tense-lax distinction on distributional, not phonetic grounds. Catford (1977) has a useful discussion of this issue:

> For vowels, the existence of such a parameter [tense — lax] is dubious, and the use of tense/lax terminology in the phonetic description of vowels is seldom if ever necessary, and should be avoided. This does not mean that the tense/lax terminology is entirely useless in *phonological* description. Here, tense and lax may, perhaps, be usefully employed as labels to designate phonetically arbitrary classes of vowels that happen to be phonologically distinct. But it should then be made quite clear that the selection of terms may be phonetically vacuous.

The term [tense] is clearly unsatisfactory. For some languages, such as English, it is, however, extremely useful. For the time being, it seems best to keep it, recognising its inadequacies. (See also the discussion on [expanded] above.)

SEMIVOWELS

A semivowel, or glide, is a moving vowel. Semivowels always occur next to a vowel. Thus [ɑj] in Figure 11.15 starts at the position of [ɑ] and moves to [i]. Similarly [jɑ] starts at [i] and moves to an [ɑ] position. The end of the glide in [ɑj] or the beginning of the glide in [jɑ] is so quick that we often cannot specify with certainty the exact point on a vowel chart.

In principle, any vowel position can be used for a glide. A subscript cap [̯] is used to show lack of syllabicity, *i.e.,* to change a vowel symbol to that of a glide, as in [ə̯ ɛ̯ ʌ̯]. Four glides [i̯ u̯ y̯ ɯ̯] are so common that they have their own symbols: [j w ɥ ɰ]. The symbol [ʍ] can be used for a voiceless [w].

Many authors write diphthongs as two vowels, as [ai] or [aɪ], rather than [aj]. Such transcriptions can obviously be converted to our system if we know whether [a] or [i] is the glide. Since [j] and [w] are common glides, but [a̯] is not, we rarely have difficulty with such transcriptions. A problem could arise, however, with a transcription such as [ui], since this could reasonably represent either [wi] or [uj].

Diphthongs with the sequence glide–vowel, as in [ja wɛ] are called **rising** diphthongs; those with the sequence vowel–glide, as in [aj ɛw], are called **falling** diphthongs. Note that falling and rising refer to prominence, not to vowel height. The glide is short and fleeting; by contrast, the vowel is longer and much more prominent.

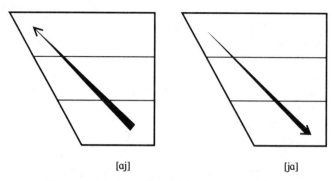

[ɑj]   [jɑ]

Figure 11.15 The diphthongs [ɑj] and [jɑ].

When two successive vowel sounds belong to different syllables, they are represented by two vowel symbols (and no glide). For example, in the English word *idea* can be pronounced [ˌajˈdiə], the first syllable contains a falling diphthong [aj], but the sequence [iə] is not a diphthong, but is represented by two vowel symbols, one for each syllable. Vowels and semivowels often alternate with each other depending on stress and speed of speech. For *idea*, both [ˌajˈdiə ˌajˈdijə] are possible pronunciations.

As we will see in Chapter 16, we do not distinguish semivowels by features, rather by their position in the syllable. Vowels always form the nucleus of a syllable and glides either precede or follow the vowel.

VOWEL SYSTEMS

The smallest known vowel systems have three vowels. Cree (/kɹi/; Canada) has a triangular pattern, whereas Adygh (Caucasus, USSR) has a linear pattern.

<table>
<tr><td>i   u</td><td>ɨ</td></tr>
<tr><td></td><td>ə</td></tr>
<tr><td>a</td><td>a</td></tr>
<tr><td>Cree</td><td>Adygh</td></tr>
</table>

Inuktitut (/ɪˈnʊktɪtʊt/; Canada, Greenland, Alaska) has a three-vowel pattern plus length, giving six vowels.

<table>
<tr><td>i   u</td><td>iː   uː</td></tr>
<tr><td>a</td><td>aː</td></tr>
</table>

Inuit

Some languages such as Margi (/ˌmɑːɹˈgi/; Africa) and Campa (/kɑmpɑ/, Peru) have four vowels:

```
    i   u                    i
    ə                        e   o
        a                        a
      Margi                    Campa
```

Five-vowel systems are by far the commonest, particularly with a V-shape.

```
    i   u          ɪ    ʊ          i y   u
    ɛ o            ɛ    ɔ              ɤ
    a              a                a
   Ainu          Yiddish      Mandarin Chinese
/ˈajnu/; Japan, USSR
```

Beembe (Congo) takes a five-vowel system, adds length and nasalisation, ending up with fifteen vowels.

```
    i   u          i:   u:          ĩ    ũ
    ɛ   ɔ          ɛ:   ɔ:          ɛ̃   ɔ̃
    a              a:               ã
                 Beembe
```

Systems with larger numbers of vowels occur. The V-shape seven-vowel system, found in Italian, is particularly common. The following examples show some of the variation found in various languages.

```
    i  u            i        u          i y ɯ u
    e  i            e        o          ɛ œ    ɔ
    a  ɑ            ɛ        ɔ              ɑ
                        a
 Persian (Iran)      Italian            Turkish
```

```
    i y  ɯ ʊ              i y  u
    ø o                   e ø  o
    ɛ                     ɛ œ  ɔ ɛ̃ œ̃ ɔ̃ ã
    a ɑ                   a   ɑ
  Azerbaijani              French
(/ˌæzəɹˌbajˈdʒɑni/)
```

Alsatian (/ˌælˈsejʃən/) German appears to take the Guinness prize for the most vowels, with ten short vowels and eleven long vowels.

```
    i y                       i: y:
    ɪ         ʊ               ɪ:        ʊ:
    e ø       o               e: ø:     o:
      œ                       ɛ: œ:
    a         ɑ               a:        ɒ:
                Alsatian German
```

TECHNICAL TERMS

back	higher	lower
backness	height	mid
cardinal vowel	International Phonetic	nasalised
cardinal vowel system	Association	primary vowel
central	International Phonetic	rhotacised
expanded	Alphabet	rising diphthong
falling diphthong	IPA	rounding
front	length	secondary vowel
high	low	tilde

EXERCISES
BASIC

1. Cardinal vowels should be learned from someone who knows them; however, you can approximate the primary vowels from the following descriptions:
   - [i] the highest completely front unrounded vowel which you can pronounce without making any audible friction
   - [e] something like the French vowel in *épée, fée*
   - [ɛ] something like the French vowel in *bête, faite*
   - [a] the lowest completely front unrounded vowel that you can make
   - [ɑ] the lowest completely back unrounded vowel that you can make. Think of saying [ɑ] in the doctor's office.
   - [ɔ] something like the French vowel in *code, note*
   - [o] something like the French vowel in *faut, eau*
   - [u] the highest completely back rounded vowel that you can make

   In all the following exercises in the rest of this book, the symbols have the value of cardinal vowels, unless otherwise specificed such as when a specific language is mentioned.
   Try saying first just the front vowels:

       i   e   ɛ   a

   Say them with a steady pitch and no glide. Ending the vowel with a sudden glottal stop can be useful in learning not to introduce a glide: [iiiiiʔ].
   Now say them with the consonant [p]:

       pi   pe   pɛ   pa

   Now say them with the following consonants: [f θ k n l b]:

   e.g.: fi   fe   fɛ   fa   etc.

2. Now try the back vowels. Remember that they are rounded except for [ɑ].

       u   o   ɔ   ɑ

   Try them now with the consonant [t]:

       tu   to   tɔ   tɑ

   Try them with other consonants: [z d m ð v g]

   e.g.: zu   zo   zɔ   zɑ

3. Now try all the primary vowels together. Be sure not to rush, saying each one clearly.

i	e	ɛ	a	ɑ	ɔ	o	u

Try other orders:

i	ɛ	e	a	u	ɔ	o	ɑ
i	u	e	o	ɛ	ɔ	a	ɑ
ɑ	a	ɔ	ɛ	o	e	u	i
i	ɑ	e	ɑ	ɛ	ɑ	a	ɑ
u	ɑ	o	ɑ	ɔ	ɑ	i	ɑ
i	a	e	a	ɛ	a	ɑ	a
u	a	o	a	ɔ	a	ɑ	a

4. Now try the secondary vowels. These are made by reversing the rounding of the primary vowels. For example, to make [y], say [i] and round your lips. To make [ɯ], say [u], and unround your lips. Make sure that the position of your tongue does not move while you are changing the rounding.

Round	[i]	to get	[y]
	[e]		[ø]
	[ɛ]		[œ]
	[a]		[Œ]
	[ɑ]		[ɒ]
Unround	[u]	to get	[ɯ]
	[o]		[ɤ]
	[ɔ]		[ʌ]

5. Practise these:

i	e	ɛ	a	ɑ	ɔ	o	u
y	œ	ø	Œ	ɒ	ʌ	ɤ	ɯ
ɯ	ɤ	ʌ	ɒ	Œ	œ	ø	u
i	e	ɛ	a	ɑ	ʌ	ɤ	ɯ
ɯ	ɤ	ʌ	ɑ	a	ɛ	e	i
u	o	ɔ	ɒ	Œ	œ	ø	y
y	ø	œ	Œ	ɒ	ɔ	o	u

6. Try the following exercises (Try them in both horizontal and vertical orders.):

zi	zy	fi	fy	pi	py	li	ly
ne	nø	ʃe	ʃø	ðe	ðø	ke	kø
dɛ	dœ	fɛ	fœ	ŋɛ	ŋœ	jɛ	jœ
va	vŒ	la	lŒ	ha	hŒ	ʒa	ʒŒ
mɑ	mɒ	bɑ	bɒ	ðɑ	ðɒ	kɑ	kɒ
ɹɔ	ɹʌ	tʃɔ	tʃʌ	zɔ	zʌ	nɔ	nʌ
ŋo	ŋɤ	ʔo	ʔɤ	do	dɤ	ʃo	ʃɤ
ɹu	ɹɯ	θu	θɯ	ʒu	ʒɯ	lu	lɯ

7. Diphthongs. In the following chart, the first symbol is a vowel and the second is a glide; *i.e.,* [ai] is the same as our usual [aj].
Make the following carefully, listening to the differences:

  ai   ae   aɛ   aɔ   ao   au

In practising the diphthongs in the following table try doing them in different patterns: across, down, diagonal — the hot-dogging diphthongist will, of course, develop fancier patterns.

ei	ɛi	ai	ɑi	ɔi	oi	ui	yi	øi	œi	Œi	ɒi	ʌi	ɤi	ɯi
ie	ɛe	ae	ɑe	ɔe	oe	ue	ye	øe	œe	Œe	ɒe	ʌe	ɤe	ɯe
iɛ	eɛ	aɛ	ɑɛ	ɔɛ	oɛ	uɛ	yɛ	øɛ	œɛ	Œɛ	ɒɛ	ʌɛ	ɤɛ	ɯɛ
ia	ea	ɛa	ɑa	ɔa	oa	ua	ya	øa	œa	Œa	ɒa	ʌa	ɤa	ɯa
iɑ	eɑ	ɛɑ	aɑ	ɔɑ	oɑ	uɑ	yɑ	øɑ	œɑ	Œɑ	ɒɑ	ʌɑ	ɤɑ	ɯɑ
iɔ	eɔ	ɛɔ	aɔ	ɑɔ	oɔ	uɔ	yɔ	øɔ	œɔ	Œɔ	ɒɔ	ʌɔ	ɤɔ	ɯɔ
io	eo	ɛo	ao	ɑo	ɔo	uo	yo	øo	œo	Œo	ɒo	ʌo	ɤo	ɯo
iu	eu	ɛu	au	ɑu	ɔu	ou	yu	øu	œu	Œu	ɒu	ʌu	ɤu	ɯu
iy	ey	ɛy	ay	ɑy	ɔy	oy	uy	øy	œy	Œy	ɒy	ʌy	ɤy	ɯy
iø	eø	ɛø	aø	ɑø	ɔø	oø	uø	yø	œø	Œø	ɒø	ʌø	ɤø	ɯø
iœ	eœ	ɛœ	aœ	ɑœ	ɔœ	oœ	uœ	yœ	øœ	Œœ	ɒœ	ʌœ	ɤœ	ɯœ
iŒ	eŒ	ɛŒ	aŒ	ɑŒ	ɔŒ	oŒ	uŒ	yŒ	øŒ	œŒ	ɒŒ	ʌŒ	ɤŒ	ɯŒ
iɒ	eɒ	ɛɒ	aɒ	ɑɒ	ɔɒ	oɒ	uɒ	yɒ	øɒ	œɒ	Œɒ	ʌɒ	ɤɒ	ɯɒ
iʌ	eʌ	ɛʌ	aʌ	ɑʌ	ɔʌ	oʌ	uʌ	yʌ	øʌ	œʌ	Œʌ	ɒʌ	ɤʌ	ɯʌ
iɤ	eɤ	ɛɤ	aɤ	ɑɤ	ɔɤ	oɤ	uɤ	yɤ	øɤ	œɤ	Œɤ	ɒɤ	ʌɤ	ɯɤ
iɯ	eɯ	ɛɯ	aɯ	ɑɯ	ɔɯ	oɯ	uɯ	yɯ	øɯ	œɯ	Œɯ	ɒɯ	ʌɯ	ɤɯ

Try the following:

  iə̰   eə̰   ɛə̰   aə̰   ɑə̰   ɔə̰   oə̰   uə̰
  yə̰   øə̰   œə̰   Œə̰   ɒə̰   ʌə̰   ɤə̰   ɯə̰

8. Try saying a sequence of [ŋŋŋgaaŋŋŋgaaŋŋŋgaɑ]. Each time you make the transition from [ŋ] to [g] or from [ɑ] to [ŋ], try to feel the velum going up or down.
Try this also with [nnndaannndaannndaɑ] and [mmmbaammmbaammmbaɑ].
Now try [dndndndn bmbmbmbm ɡŋɡŋɡŋɡŋ].
Try saying a nasal vowel and then an oral one:

  [ɑ̃ɑ̃ɑ̃ɑ̃ɑ̃] [ɑɑɑɑɑ].

See if you can alternate them:

  [ɑ ɑ̃ ɑ ɑ̃ ɑ ɑ̃ ɑ ɑ̃ ɑ ɑ̃]

Try this with other vowels: [i ĩ ɛ ɛ̃ u ũ], etc.
Practice:

bɑ	bɑ̃	lɛ	lɛ̃	dɔ	dɔ̃	ka	kɑ̃	gi	gĩ	lo	lõ
ɑsɑ̃	õfo	uʒũ	ɛ̃θɛ	bɛlõ		θẽvɔ		ɹitɔ̃		gõzɑ̃	
sĩða	dũʒɑ	pẽθɑ̃	fuʃẽ								

9. Practise the nasal vowels in Gã (/gã/; Ghana). High tone is marked [´], and mid tone is unmarked.

ʃi	to knock	ʃĩ	to leave	ké	if	kɛ̃́	certainly
ka	to hammer	kã	to lie (on the ground)				
kɔ	grass door	kɔ̃	to bite	fũ	to moulder	fu	to smell

10. Practise nasal vowels in Ijo (Nigeria). Note the nasal glide [ȷ̃].

sãlo:	gills	afãfã	a type of tree	tũ	sing	ɔ̃ȷ̃ãȷ̃ã	horse
ĩ:	yes	tɔ̃:mɔ̃:	liken	bẽĩ	be full		
ow̃ẽȷ̃	bite	sɔ̃r̃ɔ̃	five	ʊmba:	breath		

11. Practise the long vowels in Gã. High tone is marked [´], low tone is marked [`], and mid tone is unmarked.

pì	welcome	pì:	many	ba	come	bà:	leaf
tɔ̀	bottle	tɔ:	to be replete	kò	certain	kò:	forest
bú	hole	bú:	mosquito net				

12. Practise the following long vowels and consonants from Icelandic. Remember that long sounds are held longer; they are not two separate articulations.

lɛ:pja	lick	be:tʰrɔ	better
skrø:kʰva	tell a lie	tʰvɪ:svar	twice
fɪn:ɔ	find	pʰɔb:ɪ	daddy
haʰt:ʏr	hat	fɪm:ɔ	five

13. Practise the following vowel sequences, not diphthongs from Gã. Give the vowels equal weight.

bíɛ	here	káò	sweet biscuit	àbéó	mishap	kùè	neck
wùò	fishing	àkúa	girl's name	ebiɔ	he asks	ehoɔ	he cooks

14. Practise the rounded glides in Gã. For [ɥ], try saying [j] with your lips rounded.

wè	house	wɛ	to stop	wo	honey
ɥi	to avoid	ɥɛ	to cohabit	ɥere	to sit by the fire

15. Transcribe:

There was a certain mysterious presence to Aunt Maude; she did nothing but sit in front of the television for days on end and then, on Thursday night, we discovered she was dead and had been dead so long she had mummified; and then we understood why we always watched the same channel week after week after dreary week.

ADVANCED

16. Practise gliding from one vowel to another; go slowly enough to hear the intermediate vowels:

Start with [i] and gradually move through [e ɛ] to [a]:   [i e ɛ a]

— Do the same with [u] through [o ɔ] to [ɑ]:   [u o ɔ ɒ]

— Start with [y] and glide to [œ]: [y ø œ ɶ]
— Start with [ɯ] and glide to [ɑ]: [ɯ ɤ ʌ ɑ]

Now go from [a] to [i]

— from [ɒ] to [u]
— from [ɶ] to [y]
— from [ɑ] to [ɯ]

17. Practise sliding from [i] to [a] and back, and from [u] to [ɒ] and back. Now try going only from [i] to [e] and back. Do this several times, going slowly enough to hear the intermediate vowels. Try to keep the speed even.
Do the same thing for each of the following intervals:

[e — ɛ]   [ɛ — a]   [u — o]   [o — ɔ]   [ɔ — ɒ]

18. Practise again the interval [i — e]. Slide back and forth several times, and try to locate the vowel position which feels exactly half-way between [i] and [e]. Call it [i˕]. The diacritic [˕] is used to show a value slightly lower than the usual value. Now, say the sequence [i i˕ e i˕ i i˕ e]. Repeat this several times.
Repeat this procedure for the other intervals:

e	e˕	ɛ	e˕	e	e˕	ɛ	e
ɛ	ɛ˕	a	ɛ˕	ɛ	ɛ˕	a	ɛ
u	u˕	o	u˕	u	u˕	o	u
o	ɔ˕	ɔ	ɔ˕	o	ɔ˕	ɔ	o
ɔ	ɔ˕	ɒ	ɔ˕	ɔ	ɔ˕	ɒ	ɔ

Repeat each of these several times.
Now try this:

i	i˕	e	e˕	ɛ	ɛ˕	a	a	ɛ˕	ɛ	e˕	e	i˕	i
u	u˕	o	o˕	ɔ	ɔ˕	ɒ	ɒ	ɔ˕	ɔ	o˕	o	u˕	u

Note that the IPA provides special symbols for some of these in-between vowels. The symbol [ɪ] can be used for any vowel lying anywhere between cardinal vowel [i] and [e]. Thus we could have replaced [i˕] with [ɪ]. Similarly, [æ] can be used for any vowel between [a] and [ɛ], and [ʊ] for any vowel between [o] and [u]. I have not included any secondary vowels here, but there is a symbol [ʏ] for any vowel between [y] and [ø].
We could alternatively symbolise the exercise as:

i	ɪ	e	e˕	ɛ	æ	a
u	ʊ	o	o˕	ɔ	ɔ˕	ɒ

19. Many speakers of Canadian French have diphthongs instead of certain of the monophthongs presented in Chapter 7. The following exercises illustrate both monophthongs and diphthongs.

[iː]

mirer	miːre	'look at'	*dealer*	diːle	'deal (v.)'

[ɪj]

| *deal* | dɪjl | 'deal (n.)' | *fige* | fɪjʒ | 'congeals' |
| *mise* | mɪjz | 'wagers' | | | |

[ɤɥ]

| *juge* | ʒɤɥʒ | 'judges' | *abouse* | abɤyz | 'abuses' |
| *pure* | pɤyr | 'pure' | | | |

[ʊw]

| *bouge* | bʊwʒ | 'moves' | *ouvre* | ʊwvr | 'work' |
| *suit* | sʊwt | 'suit' | *rouge* | rʊwʒ | 'red' |

[eː]

| *bréquer* | breːke | 'brake' | *féquer* | feːke | 'fake' |
| *péché* | peːʃe | 'sin' | | | |

[ej]

| *break* | brejk | 'break' | *fake* | fejk | 'fakes' |
| *steak* | stejk | 'steak' | | | |

[oː]   [ow]

rosé	roːze	'rose'	*rose*	rowz	'rose'
saucer	soːse	'dunk'	*sauce*	sows	'sauce'
toaster	toːste	'toast (v.)'	*toast*	towst	'toast (n.)'

20. Try saying this short selection from Sir Walter Scott's *Young Lochinvar* in a Scottish dialect (adapted from Grant, 1913):

o ˈjʌŋ lɔxn̩ˈvaˑr	*O, young Lochinvar*
ɪz kʌm ˈʌwt əv ðə ˈwest	*is come out of the west,*
θru ˈɔl ðə ˈwaed ˈbɔrdəɹ	*Through all the wide Border*
hɪz ˈstid wəz ðə ˈbest	*his steed was the best,*
and ˈseˑv hɪz gud ˈbrɔdsɔrd	*And save his good broadsword*
hi ˈwepn̩z həd ˈnʌn	*he weapons had none;*
hi ˈrod ˈɔl ʌnˈarmd	*He rode all unarmed,*
ənd hi ˈrod ˈɔl əˈlon	*and he rode all alone.*
so ˈfeθfəl ɪn ˈlʌv	*So faithful in love,*
ənd so ˈdɔntlɪs ɪn ˈwɔˑr	*and so dauntless in war,*
ðəɹ ˈnevəɹ wəz ˈnʌjt	*There never was knight*
lʌjk ðə ˈjʌŋ lɔxn̩ˈvaˑr	*like the young Lochinvar.*
hi ˈsted nɔt fəɹ ˈbrek	*He stayed not for brake,*
ənd hi ˈstɔpt nɔt fəɹ ˈston	*and he stopped not for stone,*
hi ˈswam ðɪ ɛsk ˈrɪvəɹ	*He swam the Eske river*
hweˑr ˈford ðəɹ wəz ˈnʌn	*where ford there was non;*
bʌt, eˑr hi əˈlʌjtɪd	*But, ere he alighted*
ət ˈneðəɹbɪ ˈget	*at Netherby gate,*

ðə ˈbra̰ḛd həd kənˈsɛntɪd
ðə ˈgalənt ˈkem ˈlet
fɔr ə ˈlagərd ɪn ˈlʌv
ənd ə ˈdastəɹd ɪn ˈwɔ·r
wəz tə wɛd ðə ˈfe·r ˈɛlən
əv ˈbre·v lɔxn̩ˈvɑ·r

The bride had consented,
   the gallant came late:
For a laggard in love,
   and a dastard in war,
Was to wed the fair Ellen
   of brave Lochinvar

CHAPTER TWELVE
PLACE OF ARTICULATION

CONSONANTS are described in three ways: place, manner, and voicing. The **place of articulation**, or where they are made, is described in this chapter. The **manner of articulation**, or how they are made is the topic Chapter 13. In this chapter, we will limit ourselves primarily to three manners of articulation: stops, nasals, and fricatives. **Voicing** is described in Chapter 14.

In this chapter you will learn about:
- where consonant articulations are made
- double articulations
- secondary articulations.

PRIMARY PLACES OF ARTICULATION

The **place of articulation** is defined as the parts of the vocal tract having the greatest constriction; the **vocal tract** consists of the organs above the larynx: the phraynx, the oral cavity, and the nasal cavity. We have already learned many places of articulation from an examination of English and French. This chapter will extend our knowledge to include all the places of articulation found in languages generally.

The major constriction, which may be a complete or partial closure, is made by a lower articulator moving towards an upper articulator. The **lower articulators** are elements of the lower jaw — the lower lip, the lower teeth, and the tongue. The **upper articulators** are the upper lip, the upper teeth, the palate, the velum, the uvula and the rear wall of the pharynx. Places of articulation usually have a compound name giving the lower and upper articulators, with the name of the lower articulator first. Thus, apico-dental indicates that the lower articulator is the apex of the tongue, and the upper articulator is the upper teeth. Occasionally, when the lower articulator is obvious or unimportant, only the upper articulator is named; *e.g.*, *velar*, used alone, is interpreted as meaning *dorso-velar*. The following chart illustrates a number of terms used to describe the articulators, with their Latin or Greek equivalents.

English	Latin or Greek		
	Noun	*Combining Form*	*Adjective*
lip	labium	labio-	labial
tongue	lingua	linguo-	lingual
tip	apex	apico-	apical
blade	lamina	lamino-	laminal
front	—	—	—
back	dorsum	dorso-	dorsal
root	radix	radico-	radical
tooth	dens	denti-	dental
alveolar ridge	—	alveolo-	alveolar
(hard)palate	palatum	palato-	palatal
velum	velum	velo-	velar
mouth	os	oro-	oral
nose	nasus	naso-	nasal
throat	pharynx	pharyngo-	pharyngeal
voice box	larynx	laryngo-	laryngeal

BILABIAL

The lower lip articulates with the upper lip to form a **bilabial** consonant (Figure 12.1). The term *bilabial* is used rather than *labio-labial*. The bilabial stops are voiceless [p] and voiced [b] as in English. The fricatives are voiceless [φ] **phi** /faj/, and voiced [β] **beta** /ˈbejtə/. The nasal stop is [m] as in English. Bilabial stops and the nasal are extremely common in languages; indeed, a language without them is noteworthy. Bilabial fricatives, however, are rather uncommon; languages tend to have bilabial stops and labio-dental fricatives.

Ewe (/ˈɛˌvɛ/; Ghana /ˈgɑnə/, West Africa) is unusual in having contrasting bilabial and labio-dental fricatives. High tone here is shown by [´] and low tone by [`].

fà	*puff adder*	φà	*yeast*
fú	*feather*	φú	*bone*
vɔ̀	*to finish*	βɔ̀	*python*
vù	*to tear apart*	βù	*blood*

Ewe

Distinctive Features Bilabial and labiodental consonants are all [labial].

Acoustic Features Bilabials have an F2 transition with a transition pointing down, as shown in Chapter 11.

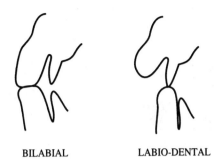

BILABIAL   LABIO-DENTAL

Figure 12.1 Bilabial and labio-dental articulations.

LABIO-DENTAL

The lower lip articulates against the upper teeth to form labio-dental consonants (Figure 12.1). Labio-dental stops and nasals do not occur distinctively although they are quite easy to make if your teeth do not have gaps. The labio-dental nasal [ɱ] occurs allophonically in English words like *symphony* [ˈsɪɱfəni] where it is a homorganic nasal agreeing as to place of articulation with the following labio-dental fricative [f] or [v]. As noted in the preceding section on bilabials, languages commonly have bilabial stops and labio-dental fricatives. The term **labial** is used to cover both bilabial and labio-dental.

Acoustic features   The transition next to a labio-dental consonant points down as with the bilabials (Figure 12.2). The fricatives have fairly faint noise in the lower frequencies (see Chapter 11).

DENTAL

Dental sounds can be made with either the tip of the tongue, **apico-dental**, or with the blade, **lamino-dental**. The dental fricatives are voiceless [θ] **theta** /ˈθejtə/ and voiced [ð] **eth** /ɛð/. Other dental sounds are shown by using the alveolar symbol with the diacritic [̪]; *e.g.*, [t̪ d̪ n̪ l̪ r̪]. Because in a given language all the stops are usually all dental or all alveolar, you will find that in discussing a particular language, the diacritic is commonly omitted with the assumption that you will know whether [t d n] represent dentals or alveolars. Dental fricatives [s̪ z̪], can be made in addition to the dentals [θ ð]. **Interdentals** are made by thrusting the tongue slightly forward so that the tip protrudes between the teeth.

Distinctive features   Dentals and alveolars are both [coronal]. Dental and alveolar stops rarely contrast with each other. Where they do, usually one place of articulation is apical and the other laminal. The feature [laminal] distinguishes those sounds made with the blade of the tongue from the apical ones. Temne /ˈtɛmni/ and Sherbro /ˈʃəɹˌbro/, two West African languages of

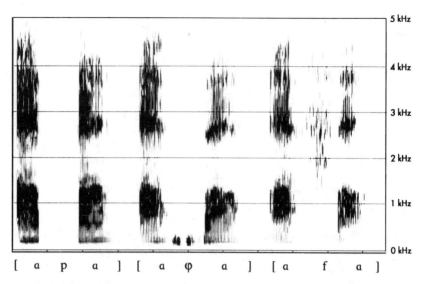

| [| α | p | α |] | [| α | φ | α |] | [| α | f | | α |] |

Figure 12.2   Spectrograms of bilabial and labio-dental stops and fricatives.

Sierra Leone /ˌsiˈɛɹə ˌliˈown/ illustrate the alternative ways of combining apical and laminal with dental and alveolar.

Temne	ṭor	*descend*	apico-dental	———
	tor	*farms*	lamino-alveolar	[laminal]
Sherbro	ṭɔk	*cloud*	lamino-dental	[laminal]
	tɔk	*wash*	apico-alveolar	———

Malayalam (/ˌmaleˈjaləm/; southern India) has a contrast between dentals and alveolars, both with apical articulation. The distinctive feature system presented here cannot account for this rare contrast.

Bilabial	Dental	Alveolar	Retroflex	Palatal	Velar
təppi	pəṭṭi	vətti	pəṭṭi		
searched	*hood*	*dried up*	*dog*		
	tʃəṭṭu	təttə	tʃəṭṭəm		
	died	*parrot*	*rule*		
pəmmi	pəṉṉi	tənnil	ənni	kəɲɲi	məŋŋi
stealthily	*pig*	*in oneself*	*link*	*gruel*	*faded*
nəmməl̠	kəṉṉu	kənni	kəṇṇi	məɲɲəl	məŋŋəl
we	*calf*	*month*	*link*	*turmeric*	*dimness*
Malayalam					

Acoustic Features   Dentals and alveolars both have a transition which is in the mid range, like that of the alveolars; see Figure 12.3. If the vowel has a high F2, the transition will tend to point down; if the F2 is low, the transition will

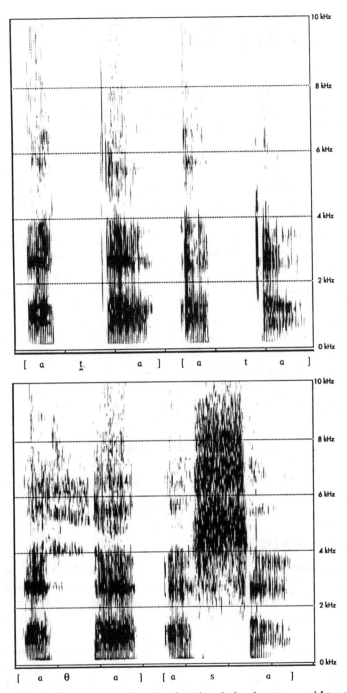

Figure 12.3 Spectrograms showing dental and alveolar stops and fricatives.

point up. With a vowel with an F2 in the mid ranges, the transition will tend to be level. The dental fricatives have a fairly faint noise pattern.

ALVEOLAR

As we saw under *dentals* above, **alveolar** sounds may be made with either the tip or blade of the tongue, known accordingly as **apico-alveolar** or **lamino-alveolar**. The symbols are [t d n s z], known to us from English.

Acoustic Features The transition for alveolar sounds is in the mid range, usually level. The fricatives [s z] have quite strong noise in the higher frequencies; see Figure 12.3.

ALVEOLO-PALATAL

The IPA lists two fricatives as having an **alveolo-palatal** /ˌæl̩viəˌloˈpælətəl/ place of articulation, different from the palato-alveolars. They can be produced with the tip of the tongue behind the upper teeth and with the blade quite close to the alveolar ridge back and to the forward part of the hard palate. Figure 12.4 shows the articulatory position of alveolo-palatals. The symbols are [ɕ] for the voiceless fricative, and [ʑ] for the voiced fricative. In recent IPA charts, these sounds have been reduced to a secondary status. Ladefoged and Mattingly (1986) refer to [ɕ ʑ] as 'palatalised postalveolars'. The distinction of palato-alveolar and alveolo-palatal, although useful for some languages, has not gained wide currency (Pullum and Ladusaw, 1986). Frequently you will find the terms used interchangeably to mean palato-alveolar; see the discussion below under palato-alveolar.

Polish has both alveolo-palatals and palato-alveolars.

ɔɕ	*axis*	ɕano	*hay*
ʑarno	*grain*	ʑima	*winter*
biteɕ	*to beat*	tɕma	*moth*
duʑɨ	*big (masc. pers. nom. pl.)*	duʒi	*big (masc. nom. sg.)*
lɛpɕɨ	*better (masc. pers. nom. pl.)*	lɛpʃi	*better (masc. nom. sg.)*

Polish

PALATO-ALVEOLAR

Palato-alveolar sounds are [posterior]. They can be made with the blade of the tongue articulating with the area at the border of the alveolar ridge and the hard palate. The blade is lower than with the alveolo-palatals. Stops are fairly rare in this region, although the fricatives [ʃ ʒ] and affricates [tʃ dʒ] are quite common in the languages of the world.

The alveolar fricatives [s z] and the palato-alveolar fricatives [ʃ ʒ] involve some difficulty in describing their point of articulation. X-rays show that both sounds are made with a variety of tongue shapes. The crucial thing seems to be to get the air-stream to hit the teeth so as to produce the appropriate turbulence. The terms

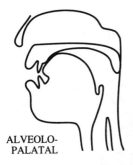 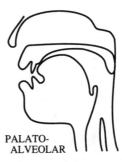

ALVEOLO-
PALATAL

PALATO-
ALVEOLAR

Figure 12.4 Alveolo-palatal and palato-alveolar places of articulation.

alveolar and palato-alveolar are not misleading, but they must be interpreted with care. Figure 12.4 shows a typical position for palato-alveolars.

Some authors refer to this point of articulation as alveolo-palatal or, with haplology (the omission of a repeated syllable), as **alveo-palatal** /ˌælviˌoˈpælətəl/. I recommend following the IPA usage, distinguishing palato-alveolar and alveolo-palatal, and not using alveo-palatal as a technical term.

Distinctive Features   Palato-alveolar sounds are [coronal] and [posterior].

Acoustic Features   The palato-alveolar fricatives have random noise in the higher frequencies, though generally not so high as the alveolars. See Figure 12.5.

RETROFLEX

Retroflex consonants can also be described as apico-palato-alveolar. The underside of the tip of the tongue articulates with the area at the border of the alveolar ridge and the hard palate, as in Figure 12.6. The body of the tongue is quite concave. The IPA uses special symbols [ʈ, ɖ, ʂ, ʐ, ɳ, ɭ, ɽ] for retroflex consonants: the alveolar symbols modified by a lower hook. I follow the common practice of using alveolar symbols with a subscript dot: [ṭ ḍ ṣ ẓ ṇ ḷ]. This is also the tradition followed in India where retroflex sounds are quite common.

Auditorily, these sounds have a rhotic, or [ɹ]-like quality, which often extends to the adjacent vowels.

Distinctive Features   The retroflex consonants are similar to the palato-alveolar ones, except that the tongue tip is up for the retroflex ones. If we need to distinguish the two types of sounds, we can use the feature [laminal] for the palato-alveolars.

Acoustic Features   With retroflex consonants, the most general acoustic characteristic is that the third formant is lowered; see Figure 12.7.

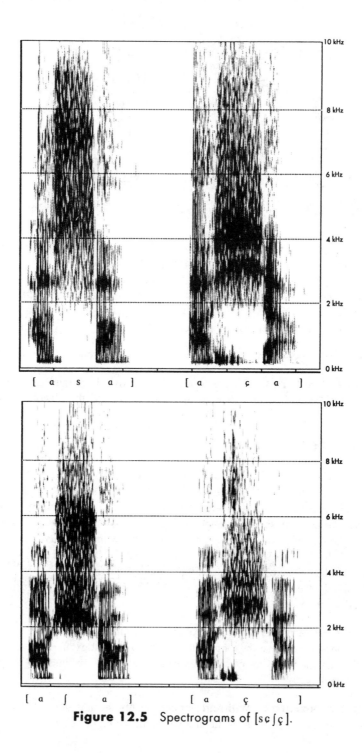

Figure 12.5 Spectrograms of [sɕʃç].

Figure 12.6 Retroflex.

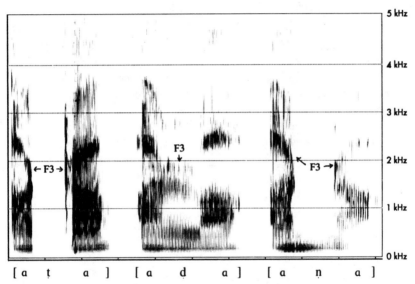

Figure 12.7 Spectrogram of retroflex consonants.

PALATAL

For **palatal** sounds, the front of the tongue articulates with the hard palate. Note that the tip of the tongue points down, often touching the lower teeth. The stops, voiceless [c] and voiced [ɟ], are fairly rare. The palatal nasal [ɲ], however, is quite common. The symbol is [ç] for the voiceless fricative and [ʝ] for the voiced fricative.

Remember that the **front** of the tongue is located behind the tip and blade. Presumably, this usage derives from the fact that this part of the tongue is used in making front vowels.

Twi (/twi/; Ghana, West Africa) contrasts alveolar, palatal, and velar stops.

àtá	*twin brother*	ɔ́dà	*he lies*
càcà	*straw mattress*	èɟá	*father*
ɔ́kà	*he bites*	àgóɹú	*play*

Twi

German has a palatal fricative [ç] contrasting with a palato-alveolar [ʃ].

vɪç	*wich*	'yielded'	vɪʃ	*wisch*	'wipe (impv.)'
fɪçt	*ficht*	'fences'	fɪʃt	*fischt*	'fishes (vb)'
mɪç	*mich*	'me'	mɪʃ	*misch*	'mix (impv.)'
dɪç	*dich*	'you'	tɪʃ	*Tisch*	'table'
kɔjç	*keuch*	'pant (impv.)'	kɔjʃ	*keusch*	'chaste'

German

Distinctive Features   Palatal consonants can be specified as [dorsal], [high], and [front].

VELAR

The full term is **dorso-velar** /ˌdoɹˌso-ˈviləɹ/, indicating that the back of the tongue articulates with the soft palate; however, the back of the tongue is the only articulator that is used to articulate with the velum, so the prefix dorso- is regularly omitted. Many people can make apico-velars, but they are not used in any language. (I have personally observed a linguist capable of placing the tip of the tongue behind the uvula!)

The stops are [k g] as in English, with the velar nasal [ŋ], **ing** /ɪŋ/. The voiceless fricative is [x], and the voiced fricative is [ɣ] **gamma** /ˈgæmə/. Scots Gaelic /ˈgælɪk ~ˈgejlɪk/ distinguishes [k g x ɣ]. Try pronouncing the examples for a challenge.

ə kuː	ə xuː	ə goər	ə ɣoər
her dog	*his dog*	*her goat*	*his goat*
xaj	xa xrədʒ	ɣaf	haxið
went	*not believe*	*took*	*happened*
ɣaxi	ahəraxəɣ	gleː ɣu	ə ɣuːxəs
homewards	*changing*	*very dark*	*his birthplace*

Scots Gaelic

The velar area is quite large. If you say the English words *key* and *caw,* you can easily hear the difference between the two [k]-sounds. The [k] of *key* is made quite far front, near the palatal region; whereas, the [k] of *caw* is made much farther back. If we want to distinguish them in transcription, the symbols [k˖ g˖] can be used for the advanced variety, and [k˗ g˗] for the retracted ones. Often the position of a velar articulation is conditioned by the neighbouring vowel; [k˖ g˖] next to front vowels, and [k˗ g˗] next to back vowels.

The diacritic [˖] used above can be generally employed after the main symbol to indicate that a sound is produced a little farther front than usual, and [˗] can be used to show a pronunciation farther back than usual. Similarly, [·] and [·] can be

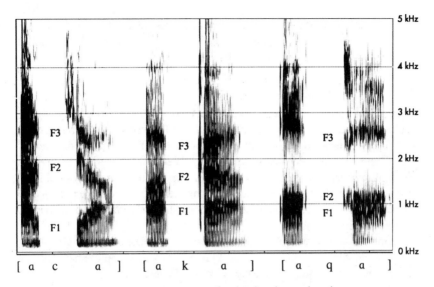

Figure 12.8 Spectrograms of palatal, velar and uvular stops.

used to show pronunciations higher and lower, respectively, than usual: *e.g.*, [e] lies between [e˔] and [e˕].

Distinctive Features The velar consonants can be specified as [dorsal] and [high].

Acoustic Features The second and third formants in a vowel preceding a velar consonant come together just at the end of the vowel (Figure 12.8).

UVULAR

For **uvular** /ˈjuvljələɹ/ consonants, the dorsum of the tongue articulates with the uvula. This feels like a velar sound made very far back in the mouth. The symbols are [q] for the voiceless stop, [ɢ] for the voiced stop, [ɴ] for the nasal, and [χ] the Greek letter **chi** /kaj/ for the voiceless fricative. The IPA uses the symbol [ʁ] for both the voiced fricative and the voiced approximant. I recommend the use of [ʁ˔] for the fricative and [ʁ] for the approximant.

Quechua (/ˈkɛtʃuə/; South America) distinguishes palatal, velar, and uvular stops.

caj	*thee*	kaj	*to be*	qan	*you*
cuŋka	*ten*	kusa	*good*	quj	*give*
cʰajna	*like that*	kʰuci	*pig*	qʰata	*slope*
		Quechua			

Distinctive Features The uvulars can be specified as [dorsal].

Acoustic Features   Lindau (1985) has observed a high third formant for uvular approximants. See Figure 12.8 where the second and third formants do not come together at the edges of the [q].

PHARYNGEAL

Pharyngeal /fəˈɹɪndʒəl/ consonants are made by moving the root of the tongue back so that it is closer to the pharyngeal wall. The full term, though rarely used, is **radico-pharyngeal** /ˌɹædɪ͵kofəˈɹɪndʒəl/. The **root** of the tongue is the vertical part, forming the forward wall of the pharyngeal cavity. Most people cannot make a complete pharyngeal closure, so only fricatives are found. A pharyngeal nasal stop is an impossibility; if the air-stream is completely blocked at the pharynx, no air can escape through the nose. The symbols are [ħ] for the voiceless fricative and [ʕ] for the voiced fricative.

Arabic has a glottal stop as well as voiced and voiceless pharyngeal fricatives. Butcher and Ahmad (1987) note that [ʕ] is often a voiced approximant with no fricative noise and often with creaky voice (see Chapter 14).

biʔr	*a well*	suʔl	*wish*
ħaːl	*condition*	ʕaːl	*fine*
qurʔaːn	*Koran*	faʔs	*axe*
ħadiːd	*iron*	wadiːʕ	*weak*

Arabic

Distinctive Features   Pharyngeals can be specified as [dorsal] and [low].

EPIGLOTTAL

Traditionally, the epiglottis has not been regarded as playing a part in phonetics. Recent studies (Laufer and Condax, 1979) have shown that in producing the voiceless pharyngeal [ħ] of Arabic and oriental Hebrew, the epiglottis is folded back. You can feel the movement of the epiglottis moving back if you swallow slowly and feel the moment of complete closure. For further details, see Catford (1988) who also mentions epiglottal stops in languages of the Caucasus.

GLOTTAL

Glottal is a curious category; it comprises two sounds, [ʔ] (**glottal stop**) and [h]. These sounds function as consonants and can be said to have a point of articulation which can be called **glottal** or **laryngeal** /ləˈɹɪndʒəl/. On the other hand, from a purely phonetic place of view, [ʔ] is a state of the glottis involving complete closure of the vocal cords, and [h] is a voiceless vowel.

Tagalog (/təˈɡɑləɡ/; Philippines) has a contrastive glottal stop and also a final [h].

Figure 12.9 Uvular.

Figure 12.10 Labial-velar.

ʔa·naj	*termite*	ha·naj	*row*
ka?o·n	*fetch*	kaho·n	*box*
ba·ta?	*child*	ba·tah	*bathrobe*
mag?alis	*remove*	magalis	*full of sores*

Tagalog

Distinctive Features Glottal stop and [h] are left unspecified as to place.

Double Articulation

It is possible to make two stops at the same time, *e.g.,* a [k] and a [p]; see Figure 12.10. Both closures are made simultaneously, and both are released simultaneously. We say that such a sound has a **double articulation**, and call it a **labial-velar**. It is symbolised as [k͡p], with the tie-bar showing that the [k] and the [p] are simultaneous. The labial-velars [k͡p, g͡b, ŋ͡m] are quite common in many language of West Africa. Occasionally we find labial-alveolars [p͡t, b͡d, m͡n], although other combinations are possible, but rarely found. Maddieson (1983) has claimed that these are all sequences of two stops at the phonemic level.

The term *labio-velar* is sometimes seen instead of *labial-velar*. Given the system of terms used here, *labio-velar* would mean that the lower lip articulates with the velum. This seems to be stretching things a bit. For the double articulation, I will use labial-velar.

The essential element of a double articulation is that it must have two different simultaneous points of articulation, each with the same degree of stricture. Thus, doubly articulated fricatives are possible, although uncommon or unknown: [v͡z, θ͡x]. The glide [w] has a double articulation of labial-velar.

Sherbro /ˈʃəɹˌbro/ contrasts [b] and [g͡b].

| bí | *have* | g͡bí | *all* |
| bàŋ | *evil* | g͡bàŋ | *hat* |

Sherbro (West Africa)

Bura (an African language; Ladefoged 1964) has the rare double articulation [p͡t] and the even rarer affricates [p͡ts] and [p͡tʃ].

p͡tá	*hare*	p͡tsa	*roast*	p͡tʃi	*sun*

Bura

Some dialects of Swedish have a simultaneous [ʃx], also symbolised as [ɧ], a voiceless palato-alveolar-velar fricative.

själ	ɧɛl	'soul'	*tjugo*	ɧʉgu	'twenty'
skjorta	ɧorṭa	'shirt'	*sköld*	ɧœld	'shield'

Swedish

Distinctive Features   Labial-velars are specified as both [labial] and [dorsal]. Similarly, labial-alveolars are specified as both [labial] and [coronal].

Secondary Articulations

Secondary articulations are the addition of a secondary, lesser constriction to the greater, **primary articulation** of a consonant. Thus, if we add lip-rounding to a [k], we get a labialised [kʷ]. The primary articulation is the velar stop; the secondary articulation is lip-rounding. A useful way of understanding secondary articulations is to think of them as adding a vowel quality to a consonant. In the case above, the vowel quality of [u] has been added to the [k]. The common secondary articulations, applied to an alveolar stop, are shown in Figure 12.11:

Secondary articulation	*Vowel quality*	*Symbol*	*Examples*
labialisation	[u]	[ʷ]	[tʷ pʷ sʷ]
palatalisation	[i]	[ʲ]	[tʲ pʲ sʲ]
velarisation	[ɤ]	[~]	[ɫ ꞇ ʁ sˠ]
and pharyngealisation	[ɑ]	(same as for velarisation)	

The IPA allows using the same symbols for velarisation and pharyngealisation. This works because languages are not known to use both. If we need to distinguish them, we can add a diacritic [ˠ] (a small superscript ram's horns [ɤ]) for velarised consonants, and a diacritic [ˤ] (a small superscript [ʕ]) for pharyngealised ones: [tˠ tˤ].

Secondary articulations may be conditioned or inherent. Consonants regularly become labialised next to rounded vowels or palatalised next to front vowels; these secondary articulations are thus conditioned by the neighbouring environment. On the other hand, they may have inherent secondary articulations. In English, for example, [ʃ] and [ɹ] are rounded no matter what vowels they are next to: *e.g., sheep* [ʃʷip], *reap* [ɹʷip].

LABIALISATION

Labialised /ˈlejbiəlˌajzd/ sounds involve lip rounding, *i.e.,* a rounded vowel quality, usually high and back. Labialised consonants are quite common. Labialised consonants can be specified [round].

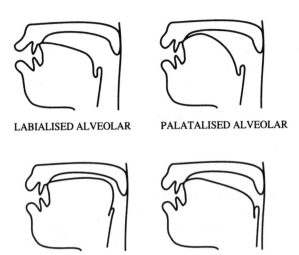

LABIALISED ALVEOLAR   PALATALISED ALVEOLAR

VELARISED ALVEOLAR   PHARYNGEALISED ALVEOLAR

Figure 12.11 Secondary articulations.

Twi contrasts plain and labialised palatals.

càcà	*straw mattress*	òcʷá?	*he cuts*
òɟá	*he leads*	òɟʷá	*he carves*
òɲá	*he finds*	ɲʷá	*snail*
ɔ̀ʃɛ́	*he puts on*	ɔ̀ʃʷɛ́	*he looks at*

Twi (West Africa)

PALATALISATION

Palatalised /ˈpælətəlˌajzd/ consonants have the front of the tongue more towards the palatal region than normal, *i.e.,* having a high front unrounded vocalic position. In many of the Slavic and Celtic languages, the consonants may be divided into plain (*i.e.,* non-palatalised) and palatalised. Palatalised consonants can be specified [high].

The term **palatalisation** is used in two quite different ways. One, as here, describes a secondary articulation. The other way describes a process which may or may not involve a secondary articulation. We may say that a certain language has a process of palatalisation. This means that under certain conditions certain sounds move towards a more palatal position. This could mean the addition of a secondary articulation: [t] → [tʲ]. Alternatively, palatalisation is commonly used to mean other changes such as [t] → [c], or [t] → [tʃ]. In these latter two cases, the sounds [c] and [tʃ] are obviously more palatal than [t], but neither has a secondary articulation.

Ukrainian contrasts plain and palatalised consonants.

lak	*varnish*	lʲak	*fright*
ʃal	*rage*	ʃalʲ	*shawl*
fɪrɪwna	*penalty*	fɪrɪwnʲa	*3-kopek coin*
kin	*public place*	kinʲ	*horse*
rasa	*race*	rʲasa	*cassock*
kruk	*raven*	krʲuk	*hook*

Ukrainian

VELARISATION

Velarised /ˈviləɹˌajzd/ consonants involve raising the tongue more towards a velar position than usual, *i.e.,* a high back unrounded vocalic position. Velarised [ɫ], known as 'dark-l' is quite common. In [ɫ], the tip of the tongue is at the alveolar ridge (or teeth), and the sides of the tongue are down as usual; however, the back of the tongue rather than being fairly flat is raised towards the velum in the position of an approximant. Velarised consonants can be specified [high] and [back].

Scots Gaelic contrasts three types of laterals and nasals: plain, velarised, and palatalised. The plain sounds are alveolar; the velarised and palatalised ones are dental.

plain		velarised		palatalised	
balə	*town*	baɫə	*ball, wall*	kal̡ʲɔx	*old woman*
ə lɔər	*his book*	ə ɫɔx	*his, her lake*	ə l̡ʲɔər	*her book*
ian	*bird*	bliəɴə	*year*	ianʲ	*John*
ə niən	*his daughter*	ə‑ɴabi	*his, her neighbour*	ə n̡ʲiən	*her daughter*

Scots Gaelic

PHARYNGEALISATION

Pharyngealised /fəˈɹɪndʒəlˌajzd/ sounds involve a lowering of the back of the tongue and a retraction of the root, thus effecting a narrowing of the pharynx. They are also transcribed with [~]. Pharyngealised sounds are not very common, although they are found in Arabic. Pharyngealised sounds can be specified [back] and [low].

mas:	*to touch*	masˁ:	*to suck*
ba:z	*falcon*	baẓ	*to be spoiled*

Arabic

TECHNICAL TERMS

alveolar	chi	eth
alveolo-palatal	dental	front
apico-alveolar	interdental	gamma
apico-dental	dorso-velar	glottal
beta	double articulation	glottal stop
bilabial	epiglottal	labial

214

labialisation
labialised
labial-velar
lamino-alveolar
lamino-dental
laryngeal
lower articulators
manner of articulation
palatal
    palatalisation

palatalised
palato-alveolar
pharyngeal
    pharyngealisation
    pharyngealised
place of articulation
primary articulation
radico-pharyngeal
retroflex

root
secondary articulation
theta
upper articulators
uvular
velar
    velarisation
    velarised
vocal tract

SYMBOLS

	bilabial	labio-dental	dental	alveolar	alveolo-palatal	palato-alveolar
stop	p b		ʈ ḍ	t d		
fricative	φ β	f v	θ ð	s z	ɕ ʑ	ʃ ʒ
nasal	m	ɱ	n̪	n		

	retroflex	palatal	velar	uvular	pharyngeal	glottal
stop	ʈ ḍ	c ɟ	k g	q ɢ		ʔ
fricative	ṣ ẓ	ç ʝ	x ɣ	χ ʁ	ħ ʕ	h
nasal	ṇ	ɲ	ŋ	N		

[ɧ] is a voiceless palato-alveolar-velar fricative, = [ʃx].

SYMBOLS WITH SPECIAL NAMES

β *beta*   ˈbejtə   ç *c-cedilla*   ˌsi səˈdɪlə   ŋ *ing*   ɪŋ
φ *phi*   faj   ɟ *curly j*   ˌkɜɹli ˈdʒej   χ *chi*   kaj
ʃ *esh*   ɛʃ   ɣ *gamma*   ˈgæmə   ʔ *glottal stop* ˌglatəl ˈstap
ʒ *ezh*   ɛʒ

DIACRITICS

 ̪ dental   ˆ raised   ‹ fronted
 . retroflex   ˬ lowered   › backed
 ⁀ simultaneous articulation

Exercises

BASIC

1. Review the exercises in chapters 5 and 6 for practice on making [β φ x ɣ].

2. Spanish has both [β] and [ɣ].

    haba   ˈaβa   *bean*   nabas   ˈnaβas   *turnips*
    avance aˈβanse *advance*   vega   ˈbeɣa   *plain, meadow*
    aguzar aɣuˈsar *sharpen*   la gula laˈɣula   *the gluttony*
    abusar aβuˈsar *abuse*   mucho gusto ˈmutʃoˈɣusto *great pleasure*

3. Now try the following nonsense words:

    xaxʌ   xɪkʌ   ɣuɣɒ   xagi   kʊxɔ   kuɣɛ

    guɣa   xægɔ   ɣɛxæ

These are a little harder.

    ˈpivʊs   ˈdiɣæʃ   mɛˈtuʒ   βɛˈðug   zæxˈɪφ   hɪˈlʌʒ

    ŋæˈθok   heˈxuɣ   ˈwæmfɔɣ   ˈʒeθxɛl   ˈŋɒφθʊd   gasˈðim

    xʌnˈsɪʃ   ˈβuŋvæɣ   ˈhɔxsæɣ

4. Place the tip of your tongue against the upper teeth and produce the apico-dental stop [t̪ d̪]. Draw the tip back to the alveolar ridge to produce apico-alveolar stops [t d]. Not pull the tip behind the alveolar ridge to produce a retroflex stop [ʈ ɖ]. In making a retroflex stop the tongue should be curled back sufficiently so that the underside of the tongue comes into contact with the upper surface.

Try the following:

    ad̪a   ada   aɖa   id̪i   idi   iɖi

    od̪o   odo   oɖo

In like manner, place the blade of the tongue against the teeth to produce a lamino-dental stop. Then pull the blade back to the alveolar ridge and produce a lamino-alveolar stop.

    ad̠a   ada   ed̠e   ede   ud̠u   udu

Try the following dentals, first make them apico-dental and then lamino-dental:

    ɛt̪i   ɔn̪ɪ   ɒl̪ɛ   æd̪ʌ   ɒl̪ɛ   un̪ʊ

    ʊta   adɔ   ʊt̪ɪ

5. If you start producing an [i], and then move the tongue higher, you will produce an approximant [j]. If you move the tongue higher until friction-like noise is present, you will produce a voiced fricative [ʝ]. Now, making sure that the tip of the tongue is near your lower teeth, move the tongue higher so as to make a complete closure and you will produce a palatal stop [ɟ].

Try pronouncing the palatals [c ɟ ç ʝ ɲ ʎ] with all eight cardinal vowels:
e.g.: [ci ce cɛ ca cɑ cɔ co cu]

Now try:

    cice   ɟaɟɛ   ɲuɲɔ   ʎɛʎæ   ɟacɔ   ʎɛɲa

    ɲiço   cuʎe   teɟi   çeɟæ   neɟu   nɔɲo

    ɲoɲe   ɟoti   ɟɛʎi   leʎa

Try these build-up patterns:

    ˈta ɟɛ ˈçe zu ˈcɛ ɲɔ   θo ˈdi cɔ ˌʎi ɟe ˈda

Now, start with an [i], and move the tongue forwards. You should produce a [ʑ].

Practise these:

    ʑi   çi   siçi   ʑiʑi   çiçi   ʑiɟi   ʑiʑi   çaʑa

    ça   ʑa   ça   ɟa   saʃa   çaʑa   aɟa   ʃasa

6. Try these nonsense words:

fɛço	çesa	ɟiva	ɟaʒo	çuxɔ	xɛçi
ʃaçe	zɛɟu	ɣɔɟe	ɟayi	ɸoçaʎ	çɔʎaɟ
ɟuɟɛç	çediɟ	ɟiɟɛc	ɟaciç		

7. German:

ziˑk	*Sieg*	'victory'	ziˑç	*siech*	'sickly'
rɛkt	*reckt*	'stretches'	reçt	*recht*	'right'
nɪkt	*nickt*	'nods'	nɪçt	*nicht*	'not'
ʃtrajk	*Streik*	'strike'	ʃtrajçt	*streicht*	'strokes'
kiˑnoˑ	*Kino*	'movie'	çeˈmi	*Chemie*	'chemistry'

8. Bengali (/ˌbɛŋˈgɑli/; India). Try the following, paying attention to the aspiration:

pʰɔl	*fruit*	tɔpʰat	*distance*	bɔropʰ	*ice*
pʰeni	*candy floss*	tʰoli	*bag*	gatʰa	*poem*
pɔtʰ	*road*	tʰana	*police station*	kʰil	*bolt*
ɔkʰil	*entire*	nokʰ	*nail*	akʰrot	*walnut*
tʰunko	*fragile*	atʰa	*glue*	katʰ	*wood*
atʰaro	*eighteen*	tʃʰobi	*picture*	atʃʰar	*to thrash*
matʃʰ	*fish*	tʃʰoto	*small*		

9. Tagalog (/təˈgaləg/, Phillipines). Practise glottal stops and initial [ŋ] in the following:

ŋaˈjon	*now*	ɲiˈti	*smile*
ˈŋaŋaʔ	*betel nut mixture*	ŋaˈwaʔ	*to cry*
ˈŋipin	*tooth*	ɲitˈɲit	*irritation*
naˈwaʔ	*may it be so*	ˈnanaʔ	*pus*

10. Georgian:

bgera	*sound*	dgas	*stands*	dʒgupi	*group*
dɣe	*day*	midzɣvna	*dedication*	pxizeli	*sober*
pkvili	*flour*	txovna	*request*	tkven	*you (pl)*
tkva	*he said*	tsxovreba	*life*	tskera	*looking*
tsxadi	*clear*	tsxviri	*nose*	tʃkari	*fast*
tʃxubi	*fight*				

11. Ewe contrasts a velar and a pharyngeal fricative: [x] and [ħ].

xexí	*umbrella*	ħà	*song*	xá	*broom*
àħò	*widow*	xɔ̀	*house*		

12. Labialisation involves lip rounding. It may occur alone or in combination with the other secondary articulations.

tʷa	dʷa	sʷa	zʷa	nʷa	lʷa
kʷɛgi	lʷaɲu	kodʷɛ	ŋʷaɾi	xeθʷa	xʷanɔ

13. Gã has labialised fricatives and affricates.

tʃa	*to dig*	tʃʷa	*to strike*	dza	*to divide*
dzʷa	*to break*	dzɛ́i	*there*	dzʷɛ́i	*rubbish*
ʃɛ	*to reach*	ʃʷɛ	*to remain*	ʃanɛ	*to slip*
ʃʷane	*afternoon*				

14. Practise the following palatalised consonants:

bʲo   fʲɛ   φʲa   βʲʌ   pʲi

For places of articulation involving the tongue, the tongue assumes a position more like a palatal articulation, *i.e.,* the front of the tongue moves more towards the palate than usual.

Try these:

tʲɑ	kʲɑ	dʲe	gʲɛ	sʲɑ	xʲe
dʲegi	tʲy	tʲɔ	nʲøkʲe	lalʲʌ	nʲɛʃu

In [sʲ], the palatalisation is simultaneous with the [s]; in [sj] there is a sequence with one sound following the other.

sʲɑ   sjɑ   sʷi   swi   fʲe   fje   θʷɛ   θwɛ

15. Practise these plain and palatalised dentals:

ˈtatʲa	ˈnʲɔnɔˈ	lʌlʲʌ	ˈdʲode
ˈtʲiteˈtʲe	tatʲaˈtɔ	ˈtʲatɔtʲu	ˈtetʲute

Remember to keep the [tʲ] one segment, and not a sequence of [tj].

Don't let palatalised sounds become affricates such as [ts — tʃ — tθ].

If labialisation occurs simultaneously with palatalisation, the resulting secondary articulation can be transcribed as [ᶣ].

tᶣa	dᶣɛ	lᶣɔ	kᶣo
tᶣɛgɒ	danᶣu	kᶣalɔ	sᶣinu

16. Velarised consonants involve a secondary velar or high back unrounded vocalic position.

Practise saying:

li   le   lɛ   lɑ   lʌ   lɣ   lɯ

Velarised [ɫ] is like the [l] of [lɯ].

Practise:

ɛɫɛ	ɲana	sɑsɑ	zʌsʌ	ɣɫ̥ɣ	ɲɛnɛ
ɫete	ɖidi	iɲɛ	tade	sɑʑi	φoɲi
ɛlɑ	bɛɫa	bɛlʲɑ	lʲeɫɑ	aφu	njaφu
naφu	nʲaφu				

17. Greek

skandzóxiros	*porcupine*	míɣðalo	*almond*
vðela	*leech*	ksirós	*dry*
exθrós	*enemy*	ɣáj ðaros	*donkey*
fθáno	*I arrive*	ɣlistró	*I slip*
sinɣnómi	*forgiveness*	ftjáno	*I make*
avɣó	*egg*	ɣambrós	*bridegroom*

18. To make double articulations, close the lips to make a [p]. Keeping them closed, make a [k]. Now, release the [k͡p]. Make sure that the two closures are released simultaneously. Try the same process with [p͡t].

| k͡pa | p͡ta | g͡ba | ek͡pe | ep͡te | eg͡be |

The tie bar [͡] indicates that the sounds are made simultaneously. Although the order given above is traditional and should be used ordinarily, practise saying them from transcriptions using the reverse order. This may correct any problem that you might have with not making the release of the stops simultaneously.

| k͡pa | p͡ka | p͡ta | t͡pa | g͡be | b͡ge | b͡de | d͡be |
| Also try | f͡sa | f͡xe | s͡xɛ | v͡zo | z͡ɣu | v͡ɣa |

19. Try the following labial-velar articulations in Gã; [´] indicates high tone, [`] indicates low tone, and mid tone is unmarked.

k͡pâî	cheeks	k͡pák͡pó	billy goat
g͡bé	road	k͡pátá	kitchen
ák͡pákí	calabash	g͡bóg͡bó	wall
g͡békɛ̃	child	ág͡bá	bivouac
ŋ͡mé	bell	éŋ͡mɔ̃mi	ocru

ADVANCED

20. Practise pronouncing the following:

ɲæmy	nyŋœ	mumo	suɯsɤ	fofʌ	ŋɒnɤ
mœny	nɤɲɯ	lœði	ɸypʌ	jæge	jeʃœ
ɹɛvœ	ɣɒça	tœʒʌ	fazɒ	xɤsɔ	hyβɯ
ɟɔɤ	çyθu				

21. [s̪ z̪]. Try making dental varieties of [s] and [z] by starting with an alveolar [s] and moving the tongue forward until it is behind the upper teeth.

| sa | s̪a | za | z̪a |

| ˈsos̪oθo | seθeˈzefe | ziˈvɛzɔ | ʃaˌnus̪o | ˈzeˈθezɛ | ðes̪ɛˌʃɛzɛ |

22. Retroflex consonants
Try the following:

| ta | ʈa | da | ɖa | na | ɳa | la | ɭa |
| sa | ʂa | za | ʐa | ɹa | ɻa | | |

aʈa	aɖa	uɳu	oɭo	ɔsɔ	eze
aɻa	ɛɻɛ	ʈɔtɛ	diɖo	ɳune	ʔɔɖa
liɭa	ɻɛɻa	ʂesa	zɔʐa	taʈiʈu	diɖanɛ
loɻena	nɛluzɔ	sosiɖe	ʐesɔli	taɻeʂu	tenɔɖa

23. Hungarian. Try the following words with palatal stops. Remember to keep the tip of your tongue pointed down.

tʃɒlaːd	salad	hɒrtʃɒ	catfish	aːtʃ	carpenter
laːndʒɒ	lance	dʒɛm	jam	cuːk	hen
kaːrcɒ	playing card	korc	gulp	ɟønɟ	pearl

219

hɔnɟɒ	*ant*	kor	*age*	ɒkɒrok	*I want*
je:g	*ice*	ɛge:r	*mouse*	haŋg	*voice*

24. Read the following selection aloud.

Seen through the stinking smoke of a smoldering straw-strewn saloon, the setting sun looked like a sorrel stack of soggy stogies, as stocky Stanfoard Stubbins, the Stanislaus Stampeder, stiffly staggered from the stuffy stagecoach; stonily stood in startled stupefaction; spontaneously saluted the still-standing Stars and Stripes; sternly stepped over the struggling scorpion; silently slew the slithering sidewinder; sadly swallowed the single swig of sickly-sweet sarsaparilla; sullenly shrugged his shrapnel-seared shoulders; suddenly stopped staring at the stolen stirrup; and sorrowfully saddled the sole surviving starving stallion...

Now read it again, substituting [ʃ] for [s].

Try it again with [ʂ ɕ ʃʷ ç]

25. For each vowel [y ø œ Œ ɑ ʌ ɤ ɯ], pronounce them after each of the following consonants:

z ʒ z̪ θ ʃ ç j̊ s̪ ð

e.g.: zy zø zœ zŒ zɑ zʌ zɤ zɯ

Now try the following vowels in the same fashion after the consonants below:

ɯ y ɤ ø œ ʌ œ ɒ Œ   l ɹ j ʔ hw l̥ t̪ hj

26. Twi (West Africa) shows labialised palatals:

caca	*mattress*	ocʷa	*he cuts*
oɟa	*he leads*	oɟʷa	*he carves*
ɔɲa	*he finds*	ɲʷa	*snail*
ɔʃɛ	*he puts on*	ɔʃʷɛ	*he looks at*

27. Pharyngealised sounds are also usually transcribed with [~]. Pharyngealisation involves a lowering of the back of the tongue and a retraction of the root, thus effecting a narrowing of the pharynx.

a. Try saying a low, back [ɑ], and then making it even lower and farther back.

b. With your thumb and finger, push gently in and down just above your adam's apple while saying [ɑ].

c. Say [ɫɑ] while doing a. and b. above. This should give you a pharyngealised [ɫɑ].

d. Some people find the following method quite succesful: think of the pharyngeal action as weak gagging. If you touch your velum with your finger, you wil usually trigger the gag reflex. What you are looking for is a very weak version of this gag reflex. Remember: nausea → success.

ɫ ɫ ɫ ɫ

ƶɑ	ȿɑ	ꞥɑ	ƀɑ	ǥɑ	đɑ

28. Try these examples from Arabic.

tiːn	*figs*	ṭiːn	*mud*
darb	*lane*	ḍarb	*striking*
seːf	*sword*	ṣeːf	*summer*
zuhuːr	*flowers*	ẓuhuːr	*appearance*
ʔisaːṣ	*punishment*	ʔisaṣha	*her stories*
taxsiːṣ	*specialisation*	ʔaṣiṣha	*he punished her*
maxṣuːṣ	*special*	ʕuṣuṣhe	*her coccyx*

CHAPTER THIRTEEN
MANNER OF ARTICULATION

In Chapter 12 we classified consonants according to their place of articulation. In this chapter, we examine the other major aspect of consonants — **manner of articulation**. A primary feature of manner is the degree of **stricture**; that is, does the air have a free passage through the mouth or is there an obstruction? By varying the degree of obstruction, we can make different sounds. **Nasality** is another way of varying sounds, by allowing air to pass out of the nose or not. As well, some sounds are **lateral** with the air passing out through the sides of the vocal tract, but not through the middle.

In this chapter you will learn about:
- how different consonants are made at the same place of articulation
- lateral and nasal consonants
- taps, flaps, and trills.

DEGREE OF STRICTURE

Say the vowel [ɑ]; notice that air passes freely out of the mouth. In saying this vowel we have the tongue low, creating as little obstruction as possible. To see your throat, doctors ask you to say [ɑ] to get the oral cavity as open as possible. Now say a long [lllllllll]. Here, air obviously passes out the mouth, but not so freely as with [ɑ]; the articulators are positioned so as to form a partial obstruction in the vocal tract. If you try a long [fffffffff], the closure is even tighter, causing a certain amount of **frication**, or friction-like noise. If you try to make a long [ppppppppp], your cheeks may puff out a bit, but no air escapes, and there is a complete closure.

Category of sound		Degree of Stricture
Consonants {	Stops	no air passes out through the mouth
	Fricatives	partial obstruction; noticeable frication
	Approximants	little obstruction; no frication
Vowels		stricture no greater than that for [i]

Figure 13.1   Degree of stricture.

We distinguish four degrees of **stricture**. Sounds made with the least stricture are vowels; the others are consonants. Figure 13.1 shows the four categories with their degree of stricture:

OBSTRUENTS

Oral stops, fricatives, and affricates together form the class of **obstruents** /'ɑbstɹuənt/. Non-obstruent sounds are called **sonorants**, comprising nasals, approximants, and vowels; the sonorant consonants are discussed below.

Stops are defined as having no air passing out through the mouth; **oral** sounds have no air passing out the nasal passage. **Oral stops**, thus, involve closure of both the oral and nasal passages. **Nasal stops** have air passing out through the nasal passage, but not through the mouth. Nasal stops are usually voiced. Oral stops may be voiced or voiceless. Nasal sounds are discussed at the end of this chapter. With voiceless stops, no sound is heard from the onset of the stop to its release. With voiced stops, the sound of the vibrating vocal cords is heard. The loudness of the voicing is often muted as the vibration has to pass through the soft tissues of the neck and cheeks. Three points about stops will be explained in Chapter 14: voicing, aspiration, and glottal stops.

With **fricatives**, the constriction in the oral cavity allows air to pass out but is close enough to cause turbulence in the air-stream producing frication. Fricatives occur at all places of articulation. The sound [h] is often called a glottal fricative. Phonologically, [h] behaves like a consonant; phonetically, however, it is a voiceless vowel with the same tongue position as the following vowel. The fricatives [s z] are called **sibilants** /'sɪbɪlənt/; [ʃ ʒ] are also called **sibilants**. Fricatives are also known as **spirants**.

Affricates consist of a stop immediately followed by a homorganic fricative. **Homorganic** /ˌhomoɹ'gænɪk/ means 'having the same place of articulation'; this is interpreted somewhat loosely so that [pɸ pf tθ ts tʃ] are all affricates, but [px kf tf qθ] are not.

Distinctive Features   Fricatives are distinguished from stops by the feature [continuant]. For affricates, the root node is divided into two trees, one for the stop and one for the fricative. The feature [strident] can be used to distinguish [s z] from [θ ð], and [f v] from [ɸ β]. Figure 13.2 shows feature trees for palatal obstruents.

Acoustic Features   Figure 13.3 shows a spectrogram of 'Peggy's speech was good'. From Chapter 9, we expect that the stops will show a gap in the acoustic pattern; we find gaps for the [p] in *Peggy's* and *speech* and for the [g] and [d] in *good*. The gap is typical of stops. The **spike** at the end of the [pʰ] is typical of the release of stops. The aspiration of the [pʰ] of *Peggy's* can be seen just at the end of the gap as a bit of random noise before the vowel. Fricatives show random noise as in the [z] of *Peggy's* and *was,* and in the [s] of *speech*.

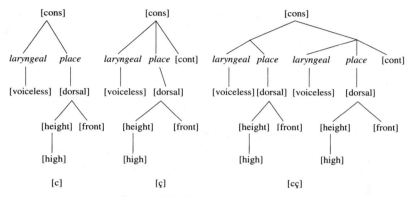

Figure 13.2 Palatal obstruents.

Affricates, such as the [tʃ] of *speech,* consist of a stop, appearing as a gap, followed by a fricative, appearing as random noise.

APPROXIMANTS

Approximants have an articulatory constriction closer than the vowel [i], yet without the frication of fricatives. Any fricative can be turned into an approximant by widening the constriction until the frication ceases. Try making a [v]; gradually increase the opening until the frication ceases. The sound you are now making is a voiced labio-dental approximant [ʋ]. Semivowels are classified as approximants. Approximants are usually voiced.

Quite a number of approximants are laterals which are discussed separately below. Although we can make approximants at any place of articulation, only certain ones are common; the symbols for fricatives and approximants are shown below:

	bi-labial	labio-dental	dental	alveo-lar	palato-alveolar	retro-flex	palatal
fricative	φ β	f v	θ ð	s z	ʃ ʒ	ʂ ʐ	ç ʝ
approximant		ʋ				ɻ, ɭ	j

	velar	uvular	pharyn-geal	labial-palatal	labial-velar
fricative	x ɣ	χ ʁ˕	ħ ʕ	ɥ˕ ɥ˕	ʍ˕ w˕
approximant	ɰ ɰ	ʁ		ɥ ɥ	ʍ w

The symbols [ɹ] and [ɻ] can be used to distinguish two types of rhotic sounds: [ɹ] for a more advanced post-alveolar approximant, and [ɻ] for a more retracted, retroflexed sound. The symbol [ʍ] represents a voiceless [w].

Rhotic sounds are ones with an r-like quality. They include [ɹ], [ɻ], and [ʁ], as well as the taps and trills discussed below. As we pointed out in Chapter 3, the

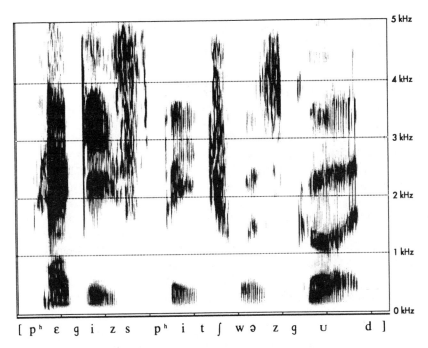

Figure 13.3 'Peggy's speech was good.'

[pʰ ɛ g i z s pʰ i t ʃ w ə z g ʊ d]

retroflex [ɻ], as in English, can be made either with the tongue tip up or with it down.

Liquids include lateral and rhotic sounds.

The semivowels [j ɥ w ɯ] are considered to be approximants, having respectively palatal, labial-palatal, labial-velar, and velar places of articulation.

Note that [ɥ w] are used by the IPA for approximants, and [ʁˠ] for a fricative. I suggest using the plain symbols [ɥ w ʁ] for the approximants, and [ɥˠ wˠ ʁˠ] for the fricatives.

Distinctive features Figure 13.4 shows a feature tree for a uvular approximant.

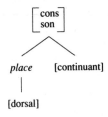

Figure 13.4 Uvular approximant.

Acoustic features   The approximants are very similar to the vowels and thus have acoustic characteristics like the corresponding vowels; compare Figure 13.5.

TRILLS, TAPS, AND FLAPS
TRILLS

Two types of **trill** are commonly found: one with the tip of the tongue at the dental [r̪] or alveolar [r] region. The other trill is uvular [ʀ]. In the dental and alveolar trills, the tongue tip strikes the alveolar ridge several times very quickly.

Trills are not made by consciously controlling the motion of the tongue; rather, the tongue is placed in the approximate position and tension, air is blown through the gap, and aerodynamic forces cause the tongue to vibrate rapidly against the upper articulator. The aerodynamic forces involved in making a trill involve the Bernoulli effect which is explained in Chapter 14. The Bernoulli effect pulls the articulators together, and the air-stream from the lungs pushes them apart again. This sequence of events happens several times rapidly causing the trill.

The uvular trill is made by raising the back of the tongue so that the airstream causes the uvula to vibrate against it. Snoring often involves a uvular trill made while breathing in. Figure 13.6 shows an alveolar and a uvular trill.

An alveolar fricative trill [r̝] occurs in Czech, as in the name of the composer Dvořák ['dvor̝ak]. Here the body of the tongue is raised higher towards the postalveolar region than for the sonorant trill, producing frication.

A bilabial trill is reported as occurring very rarely as a consonant; it is reported more often as occurring in impolite society. If needed, it can be written with a [ʙ]. The contrast between a bilabial trill and a bilabial stop is shown in the following examples from Ngwe (Camerouns; Ladefoged, 1971).

mʙɤ	*tadpoles*	mbɛm	*seed*

Ngwe

TAPS

In Chapter 3, we learned that the typical North American English intervocalic allophone of /t/ is usually a voiced tap [ɾ]. **Taps** are often described as a trill of one vibration. The sensation is that the tongue is flicked against the upper articulator like a ballistic missile in that the speaker does not exercise control over its movement once the action begins. A stop, in contrast, is like a guided missile in which the action is under the control of the speaker for the duration of the sound.

Spanish contrasts a dental tap with a dental trill .

caro	kaɾo	'dear'	*carro*	karo	'cart'
pero	peɾo	'but'	*perro*	pero	'dog'
fiero	fjeɾo	'fierce'	*fierro*	fjero	'shoe (a horse)'
yero	jeɾo	'lentil'	*hierro*	jero	'iron'

Spanish

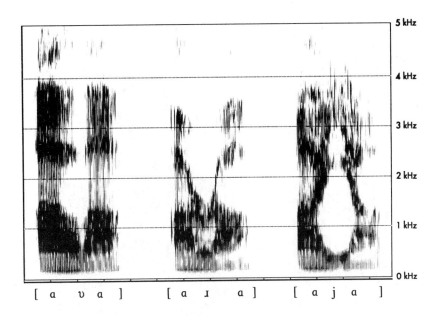

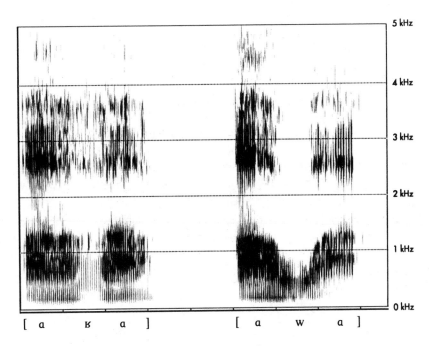

Figure 13.5 Spectrograms of approximants.

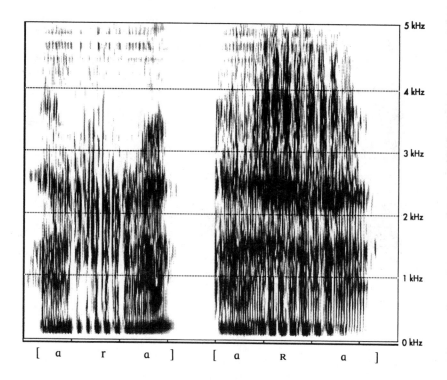

[ɑ   r   ɑ   ]   [ɑ   R   ɑ   ]

Figure 13.6   Spectrogram of an alveolar and a uvular trill.

FLAPS

With a tap, the active articulator returns to its point of origin. With a **flap** the active articulator starts in one position, strikes the place of articulation in passing, and ends the movement in a position different from which it began. Three flaps are known to occur. For an apical flap, the tip of the tongue is curled back in the oral cavity; then, it moves forward striking the upper surface of the mouth, and ends with the tip forward in the mouth. The place of articulation is usually retroflex: [ɽ]. Hausa (/ˈhawsə/; Nigeria, West Africa) contrasts a flap and a tap:

bár̠à   *servant*   bárà   *begging*

Hausa

Japanese has an alveolar lateral flap [ɺ]. This is like the alveolar tap [ɾ] except that the tongue does not make contact at the sides, allowing air to flow over the sides of the tongue in a lateral fashion.

ɺiku   *land*   aɺimas   *there is*
kiɺi   *gimlet*   ɺjokoː   *journey*

Japanese

A labio-dental flap, although rare, occurs in Shona (Ladefoged, 1971). The lower lip is curled back and strikes the upper teeth in passing as it moves forward. The labio-dental flap in Shona (/ˈʃownə/; southern Africa) is shown here as [*].

ko*ó   *blackness*
wó*o   *movement*

Shona

LATERALS

Laterals are made with the sides of the constriction open allowing air to escape. We have discussed the English alveolar lateral [l] in Chapter 3. Other laterals are shown below:

	dental	alveolar	retroflex	palatal	velar
laterals	l̪	l	ɭ	ʎ	L

The dental, alveolar, and retroflex laterals are made by placing the tip of the tongue at each place of articulation and allowing air to escape along the sides. The palatal lateral is formed by raising the medial portion of the front of the tongue to the palate and allowing air to escape out the sides. A similar movement with the medial portion of the back of the tongue against the velum produces the velar lateral.

The dental and alveolar laterals can take on the colour of any vowel: *e.g.,* [lⁱ lʸ lᵉ lᵃ lᵒ lᵘ lᵚ], where the raised vowel indicates the vowel quality. The tip of the tongue is at the teeth or alveolar ridge, and the body of the tongue assumes the various vowel shapes. In fact, it is sufficient to distinguish only two vowel qualities: front unrounded [lⁱ] and back unrounded [lᵚ]. These are known respectively as **clear-l** and **dark-l**. The back unrounded quality of dark-l can be thought of as velarisation. Normally, clear-l is transcribed as [l], and dark-l as [ɫ], using [~], the normal diacritic for velarisation.

Laterals are not necessarily approximants (Maddieson and Emmorey, 1984). For each lateral sonorant, there is a corresponding fricative. The voiced dental and alveolar lateral have special symbols, [ɮ̪] and [ɮ]. Approximant laterals can be syllabic.

Bilabial laterals are easily made but are not found in languages of the world. Velar laterals are extremely rare, but they are found in Melpa, a language of Papua New Guinea (Ladefoged, Cochrane, &. Disner, 1977).

		dental	alveolar	retroflex	palatal
fricatives	voiced	ɮ̪	ɮ	ɭˑ	ʎˑ
	voiceless	ɬ̪	ɬ	ɭˑ̥	ʎˑ̥
approximants	voiced	l̪	l	ɭ	ʎ
	voiceless	l̪̥	l̥	ɭ̥	ʎ̥

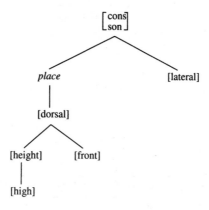

Figure 13.7 Palatal lateral.

The voiceless lateral [ɬ] in Welsh, spelled *ll*, is frequently unilateral, or open only at one side.

ɬan	*church*	araɬ	*other*
ɬin	*ship*	ɬond	*full*

Welsh

Distinctive Features   All laterals are specified [lateral]. Figure 13.7 shows a feature tree for a palatal lateral [ʎ].

Acoustic Features   Laterals generally have weak formants at frequencies around 250, 1200, and 2400 Hz.

NASALS

Nasals are made with a velic opening with air going out through the nasal passage. The term **nasal**, used alone, means *nasal stop*. Otherwise the type of sound must be specified, as in *nasal fricative, nasal lateral,* etc. Nasal fricatives and approximants occur, but usually as the result of being next to a nasal vowel. Nasal stops are ordinarily voiced. Nasals can be syllabic. The symbols are:

	bilabial	labio-dental	dental	alveolar	retro-flex	palatal	velar	uvular
nasal	m	ɱ	n̪	n	ɳ	ɲ	ŋ	N

Distinctive Features   The feature tree for a velar nasal [ŋ] is shown in Figure 13.9.

Acoustic Features   Nasals show weak formant-like patterns, with one formant around 250 Hz and one typically at about 2200 Hz.

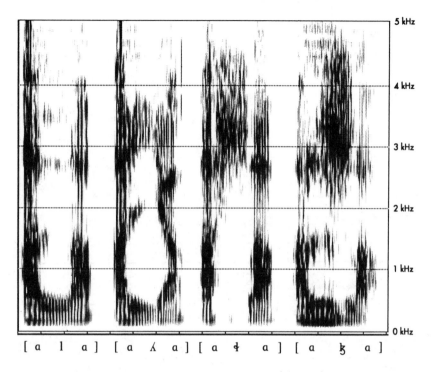

[ɑ   l   ɑ]   [ɑ   ʎ   ɑ]   [ɑ   ɬ   ɑ]   [ɑ   ɮ   ɑ]

Figure 13.8 Spectrograms of laterals.

TECHNICAL TERMS

affricate	oral
approximant	rhotic
clear-l	sibilant
dark-l	shibilant
flap	sonorant
fricative	spike
homorganic	spirant
lateral	stop
liquid	nasal stop
manner of articulation	oral stop
nasal	stricture
nasality	tap
obstruents	trill

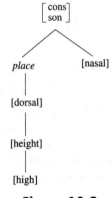

Figure 13.9
Velar nasal.

SYMBOLS

	bilabial	labio-dental	dental	alveolar	alveolo-palatal	palato-alveolar
stop	p b		t d̪	t d		
fricative	ɸ β	f v	θ ð	s z	ɕ ʑ	ʃ ʒ
approximant		ʋ				
nasal	m	ɱ	n̪	n		

	retro-flex	palatal	velar	uvular	pharyn-geal	glottal
stop	ʈ ɖ	c ɟ	k g	q ɢ		ʔ
fricative	ʂ ʐ	ç ʝ	x ɣ	χ ʁ	ħ ʕ	h
approximant	ɻ, ɻ̡	j	ɰ	ʁ		
nasal	ɳ	ɲ	ŋ	N		

DOUBLE ARTICULATIONS

	labial-alveolar	labial-palatal	labial-velar
stop	p͡t b͡d	p͡c b͡ɟ	k͡p g͡b
fricative		ɥ̊ˆ ɥˆ	ʍˆ wˆ
approximant		ɥ̊ ɥ	ʍ w
nasal	m͡n	m͡ɲ	ŋ͡m

LATERALS

		dental	alveolar	retroflex	palatal
fricatives	voiced	ɮ̪	ɮ	ɭˆ	ʎˆ
	voiceless	ɬ̪	ɬ	ɭ̊ˆ	ʎ̥ˆ
approximants	voiced	l̪	l	ɭ	ʎ
	voiceless	l̪̥	l̥	ɭ̊	ʎ̥

RHOTIC SOUNDS

dental trill	r̪
alveolar trill	r
alveolar fricative trill	r̝
uvular trill	ʀ
bilabial trill	ʙ
alveolar tap	ɾ
retroflex flap	ɽ
lateral flap	ɺ

EXERCISES

BASIC

1. Review:

ɸiʔɑ	xɔɣɑ	ʔæβɑ	βɛxɔ	ɣɒβɑ	ɸʌɣɒ
xɑʔɒ	ɣɑɸɔ	ʔɔɸʌ	ɸɒxɔ	βɒɸæ	βɔʔɒ

2. German:

tawkt	*is of use*	tawxt	*dips*
dɔk	*dock*	dɔx	*but*
ʃtaːkən	*stuck (pl)*	ʃtaːxən	*pricked (pl)*
nakt	*naked*	naxt	*night*
pɔkən	*pockmarks*	pɔxən	*beat*
lɔkt	*entices*	lɔxt	*perforates*
buːk	*baked*	buːx	*book*
pawkən	*practise*	hawxən	*breathe*

3. Build-up:

ˈgɑ lu ˈŋɔ ɹɪ ˈθæ sɒ   ˈxo n̪i hʊ ˈtʃej vu ˈβʌ

dʊ ˌɣɒ ɾɛ ɸow ˈvɪ ʔe

Try the build-up starting at the left and at the right side.

4. Affricates.

Pronounce:

tʃɑ	dʒu	tsɑ	dzu	pfɑ
pɸɑ	bβu	t̪θɑ	d̪ðu	cçɑ
kxɑ	gɣu	bvu	ɟʝɑ	tʃɒ

Build-up exercises:

ˈpfɑ gɣe ˈpɸo dzɛ ˈcçɔ t̪θi

kxi ˈd̪ðɔ tse ˈɟʝ otʃɑ ˌbβɛ

Remember to try starting the build-up from both ends.

Now try these:

ˈpfɛkɑdʒ   ˈbβeɹits   ˈd̪ðem̩ɔcç   ˈɟʝulidʒ   ˈt̪θonagɣ   ˈbvoʒɛtʃ

And these reversed affricates:

eɸp	ɛvb	ɛθt̪	ɛzd	ɛʃt
ɛɟʝ	ɛxk	oɣg	oçc	oʒd
ost	oðd̪	ofp	oβb	ozd

5. Try these Ewe words:

tsà	*to wander*	dzè	*salt*	tsò	*to cut*
dzà	*to fall (rain)*	tsù	*madness*	dzò	*fire*
tsé	*to bear fruit*	dzù	*to insult*	tsì	*water*
dzì	*heart*				

6. Try the affricates in these German words:

ˈpfʊnt	*pound*	ˈpsɑlm	*psalm*
ˈpflawmə	*plum*	ˈtsɑːl	*number*
ˈtʃɛçə	*Czech*	ˈtsyndən	*ignite*
ˈtsvɛtʃɡərn	*damsons*	ˈpsyçologi	*psychology*

7. Pig Latin is good dexterity practice. One variety moves an initial consonant (cluster) to the end of the word, and then the suffix [ej] is added:

key	ikej	*book*	ʊkbej
damage	æmɪdʒdej	*stop*	ɑpstej
thwart	ɑɹtθwej	*watch*	atʃwej

Read the following passage aloud:

ənɛsəzvej ɪʒənvej evej æpɪnıshej əzwej owsklej ʊtej iɪŋbeɪ aɹdmej aɪbej ɪnstənzwej ʌnfoɹtʃənətej ɛfərənspɹej əɹfej ændkej agdej udfej æθəɹɹej ænðej əɹfej əɹhej itmej owfleɪ, əðej ɛsıpiɹej əvej ɪtʃwej iʃej ədhej ɪvənstɹej owsej aŋlej ətej əɹfɛktpeɪ, alðowej ɪtej ʊdʃej ibej owtɪdnej ətðej ihej ɪddej owgej ɪnej əɹfej əðej ɛɹəɹbeɪ ændzbɹej əndej atnej ætðej iptʃej ʌfsteɪ.

8. Practise these nonsense forms. Be sure not to rush — aim for accuracy, not speed.

ˈpɯʧynɑ	ˈtʀʒamɤ	ˈdiɣɒŋɶ	ˈkɒβɛɲɶ	ˌɡeça'dy	ˌløxi'n̩ɔ
ˌbʌʔɤmɯ	ˌtøʒe'θu	ʔʌˈsɑɸɯ	ʒɶˈɣɔl̩ɒ	ˈtɶˌpofe	mʌˈcyxɛ

And these:

ˈladʒiˌpʰɛ	ˈpfeṣaˌcʰu	ˈbβɛtiˌɟɔ	kɔˈɲece	ɲeˈdlɛtɔ	ẓeˈlokxa
ˌliɟjaˈɹu	ˌcçadeˈɟa	ˌtʰɔŋoˈçi			

9. Uvular stops are made with the back of the tongue against the uvula. To make these, start with [ki ke kɛkɑ]; feel the place of articulation moving steadily back. Now starting with [kɑ], try to move the stop back as far as it will go. You should be producing a uvular [qɑ].
Practise:

qɑ	qɑ .	qɑ	qɔ	qo	qu

Try these, being very careful not to move the tongue forward:

qɑ	qɑ	qɛ	qe	qi

Now try the voiced stop:

ɢɑ	ɢɔ	ɢo	ɢu
ɢa	ɢɛ	ɢe	ɢi

10. The uvular fricatives are made by opening the closure slightly. Try starting with a velar [xɑ] and moving it back to [ʁ]. Then, do the same going from [ɣɑ] to [ʁ˗].

χɑ	χɔ	χo	χa	χu	χɒ
χi	χɛ	ʁ˗ɑ	ʁ˗o	ʁ˗ɔ	ʁ˗a
ʁ˗u	ʁ˗ɒ	ʁ˗i	ʁ˗ɛ		

11. The uvular approximant [ʁ] is made like a weak version of [ʁˠ]. Start with [ʁˠ] and lessen the constriction until the friction is much reduced. To make the nasal [ɴ], start with [ɢ], and lower the velum to allow air to pass through the nose.

ʁi	ʁy	ʁɛ	ʁɑ	ʁo	ʁu

Practise the uvular fricative in French; note that some are voiceless.

rose	ʁoz	'rose'	*tour*	tuʁ	'turn'
rat	ʁa	'rat'	*part*	paʁ	'leaves'
arbre	aʁbʁ	'tree'	*poutre*	putʁ̥	'girder'
trente	tʁɑ̃t	'thirty'	*Paris*	paʁi	'Paris'

Practise:

qɑ	qi	ɢoʏe	χoχɛ	ʁˠɑʁˠɛ	ɴɑɴe
qaɢi	ɢoɴa	ɴeχa	xɔχe	ʁˠɔɟ	qaʁi
χuʁi	ɴeʁˠi	qoɢɛ	qɔɢu	ŋɔɴu	χexɑ
ʏaʁˠɛ	ʏeʁi	qaqi	ɴwɲa	ʁɔʏɑ	xoʁˠɛ

12. The trills are not so much the result of conscious movement as of arranging the tongue appropriately and then blowing air out.

To make the alveolar trill [r], try these suggestions:

a. Place the tip of your tongue at the back of the alveolar ridge. Blow fairly hard out your mouth. Try to relax your tongue.

b. Many children make this sound to imitate airplanes, engines, machine guns, etc.

c. Some people find trills easier after [p]: [pr pr]

r r r r r

prɑ	ɹɑ	trɑ	krɑ	ri	re
rɛ	ra	rɑ	rɔ	ro	ru
ɑrɑ	ɑɾɑ	ɑɹɑ	ɑrɑ	eru	ori
irɔ	eɾo	ɑrɛ	ɛɾɔ	eɹɑ	aro

13. The uvular trill is made with the back of the tongue close to the uvula. The symbol is [ʀ]. Most people make an uvular trill when gargling. Try gargling with some water to get the feel of the uvular trill; then, try gargling only with saliva. This should produce a uvular trill.

Some people have luck starting from snoring. First try snoring while breathing in, and then try snoring while breathing out. Try the following steps:

a. Hold your fingers over your nostrils. Snore. Breathe out without changing anything else. Keep the back of your mouth very relaxed.

b. Try the uvula trill after [g]: [gʀ gʀ].

c. Try a voiced uvular fricative [ʁˠ]; then relax the tongue.

d. Sitting in a chair with a fairly high back, lean your head back until it is supported by the chair-back. It is important to be relaxed. Now try [ʀ].

e. Be patient. Rome was not trilled in a day.

Practise:

ʀ ʀ ʀ ʀ ʀ

gʀɑ	kʀɑ	bʀɑ	dʀɑ	tʀɑ
ɑʀɑ	eʀe	oʀo	uʀɔ	eʀɑ
eɾe	eɾe	eɾe	eɹe	eʀe
ʀɑʀo	ɾɑʀo	ʀɑɾo	ʀɑɾo	ɹɑʀo

14. The bilabial trill is rare, but fun; it can be transcribed as [ʙ].

ʙ ʙ ʙ ʙ ʙ   r r r r r   ʀ ʀ ʀ ʀ ʀ

To entertain and amuse your friends, try a uvular trill; keep it going and add an alveolar trill; keep both going and add a bilabial trill. This sounds like a motorboat starting or a ruffed grouse in heat. Practise at home before attempting this at cocktail parties. You're sure to get compliments on your progress in phonetics.

Advanced

15. Be sure to keep these distinct [ø œ ə]:

| œ ø ə | œ ə ø | œ œ ə | ə ø œ | møbə | sœlə |
| fœɲə | sədœ | nəkø | ʒøpə | ŋœlø | ɹəfø |

16. Central vowels lie between front and back vowels
    Practise sliding front to back and from back to front.

i — ɯ	e — ɤ	ɛ — ʌ	a — ɑ	y — u	ø — o
œ — ɔ	ɶ — ɒ	ɯ — i	ɤ — e	ʌ — e	ɑ — a
u — y	o — ø	ɔ — œ	ɒ — ɶ		

17. Practise

i ɨ ɯ	ɯ ɨ i	y ʉ u	u ʉ y	i y i	ɨ ʉ ɨ
ɯ ʉ ɨ	ɨ i ɯ	ø o ø	o ɤ ø	ʉ ø o	ø ɤ u
e ə ɤ	ɤ ə e	o ə œ	ø ə ɛ	a ɐ ɑ	ɑ ɐ a
ɨ ə a	ɐ a ɨ	miʃi	ɸuzʉ	bosə	ɸeʔo
kʉfɨ	cɐɹə	jəxɐ	ɲadʒɐ	lavʌ	piðʉ
nɯŋɨ	weʝə	sotʃə	xɒdza	ʒɨɣɐ	θugʉ

18. Two pharyngeal fricatives are possible: voiceless [ħ] and voiced [ʕ].
    Production hints:

a. Try saying [ɑ] and make it as low and as far back as possible. Your pharynx should feel tense.

b. With your thumb and forefinger press gently down and back on your adam's apple.

c. Try the voiceless [ħ] first, and then the voiced [ʕ].

ħa	ħaħa	ħo	ħoħo	ʕa	ʕaʕa
ʕɛ	ʕɛʕɛ	aħa	aħa	aʕa	aʁˤɑ
aħa	aχa	axa	aʕa	aħa	aʔa
aħɔ	ɛʕɒ	aʕe	oħa	ɛʕa	

19. Try the labio-dental flap [*] found in Gbeya (/ˈɡbeja/; Central African Republic):

gu*uuŋ	*deep place in river*	hɔ*ɔk	*passing out of sight*
*ɔŋ	*hitting something*	hɔ*ɔ*ɔ	*shout of victory*

20. Inuktitut (/ɪˈnʊktɪtʊt/; Northwest Territories) is known for its uvulars and long words. Be sure not to rush.

uqsuaʀnigaa	*The sea is calm and flat.*
qaumaakkirnigaa	*It is dawning.*
punniliurutiniariipkin	*I will make bread for you.*
uqallautiniariipkin	*I will tell you.*
anurauvallaarniqtuaq	*It is too windy.*
tigusunngitaa	*He does not want to take it.*
jaraiqsiqaaqtuaq	*He is going to get ice.*
siniktiɹiiqpauŋ	*Is he keeping him from sleeping?*
tuktulaigaqsijuami	*I am going to hunt caribou.*
aŋaatdʒliaqtuaq	*He went to church.*
uqaqsuqtuaq	*She used an interpreter.*
qamrulgujuq	*He snores a lot.*

21. The following story is one used extensively by the IPA as a standard short text; it has been translated and transcribed in hundreds of languages and dialects. Practise reading the following RP transcription.

[ˈðə ˈnɔθ ˈwɪnd ən ðə ˈsʌn]

[ˈðə ˈnɔθ ˈwɪnd ən ðə ˈsʌn wə dɪsˈpjutɪŋ ˈwɪtʃ wəz ðə ˈstɹɑŋgə, wən ə ˈtɹævlə kejm əˈlɒŋ ˈɹæpt ɪn ə ˈwɔm ˈkləwk. ðej əˈgɹiːd ðət ðə ˈwʌn hu ˈfəst səkˈsɪdɪd ɪn ˈmejkɪŋ ðə ˈtɹævlə tejk ɪz ˈkləwk ɒf ʃʊd bi kənˈsɪdəd ˈstɹɒŋgə ðən ðɪ ˈʌðə. ˈðen də ˈnɔθ ˈwɪnd ˈblu əz ˈhɑd əz i ˈkʊd, bət ðə ˈmɔɹ i ˈblu ðə mɔ ˈkləwslɪ dɪd ðə ˈtɹævlə ˈfəwld ɪz ˈkləwk əˈɹawnd im; ənd ət ˈlɑst ðə ˈnɔθ ˈwɪnd gejv ˈʌp ði əˈtempt. ðen ðə ˈsʌn ʃɒn ˈawt ˈwɔmlɪ ənd ɪˈmidʒətlɪ ðə ˈtɹævlə tʊk ˈɔf ɪz ˈkləwk. ən ˈsəw ðə ˈnɔθ ˈwɪnd wəz əˈblajdʒd tə kənˈfes ðət ðə ˈsʌn wəz ðə ˈstɹɒŋgəɹ əv ðə ˈtu.]

CHAPTER FOURTEEN
PHONATION

In the three preceding chapters, we have examined how the vocal tract is shaped to produce the various sounds of language. We now turn our attention to the activities of the vocal cords which are collectively known as **phonation** /ˌfoˈnejʃən/.

In this chapter you will learn about:

- anatomy of the larynx
- various adjustments of the vocal cords
- voice onset time.

ANATOMY

The **larynx** /ˈleɹɪŋks/ (Figures 14.1 and 14.2) is a complex structure, cylindrical in shape, composed of cartilages held together by ligaments, and supporting several muscles. Crucial to sound production are the **vocal cords**. These are two shelves of muscle and ligament lying horizontally just behind the adam's apple. They assume a variety of positions so as to affect the airstream coming from the lungs. We are already familiar with the voiced and voiceless states of the vocal cords, phonetically their most important adjustments.

Apart from speech, the role of the vocal cords is to open, allowing air to pass in and out. When closed, the vocal cords prevent foreign objects from entering the lungs. Also, when closed, they stabilise the rib cage when the lungs are inflated. This is useful in lifting heavy objects, in defecation, and in child-birth.

The larynx (Figure 14.1) sits atop the **trachea** /ˈtɹejkɹə/, a tube made up of a series of cartilagenous rings and resembling a vacuum-sweeper hose coming up from the lungs. Immediately above the trachea is the **cricoid cartilage** /ˈkɹaj̩kɔjd/, shaped like a signet ring with the shield at the back. You can feel the top of the trachea by placing a finger at the top of your chest in the notch between the collarbones. If you press gently, the cricoid cartilage is the larger ring protruding slightly forward. Just above the cricoid cartilage is a plough-shaped cartilage called the **thyroid cartilage** /ˈθaj̩ɹɔjd/. The forward point of the thyroid cartilage is easily identified as the adam's apple. At its rear, the thyroid cartilage

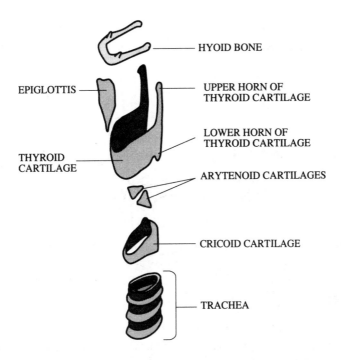

Figure 14.1 The parts of the larynx.

has two horns pointing down and two pointing up. The two lower horns attach to the outer edges of the cricoid cartilage in such a way that the thyroid cartilage can pivot forwards and backwards on the cricoid cartilage. The thyroid cartilage provides a shield for the vocal cords, which are attached at the rear of the point forming the adam's apple. The **arytenoid cartilages** /ˌeɹɪˈtiˌnɔjd/ are small and pyramid-shaped. They sit atop the rear of the cricoid cartilage on either side.

A spoon-shaped object in the pharynx, the **epiglottis** /ˌɛpɪˈglatɪs/, forms something of a hood over the main part of the larynx. Its function in the human body is uncertain, and its presence is a hindrance to observation of the larynx. Behind the chin is the **hyoid bone** /ˈhajˌɔjd/, shaped like a horseshoe. The hyoid bone provides support for the muscles of the tongue sitting above it, and it is connected by muscles to the larynx below. The hyoid bone has the small distinction of being the only bone in the body not immediately attached to another bone.

Figure 14.1 shows the parts of the larynx separated from each other. Figure 14.2 provides a side view of the larynx. The front of the larynx is to the left. Notice that the lower horns of the thyroid cartilage are fastened to the outer rim of the cricoid cartilage. This attachment allows the thyroid cartilage to rock back and forth. The vocal cords and arytenoid cartilages are shown by broken lines as they are hidden from view by the wall of the thyroid cartilage.

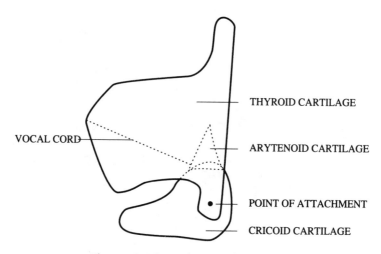

THYROID CARTILAGE

VOCAL CORD

ARYTENOID CARTILAGE

POINT OF ATTACHMENT

CRICOID CARTILAGE

Figure 14.2 Side view of the larynx.

GLOTTIS

The **vocal cords** (Figures 14.3 and 14.4) are two horizontal shelves of ligament and muscles joined together in front to the thyroid cartilage and in back to each of the arytenoid cartilages. Together with the arytenoid cartilages, they form a triangular space known as the **glottis** /ˈglɑtɪs/, through which air passes as it comes up from the lungs. The part of the glottis between the vocal cords is called the **ligamental glottis** /ˌlɪgəˈmɛntəl/, and the part lying between the arytenoid cartilages is called the **cartilagenous glottis** /ˌkɑɹtɪˈlædʒɪnəs/. The shape of the glottis is controlled by a number of muscles. The arytenoid cartilages can rotate on their base, and they can move forwards and backwards slightly. These movements give the glottis a variety of shapes which produce various sounds as we shall see later in this chapter.

From physics we know that the vibrating frequency of a string depends on two properties: length and tension. A longer string vibrates at a lower frequency than a shorter one; a lax string vibrates at a lower frequency than a taut one. Both the length and the tension of the vocal cords can be varied, but varying the tension of the vocal cords is the primary means of changing the vibration rate. The length and tension of the vocal cords can be altered in three ways: (1) the thyroid cartilage can be tilted forward stretching the vocal cords, (2) the position of the arytenoid cartilages can be moved, changing the length and tension of the vocal cords, and (3) the vocal cords themselves consist partially of muscles which can be tensed.

The vibration rate of the vocal cords controls the fundamental frequency of a sound and thus its perceived pitch. Men have longer vocal cords than women and children and thus have lower-pitched voices. Lengthening of the vocal cords

FRONT

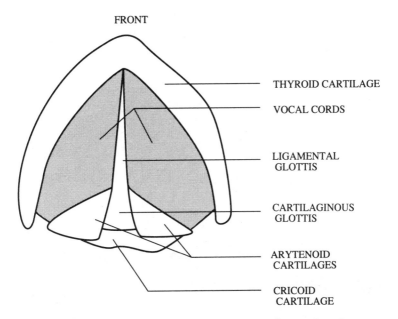

THYROID CARTILAGE

VOCAL CORDS

LIGAMENTAL
GLOTTIS

CARTILAGINOUS
GLOTTIS

ARYTENOID
CARTILAGES

CRICOID
CARTILAGE

Figure 14.3 View looking down at the larynx. The vocal cords are nearly closed with only a small triangular gap between the arytenoid cartilages.

occurs in males at puberty along with the growth of the beard and other secondary sexual characteristics. Boys often experience the so-called 'breaking' in their voice, a sign that they have not yet become used to the new length of their vocal cords.

Figure 14.4 shows a vertical cross-section of the larynx. You can see the vocal cords as shelves of muscles. Above them are overhanging folds known as the **false vocal cords**. Between the vocal cords and the false vocal cords is a cavity known as the **Ventricle of Morgagni** /ˌvɛntɹɪkəl əv ˌmoɹˈɡɑnji/.

The false vocal cords are generally not used distinctively in speech. Catford (1977) reports them used in the type of singing known as 'scat' singing which was used by a 1930's jazz singer Cab Calloway, and also in the singing of certain Tibetan monks. He also reports Chechen, a Caucasian language, as having the interesting contrast [daʔa] 'eat', with a plain glottal stop and [daʕʔa] 'castrate', where [ʕʔ] indicates a simultaneous closure of the vocal cords and the false vocal cords.

A Bushman language !Xóo (Southern Africa) uses **ventricular** /vɛnˈtɹɪkjuləɹ/ voice, made by tightening the upper part of the larynx. X-ray photgraphs of !Xóo speakers show that certain muscles in their upper larynx are much more developed than in speakers of other languages (Ladefoged, 1983). Such 'overdevelopment' is unusual. Ordinarily, we do not find statistically significant anatomical variation as a result of speaking different languages.

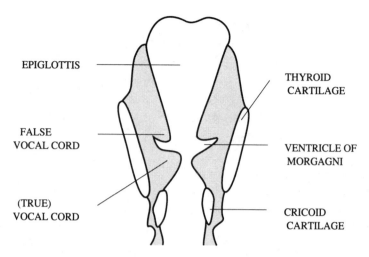

EPIGLOTTIS

THYROID
CARTILAGE

FALSE
VOCAL CORD

VENTRICLE OF
MORGAGNI

(TRUE)
VOCAL CORD

CRICOID
CARTILAGE

Figure 14.4 Cross-sectional view of the larynx from behind.

STATES OF THE GLOTTIS

The glottis can be shaped in a variety of ways, some used in languages and some not. The basic states of the glottis are glottal stop, voiceless and voiced. We will examine these first and then look at the other states.

BASIC STATES

GLOTTAL STOP   The entire glottis is closed for the **glottal stop** [ʔ]. Glottal stops are generally easy to make; just hold your breath with your mouth open. They are, however, harder for English speakers to control and to hear. Many speakers of English have special forms to indicate 'no' [ˈʔʌ̃ʔʌ̃] or [ˈʔm̃ʔm̃]. In both cases, the form begins with a glottal stop, and another glottal stop occurs in the middle of the form. If you use such forms for 'no', try saying them deliberately to get a better feel for glottal stops.

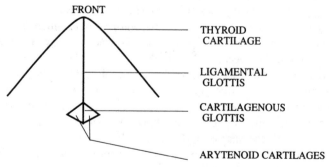

FRONT

THYROID
CARTILAGE

LIGAMENTAL
GLOTTIS

CARTILAGENOUS
GLOTTIS

ARYTENOID CARTILAGES

Figure 14.5 Glottal stop.

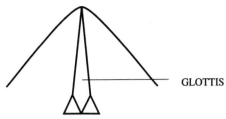

Figure 14.6 Voiceless.

Figure 14.5 shows a schematic glottis, positioned for a glottal stop. The vocal cords are together and thus shown as a single line; the arytenoid cartilages are shown as two triangles. The entire glottis is closed and no air can pass through.

Distinctive Features A glottal stop is unspecified as to place. It is specified as voiceless.

Acoustic features Glottal stops are marked by a complete absence of energy, with no strong transitional distinctions in the neighbouring sounds.

VOICELESS For **voiceless** sounds, the vocal cords are partially open, although not so completely open as possible. Say a long [hhhhh] with the vowel quality of [ɑ]; this is simply a voiceless vowel [ɑ̥]. You can hear the soft frication noise of voicelessness. Voiceless sounds involve considerably greater airflow than voiced sounds (Lieberman & Blumstein, 1988). Figure 14.6 shows the vocal cords positioned for a voiceless sound. The ligamental glottis is slightly open as is the cartilagenous glottis. Air can pass through creating the kind of noise heard in an [h]. Note that voiceless is a specific adjustment of the glottis and not just the absence of voicing.

Obstruents often occur both voiceless and voiced. Sonorants are rarely voiceless although Burmese contrasts voiced and voiceless sounds.

laʔ	be bare	l̥aʔ	uncover
lu	almost	l̥u	set free
maʔ	be steep	m̥ã	estimate
mi	inadvertently	m̥owʔ	blow
naʔ	be fully cooked	n̥a	nose
now	be awake	n̥owʔ	month

Burmese

Vowels are normally voiced; high vowels become voiceless in Japanese when surrounded by voiceless consonants.

çi̥to	person	haha	mother
ɸɯ̥kai	deep	aki̥kaze	autumn wind
kɯ̥suɰli	medicine	aɾimaçi̥tḁ	it was there

Japanese

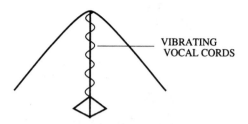

VIBRATING
VOCAL CORDS

Figure 14. 7 Voicing.

Distinctive Features   Voiceless sounds are specified [voiceless].

Acoustic Features   Voiceless sounds are characterised by low energy, usually without a formant pattern; see Figure 14.8.

VOICED   In voicing (Figure 14.7), the cartilaginous glottis is closed. The vocal cords vibrate allowing the air to escape from the lungs in brief puffs. Figure 14.7 gives a schematic picture of the glottis during voicing. The cartilagenous glottis is shut, and the wavy line indicates that the vocal cords are vibrating. During vibrations the vocal cords come together and then open in a wave-like motion.

The mechanism of voicing is fairly complex. To understand voicing, we need to learn about the **Bernoulli principle** /bəɹˈnuli/ first. According to this principle, a moving stream of gas or liquid will tend to pull objects from the sides of the stream to the middle. The faster the stream flows, the stronger the pull. You have probably experienced the phenomenon of a classroom door that opens into the room suddenly blowing shut when a breeze blows down the corridor pulling the door towards the stream of air. Similarly, when you turn on a bathroom shower and create a stream of water, a shower curtain will swing inwards.

In voicing, the vocal cords are held fairly closely together. When a stream of air from the lungs passes between them, the Bernoulli effect pulls them together. As soon as they are together, the Bernoulli effect ceases and force of the airstream from below pushes them apart again. As soon as they are apart, the Bernoulli effect comes into play again and pulls them together, and the process continues.

Thus, to produce voicing, the speaker positions the vocal cords appropriately with a suitable tension and then pushes air out of the lungs through them. We have already noted that the frequency of a sound is dependent on the vibration rate of the vocal cords which can be varied by changing the subglottal pressure. Greater air pressure results in a higher frequency and thus a higher pitch.

The result of the actions of the vocal cords is to impose a wave-like pattern of alternating pressures on the airstream as it enters the upper vocal tract which acts as a resonator on the airstream.

Obstruents regularly occur in both voiced and voiceless forms. Sonorants and vowels are usually voiced.

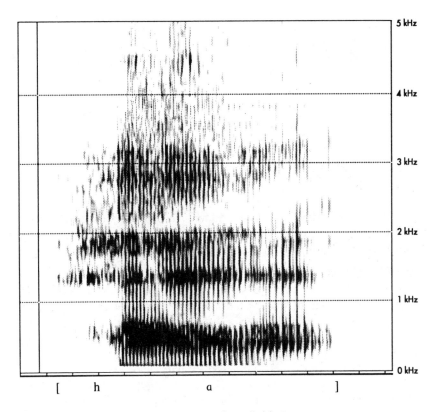

Figure 14.8 The syllable [hɑ].

Distinctive Features Voiced sounds are unspecified at the laryngeal node.

Acoustic Features Voicing involves a series of bursts of energy, organised in formant patterns. On a broadband spectrogram, voicing is identifiable as vertical striations during the voiced portions. Figure 14.8 shows a pronunciation of the syllable [hɑ]. During the [ɑ], we see the striations typical of voicing. Since the striations correspond to bursts of air coming through the glottis as it vibrates, we could measure the time elapsed between striations and calculate the frequency of the vocal cord vibration at that moment of time.

OTHER ADJUSTMENTS OF THE GLOTTIS

DEEP BREATHING For deep breathing, the glottis is opened as far as possible, allowing air to pass freely in and out. Frication may be heard if the air passes the edge of the vocal cords at a high velocity. Figure 14.9 shows the glottis wide open for deep breathing.

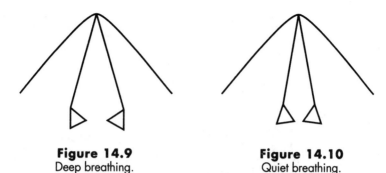

Figure 14.9
Deep breathing.

Figure 14.10
Quiet breathing.

QUIET BREATHING   In quiet breathing, the glottis is more open than for voiceless, yet more closed than for deep breathing. The pressure is not strong enough to cause frication. Figure 14.10 shows the glottis for quiet breathing.

MURMUR   Murmur is sometimes described as 'breathy voice'; there is vibration as in voicing, but there is a breathy quality as well. Intervocalic /h/ in English is murmured [ɦ], as in *ahead, ahoy*. Two types of mechanisms for producing murmur occur. In one, the vocal cords are vibrating, but are positioned far enough apart that they do not close completely allowing air to escape giving the breathy quality. The other type of murmur is produced by having the vocal cords vibrate, but with an open cartilagenous glottis allowing the air to escape. The two mechanisms for murmur are shown in Figure 14.11. Murmur$_1$ has the vocal cords vibrating, but slightly apart; murmur$_2$ has the vocal cords vibrating as in voicing, but with the cartilaginous glottis open.

Murmur is not used for extended stretches of speech, but languages sometimes have individual murmured sounds. (Actors imitating the late John Diefenbaker often use murmur.) The diacritic for murmur is two subscript dots [..] with a voiced symbol. Murmured sounds are well known in languages of the Indian subcontinent. The following examples from Hindi (/ˈhɪndi/; India) show contrastive voiced and murmured stops and affricates.

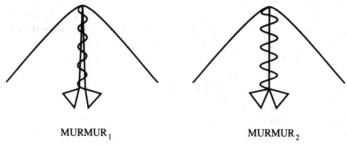

MURMUR$_1$

MURMUR$_2$

Figure 14.11   Murmur.

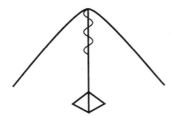

Figure 14.12 Creaky voice.

bal	hair	ḅal	forehead
ḓan	charity	ḍan	paddy
ḓal	branch	ḍan	shield
dʒəl	water	ḍʒəl	glimmer
gan	song	g̣an	kind of bundle

Hindi

CREAKY VOICE With **creaky voice**, the arytenoids are tightly closed, allowing only the forward portion of the vocal cords to vibrate (Figures 14.12 and 13). The result is a very low pitched vibration. The sound of creaky voice is often described as similar to the noise a stick makes when run along a picket fence. Creaky voice is not ordinarily used for extended speech, but in some languages, individual sounds are made with creaky voice. Some RP speakers trail off sentences with creaky voice; the social effect is often associated with snobbery. The diacritic for creaky voice is a subscript tilde [˷].

Margi (/ˌmaɹˈgi/; Nigeria; Hoffman, 1963) has various sounds with creaky voice.

bəlam	baboon	bəḅu	walk
dəgəl	bed	dəfɯ	mush
jɯ	love	j ɯ	do
wa	who?	wal	great

Margi

FALSETTO In **falsetto** /ˌfɑlˈsɛto/, the vocal cords are held very tightly allowing vibration only at the edges (Catford, 1977). Falsetto is not used distinctively in speech. Male singers often use falsetto to sing notes higher than their normal range. Yodelling involves a singing alternation between regular voice and falsetto.

WHISPER I will distinguish **whisper**, a state of the glottis, from **whispering**, a way of speaking quietly. Whisper involves an open cartilaginous glottis with no ligamental vibration. When you are whispering, you can feel your adam's apple to verify that your vocal cords do not vibrate and that thus there are no voiced sounds in whispering. Nevertheless, you can easily verify that in

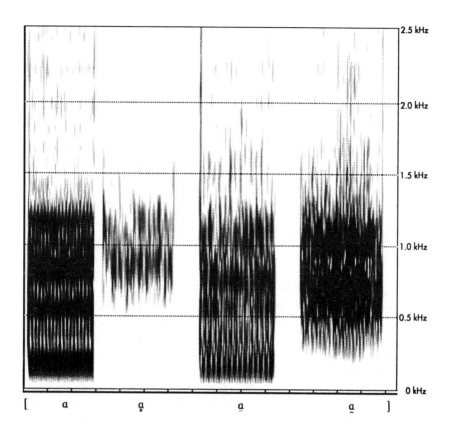

Figure 14.13 Spectrograms of various glottal adjustments.

whispering the words *seal* and *zeal* are distinct. If nothing is voiced, how then is a [z] distinct from an [s]? The answer is that in whispering, voicing is replaced by another adjustment of the vocal cords — whisper. There is no standard diacritic for whisper; I use three subscript dots [͟]. Whisper is not used in ordinary speech, although whispering is a human universal.

	Ordinary speech	**Whispering**
/s/	[s] voiceless	[s] voiceless
/z/	[z] voiced	[z] whisper

Figure 14.14
Whisper.

VOICE ONSET TIME   Most languages have two sets of stops — voiced and voiceless. It is not always simply the case that one set uses the voiced glottal adjustment and the other uses voiceless. French, English and Scots Gaelic all contrast two sounds [t] and [d] in word initial position, but in different ways. In

French, the two sounds are simply voiced and voiceless. In English, [d] is partially voiceless, and [t] is completely voiceless. In Scots Gaelic, both [d] and [t] are completely voiceless. The languages differ in the timing of the onset of voicing.

In Figure 14.15, time moves from left to right. The line labelled 'tongue opening' shows a single line to show that the tongue forms a stop. At the point where the stop is released, the line is divided in two. In the line labelled 'voicing', a straight line shows voicelessness, and the wavy line voicing. Pay particular attention to the relative timing of events. The notion of **voice onset time** (**VOT**) is useful in characterising the phonetic facts clearly. Voice onset time refers to the time at which voicing occurs in relation to the release of the stop.

Looking first at the onset of voicing for /d/ in Figure 14.15, we see that in French voicing starts immediately at the beginning of the stop, phonetically a straight-forward [d]. In English, voicing starts mid-way through the stop; we can represent this as [d̥d] showing the voiceless onset. (Recall that [d̥] = [t].) In Scots Gaelic voicing starts at the release of the stop, producing a phonetic [t].

If we now look at the onset of voicing for /t/, we see that in French voicing starts immediately at the release of the stop, producing a straight-forward [t]. In English, the voiceless period persists into the vowel, and the VOT is slightly after the release of the stop, giving an aspirated [tʰ]. In Scots Gaelic, the delay of VOT is even greater than for English, with a strongly aspirated stop, which we can symbolise as [tʰʰ].

We see that French /t/ and Scots Gaelic /d/ are identical in their glottal behaviour although one is called 'voiced' and the other 'voiceless'. The terms *voiced* and *voiceless* when used with consonants often represent a difference in VOT, rather than an absolute description of vocal cord activity. Voiced sounds have an earlier VOT than voiceless sounds.

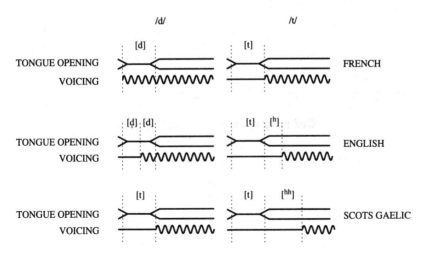

Figure 14.15 VOT of /d/ and /t/ in French, English and Scots Gaelic.

Dutch

p	t	k		b	d	g
10	15	25		-85	-80	25

Cantonese

p	t	k		pʰ	tʰ	kʰ
9	14	34		77	75	87

English

pʰ	tʰ	kʰ		b	d	g
58	70	80		-101	-102	-88

Thai

b	d			p	t	k		pʰ	tʰ	kʰ
-96	-102			3	15	30		78	59	98

Hindi

b	d	ḍ	g	p	t	ṭ	k	pʰ	tʰ	ṭʰ	kʰ
-85	-87	-76	-63	13	15	9	18	70	67	60	92

Figure 14.16 VOT for several languages (times in msec).

Sounds, like the English or Scots Gaelic /t/, with the stop voiceless and the voicelessness carrying on into the following segment are called **aspirated** /ˈæspɪˌɹejtɪd/. Note that the following segment may be a vowel, *pay* [p̥eej], or a sonorant, *play* [p̥lej]. English has light aspiration, whereas Scots Gaelic has heavy aspiration. In an English word like *stop,* with an unaspirated [t], the VOT is at the release of the stop and thus similar to that of a French /t/ or Scots Gaelic /d/.

Figure 14.16 (Abramson & Lisker, 1964) gives the voice onset times for a number of languages. Dutch, Cantonese, and English have a two-way contrast in VOT. Thai and Hindi have a three-way contrast. No language is known to have a four-way contrast of voice onset time. A positive value for VOT means that voicing onset occurs after the release of the stop; a negative value means that voicing onset precedes the release of the stop.

Voice onset time is not the only attribute of aspiration. Aspiration also may involve greater subglottal force. This force holds the vocal cords apart longer, thus preventing voicing.

Scots Gaelic also has preaspiration before medial and final voiceless stops: [ʰp ʰt]. Before [k], the aspiration is usually realised as a velar fricative [xk].

kɔʰp	*foam*	ˈʃnʲɛːʰpən	*turnips*
kaʰt	*cat*	ˈkrɔʰtəɬ	*lichen*
maxk	*son*	ˈfaxkəɬ	*word*

Scots Gaelic

Korean has an unusual three-way series of stops. According to Kim (1965, 1970), the set [p t k] are lax. The other stops are tense: [p* t* k*] are unaspirated, and [pʰ tʰ kʰ] are aspirated. Tenseness here is manifested as greater length and greater air pressure.

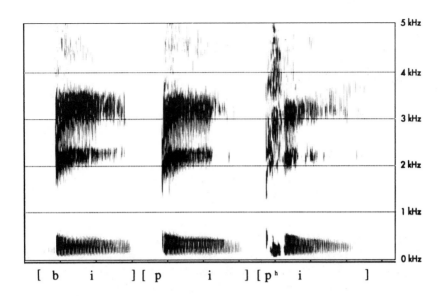

[b   i   ] [p   i   ] [pʰ   i   ]

Figure 14.17 A three-way distinction in VOT.

pam	night	pə:r	bee
p*ul	horn	p*aɯda	be quick
pʰar	arm	pʰi	blood
tal	moon	to:l	stone
t*al	daughter	t*am	a crack
tʰa:l	mask	tʰək	chin
kat	hat	kot	place
k*ul	honey	tʰok*i	rabbit
kʰo	nose	kʰoŋ	bean

Korean

Distinctive Features   Voicelessness is specified as [voiceless], no matter what the voice onset time. The feature [aspirated] is used to mark the aspirated stops in three-way contrasts. Some authors have used [tense] as equivalent to [voiceless]. The use of the word *tense* is so confused in phonetics and phonology, that it is perhaps better to stick with [voiceless].

Acoustic Features   Voice onset time is fairly easily measured from a waveform or a spectrogram. Aspiration appears as a fairly faint burst of energy on a spectrogram. Figure 14.17 shows a spectrogram of voiced, voiceless plain and aspirated bilabial stops. Notice the noise after the release of the aspirated stop which is absent in the release of the plain stop.

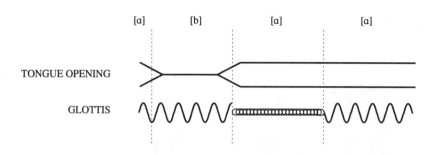

Figure 14.18 Murmured stop.

MURMURED STOPS

We discussed murmur earlier in this chapter. This adjustment of the glottis is used in many of the languages of India which typically have four kinds of constrastive stops. Three kinds are familiar to us. The stops [p b pʰ] are voiceless, voiced and voiceless aspirated. The fourth kind is murmured. It has often been referred to as a voiced aspirate. In our terms aspirates are always voiceless, so a voiced aspirated stop is a contradiction in terms. Ladefoged (1982) has argued that the stop portion of these sounds is voiced, but there is a following portion (occupying the same time portion as aspiration with the aspirated stops) in which the vocal cords assume a murmured position. Figure 14.18 shows the timing of the events for a murmured bilabial stop.

TECHNICAL TERMS

arytenoid cartilages	falsetto	trachea
aspiration	glottal stop	ventricle of Morgagni
aspirated	glottis	ventricular
Bernoulli principle	hyoid bone	vocal cords
cartilagenous glottis	larynx	voiceless
creaky voice	ligamental glottis	voice onset time
cricoid cartilage	murmur	VOT
epiglottis	phonation	whisper
false vocal cords	thyroid cartilage	whispering

SYMBOLS

[ɦ]   murmured vowel (glottal fricative)

DIACRITICS

[˷]   creaky
[¨]   murmur
[͟]   whisper

EXERCISES

BASIC

1. Practise the following:

   fffffff vvvvvvvvv fffffffff   sssssssssss zzzzzzzzz sssssssssss

   ðððððððð θθθθθθθ ðððððððð   ʒʒʒʒʒʒʒʒ ʃʃʃʃʃʃʃʃʃ ʒʒʒʒʒʒʒ

   Now try:

   f v f v f v   s z s z s z   ʃ ʒ ʃ ʒ ʃ ʒ   θ ð θ ð θ ð

2. Practise changing the voicing with sonorants:

   l̥ l l̥ l l̥ l l̥ l l̥ l l̥ l   m m̥ m m̥ m m̥ m m̥ m m̥ m m̥ m

   ɹ l̥ ɹ l̥ ɹ l̥ ɹ l̥ ɹ l̥ ɹ l̥ ɹ   n n̥ n n̥ n n̥ n n̥ n n̥ n

   nɛn̥   lil̥   nun̥   m̥em   mɑm̥   lul̥   ɹɔɹ̥   nin̥

3. Practise:

   dɛlθz   maslf   slfɑn   sl̥ifp   fm̥og   kɹɛn̥   hifts   vtɔkn̥ul

4. Gradual changes. Start at the top of each column and work down:

ˈpiðukælmɔ	ˈʔisuɹdɛnoˈɣu
ˈpɹðukælmɒ	ˈʔisuɹtenoˈɣu
ˈpɹðukelmɒ	ˈʔizuɹten̥oˈɣu
ˈpɹðukelmɒ	ˈʔizulten̥oˈɣu
ˈbɹðukelmɒ	ˈʔɪzultæn̥oˈɣu
ˈbɹðugelmɒ	ˈʔɪzuɹtæn̥oˈɣʊ

5. Now try the fricative laterals; the voiced one is written [ɮ], and the voiceless one is [ɬ]. Start with a voiceless [l̥] You should not have any more friction than you would have with [h].
   Practise the following:

   l l l l l   l̥ l̥ l̥ l̥ l̥

   ɑlɑ   ɛlɛ   ili   olo   lɑl̥o   l̥ulɛ   lil̥ɛ   lɔlɑ

   Start with [l l l l l]; gradually raise the body of the tongue (not the tip) to produce a strong fricative [ɮ ɮ ɮ ɮ ɮ]. Make sure that the tip of the tongue remains against the alveolar ridge.

   ɮo   ɮi   ɮɑ   loɮi   ɮeʒa   ɮeli   luɮa   ɮelɔ

   Now say [l]; devoice it to [l̥]; raise the body of the tongue to get a strong fricative [ɬ]. Alternatively, start with [l]; raise the tongue to get [ɮ]; now devoice it to [ɬ].

   ɬɬɬɬɬɬɬɬɬ   ɮɮɮɮɮɮɮɮɮ

   ɬɛ   ɬu   ɬɔ   ɬo   ɮe   l̥i   lɑ   l̥ɛ

   luɬɑ   ɮoɬe   laɮe   lɛl̥i   lɛɬi   lɛɬa

   ɬale   ɬoɮa   ɬil̥ɔ

6. Murmur. In English, /h/ between vowels is usually murmured [ɦ]. Try saying *aha, ahead, ahoy*. Now try to prolong the [ɦ]: [aˈɦa — aˈɦɦɦɦɦɦa]. Now try to eliminate first the initial vowel and then the final one, ending up with just [ɦɦɦɦɦ]. Murmur with other consonants is often written with [◌̤] underneath.
   Try:

ɦa	ɦɛ	ɦi	ɦo	ɦu	ɦe
ba̤	da̤	ga̤	bo̤	do̤	go̤
be̤di	gṳbɔ	da̤gɛ			

7. Gujarati (/ˌgudʒəˈɹati/; India) distinguishes murmured stops and vowels:

baɾ	*twelve*	pɔɾ	*last year*
ba̤ɾ	*outside*	pɔ̤ɾ	*early morning*
ba̤ɾ	*burden*	pʰɔdz	*army*
a̤ɾ	*obstruction*	a̤ ɾ̤	*bones*

8. Bhojpuri (/ˌbowdʒˈpuɹi/; India) has murmured nasals: practise these:

samar	*battle*	sama̤r	*be careful*
ana:r	*pomegranate*	ana̤:r	*darkness*
ba:nar	*monkey*	a:na̤r	*blind*
ka:n	*ear*	ka:n̤	*shoulder*

9. Bengali (/bɛŋˈgali/; India) has murmured stops:

ba̤g	*part*	go̤bir	*deep*
lo̤b	*greed*	bṳbon	*earth*
do̤nuk	*bow*	di̤da	*doubt*
kā̤d	*shoulder*	dṳp	*incense*
gɔr	*room*	aga̤t	*blow*
ba̤g	*tiger*	gṳgu	*dove*

10. Creaky voice sounds like a stick on a picket fence. Open the mouth wide, and say [ɑː]. Start at a low pitch, and try to go as low as you can; now try to go even lower. This often results in creaky voice. We will symbolise creaky voice with [◌̰].

    a̰ ḭ o̰ ḛ ṵ ḛ ɑ̰ ɔ̰

11. Lango (/ˈlaŋˌgo/; Africa) has both creaky vowels and creaky consonants:

lee	*animal*	lḛḛ	*axe*
man	*this*	ma̰n̰	*testicles*
kor	*chest*	ko̰r̰	*hen's nest*
tur	*break*	tṵr̰	*high ground*

12. Transcribe:
    How little could I foresee, as I sat nervously awaiting the employment interviewer's seemingly endless perusal of my application for junior laundress to the House of Commons, of my sixteen never-to-be-forgotten years of warmth, humour, and humanity to come in the corridors of power.

ADVANCED

13. Whisper. We will symbolise this with [̤].
    Try whispering the sentence below. Listen to the shifts between voiceless and whisper:

Where	can	he	find	it?
we̤ɹ	kə̤n̤	hi̤	fa̤ɪn̤d̤	ɪ̤t

    Try whispering these pairs, concentrating on the sounds with whisper.

    seal zeal   ether either   fat vat   pressure pleasure

14. Try the following Bengali retroflex and palato-alveolar sounds. Note especially the aspirated and murmured stops.

tʰunko	fragile	aʈʰa	glue	katʰ	wood
aʈʰaro	eighteen	ɖak	drum	ɖal	shield
ɔɖel	sufficient	ɖima	slow	tʃʰobi	picture
aʈʃʰar	to thrash	matʃʰ	fish	tʃʰoʈo	small
dʒop	bush	nirdʒɔr	spring	maɖʒ	middle
dʒinuk	oyster				

15. Try the following alveolo-palatals from Japanese:

tɕi	blood	kɯ̥tɕi	mouth
tɕisei	topography	ɕima	island
ɕḁɕin	photograph	anɕin	peace of mind
ɕi̥sei	municipal government		

16. Abi Dabi /ˈabiˌdabi/ is considered by many to be a gourmet pig latin. The rule is that the sequence [əb] is inserted before each vowel or diphthong.

cat	kəbæt	dog	dəbɑg	try	tɹəbaj
at	əbæt	strip	stɹəbɪp	flat	fləbæt
lousy	ləbawzəbi	carcinogenic	kəbɑɹsəbɪnəbədʒəbenəbɪk		

    Decode the following Abi Dabi utterances:

    ### SIGNS FOUND IN PUBLIC PLACES

    ðəbə ləbɪft əbɪz bəbiəbɪŋ fəbɪkst fəbəɹ ðəbə nəbekst fjəbu dəbejz. dəbuɹəbɪŋ ðəbæt təbajm wəbi rəbɪgɹəbet ðəbət jəbu wəbɪl bəbi əbʌnbəbeɹəbəbəbəl.

    ðəbə pəbəɹəbejd təbəməbaɹəbow wəbɪl təbejk pləbejs əbɪn ðəbə məboɹnəbɪŋ əbɪf əbɪt rəbejnz əbɪn ðəbə əbæftəbəɹnəbun.

    nəbow tʃəbɪldɹəbən əbələbawd əbɪn ðəbə məbətəbəɹnəbɪtəbi wəbaɹdz.

    əbæz fəbəɹ ðəbə tɹəbawt səbəɹvd jəbu əbæt ðəbə həbowtəbel məbanəbəpəbowl, jəbu wəbɪl bəbi səbɪŋəbɪŋ əbɪts prəbejzəbɪz təbə jəbəɹ gɹəbændtʃəbɪldɹəbən əbæz jəbu ləbaj əban jəbəɹ dəbeθbəbed.

17. Transcribe and practise with an RP accent. Use a British dictionary to help you.

    Harriet seemed to have an almost theological halo about her head as she ambled towards him in the fading moonlight with that peculiarly sexy way of walking which was really due to an old spinal injury and incipient arthritis.

CHAPTER FIFTEEN
AIRSTREAM MECHANISMS

In our discussion of sounds so far, we have simply assumed that the lungs produce an airstream which is modified by the larynx and vocal tract. This is, indeed, the way the vast majority of phonetic sounds are produced. In this chapter, we will discuss other ways which are used to move air in and out of the body.

For phonetic sounds to occur, air must move past the articulators. This moving air is called the **airstream**; it is set in motion by the **airstream mechanism**. The anatomical organ whose action sets the airstream in motion is called the **initiator**. The airstream may be **egressive** /ˌiˈɡɹɛsɪv/, flowing out of the body, or **ingressive** /ˌɪŋˈɡɹɛsɪv/, flowing into the body.

In this chapter you will learn about:
* the various ways languages move air in and out of the body
* the kinds of sounds made by different airstream mechanisms.

AIR PRESSURE

All airstream mechanisms work by changing the air pressure in the vocal tract. A basic principle of physics, **Boyle's Law**, says that the pressure of a gas varies inversely with its volume. A second principle is that, if possible, gas will move so as to equalise different pressures.

Consider Figure 15.1, which shows an experiment with a container having a movable top and a door in the side. At the beginning of the experiment (Figure 15.1a) the door is open, and the air pressure is the same both inside the container and outside (arbitrarily shown as [0]). In Figure 15.1b the door is closed; then in Figure 15.1c the top of the container is lowered to make the container smaller. According to Boyle's Law, if the volume is thus decreased, the air pressure is increased. The resulting air pressures are shown in Figure 15.1c. The outside air pressure remains at [0]; however, the inside pressure is now greater, shown as [+]. If the door is now opened (1d), the air will rush out to equalise the pressure inside the container with that outside.

In a second experiment shown in Figure 15.2, the door is again open (2a), and

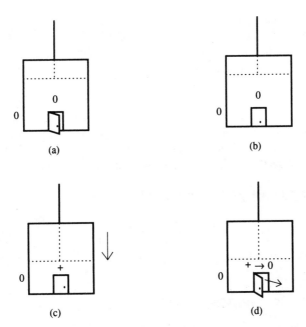

Figure 15.1 A reduction in the size of the container causes an increase in the pressure within the container. On opening, air rushes out.

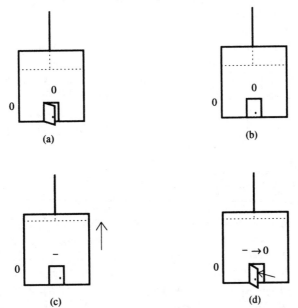

Figure 15.2 An increase in the size of the container causes a decrease in the pressure within the container. On opening, air rushes in.

the air pressure both inside and outside the container is [0]. In Figure 15.2b, the door is shut, and in Figure 15.2c, the top of the container is raised thus increasing the volume of the container. Boyle's law says that if the volume is increased, the pressure is decreased, here shown as [–]. In Figure 15.2d, the door is opened and air rushes in to equalise air pressures inside and outside the container.

In phonetics, our body is the container, and the door is our mouth and nose, opening to the outside world. By changing the volume of our lungs, we can change the air pressure; if our oral or nasal passage is open, air moves in or out of our body. If we expand our chest cavity, pressure inside is lowered, and air flows in. If we contract our chest cavity, pressure inside is raised, and air flows out.

AIRSTREAM MECHANISMS

Three airstream mechanisms occur ordinarily in language. The mechanisms are known as **pulmonic**, **glottalic**, and **velaric**. The initiators for these mechanisms are, respectively, the lungs, the glottis, and the velum. Each of these mechanisms can occur with an egressive or ingressive airstream.

PULMONIC AIRSTREAM MECHANISM

The primary airstream mechanism for speech is **pulmonic** /ˌpʊlˈmɑnɪk/ with the lungs as initiator. All sounds of English are pulmonic. In fact, most languages in the world use only pulmonic egressive sounds; and of those languages that use other kinds of airstream mechanisms, the great majority of their sounds are still pulmonic egressive.

The primary function of the lungs is, of course, for breathing; speech is a secondary phenomenon and accompanies breathing. When the lungs are contracted, the air pressure is increased, and air flows out. When the lungs are expanded, the air pressure is decreased and air flows in.

The two lungs sit inside the rib cage (Figure 15.3). They consist of soft, non-muscular tissue and have an elastic property, like a sponge, allowing them to be expanded and contracted. As with a sponge, if the size of the lungs is altered, the elastic property exerts a force to return the lungs to their resting size. The two lungs are independent, so if one is injured, we can still breathe with the other one. The right lung is slightly larger than the left one.

The tiny tubes within the lungs are supplied with air by a pair of tubes, one for each lung, called a **bronchus** /ˈbɹɑŋkəs/. The two **bronchi** /ˈbɹɑŋki/ join to form the **trachea** /ˈtɹejkiə/, which is formed of rings of **cartilages** /ˈkɑɹtɪlɪdʒ/. The cartilagenous /ˌkɑɹtɪˈlædʒɪnəs/ rings are not complete, but are closed at the rear by membrane. Just behind the trachea is a tube called the **œsophagus** /əˈsɑfəgəs/, which carries food from the mouth to the stomach. Having the trachea formed of rings rather than being a solid tube is useful in allowing us to bend our neck more easily.

Several muscles control the ribcage. Certain of these, the **external intercostals** /ˌɪntəɹˈkɑstəl/, lift the ribcage and hold it up, inflating the lungs. These

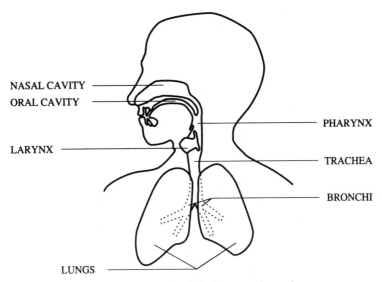

NASAL CAVITY

ORAL CAVITY

PHARYNX

LARYNX

TRACHEA

BRONCHI

LUNGS

Figure 15.3 A view of the lungs and vocal tract.

can be termed the ingressive muscles. Other muscles, the **internal intercostals** pull the ribcage down and deflate the lungs. The **abdominal muscles** /ˌæbˈdɑmɪnəl/ also help deflate the lungs. These can be termed the egressive muscles. As explained above, the lungs are elastic and will resist expansion and contraction, attempting to return to their resting size.

Singing teachers often claim that the **diaphragm** /ˈdajəˌfɹæm/, a large dome-shaped muscle lying just below the lungs, is very important in sound production; however, physiological research (Bouhuys, 1974) has shown that it plays little role in either speech or singing.

The maximum capacity of the lungs is about seven litres. If you breathe out as much as you can, some two litres of air still remain in the lungs. Thus, at a maximum, you have the use of five litres of air for speech. At rest, we breathe slowly both in and out. In speaking, however, we breathe in quickly and then breathe out over a prolonged period, using the egressive air for speech.

Draper, *et al.* (1960) found that we use the ingressive muscles to inflate the lungs and then we continue using them in breathing out to slow down the contraction of the lungs which results from their inherent elastic property. In exhaling, after the lungs pass their point of rest, we bring the egressive muscles increasingly into play to push the air out and to overcome the increasing elastic force which resists compression.

Figure 15.4 presents a stylised chart which we will use to show the various types of airstream mechanisms. The outside air pressure is arbitrarily set at [0]. Air pressure is marked in the lungs, pharynx, and mouth; [+] indicates a pressure higher than the outside air pressure, and [–] indicates a pressure lower than the outside air pressure.

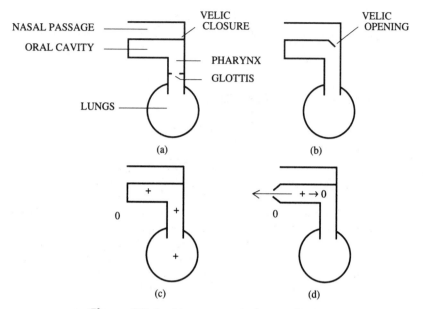

Figure 15.4 Air pressures in the vocal tract.

Look at Figures 15.4a and 15.4b to understand how this diagram represents the vocal tract. Figure 15.4a shows a bilabial stop with closure at the left end of the oral cavity. Figure 15.4b shows a bilabial nasal with velic opening so that air can pass out the nose.

Figure 15.4c shows a **plosive** /'plowsɪv/, that is, an egressive pulmonic stop, before its release. The chest cavity has been contracted with the result that the air pressure in the lungs is greater than the outside air pressure. Since there are no obstructions, this increased air pressure has spread to the pharynx and oral cavity as well. Figure 15.4d shows the plosive at the moment of release. When the lips open, the greater air pressure inside the vocal tract causes air to flow outwards until the air pressure inside the vocal tract equals that of the outside.

Pulmonic ingressive sounds are quite easy to make. Speakers occasionally use that airstream mechanism for short utterances so as to continue talking while breathing in, as in counting. The vocal cords do not vibrate well with ingressive air, so voiced sounds are a bit odd. Boys in Switzerland are reported using ingressive air while courting girls outside their bedroom window; their intent is to avoid identification by the girls' parents (Dieth 1950).

Figure 15.5 shows the production of a pulmonic ingressive stop. While a stop is being produced, the chest cavity has been enlarged, lowering the air pressure inside. When the stop is released, air flows into the body until the inside and outside air pressures are equalised.

Languages rarely use pulmonic ingressive sounds as regular speech sounds; however, Danin, a ritual language of the Lardil in Australia, according to Hale

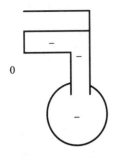

Figure 15.5
Pulmonic ingressive stop.

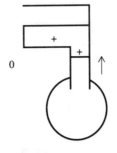

Figure 15.6
Ejective.

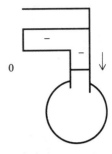

Figure 15.7
Glottalic Ingressive.

(Catford, 1977), has a pulmonic ingressive [l]. S.G. Thomason (p.c.) reports that a Taiwanese dialect of Chinese has two pulmonic ingressive fricatives as variants initially before a glottal stop. Speakers in Newfoundland sometimes pronounce *yeah* in the sense of 'yes' with an ingressive pulmonic airstream; the same thing happens in Swedish, where /ja/ 'yes' is frequently heard with an ingressive pulmonic airstream.

GLOTTALIC AIRSTREAM MECHANISM

The larynx can move up and down in the neck. If you put your fingers lightly on your adam's apple and swallow, you will feel the larynx move upward for a short distance and then back down. Figure 15.6 shows that if the vocal cords are closed in a glottal stop and the larynx then raised, the air pressure of the pharynx and mouth is raised. (We are not concerned here with the air pressure in the lungs.) This forms our second airstream mechanism, **glottalic** /ˌglɑˈtælɪk/, in which the glottis acts as the initiator. Because of the small size of the supralaryngeal vocal tract, the glottalic airstream mechanism cannot be continued very long, but it can create quite high pressures.

Glottalic egressive stops are called **ejectives** /ˌiˈdʒɛktɪv/. They are transcribed with the symbol for a voiceless stop, with the diacritic [ˀ]: [pˀ tˀ cˀ kˀ qˀ]. Glottalic egressive fricatives and affricates are also possible: [fˀ sˀ ʃ tθˀ tsˀ tʃˀ].

tˀanta	*bread*	tˀaqa	*group*
cˀakij	*to be thirsty*	cˀuʎu	*cap*
kˀucu	*corner*	hajkˀa	*how many*
wisqˀaj	*to close*	qˀupi	*warm*

Quechua (/ˈkɛtʃuə/; South America)

Glottalic ingressive sounds, Figure 15.7, can be made without a great deal of difficulty. The glottis is closed, and then the larynx is lowered prior to release. In fact, however, these sounds seem not to occur, although Pike (1963) reports them in Tojolabal /ˌtoholɑˈbɑl/ of Guatemala.

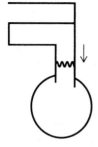

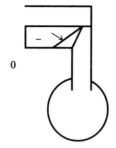

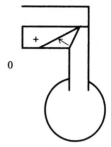

Figure 15.8	**Figure 15.9**	**Figure 15.10**
Implosive.	Click. The body of the tongue is drawn back as shown by the arrow, enlarging the oral cavity.	Velaric egressive stop.

Although pure glottalic ingressives are rare, a somewhat related mechanism producing sounds called implosives is occasionaly found. **Implosives** /ˌɪmˈplowsɪv/ involve a downward-moving larynx. Normally, voicing occurs when air is pushed upwards through the glottis. With implosives, the vocal cords vibrate as the larynx is pushed downwards through the air. Figure 15.8 illustrates this with a wavy line showing the vibrating vocal cords. Implosives are transcribed with modified forms of the voiced stops: [ɓ ɗ ɠ].

Gbeya /ɠbɛjɑ/ (Central African Republic) has bilabial and apico-postdental implosives. The term *apico-postdental* means that the tip of the tongue is at the boundary of the teeth and alveolar ridge. The exercises at the end of the chapter give help in learning to pronounce implosives.

ba	*to take*	ɓa	*to disavow*
bi	*to extinguish*	ɓi	*to pick fruit*
dik	*to thunder*	ɗik	*to sift*
dɔk	*to be muck*	ɗɔk	*to be weak*
gede	*certain tree*	geɗe	*buttock*

Gbeya

VELARIC AIRSTREAM MECHANISM

The third airstream mechanism we encounter is **velaric** /vəˈleːɪk/. The back of the tongue and the velum act as the initiator. Velaric ingressive stops are known as **clicks**. These are shown in Figure 15.9; here the diagonal lines show the tongue making a dorso-velar closure; this closure is always present in velaric sounds. Simultaneously, a closure is made farther forward, *e.g.*, the lips, to seal the oral cavity. Then the tongue is pulled down and back, enlarging the cavity and thus lowering the air pressure inside the oral cavity. When the lips are opened, air flows in. The resulting sound is called a bilabial click, or more commonly, a kiss.

As ordinary consonants, clicks are found only in the languages of southern Africa. In many other cultures, however they are used as special sounds. In

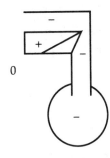

Figure 15.11
A velaric egressive airstream simultaneous with an ingressive pulmonic airstream with velic opening.

English, a dental click [ǀ], often written *tsk-tsk,* is used to indicate displeasure or concern. A palato-alveolar click is symbolised [ǂ]. An alveolar lateral click [ǁ] is used to urge on horses. In the release of this click, only one side of the tongue is lowered on release. For an alveolar or postalveolar click the symbol [!] is used. The bilabial click is transcribed [☉].

Velaric egressive sounds (Figure 15.10) are not found as speech sounds. Many people, however, use them when trying to remove a hair from the tip of their tongue. It is possible to use the velaric airstream mechanism simultaneously with a pulmonic airstream mechanism. Try saying a string of *tsk-tsk-tsk* [ǀ ǀ ǀ] and simultaneously breathe in and out through the nose; you can easily observe that the two events are independent of each other.

Bagpipes are constructed so that an inflated bag is pressed to act as the initiator of the air-mechanism forming the sound. Since the bag is the initiator, the player is free to breathe at will, blowing through a tube to inflate the bag as required. Bagpipe music, thus, is written without any pauses for breathing. Bagpipe players often practise with a chanter, a special instrument without a bag, similar to a recorder or clarinette. Ordinarily, of course, the chanter is played with pulmonic egressive air. To produce the sustained notes of bagpipe music, however, and to breathe as well, the musician learns to use a glottalic egressive airstream to keep the music going, while simultaneously using a pulmonic ingressive air–stream through the nasal passage to replenish the air supply in the lungs (Figure 15.11).

In a similar fashion, some smokers, after drawing the smoke into the mouth, use an egressive velaric mechanism to eject the smoke out of the mouth while simultaneously employing a pulmonic ingressive mechanism with velic opening pulling the smoke up through the nostrils and down into the lungs.

Languages with clicks often have an amazing number of them. A voiced click, for example, involves a pulmonic [g] so that the vocal cords are vibrating simultaneously with the click. In nasal clicks (Figure 15.11), a pulmonic /ŋ/ is made simultaneously with the click.

Ladefoged and Traill (1984) describe Nama, a language of southern Africa as having 20 clicks (Figure 15.12). Here, [!] is used to represent an alveolar click.

ŒSOPHAGIC AIRSTREAM MECHANISM Individuals sometimes develop cancer or other ailments in their larynx, requiring surgery which restructures the air tract so that they breathe through a hole in the neck. Such people obviously cannot use the pulmonic airstream mechanism to produce sounds. Sometimes they learn to swallow air and then to belch in a controlled fashion using this air for speech (Figure 15.13). This airstream mechanism is known as

	voiceless unaspirated	voiceless aspirated	delayed aspiration	voiced nasal	glottal closure
Dental	ǀgoɑ *put into*	ǀkho *play an instrument*	ǀho *push into*	ǀno *measure*	ǀo *sound*
Palatal	ǂgais *calling*	ǂkharis *small one*	ǂhais *baboon's arse*	ǂnais *turtledove*	ǂais *gold*
Alveolar	ǃgoɑs *hollow*	ǃkhoɑs *belt*	ǃhoɑs *narrating*	ǃnorɑs *pluck maize seeds*	ǃorɑs *meeting*
Lateral	ǁgɑros *writing*	ǁkhɑos *strike*	ǁnaos *special cooking place*	ǁnaes *pointing*	ǁaos *reject a present*

Figure 15.12 Nama.

œsophagic /ˌɛsəˈfejdʒɪk/ because it uses the **œsophagus** /əˈsɑfəgəs/, the tube from the mouth to the stomach.

The œsophagus is a soft tube lying behind the trachea. It is normally flat when not in use carrying food to the stomach. The top of the tube is just above and behind the larynx. Any air coming from the stomach misses the vocal cords, but passes through the oral and nasal cavities. In œsophagic speech, voicing is missing, but normal articulations can take place in the upper vocal tract, which acts as a resonating chamber, as in normal speech. Obviously, the quality of this sort of speech lacks a good deal, but it may be the best alternative available.

TECHNICAL TERMS

abdominal
air pressure
airstream
   airstream mechanism
Boyle's Law
bronchus
   bronchi
cartilages

click
diaphragm
egressive
ejective
external intercostals
glottalic
implosive
ingressive

initiator
internal intercostals
œsophagus
   œsophagic
plosive
pulmonic
trachea
velaric

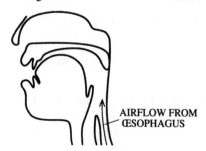

AIRFLOW FROM ŒSOPHAGUS

Figure 15.13 Œsophagic airstream.

	Pulmonic	**Glottalic**	**Velaric**
Egressive	*Plosives* p t k	*Ejectives* pʼ tʼ kʼ	————
Ingressive	————	*Implosives* ɓ ɗ ɠ	*Clicks* ʘ ǀ ! ǁ ǂ

* As described in the text, implosives are not made with a glottalic ingressive mechanism; it is convenient and traditional, however, to show them on a chart in this slot.

EXERCISES

BASIC

1. Review

pʌzɛ	bɛxo	n̥otʊ	geθaw	ɲi̯aj	ʃatʒej
hɪvɔ	dʒɪl̥e	keʒɔ	mowɸaw	ɣɒræ	ɹæno
ʔɒd̥ʊ	ɹ̥ejɣɛ	n̥ʊʃa	ðajʔi	d̥owm	ð̥ɒl̥ʊ
huŋo	l̥ibɛ				

2. Take a slow breath in and then a slow breath out. Most people find it fairly easy to speak with an ingressive airstream, although voicing does not work well. Try saying the following while breathing in:

   [ˈtɹajɪŋ tə ˈtɑk wajl ˈbɹiˈðɪŋ ɪn ɪz bɪˈzaɹ].

3. Ejectives are made by lowering the larynx, closing the vocal cords, forming the articulatory closure, and raising the larynx, creating a higher pressure between the vocal cords and the articulatory closure. Perhaps this description worked for you; it sure doesn't for most people. It is, however, quite useful once you start to get the basic feel of an ejective. Ejectives are not difficult to produce, but they involve a number of activities which are hard to coordinate at first. Be patient, eventually you'll get there.

   Hints:

   a. Pretend you have a hair on the tip of your tongue. Extend the tip of your tongue just beyond the lips and try to spit the hair off. With luck, you may be using the glottalic egressive air stream. Now, try this without extending your tongue to produce [pʼ pʼ pʼ].

   b. To feel your larynx move, touch your finger lightly to your adam's apple and swallow. You will feel your larynx go up and down. Now try to get the same effect without swallowing.

   c. Now:
      i. Start to make a [k].
      ii. Hold your breath.
      iii. Try to get the adam's apple up. Thinking that you are about to swallow may help.
      iv. Push the [kʼ] out.

d. Some children use an ejective [p'] to imitate a gunshot as in [p'aw]. Notice that the ejective makes a noticeable pop.

Once you have some success with an ejective, try different places of articulation.

p'p'p'   t't't'   c'c'c'   k'k'k'

Now try to put a vowel with the ejective:

p'a   t'a   c'a   k'a

Try these:

ap'ɛ   ot'u   ik'a   nut'a   k'ele   p'ɔk'i   tok'   p'oc'u

Try an ejective fricative:

f'f'f'   s's's'   ʃ'ʃ'ʃ'   ç'ç'ç'

f'o   f'ɪ   f'ə   s'i   s'a   s'ɛ

ʃ'o   ʃ'u   ʃ'æ   ç'ɛ   ç'a   ç'ɔ

4. Try these from Bearlake Slave (/ˈslejvi/, Northwest Territories). The acute accent [´] indicates high tone; low tone is unmarked (Rice, p.c.).

petʰá	*his/her father*	petá	*his/her eye*	pet'álé	*its wing*
kʰő	*fire*	kõ	*reeds*	k'o	*cloud*
tsʰẽ	*dirt*	tsine	*day*	ts'éré	*blanket*
tʃʰõ	*rain*	tʃõ	*here*	tʃ'õ	*porcupine*
kʷʰa	*carrot*	nakʷe	*he/she lives*	kʷ'a	*diaper*
tɬʰe	*grease, lard*	tɬa	*water plant*	tɬ'a	*grass*

5. Implosives involve lowering the larynx. They have special symbols: [ɓ ɗ ɠ]. Hints:

a. If possible, listen to someone who can make ejectives.

b. Some people use [ɠ] when imitating frogs, pouring water, or just when acting silly.

c. Try to make a [b] with extra heavy voicing. Many people make an implosive [ɓ] when trying this.

d. Most learners raise their eyebrows while making implosives. Do not interfere with any supercilious activity; it may be crucial.

When you finally get a bit of an implosive going, try practising these:

ɓɓɓɓɓ   ɗɗɗɗɗ   ɠɠɠɠɠ

ɓa ɗa ɠa   ɓu ɗe ɠo   ɠɛ ɗi ɓæ

ɓaɓɛ	baɓɛ	ɓabɛ	duɗa	ɗuda
tɛɓu	laɠe	ɹiɗo	ɗegi	ɠoɠu
ɠla	ɗɹib	aɓnu	anɓu	poɓe

6. Clicks are not particularly difficult. The trick is to integrate them smoothly in a string of other sounds. Slow and steady practice is the only method for success.

a. Bilabial. A bilabial click is essentially a kiss. The symbol is [ʘ]. Place your forefinger (either hand) horizontally, just touching your lips and kiss your finger. This is a bilabial click. Now remove your finger and try several of these clicks in a row.

ʘ ʘ ʘ ʘ ʘ

ʘi	ʘe	ʘɛ	ʘa	ʘɑ	ʘɔ	ʘo	ʘu
aʘu	oʘe	eʘɑ	ɔʘɛ	ʘiʘu	ʘɛʘɔ	ʘaʘɑ	ʘoʘeʘ

If you are practising with a partner, you may want to try a few quadrilabial clicks.

b. The dental click is symbolised as [ǀ]. In its reduplicated form, it is used in English as a sign of disapproval or regret, often written *tsk-tsk*.

c. The alveolar lateral click is made by putting the tip of the tongue at the alveolar ridge with a velaric ingressive airstream mechanism with a lateral release; in English, its reduplicated form is frequently written *gitty-up*. The symbol is [ǁ].

ǁ ǁ ǁ ǁ ǁ

ǁi	ǁe	ǁɛ	ǁa	ǁɑ	ǁɔ	ǁo	ǁu
iǁɑ	aǁo	eǁi	aǁɛ	ǁɔǁo	ǁaǁɑ	ǁuǁɛ	ǁiǁeǁ

d. Lateral clicks can be made with central, alveolar, or post-alveolar tongue positions.

   A postalveolar or palatal click is written [ǃ]. The tongue tip is at the back of the alveolar ridge.

ǃ ǃ ǃ ǃ ǃ

ǃi	ǃe	ǃɛ	ǃa	ǃɑ	ǃɔ	ǃo	ǃu
eǃo	ɔǃo	aǃi	uǃɛ	ǃoǃɔ	ǃɛǃa	ǃoǃɛ	ǃuǃeǃ

Try these:

ǀitɔ	ǃako	ʘole	neǁu	ɳaǃo	ǀaou	ǃeǀa	ǁeǃo
ʘɔǁɛ	ǀiǃa	ǁoou	ʘaǁɔ	aʘaǀaǁ	ɔǃekuʘ	oǁaɳiʘa	uǀiǁoʘɛǃa

e. Clicks can be combined with various other phonetic phenomena such as voicing, murmur, nasalisation. We will look at nasal clicks here.

   Try saying a sequence of [ʘ ʘ ʘ ʘ ʘ ǀ ǀ ǀ ǀ ǀ ǁ ǁ ǁ ǁ ǁ ǃ ǃ ǃ ǃ ǃ] while simultaneously slowly breathing in and out. It is clear that both pulmonic and velaric airstreams can occur at the same time.

   Now say a long [ŋŋŋŋŋŋ].

   Say a long [ŋŋŋŋŋ] and a series of clicks [ǁǁǁǁ] at the same time. Each of these is a nasal click and can be written [ŋǁ].

   Now try a series of these:

ŋǀɛ	ŋǀu	ŋǀɑ	ŋǁa	ŋǀi	ŋǁo
ŋ͡ǀu	ŋǀa	ŋǀe	ŋ͡ɔɔ	ŋ͡ɔe	ŋ͡ʘa
ŋǁeta	ŋǀoka	ŋǁaɳi	oŋ͡ʘaɳu	iŋǁaǃo	uŋǃoʘe

ADVANCED

7. Try the following ejectives from Amharic (/ˌæmˈheɹɪk/; Ethiopia):

tʼɨl	tɨl	dɨl
quarrel	warm	victory
kʼɨr	kɨr	gərr
stay away	thread	innocent
mətʼ	mətʃ	mədʒ
one who comes	when	grinding stone
sʼəgga	səgga	zəgga
grace	to worry	to close

8. The double articulation [g͡b] is a common sound in many languages. The [g] and the [b] are simultaneous, and the whole sound is often an implosive. Practise distinguishing [g͡b], [g], and [b].

g͡bi	g͡be	g͡ba	g͡bo
gɛg͡bu	g͡beg͡bo	bag͡bu	g͡babɛ
gigɔ	ɓɛg͡bu	g͡bɛɓɪ	g͡bogu

9. Vietnamese has implosives. Pay particular attention to the back unrounded vowels; [ɯ] and [ɤ] are the unrounded equivalents of [u] and [o]. (Tone is not marked.)

ɓɛn	*side*	bɤ	*shore*
ɓæn	*to shoot*	ba	*three*
ɗi	*go*	ɗa	*stone*
ɗo	*be red*	ɗɤn	*application*
ŋɯi	*sniff*	ɯa	*to like*
ɗɯt	*to break*	ɗɯŋ	*don't*
mɤi	*invite*	xɤp	*joint*
sɤm	*be early*	ɯɤt	*be wet*

10. Chilcotin (/ˌtʃɪlˈkowtɪn/; B.C.). Practise the labialised consonants:

kʷixkʷix	*Steller's Jay*	nætsʼɛdɛtɛlkwix	*whooping cough*
sɛkʷˀɛ̃d	*my kidney*	dɛtʃɛndɛɬkwʼɛð	*woodpecker*
tʃɛgʷix	*blouse*	ɛgʷɛ̃ð	*back the same way*
gʷɛdɛðkʼæn	*it is burning*	tɛnahʷɛð	*gooseberry*
hʷɛθ	*cactus, thorn*	xʷɔstɛstæðtʼe	*suspenders*
nɛntasgweθ	*I will tickle you*	sɛgʷɛð	*my leg muscle*
nosgʷɛθ	*I want to tickle you*	ɛgiðgʷɛt	*eggshell*

11. Practise the lateral affricates in Rae Dogrib (/ˌɹej ˈdɑɡˌɹɪb/, N.W.T):

ɬo	smoke	ɬo	much
kʔaɬa	still, yet	natɬa	he walks
tlĭa	mouse	tɬĭ	dog
tla	water-grass	la	work

CHAPTER SIXTEEN

SYLLABLES AND SUPRASEGMENTALS

The **segments** of a language are the consonants and vowels. The **supraseg-mentals** comprise several linguistically important phenomena which are not segmental, such as length, stress, pitch, and intonation. The term suprasegmental derives from the fact that these elements often extend over a string of segments. Suprasegmentals are often defined in terms of syllables, so we will begin with a general consideration of the syllable.

In this chapter you will learn about:
- the nature of the syllable
- long vowels and consonants
- the use of pitch in speech
- metrical theory of stress.

SYLLABLE

The **syllable** /ˈsɪləbəl/ is a phonological unit of organisation containing one or more segments. Syllables are found in all languages; that is, all languages organise sounds in terms of syllables. They are usually easy to count. Almost everyone will agree that the words *book, table, carnation, particular, lackadaisical,* and *compatibility* have one to six syllables, respectively. Even in a language which you do not know, you can often count the syllables in a word.

Although it may be easy to count syllables, it is not always easy to divide a word into syllables. The word *kidnap* has two syllables. Almost all English speakers will divide those syllables as /kɪd – næp/. The word *very* also has two syllables, but it is difficult to know where to divide it. Neither /vɛ – ɹi/ nor /vɛɹ – i/ seems satisfactory, or, in another sense, both seem satisfactory.

STRUCTURE OF THE SYLLABLE

In Chapter 6, we learned the basic terms for parts of the syllable; they are shown here again in Figure 16.1. A lower-case Greek sigma [σ] is often used as a symbol for a syllable.

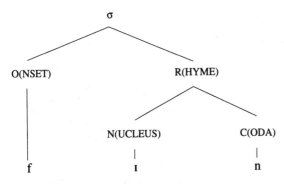

Figure 16.1 Structure of the Syllable.

Typically, the **nucleus** of a syllable is the vowel; the **onset** is the preceding consonant, and the **coda** is the consonant after the vowel. Together, the nucleus and the coda form the **rhyme**. Any of these elements may branch, that is, have more than one unit. In *fling,* the onset branches; in *belt,* the coda branches (Figure 16.2).

In a syllable containing a diphthong, such as *bait* /bejt/, the nucleus branches (Figure 16.3). In languages with distinctive long and short vowels, a long vowel such as German /raːt/ 'advice', is often analysed as having a branching nucleus with a series of two identical vowels /raat/. Two adjacent identical segments are called **geminates** /ˈdʒemɪnət/.

The nucleus of a syllable is ordinarily a vowel or diphthong. However, sonorant consonants sometimes form the nucleus and are then known as **syllabic consonants**. These are indicated by a short stroke under the consonant, as in [l̩ n̩ m̩]. As we see in Figure 16.4, English *table* [ˈtejbl̩] has a syllablic [l̩] in its second syllable.

An **open** syllable is one that has no coda, *i.e.,* no final consonant: *e.g.,* [ʌ], [tu], [splæ]. A **closed** syllable has one or more final consonants: *e.g.,* [ik], [nʊdʒ], [dɛlps]. The terms **light** and **heavy** syllables are common, although their definition varies slightly depending on what language is being analysed. A syllable with a branching nucleus or with a branching coda is heavy. A syllable with an unbranched

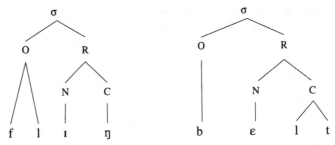

Figure 16.2 Branching onset and coda.

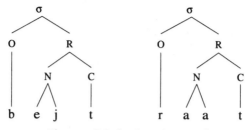

Figure 16.3 Branching nuclei.

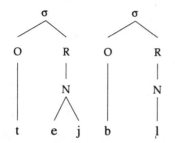

Figure 16.4 Syllabic consonant in English *table*.

nucleus and no coda is light. A syllable with an unbranched nucleus and a single consonant in the coda, *e.g.*, [lʌg] functions as a heavy syllable in some languages and as a light syllable in others (Figure 16.5). The onset is irrelevant to the distinction of heavy and light.

The last syllable of a word is known as the **ultimate syllable** or **ultima** /ˈʌltɪmə/. The second last is the **penultimate** /pɪnˈʌltɪmət/ **syllable** or **penult** /ˈpiˌnʌlt/. The third last syllable is known as the **antepenultimate** /ˌæntɪpɪnˈʌltɪmət/ **syllable** or **antepenult** /ˌæntiˈpinʌlt/.

For example:

conversation

ˌkɑn	–	vəɹ	–	ˈsej	–	ʃən
		antepen.		*penult.*		*ultima*

PRODUCTION OF THE SYLLABLE

We would like to be able to state just how a syllable is produced. Unfortunately, there is no satisfactory, general explanation of how syllables are produced. Clearly, however, the production of syllables involves at least in part the way in which the lungs move air out of the body.

Some years ago, Stetson (1928, 1951) put forward a theory that syllables were

light	heavy
V	VV
CV	CVV
	CVCC
	CVVCC

← (CVC) →

Figure 16.5 Light and heavy syllables. C represents a consonant; V, a vowel. CVC syllables may be heavy or light, depending on the language.

Figure 16.6 Waveform of English *loving*.

formed by a **chest pulse**. By this, he meant a single contraction of the ribcage. In particular, he suggested that the **external intercostal** /ˌɪntəɹˈkɑstəl/ muscles, located between the ribs, act to pull the ribcage down and thereby push air out of the lungs. Stetson suggested that each chest pulse pushes a bit of air out which forms the air flow used for a single syllable. Later work (*e.g.*, Draper *et al.*, 1957, 1958, 1960) showed Stetson's chest pulse theory unworkable. First, words like *very* have only one chest pulse, and words like *sport* have two chest pulses. It was further shown that the external intercostal muscles are inactive in much of speech. In the first part of a breath-group, the elastic force of the lungs, which tries to decrease the expanded lungs to normal (see Chapter 15), is used to move air out of the lungs. The external intercostals only come into play after the lungs reach the elastic mid-point and then are used to push air out.

PERCEPTION OF THE SYLLABLE

Sonority refers to the relative loudness of sounds. If we look at the waveform of the word *loving* (Figure 16.6), we can easily see that the intensity (which we perceive as loudness) of the vowels are much greater than that of the neighbouring consonants.

Phonologists have proposed the notion of a sonority hierarchy (Figure 16.7, after Selkirk, 1984). This hierarchy categorises groups of sounds by their relative sonority. The values in the index are relative. Two articulatory factors generally

Sound	Sonority Index
Low vowels	10
Mid vowels	9
High vowels	8
ɹ	7
l	6
Nasals	5
s	4
Voiced fricatives	3
Voiceless fricatives (not [s])	2
Voiced stops	1
Voiceless stops	0.5

Figure 16.7 Sonority hierarchy.

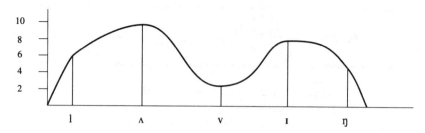

Figure 16.8 Sonority curve of English *loving.*

contribute to sonority: an open vocal tract and voicing. We perceive greater sonority as greater **prominence**. More sonorant sounds stand out and are perceptually more prominent than their neighbours.

In Figure 16.8, the sonority values for the word *loving* have been predicted. Sonority is the vertical dimension. When the individual lines of relative sonority are joined, the resulting pattern is called a **sonority curve**. From these sonorities, we would predict that *loving* would have a sonority curve as shown in Figure 16.8. This curve is, in fact, fairly close to the intensities shown in the waveform of Figure 16.6.

The sonority theory holds that a peak of sonority defines a syllable. In Figure 16.8, there are two peaks, so the theory correctly predicts that we will perceive *loving* as having two syllables.

This theory generally works, with peaks of sonority corresponding to the nuclei of syllables, and troughs of sonority corresponding to the onsets and codas of syllables. Figure 16.9 shows sonority curves for the words *flit* and *pruned*. In *flit,* the /l/ is more sonorous than the /f/; the peak of sonority is in the vowel; and the final /t/ has very little sonority at all. In *pruned,* the peak of sonority is in the vowel; the consonants surrounding the vowel, /ɹ/ and /n/, are less sonorous, and the consonants at the extreme edges of the word, /p/ and /d/, are least sonorous of all. These words have a relatively complex syllable structure, but the sonority theory agrees with the position of each segment in the syllable.

If we plot the sonority curve for a word like *split,* however, we see that the

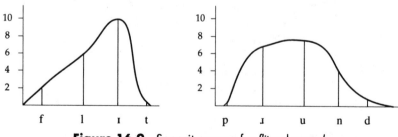

Figure 16.9 Sonority curves for *flit* and *pruned.*

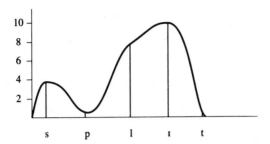

Figure 16.10 Predicted sonority of English *split*.

curve (Figure 16.10) has two peaks of sonority: one for the [s], and one for the vowel; yet *split* clearly consists of only one syllable.

The sonority theory thus does not work for syllables beginning with [s]–stop clusters. There is no obvious explanation for this; however, we can note that in many languages /s/ forms clusters with other consonants as in English. There seems to be something special about the ability of /s/ to form consonant clusters without creating a peak of sonority.

A second problem for the sonorant theory appears if we examine the syllabic structure for English and French *table*. English *table* has two syllables with its syllabic /l/, but French *table* has only one syllable, as the /l/ is not syllabic. The sonority theory gives the same sonority curve (Figure 16.11) for both languages and predicts two syllables for both.

Although the sonority theory meets with very wide success in explaining how syllables are perceived, it needs to be refined further to cover certain cases.

SYLLABLES AND MORÆ

If we apply our notions of sonority to Japanese, we can readily divide words into syllables. Syllables have the general pattern of consonant — vowel, with an optional consonant in the coda.

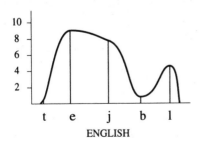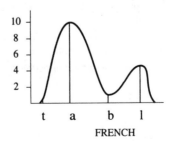

Figure 16.11 Predicted sonority of English *table* and French *table*.

ha-ʃi	*edge*
kek-koŋ	*marriage*
ʃoo-kai	*introduction*
mu-ra-sa-kii-ro	*purple*

Japanese

Note that /ŋ/ and a homorganic obstruent are the only permissable syllable codas. A syllable nucleus may branch: /oo/, /ai/, /ii/.

Japanese has, however, traditionally recognised a unit called the **mora** /ˈmoɹə/ (pl. **moræ** /ˈmoɹi/), rather than the syllable. The difference between syllables and moræ is that a consonant in the coda forms a mora of its own, and a branching nucleus forms two moræ. The words from the list above are given again below, this time divided into moræ.

> ha-ʃi
> ke-k-ko-ŋ
> ʃo-o-ka-i
> mu-ra-sa-ki-i-ro

The traditional view for Japanese (*e.g.*, Bloch, 1950; Ladefoged, 1982) has been that each mora takes about the same amount of time to be pronounced. Thus, /kekkoŋ/ and /ʃookai/ take twice as long as /haʃi/, and /murasakiiro/ with six moræ takes three times as long.

Japanese speakers are clearly aware of the mora as a phonological unit. Japanese poetic rhythm is defined by the number of moræ. A *haiku* poem, for example, is written in 17 moræ.

ha-ru ta-tsu ja	'Spring starts;
ʃi-n-ne-n fu-ru-ki	new year; old rice;
ko-me go ʃo-o	five quarts'
	— Matsuo Bashō, 1684

Beckman (1982) found evidence contradicting the traditional view; her study showed no convincing evidence for the existence of the mora as a unit of timing. In written Japanese, each mora is written with a separate *kana* symbol. Beckman suggests that the ability to conceptualise Japanese in terms of morae is due in large part to familiarity with the writing system. The mora, in any case, seems to play a part in the phonological behaviour of Japanese (Vance, 1987; also below in this chapter under *pitch accent*).

LENGTH

Length refers to the duration of a sounds. We saw in Chapter 4 that English has noncontrastive variation of length: vowels are longer before a voiced consonant than before a voiceless one. Many languages have contrastive distinctions of length, particularly in the vowels. Length is transcribed by a colon [ː], following the long segment. If it is necessary to show various lengths, a raised dot [·] can be used for length intermediate between short (unmarked) and long [:].

As we saw earlier in this chapter, if we consider vowels as a part of the syllable, they are often analysed in phonology as geminates: *e.g.* [ee]. In such an analysis, the nucleus branches to include two identical vowels.

In many languages, for example Ewe, long and short vowels contrast.

ba	*mud*	ba:	*wide open*
bi	*bend*	bi:	*narrow*
bliba	*make dirty*	bliba:	*dirty, soiled*
bala	*climb*	bala:	*moving quitely*

Ewe

Contrasts of length are often accompanied by small alterations of quality. In German, the long vowels have a different articulation from the short vowels, generally higher and more peripheral.

biete	bi:tə	'offer (impv.)'	*Bitte*	bɪtə	'request'
Beet	be:t	'(flower)bed'	*Bett*	bɛt	'(sleeping) bed'
fühlen	fy:lən	'feel'	*füllen*	fʏlən	'fill'
Höhle	hø:lə	'cave'	*Hölle*	hœlə	'hell'
Fuß	fu:s	'foot'	*Fluß*	flʊs	'river'
Schoß	ʃo:s	'lap'	*schoß*	ʃɔs	'shot (past)'
Staat	ʃtɑ:t	'state'	*Stadt*	ʃtat	'city'

German

Consonants may also be long. Phonetically, in the English word *penknife*, we find a long /n/. On closer examination, however, we discover that the first /n/ belongs to one morpheme *pen*, and the second /n/ belongs to a different morpheme *knife*. In fact, in English, we can find no geminates (*i.e.,* long) consonants *within* a morpheme.

Italian is a language which has contrastive long and short consonants within morphemes.

fato	*fate*	fatto	*done*
akanto	*acanthus*	akkanto	*alongside*
ara	*altar*	arra	*guarantee*
kolo	*sieve*	kollo	*neck*

Italian

PITCH AND TONE

All languages use pitch and stress to some degree. Some languages make very extensive use of pitch or stress. In the following sections, we will look at some of the ways in which these properties are used in language.

'mother' ma	⌐	ma^1	mha	mā
'hemp' ma	⌐	ma^2	ma	má
'horse' ma	⌐	ma^3	maa	mǎ
'scold' ma	√	ma^4	mah	mà
	a	b	c	d

Figure 16.12 Mandarin Chinese tone.

We perceive changes in the fundamental frequency as changes in **pitch**. In phonetics, pitch is often referred to as **tone**, particularly when pitch distinguishes different words in a language. Languages which contrast lexical items with tone alone are called **tone languages**. For example, in Sherbro, a West-African language, [ná] spoken with a high tone means 'cow', whereas [nà] with a low tone means 'spider'. English speakers are usually somewhat surprised to learn that most languages in the world are tone languages.

Note that *high* and *low* are relative terms. A high tone for an adult man may have the same pitch as a low tone for a child. Apparently, listeners identify the pitch range of a speaker quickly and adjust their notion of high and low for that speaker accordingly.

We have already noted in Chapter 14 that the fundamental frequency of a phonetic sound is determined by the vibration rate of the vocal cords, and we examined the ways in which the larynx acts to vary this vibration rate. Every sound with vibrating vocal cords has a pitch. Most commonly, a pitch pattern extends over a syllable.

The Mandarin dialect of Chinese has four distinctive tones which can be illustrated with the segments /ma/. When [mā] is spoken with a high level tone, it means 'mother'. Spoken with a high rising tone, /má/ means 'hemp'. With a tone that first falls and then rises, /mǎ/ means 'horse', and with a low falling tone, /mà/ means 'scold'. Figure 16.12 shows different ways that have been used to transcribe the tones of this dialect.

One way to indicate tone (12a) uses a vertical mark to indicate the vocal range and places a second line next to this to show the tone, something like musical notation. Although clumsy to write, this system gives a clear visual image of the tone pattern. Superscript numerals (12b) are occasionally used to mark tone. This system, known as the *Wade-Giles* system, was commonly used in the past with Chinese; unfortunately, such marks have little mnemonic value and are often omitted. Another scheme (12c) indicates the tones of Chinese using extra consonants and vowels. In 1958, China officially adopted the transcription system known as *Pinyin* /ˌpinˈjin/, which uses accents (12d); the shape of the accents suggests the tonal pattern.

In general, the notation of Figure 16.12a above is useful when first analysing the language. After the tonal system of a language is determined, other marks such as accents are more convenient. In a two-tone system with high and low, an **acute accent** [´] marks a high tone, and a **grave accent** [`] /gɹɑv ~ gɹejv/ marks a low tone. In a three-tone system, a **macron** /ˈmejkɹən/ [¯] is used for a mid-tone. A **circumflex accent** [ˆ] /ˈsəɹkəmˌflɛks/ is often used to mark a falling tone, and a **haček** [ˇ] /ˈhɑˌtʃɛk/ is used to mark a rising tone. (In the Pinyin system for Chinese, a **breve** [˘] /bɹiv ~ bɹɛv/, with a rounded bottom, is used instead of a haček.) Often (H) and (L) are used to indicate high and low tones. Usage in transcribing tone varies, so if you find accents, you will have to determine whether they represent tone, stress, or something else, and then determine what value each accent is used for.

REGISTER AND CONTOUR TONE LANGUAGES

In Chinese, the tones have a specific shape at a particular point on the musical scale: high level, low falling, etc. Such tones are called **contour tones.** Vietnamese has a contour system with six tones, as shown below (Thompson, 1965). Note that laryngeal quality and glottal stops are associated with certain of the tones.

a. Mid level, with falling final

    [ɗʌm] 'stab', [tɯ] 'fourth', [ma] 'ghost'

b. Long low falling, breathy voice

    [gʌn] 'near', [ɗɯŋ] 'don't', [ma] 'that'

c. High rising

    [rʌt] 'very', [sɯk] 'strength', [ma] 'cheek'

d. Short low falling, ending in glottal stop

    [ɲʌp] 'flooded', [ŋɯə] 'horse', [ma] 'rice seedling'

e. Falling rising

    [fʌj] 'comma', [tʰɯ] 'try', [ma] 'grave'

f. High rising, broken, ending in glottal stop

    [ɗʌj] 'be fat', [cɯ] 'written word', [ɗa] 'anterior tense marker'

In contrast to contour tones, **register tones** are always level. Languages with register tone typically distinguish only two or three levels. Sherbro is a register tone language with two levels. In Figure 16.13 we see a typical utterance. Note the allophonic variation which causes a final high tone to be mid after a low tone.

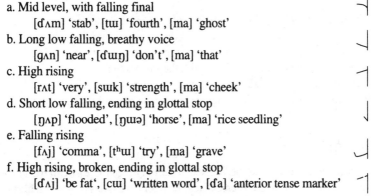

HIGH								
LOW								
jà	mɔ́	kí	já	jèn	dʒɔ́	ì	- ʃɔ́
I	you	future	cook for	some- thing	eat	morning	

I will cook something for you to eat this morning.

Figure 16.13 Register tones in Sherbro.

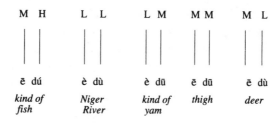

Figure 16.14   Tones in Nupe.

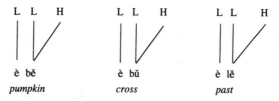

Figure 16.15   Rising tones in Nupe.

Nupe ('nu₍pe/; Nigeria) is register tone language with three tones:

Phonetic rising tones (marked as [ˇ]) occur in some words. In such cases, phonologists have argued that the correct representation for these rising tones to have a low-high sequence associated with the same syllable.

Although rising and falling tones occur in register tone languages, they are analysed as the result of a low-high or a high-low tone sequence on the same vowel.

DRIFT AND STEP

A phenomenon found in some register tone languages is **downdrift**. For example, Igbo (/ˈiˌbo/; Ghana, West Africa; Hyman, 1975) has two tones: high and low. The first syllable is high (H), and the second is low (L). The third syllable is high, but not quite so high as with the first syllable. With downdrift, the level of *high* is reset just a little lower after a low tone. The result is that the actual value

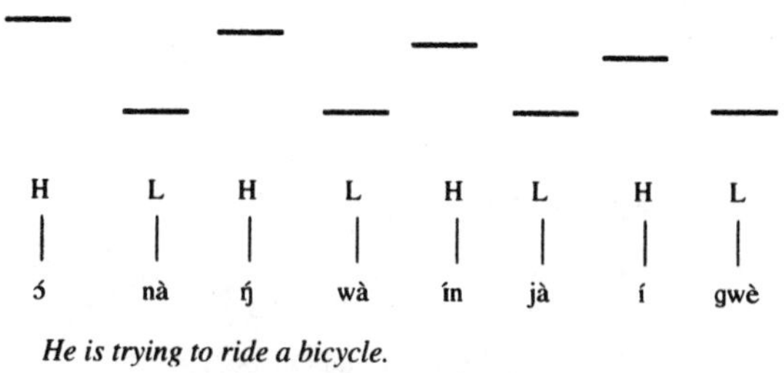

He is trying to ride a bicycle.

Figure 16.16   Downdrift in Igbo.

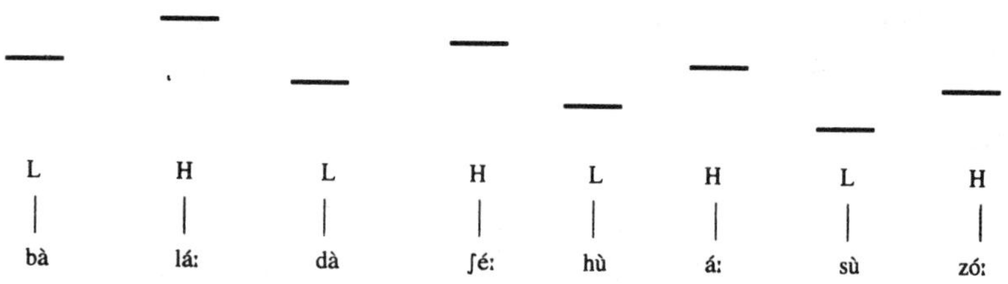

L	H	L	H	L	H	L	H
bà	lá:	dà	ʃé:	hù	á:	sù	zó:

Bala and Shehu will come.

Figure 16.17 Downdrift in Hausa.

of high drifts downwards (Figure 16.16). The level of the low tone may drift lower as well.

In Hausa (/ˈhawsə/; Nigeria, West Africa), a high tone can actually drift phonetically lower than a low tone which occurs early in the sentence.

DOWNSTEP Some languages, such as Coatzospan Mixtec (Figure 16.18), exhibit **downstep**. In such languages, the high-tone level becomes increasingly lower, but the mechanism is different from that of downdrift. Each syllable is specified as *high, low,* or *downstep* [↓]. After a high tone, a syllable with downstep is slightly lower in pitch than the previous high tone, and this level becomes the new level for later high tones. Note in Figure 16.14 that the high-tone level drops after every occurrence of downstep.

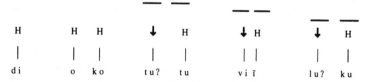

H		H	H		↓	H		↓	H		↓	H
d i		o	k o		t u ?	t u		v i ī			l u ?	k u

I want crazy cold paper.

Figure 16.18 Downstep in Coatzospan Mixtec.

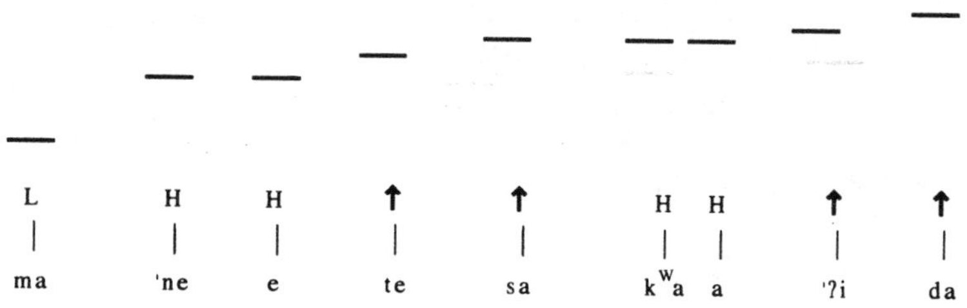

L	H	H	↑	↑		H	H	↑	↑
m a	ʼne	e	t e	s a		kʷa	a	ʼʔi	d a

He will not skin the deer the day after tomorrow.

Figure 16.19 Upstep in Acatlán Mixtec.

UPSTEP Acatlán Mixtec (Suárez, 1983) has **upstep**, the reverse of downstep. Here, certain syllables, marked [↑], are higher after a previous unstepped tone.

PITCH ACCENT

In Japanese, many words, traditionally called unaccented, conform to a pattern of having a low tone on the first mora and a high tone on subsequent moræ; a one-mora word has a high tone (McCawley, 1968; Vance, 1987). In the examples below, a word is given in its basic form and then with a suffix added — /wa/ (marking the topic of a clause); the relevance of the suffix will become clear later. Tone is indicated with H for high tone, and L for low tone; the hyphens divide moræ.

ki	H	*spirit*	ki-wa	LH
ha-ʃi	LH	*edge*	ha-ʃi-wa	LHH
to-mo-da-ti	LHHH	*friend*	to-mo-da-ti-wa	LHHHH
mu-ra-sa-ki-i-ro	LHHHHH	*purple*	mu-ra-sa-ki-i-ro-wa	LHHHHHH

With other words, called accented words, there is a fall from high to low tone. This fall, traditionally known as *accent,* is phonologically unpredictable and is marked here with /ˈ/. The basic tone pattern prevails (the first mora has low tone, and subsequent moræ have high tone), except that the mora immediately preceding /ˈ/ has high tone, and all moræ following /ˈ/ have low tone.

kiˈ	H	*tree*	kiˈ-wa	HL
aˈ-sa	HL	*morning*	aˈ-sa-wa	HLL
o-kaˈ-a-sa-ma	LHLLL	*mother*	o-kaˈ-a-sa-ma-wa	LHLLLL
ya-ma-zaˈ-ku-ra	LHHLL	*wild cherry tree*	ya-ma-zaˈ-ku-ra-wa	LHHLLL
ta-n-sa-ŋ-gaˈ-su	LHHHHL	*carbon dioxide*	ta-n-sa-ŋ-gaˈ-su-wa	LHHHHLL

Note that /haʃiˈ/ 'bridge' and /haʃi/ 'edge' both have the same tone pattern LH in isolation; it is only with a suffix that we can distinguish them.

ha-ʃiˈ	LH	*bridge*	ha-ʃiˈ-wa	LHL
ha-ʃi	LH	*edge*	ha-ʃi-wa	LHH

Japanese is not a tone language in the sense that each mora can independently have a high tone or a low tone. Rather, there is an overall tonal pattern for words and a linguistically determined lexical accent /ˈ/ which overrides the pattern with a fall from high to low. Languages with tonal patterns like that of Japanese have been called **pitch-accent** languages.

TONE IN SWEDISH

Swedish intonation often strikes English ears as 'musical' or 'lilting'. We could easily imagine that pitch might play a distinctive role in Swedish. Indeed, we do find a few hundred pairs of words which are contrasted by means of

PATTERN I   PATTERN II

Figure 16.20   Contrastive tones in Swedish.

pitch. The two pitch patterns are shown in Figure 16.20 with examples below. Both patterns have a relatively level pitch at the beginning of the word. Pattern I simply falls at the end. Pattern II falls somewhat, rises, and then falls again.

Pattern I		**Pattern II**	
reːgel	*rule*	reːgel	*bolt*
anden	*the duck*	anden	*the spirit*
viːken	*the bay*	viːken	*folded*
taŋken	*the tank*	taŋken	*the thought*

Swedish

Does this type of contrast make Swedish a tone language? Not really. The basic suprasegmental pattern of Swedish is intonational, like English, although the intonational patterns are phonetically quite different from those of English. The contrastive use of tone is only a very small part of a much larger pattern. Compare Chinese, where tone forms a crucial part of every lexical item. Outside Sweden, Swedish is also the native language of a small minority of people in Finland. Interestingly, the Finnish dialect of Swedish does not have the tone pattern typical of Swedish and does not distinguish the pairs shown above. Norwegian has a tone system similar to that of Swedish.

STRESS

Phonetically, **stress** is the perceived prominence of one syllable over another; the prominence is due to an interplay of greater loudness, higher pitch, and longer duration. At the phonetic level, we can measure the factors contributing to the prominence and rank syllables in terms of levels of stress as we did for English in Chapter 5.

In the last decade, phonologists have explored the patterning of stress in many languages and have revealed a very rich and intricate part of certain languages. The section give an introduction to some of this work. Our concern here is to show some of the basic ways in which stress patterns in languages and how linguists have attempted to account for that patterning. The approach and notation taken here is somewhat similar to that of Halle and Vergnaud (1987).

In this section, I will follow a tradition of marking stress over the vowel of the stressed syllable. An acute accent [´] indicates a primary stress, and a grave accent [`] indicates a secondary stress; unstressed syllables are left unmarked.

Typically, in a word, one syllable stands out as more prominent than the others. This is true for all languages. Some languages have only one stress per word with the location determined by a general principle. In French stress falls on the ultima, with little variation in the relative prominence of the other syllables:

culture	[kʏltsýr]	'culture'
agrafer	[agrafé]	'staple'
épouvantable	[epuvɑ̃tábl]	'terrible'
prononciation	[prɔnɔ̃sjasjɔ̃]	'pronunciation'
électrocardiogramme	[elɛktrokardzjɔgrám]	'electrocardiogram'

In other languages, such as English, we find a pattern of alternating stresses. In *propaganda,* for example, the primary stress is on the penultimate syllable; there is, however, as well, a secondary stress on the first syllable /pɹɑ̀pəgǽndə/. In a longer word, such *unreliability* [ʌnɹɪlàjəbílɪti], there are two secondary stresses, on the first and third syllables as well. We observe then that in many words, English has a pattern of alternating stress, with some sort of stress on every other syllable.

In many languages, the position of stress is predictable and need not be indicated in the lexicon. In French, we can automatically stress the final syllable in every word. In Scots Gaelic, stress always falls on the first syllable of a word:

ʃéxəd̯	*past*	mɔ́ːn̯ʲə	*peat*
bðébəd̯að	*weaver*	píːbəðɔxg	*piping*
d̯ʒíxən̯ʲixəɣ	*forgetting*	áhəraxəɣ	*changing*

Scots Gaelic

The patterning of stress, however, is frequently more complex than that found in French or Scots Gaelic. In many languages, a word has more than one stress. In Weri, a language of New Guinea, stress falls on odd-numbered syllables counting from the right. The rightmost stress is primary [´]; the other stresses are secondary [`].

ʊlð̀amít	*mist*	àkʊnètepál	*times*

Weri

We can see that Weri has an alternating stress pattern — one syllable with stress, the next unstressed. Phonologists have analysed such patterns by dividing words into constituents called **feet**, each consisting of two syllables. In Weri, the feet are constructed by dividing the word into two-syllable units, starting at the right edge of the word and moving to the left. The division into feet is shown below by parentheses. The stressed syllable, or **head**, of each foot is indicated by an asterisk in the line above, called the **foot line**. Note that in words with an odd number of syllables (*e.g.,* /àkʊnètepál/), the remaining syllable [à] (at the beginning of the word) forms a foot of its own. Such a foot, without the normal number of syllables, is said to be **degenerate**.

```
(  *)( * )        (*)(  *)(  *)              foot
ʊ-lʊ̀ -a-mít      à - kʊ-nè -te-pál
```

We still have to account for the fact that the last stress is primary, but the preceding ones are secondary. We do this by constructing another line, the **word line**, above the foot line. The word line comines all the feet into a single unit and thus has only one set of parentheses. In order to make the stress of the last foot stronger than the others, we place an asterisk above the asterisk of the last foot. We can now interpret our analysis phonetically. A syllable with two asterisks receives primary stress, a syllable with one asterisk receives secondary stress, and a syllable with no asterisk is unstressed.

```
(         * )          (              * )    word
(  *)( * )             (*)(   *)(  * )        foot
ʊ-lʊ̀ -a-mít           à - kʊ-nè -te-pál
```

Comparing our analyses of Weri, French, and Scots Gaelic, we see that the feet of Weri have a fixed number of syllables (in our examples two); such feet are called **bounded**. We can also apply our system of analysis to French or to Scots Gaelic. In both languages, all the syllables of a word belong to a single foot. In French, the rightmost syllable receives an asterisk; in Scots Gaelic the leftmost syllable receives and asterisk. The feet of French and Scots Gaelic are **unbounded**, in that they can have any number of syllables. In this book, we use the term *bounded* only to describe feet of two syllables.

```
(         *  )         ( *           )        foot
e - pu - vã - tabl     bˀðe - bə - dað
     French              Scots Gaelic
```

In both French and Weri, the rightmost syllable of a foot is the head, receiving stress; in Scots Gaelic, the leftmost syllable is the head. In Weri, we need a separate word line to distinguish between different levels of stress. In French and Scots Gaelic, the word line adds no new information.

If we now look at Maranungku, an Australian language, we find a pattern like Weri, but reversed; in Maranungku, stress falls on odd-numbered syllables counting from the left.

```
(*          )          (*                    )    word
(*    )(*   )(*)        (*   )(*   )(*        )    foot
1   2   3   4   5       1   2   3   4   5   6
láŋ - ka - rà - te - tì̀    wé - le - pè - ne - màn - ta
prawn                  kind of duck
```

Maranungku

We see that the foot in Maranungku is bounded, left-headed, and formed from left to right. Since primary stress is on the leftmost foot, the word is left-headed.

The observations that we just stated for Maranungku are called **stress**

parameters /pəˈræmətəɹ/; they govern the placement of stress. For each language, we have to establish the parameters. We have to determine if the feet are bounded or unbounded? Are the feet right-headed or left-headed? If the feet are bounded, we further have to determine the direction: are they established from left to right or right to left? And finally, is the word right- or left-headed? For the languages we have examined so far in this section, the parameters are shown in the table below.

	French	Scots Gaelic	Weri	Maranungku
bounded or **unbounded**	unbounded	unbounded	bounded	bounded
head of foot	right	left	right	left
direction	——	——	r → l	l → r
head of word	——	——	right	left

EXTRAMETRICALITY

In Polish, a word has only one stress falling on the penultimate syllable. The following examples show that stress moves as more syllables are added after the . root:

hippopotamus	hi-po-pó-tam	nominative singular
	hi-po-po-tá-ma	genitive singular
	hi-po-po-ta-má-mi	instrumental plural

Polish

In Polish, we find only one unbounded foot, but it is not right-headed; rather, the stress falls one syllable back from the right end. Phonologists have introduced a new parameter, called **extrametricality** /ˌɛkstɹəˌˌmɛtɹɪˈkælɪti/, to account for such phenomena. We say that in Polish, the final syllable of a word is extrametrical and does not form part of a foot. We enclose an extrametrical foot in angled brackets — < >.

(*)	(*)	(*)	**foot**
hi-po-pó-<tam>	hi-po-po-tá-<ma>	hi-po-po-ta-má-<mi>	

We can now state the parameters of Polish as:
  a. The final syllable is extrametrical.
  b. Feet are unbounded.
  c. Feet are right-headed.

Extrametricality may look like a trick to get us out of hard spot, but phonologists have found that extrametricality is an important concept in many languages. Note that only one syllable in a word may be extrametrical. For any language, only the first or last syllable can be extrametrical; further, the extrametrical syllable cannot be the first for some words and the last for others in the same language. Note that a degenerate foot arises when an extra syllable is left over at the end of foot-formation, whereas an extrametrical syllable is one that is overlooked at the beginning of foot-formation.

Koya (India; Tyler, 1969) is a language in which the internal nature of the syllable is important. In Koya, primary stress falls on the first syllable and secondary stress is found on every subsequent heavy syllable (*i.e.*, having either a long vowel or a consonant in the coda). In the examples below, unbounded feet are constructed in the foot line. The leftmost syllable is given an asterisk, as is every heavy syllable. On the word level, an asterisk is added for the leftmost syllable. Thus, syllables with two asterisks receive primary stress; syllables with one asterisk receive secondary stress; and the others are unstressed.

(*)	(*)	(*) **word**
(*)	(* *)	(* *) **foot**
nú - du - ru	nú - dùr - ku	ée - làa - ḍi
forehead	*foreheads*	*younger sister*

(*)	(*)	(*) **word**
(* *)	(* *)	(* *) **foot**
náa - tòn - ṭe	lé - dʒòoṇ - ḍu	mút - tʃa - tòṇ - ḍu
along with me	*young man*	*leper*

(*)	(*)	(*) **word**
(* * *)	(* * * *)	(* * *) **foot**
méṭ - tàat - pòr - ro	pée - tʃòo - mìn - nàa - na	kén - ja - kòn - tàa - na
on the mountain	*I am starting*	*I will hear for myself*

Koya

We can now state the parameters of Koya:

    a. No extrametricality
    b. Unbounded feet
    c. Left-headed; heavy syllables are stressed
    d. Left to right
    e. Word: left-headed

INTONATION

Intonation is the use of pitch distinctively over a phrase. Whereas tone languages distinguish two lexical items by tone, such as /ná/ 'cow' and /nà/ 'spider' in Sherbro, intonation generally conveys different sorts of meaning. Intonational differences may distinguish statements from questions, or from commands, or intonation may add a meaning such as doubt, politeness, or boredom.

Even in a language as widely studied as English, research into intonation has not produced a clear understanding of how it works. Nevertheless, Cruttenden (1986) showed that various intonational languages use intonations that have an overall falling pattern for certain purposes and intonations with an overall rising pattern for others.

Falling	*Rising*
Neutral statement	Tentative statement
Wh-question	Yes-No question
Command	Request

Try to find a native speaker of German, an intonational language, and compare the intonational patterns of the following English and German sentences.

Falling Intonation
    Neutral statement
    My parents won't arrive until Monday.
    Meine Eltern kommen erst am Montag an.

    Wh-question
    Where are you going now?
    Wo gehen Sie jetzt hin?

    Command
    Be nice to each other!
    Seid nett zueinander!

Rising intonation
    Tentative statement
    She's leaving today?
    Reist sie heute vielleicht ab?

    Yes-no question
    Did the dog bite your leg?
    Hat der Hund dir ins Bein gebissen?

    Request
    Would you please accompany us.
    Möchten Sie bitte mitkommen.

(Wh-questions ask for a blank to be filled in; in English, they generally begin with words in *wh: who, what, where,* etc. Yes-no questions ask for a response of 'yes' or 'no'.) For me, although a falling intonation pattern with yes-no questions is normal, a rising intonation is possible, particularly with contrastive meaning: 'Did the dog bite your *leg?*' (not your hand). See Chapter 5.

The attitudinal meaning of intonation can be exceedingly subtle. Very often, you will find various intonation patterns with slightly different nuances.

TONE LANGUAGES AND INTONATION

A tone language can have intonation just as a non-tonal language does. Consider the following utterances (Figure 16.21) from Hausa (from Schuh, 1978). We see that Hausa has two register tones with downdrift. In the statement, the tones

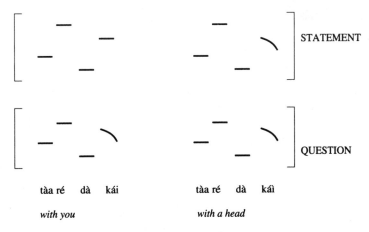

Figure 16.21 Statement and question in Hausa.

generally move from the middle to the lower portion of the speaker's pitch range (shown by the brackets). In the question form, two things happen: 1) the final high syllable falls, and 2) the entire utterance is in the upper part of the range with downdrift suspended. The second utterance is similar, except that the final syllable falls even in the statement.

TECHNICAL TERMS

acute accent
antepenult
antepenultimate syllable
bounded
breve
chest pulse
circumflex accent
closed syllable
coda
contour tone
degenerate
downdrift
downstep
external intercostals
extrametrical
head
foot
  foot line
geminate
grave accent
haček
heavy syllable
intonation

length
light syllable
macron
mora
  moræ
nucleus
onset
open syllable
parameter
penult
penultimate syllable
pitch
pitch accent
register tone
rhyme
segment
sonority
  sonority curve
stress
  stress languages
  stress parameter
suprasegmental
syllabic consonants

syllable
tone
  tone language
tonic stress
ultima
  ultimate syllable
unbounded
upstep
word line
  word stress

EXERCISES
BASIC

1. Tone. Practise these.

   bàbá   sósò   fìfí   gúgù   nèlé   θázà   ʒɔ̀kɔ́   xèŋú
   φèʔɔ́   hàðè   ɹòdʒí   jáʃú

   Now try these. Try each form with the various tone patterns.

   fʊlika   dɔgiφu   naʃeðɛ

   e.g.: fólìkà   fʊlìká   fólíkà   fʊlìkà etc.

   ˊ ˋ ˋ   ˋ ˋ ˊ   ˋ ˊ ˊ

   ˋ ˋ ˊ   ˊ ˊ ˋ   ˊ ˊ ˊ

   ˊ ˊ ˋ   ˊ ˋ ˋ   ˋ ˊ ˋ

   ˋ ˋ ˋ   ˋ ˊ ˋ   ˋ ˋ ˋ

   ˋ ˋ ˊ   ˋ ˊ ˋ   ˊ ˊ ˋ

   ˋ ˊ ˊ   ˊ ˋ ˊ   ˊ ˋ ˋ

   Now try saying these:

   níilùdʒà   ʁèʃɔ́ríi   wèʔàtʃù   ɹèkàzɔ́
   ɣàhèφò   ŋèpòʔà   βàfìɾɔ́   gòðèxà

2. The mid tone is a level tone half way between a high tone and a low one; it is marked [ˉ].

   Pronounce [lafiku] with each of the tone patterns below.

   e.g.: [láfīkū — láfīkú], etc.

   ˊ ˋ ˉ   ˊ ˋ ˋ   ˋ ˋ ˉ   ˋ ˋ ˉ   ˉ ˋ ˉ
   ˋ ˉ ˋ   ˋ ˋ ˋ   ˉ ˋ ˋ   ˉ ˋ ˋ   ˉ ˋ ˋ
   ˉ ˉ ˋ   ˉ ˋ ˋ   ˉ ˋ ˉ   ˋ ˉ ˋ   ˋ ˉ ˉ
   ˋ ˋ ˉ   ˋ ˉ ˋ   ˉ ˋ ˋ   ˉ ˋ ˉ   ˉ ˋ ˉ

   Similarly, pronounce [bomeʔikʌ] with each of the tone patterns belows:

   e.g.: [bómēʔɪkʌ̄ — bóméʔíkʌ̀], etc.

   ˋ ˉ ˋ ˉ   ˊ ˋ ˋ ˋ   ˋ ˋ ˋ ˉ   ˋ ˋ ˋ ˉ   ˋ ˉ ˋ ˋ
   ˋ ˋ ˋ ˉ   ˋ ˉ ˋ ˉ   ˋ ˉ ˋ ˋ   ˋ ˋ ˋ ˉ   ˋ ˉ ˉ ˋ
   ˋ ˉ ˋ ˋ   ˋ ˋ ˉ ˉ   ˋ ˉ ˋ ˉ   ˋ ˉ ˋ ˋ   ˋ ˋ ˋ ˋ
   ˉ ˋ ˋ ˋ   ˉ ˋ ˋ ˋ   ˉ ˋ ˋ ˋ   ˋ ˋ ˋ ˋ   ˉ ˋ ˋ ˋ

   Take your time in practising. Ability with tone is not developed overnight. Your progress will be gradual, not dramatic. Just try to improve; don't try to compete with others. Some rather annoying people seem naturally better at tone than the rest of us — maybe they have ingrown toenails as compensation.

3. Practise saying [fomekinɑ] with the following tones:

   e.g.: fómèkínà

   ˊ ˋ ˊ ˋ   ˊ ˊ ˊ ˋ   ˊ ˊ ˋ ˊ   ˊ ˊ ˊ ˋ

   ˊ ˋ ˊ ˊ   ˊ ˋ ˊ ˋ   ˊ ˋ ˋ ˊ   ˊ ˋ ˋ ˋ

   ˋ ˊ ˊ ˊ   ˋ ˊ ˊ ˋ   ˋ ˊ ˋ ˊ   ˋ ˊ ˋ ˋ

   ˋ ˋ ˊ ˊ   ˋ ˋ ˊ ˋ   ˋ ˋ ˊ ˊ   ˋ ˋ ˋ ˋ

Try these:

tíɣáɸèṣù	tʒɔ̀l̩éɟj˞ɔ́dɔ̀	sà̰ðèl̩ɔ́ŋà	vòpɸìçáɹ̩ú
jèʔéçódé	gáɹ̩èbvùxɔ́	hèʃítṣéɹ̩à	hjútd̩ðíʒóβè

4. Moving tones fall from high to low or rise from low to high. Falling tones are shown with [ˆ] over the vowel, and rising tones with [ˇ].

First practise a long fall [â]:

â	â	â	â				
î	ê	ɛ̂	â	ɑ̂	ɔ̂	ô	û
bî	bê	bɛ̂	bâ	bɑ̂	bɔ̂	bô	bû

And now a long rise [ǎ]:

ǎ	ǎ	ǎ	ǎ				
ǐ	ě	ɛ̌	ǎ	ɑ̌	ɔ̌	ǒ	ǔ
bǐ	bě	bɛ̌	bǎ	bɑ̌	bɔ̌	bǒ	bǔ

Now try:

ɹékê	ɲɔɸǒ	wàsǐ	félǔ
m̩ɔ̀zǎ	çòkê	fàɣú	βéɟˀɔ̂

Now try [dolifu] with each of the following tone patterns:

e.g.: dòlǐfú	dólífú	dólífû
´ ˇ `	´ ´ ´	´ ´ ˆ	´ ˆ ˇ	ˆ ˇ ´
` ˇ ´	ˇ ´ `	ˇ ` ´	ˇ ´ ˆ	ˇ ´ ˆ
ˆ ` ˇ	´ ` ˆ	ˇ ˆ ´	` ` ´	´ ´ ˇ
ˆ ˆ `	ˇ ` ˇ	ˆ ˆ ˆ	ˇ ˇ ˇ	` ˇ ˇ

5. Vowel length

a aː	o oː	u uː	ɛ ɛː	iː i	uː u	ɑː ɑ	eː e
ɔpɔ:	aka:	o:do	efe:	e:fe	ɛʃɛ:	ɑ:ba	idi:
bɛ:vɔ	pufa:	tɑ:θɛ:	daðˀa:	ti:sɔ:	dizu:	kaxe	ɡo:ɣe:

6. Long consonants. How do you pronounce *fourteen* and *eighteen*? Consider the length of the [t] in these words carefully?

Practise the following words:

nː	lː	ɹː	sː	mː	ɑnɑ	ɑnːɑ	olːo
o:lo:	ɛɹɛː	ib:u	ɑ:ɡo	ɛk:a	es:u	ʁɣ:o	

Try the following pairs of short and long consonants in Italian:

fato	*fate*	fatto	*done*
kade	*he falls*	kadde	*he fell*
fola	*fable*	folla	*crowd*
nono	*ninth*	nonno	*grandfather*

7. Yoruba (Bamgboṣe, 1966) is a register tone language with three levels. High tone is marked by [´], low tone by [`], and mid tone is unmarked. Practise the single words first, and then the sentences. Be sure to take your time; speak slowly at first, exaggerating the tones. A useful exercise is to tape record yourself, and then to transcribe the tones of your speech. Then compare your

transcription with the original below. After doing this a few times, your should improve in both your ability and your confidence at producing and transcribing tones.

iʃé	work	ìʃé	poverty
awo	cult	àwo	plate
ɔwɔ́	broom	ɔ̀wɔ̀	respect

àwɔn èǹjɔn wa àg͡bè ni wɔ́n	*Our people are farmers*
wɔ́n raʃɔ tó pɔ̀ ʃùg͡bɔ́n wɔn	*They bought many cloths, but*
ò rówó sɔn	*they could not pay for them.*
ilé tó tóbi tó léwà tó sì dára	*A big, fine and good house*
wɔ́n rɛja ɛrɔn àtèfɔ́	*They bought fish, meat,*
	and vegetables.
wɔn ò fɛkó ʃòfò	*They do not want it; let it be*
	wasted.

ADVANCED

8. In the following words, try to control stress and pitch separately. The accents indicate tone.

ˈlómè	lòˈmé	ˈfákìsè	ˈfàkìsé	fàˈkísè	fáˈkísè
ˈlòmé	lóˈmè	ˈfàkísè	ˈfàkísé	fàˈkìsé	fáˈkìsé

9. Given the following parameters, contruct foot and word lines for the words below, and assign the proper stress.

> bounded (two syllables to a foot) ultima extrametrical
> right-headed foot right to left
> left-headed word

lamikɛ   tozɛ   defoniʃupanikɔ   mɑkɔɲizu

10. From the forms below, describe the parameters necessary to account for stress in this language.

dɔnífuŋ   lemnókɔnne   sɔné   rizénomvusʌŋ

11. From the forms below, describe the parameters necessary to account for stress in this language.

léʒupàŋ   ŋɔfúlzimtè   tídʒolèðultè   fumé

12. The tonal system of Cantonese (a dialect of Chinese spoken in southern China, including Hong Kong) is very complex. It has at least six tones. Practise the following words.

1. ⌐	53	**2.** ⌐	35	**3.** ⊣	33
ka	*home*	ka	*false*	ka	*frame*
saj	*west*	saj	*wash*	saj	*small*
kaw	*ditch*	kaw	*nine*	kaw	*enough*
kam	*present*	kam	*so (manner)*	kam	*so (degree)*
pin	*border*	pin	*flat, thin*	pin	*change*
fan	*divide*	fan	*powder*	fan	*advise*

4. ⌐	21	5. ⌐	21	6. ⌐	22
ma	*hemp*	ma	*horse*	ma	*scold*
laj	*come*	laj	*propriety*	laj	*example*
lam	*blue*	lam	*behold*	lam	*warship*
jyn	*round*	jyn	*far*	jyn	*court*
fan	*grave*	fan	*excited*	fan	*share*

13. Thai /taj/ distinguishes voiced, plain voiceless, and aspirated voiceless stops and fricatives:

pʰàa	*split*	tʰam	*do*	kʰàt	*interrupt*
pàa	*forest*	tam	*pound*	kàt	*bite*
bàa	*shoulder*	dam	*black*		
zãn	*levitation*	zauŋ	*edge*		
sãn	*example*	sauŋ	*harp*		
sʰãn	*rice*	sʰauŋ	*winter*		

14. Practise aspiration and retroflex consonants in Bengali:

kɑl	*tomorrow*	kʰɑl	*canal*
gɑl	*cheek*	gʰɑl	*wounded*
bɑg	*behind part*	bɑgʰ	*tiger*
ʃap	*snake*	ʃapʰ	*clean*
sɒtʰɑ	*proposition*	ʃudʰu	*only*
dɔpʰtor	*office*	skʰlɔlon	*fault*
stʰir	*quiet*	spʰuliŋgo	*sport*
ʈɑt	*mat*	tɑt	*heat*
ɖɑn	*right side*	dɑn	*gift*
beɖ	*flower bed*	bed	*Vedas*

15. Nasal Onset. Practise saying the following words from Central Carrier (an Athabaskan /ˌæθəˈbæskən/ language, spoken in British Columbia) with nasal onset. At first, make the nasal a separate syllable: [m - bət]. Then try to make the nasal a part of the the same syllable as the following oral stop: [mbət].

mbət	*your stomach*	ndaj	*what*
ntʃa	*big*	ŋgan	*your arm*
ŋʷgʷət	*your knee*	ŋgeni	*that*

Try the following words from Gbeya (/ˈɡɓejɑ/, Central African Republic; Samarin 1966).

ba	*to take*	mba	*to greet*
dak	*to extract*	ndak	*to chase*
guri	*to smoke meat*	ŋguti	*to burst (intr)*
nɔ	*to drink*	ndɔ	*to have sexual intercourse*
ɲ̂mãj	*to split*	ɲ̂mgban	*to uproot*

CHAPTER SEVENTEEN
HEARING AND PERCEPTION

The ear, as we all know, is the organ of hearing. A general theory of phonetics has to describe how the ear converts sound waves into sound signals for the brain and then how the brain interprets these signals as language. Scientists do not now have a very complete understanding of the processes involved. This chapter reviews what we know about hearing and speech perception, starting with the structure of the ear.

In this chapter you will learn about:
• how we hear sounds
• various theories about how we perceive sound as language.

HEARING

THE EAR

The ear is divided into three separate parts, known as the **outer**, **middle**, and **inner ears**. From Figure 17.1 you can see that the outer ear consists of the **pinna** /ˈpɪnə/ (the visible part) and the **ear canal**. The outer ear plays only a minor role in hearing. The pinna gathers sounds, and the ear canal amplifies higher frequencies slightly. The ear canal serves to protect the delicate apparatus of the inner ear.

The **outer ear** and **inner ear** are separated by a round membrane known as the **eardrum**. Variations in air pressure travel along the ear canal and cause the eardrum to vibrate. Three small bones located in the **middle ear** transmit these vibrations to the inner ear. These bones, in sequence, are the **hammer**, the **anvil**, and the **stirrup**. The footplate of the stirrup covers the **oval window** which leads to the inner ear.

The middle ear cavity is linked with the upper pharynx by the **eustachian tube** /juˈstejʃən/. This tube equalises pressure with the surrounding air. It is normally closed, often opening when we swallow. In a airplane or long elevator ride, your ears may have 'popped'. This pop is caused when the eustachian tube opens to equalise the difference in air pressures resulting from the change in altitude. The mechanical action of the bones of the middle ear amplifies the

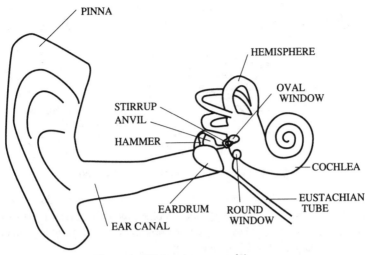

Figure 17.1 Anatomy of the ear.

vibrations passing through it. Also, the middle ear acts to protect us somewhat from damage resulting from loud noises.

The **inner ear** is a set of cavities filled with fluid in the bone of the skull. The three **hemispheres** at the top shown in Figure 17.1 are responsible for our equilibrium. In hearing, the vibrations from the middle ear are transmitted across the oval window to the **cochlea** /ˈkowkliə ~ ˈkɑkliə/, a spiral-shaped cavity.

The cochlea is easier to visualise if we imagine that it were unrolled as in Figure 17.2. Unrolled, the cochlea appears as a long two-chambered structure with a passageway between the chambers at the far end. Vibrations come in from the **oval window**, pass along the **scala vestibuli** /ˌskɑlə ˌvɛsˈtɪbjəli/, turn around through the gap at the end called the **helicotrema** /ˌhɛliˌkoˈtrimə/, and return along the **scala tympani** /ˌskɑlə ˌtɪmˈpɑni/ to the **round window**.

Figure 17.3 shows a cross-section of the cochlear tube. Lying between the scala vestibuli and the scala tympani, is a third area called the **cochlear duct**. Within this duct lies the **organ of Corti** /ˈkoɹˌti/, which is connected to the **auditory nerve**.

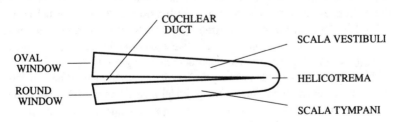

Figure 17.2 The cochlea unrolled.

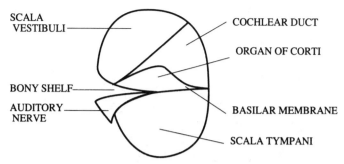

SCALA VESTIBULI

COCHLEAR DUCT

ORGAN OF CORTI

BONY SHELF

AUDITORY NERVE

BASILAR MEMBRANE

SCALA TYMPANI

Figure 17.3 Cross-section of the cochlea.

The **bony shelf**, lying between the scala tympani and the cochlear duct, is quite thick at the end near the middle ear and become gradually thinner towards the helicotrema. Conversely, the **basilar membrane** /ˈbæzɪləɹ/ is narrow near the middle ear, becoming larger towards the helicotrema.

The basilar membrane responds to the vibrations passing through the inner ear, with different parts of the membrane responding to different sounds. Generally the end near the middle ear responds more to high pitched sounds and the end at the helicotrema responds to low pitched sounds. As the different parts of the basilar membrane respond to different sounds, the organ of Corti adjacent to that part responds as well and sends a signal along the auditory nerve to the brain.

Much remains to be understood about human hearing. Because of its location in the skull bones, the inner ear is not easy to observe. Much of the work on hearing has been done on other animals, such as cats and chinchillas, which do not have language.

PERCEPTION

Humans can perceive sounds between about 20 Hz and 20,000 Hz. Actually, our ability to hear different frequencies depends on their intensity. Figure 17.4 shows this relationship. Sounds with great intensity cause pain. With intensities below the limit, the sound is inaudible. Other animals have different hearing abilities. Dogs, for example, can hear higher frequencies than humans can. Our hearing ability declines somewhat after the age of 30. Exposure to loud noise, such as from jet airplanes or rock bands, is known to cause hearing loss. With age, the nerve endings of the cochlea become less sensitive at the middle-ear end, reducing the ability to hear high-pitched sounds later in life.

Note that frequency and intensity are physical measurements. Our perception does not, however, always match the physical measurements. The **mel scale** is frequently used to give a more accurate representation of the way humans perceive frequency as pitch. This scale shows perceptually equal intervals of pitch as equal distances on the scale. The usual statement in physics is that one sound is

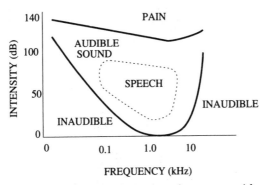

Figure 17.4 The auditory relationship of intensity and frequency.

an octave higher than another if the first has a frequency twice that of the second. Thus we would expect two sounds 1000 Hz and 2000 Hz to be one octave apart. Psychological studies have shown that if we start with a sound with a frequency of 1000 Hz, the sound which is perceptually an octave higher has a frequency of approximately 3120 Hz, not 2000 Hz as we would have expected. The mel scale spaces the perceived octaves 1000 mels apart, corresponding to our perception of pitch. The entire mel scale has been worked out relating pitch to frequency, as in Figure 17.5; it is sometimes used in phonetics instead of frequency.

MASKING

We know that it is hard to hear a sound if there is another sound present. It is harder to use a telephone at a busy intersection than in a quiet room. Sounds are said to **mask** other sounds by making them harder to hear. Tests have shown that one tone is better at masking another if it is closer in frequency to the masked tone. Also, low-frequency tones are more effective at masking other sounds than are high-frequency tones.

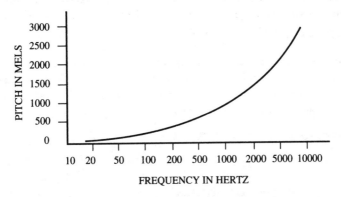

Figure 17.5 Frequency and mels, with 1000 mels = 1000 Hz.

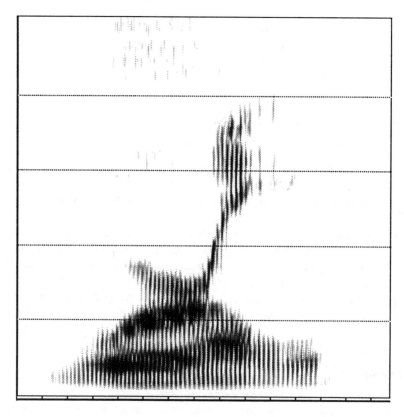

Figure 17.6 Spectrogram of *whirl*.

BINAURALNESS

We use both ears together in **binaural** /ˌbajˈnɑɹəl/ hearing to locate the direction from which sounds come. In addition, we perceive sounds to be 5–6 dB louder when both ears are used together.

SEGMENTATION

An acoustic signal is continuous. The segmentation of a word like *whirl* is difficult to do by looking at a spectrogram alone. On a spectrogram (Figure 17.6), the points of division occasionally seem arbitrary. Our mind, however, invariably divides utterances into discrete segments — /w ə ɹ l/.

CATEGORICAL PERCEPTION

We perceive individual colours as part of a continuum. We may refer to a specific colour as 'blue', 'blue with a little green', 'blue-green', 'bluish green, but with a little more green than on Aunt Ethel's afghan'. We do not perceive speech sounds this way; we perceive them categorically, that is, as clearly a member of category

X or of category Y. A primary difference in English intervocalic stops is that voiced stops are shorter than voiceless ones. One experiment (Lisker and Abramson, 1971) took a recording of a word with an intervocalic /b/ and artificially varied the length of the gap forming the stop between two vowels. Subjects were asked to identify the sound as /p/ or as /b/. When the gap was greater than 4 csec, the subjects perceived the gap as /p/; when the gap was shorter than 1 csec, they perceived it as /b/. There was almost no confusion. Speakers of English are very good at distinguishing very small differences of timing in the region between 1–5 csec. On the other hand, they are not particularly good at similar distinctions of timing at different points, *e.g.,* 10 csec from 13 csec. It seems that English speakers are particularly attuned to certain distinctions of timing and oblivious to others.

RATE

Typically, we speak at a **rate** of about 8–12 phonemes per second, with a maximum possible production rate of about 15 phonemes per second. Experiments with artificially speeded-up utterances have shown that we can understand speech up to 30 phonemes per second. Note that a rate of about 10 phonemes per second, we speak with little or no conscious attention paid to speaking or listening; our minds are usually focussed entirely on the meaning and significance of the message.

By contrast, consider how we perceive non-speech sounds. Suppose we hear a simple tap repeated at even intervals. If the rate of tapping is increased, we hear the individual taps until the rate exceeds about 15 per second. At rates higher than this, we only hear a steady buzz. Note, by comparison, that in listening to speech, we not only hear individual speech sounds, but we also identify and distinguish each one from other possible sounds.

This type of evidence has led to the belief that we perceive speech differently from the way we perceive other sounds, that somehow, our brain is wired to deal specially with language.

LATERALISATION

The brain is divided from front to back into two lateral **hemispheres** (Figure 17.7). In most people the right side of the body is controlled by the left hemisphere of the brain, and the left side of the body is controlled by the right hemisphere. Studies have shown that for most people (98%), language is **lateralised**, or located, on the left side of the brain. Non-linguistic sounds, such as music or the noise of a siren, are processed on the right side of the brain.

Although we are a long way from a full understanding of how language is processed in the brain, certain areas of the left hemisphere have been identified as particularly important for language. Much of the research derives from studies of people who have suffered a stroke. A stroke damages the brain by cutting off the oxygen supply to certain areas. If the stroke affects an area responsible for language, some loss of speech, or **aphasia** /əˈfejʒə/, may result.

299

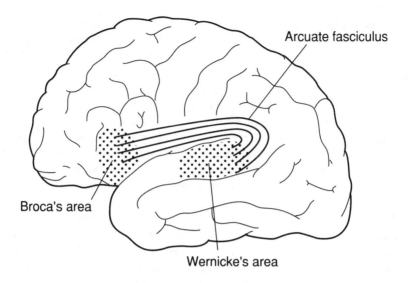

Figure 17.7 The left hemisphere of the brain.
(O'Grady and Dobrovolsky, 1987, by permission).

Several different aphasias have been identified and associated with different areas of the brain. **Broca's aphasia** /ˈbrowkə/ is associated with **Broca's area**; this aphasia may result in poor articulation and loss of inflectional morphemes, such as 'plural', although the speech is still meaningful. Damage in **Wernicke's area** /ˈveɹnɪkə/ is associated with **Wernicke's aphasia**, chacterised by comprehension disorders and by fluent, but nonsensical speech. The **arcuate fasciculus** /ˈaɹkjuət fəˈsɪkjələs/ connects Broca's area and Wernicke's area; damage here may impair the ability to repeat an utterance.

THEORIES OF PERCEPTION

Encoding or production is the process of giving an acoustic shape to a particular linguistic message. **Decoding** is the reverse: giving a meaning to a specific acoustic signal. Almost all theories of perception and production assume that speech sounds are coded at several levels of representation. The following is a list of levels of representation often posited for encoding and decoding.

a. acoustic signal: the waveform as it is transmitted through the air, and received by the ear
b. spectral analysis of the waveform showing formants, noise, etc.
c. motor signal: neural signals which, if activated, would cause the muscles to behave in a certain fashion

d. vocal tract shape: representation of the shape of the vocal tract for each sound produced

e. phonetic representation: phonetic detail represented either as features or as segments (narrow transcription)

f. phonological representation: phonological transcription either as features or as segments (broad transcription)

A large variety of theories have been advanced to explain how we perceive speech. Theories differ essentially in which levels they see as crucial and in how the levels relate to each other. In general the theories can be divided into passive and active theories.

PASSIVE THEORIES

The **passive** theories hold that the listener decodes the utterance without using any knowledge of the language or of speech production. Such theories have generally followed one of two courses, involving either a phonetic matrix or a specific feature detector.

PHONETIC MATRIX

In the **phonetic matrix theory**, the acoustic signal undergoes spectral analysis (stage b), and the results of this analysis are then compared to standard matrices for each sound in the language. When a match is found, the sound is registered (stages e and f), and the matching process goes on to the next sound.

FEATURE DETECTORS According to the **feature detector theory**, human beings have detectors which are sensitive to specific phonetic cues. Such phenomena are known among other species. Certain frogs, for example, have built-in detectors which are sensitive only to the specific sounds of the mating calls of their own species. It is thus possible to imagine that we have feature detectors which are sensitive to certain important features of speech. Such detectors might be sensitive to the voice-onset time of stops, or to the formant frequencies of vowels. Feature detectors would explain categorical perception.

DISCUSSION The passive theories are straightforward and easy to understand. They are less easy, however, to verify experimentally. Researchers have not established feature detectors with the reliability that we would like to see. Further, these theories do not explain the fact that information about the identity of one sound is often found in the phonetic detail of another. They do not explain how segmentation occurs, nor do they explain how we easily understand speakers with a wide variety of speech qualities, such as a foreign accent.

ACTIVE THEORIES

The **active** theories suppose that perception involves active participation of the hearer's brain and knowledge of the language. Two theories of this sort have been widely considered.

MOTOR THEORY OF SPEECH PERCEPTION The **motor theory of speech perception** supposes that, as we hear sounds, we go partly through the process of speech production. When we hear *bill,* we form a mental representation or model of the vocal tract (stage d above). In some sense, we then activate this model to determine what sound it would produce. We then compare the sound of our mental model with what we actually hear. If we are correct, we register the sounds and go on to the next sound. Thus we use our knowledge of how sounds are produced to perceive what we hear, or as it might be more technically put: the auditory signal is interpreted neurally in terms of the motor commands necessary to produce the signal.

You must not get the idea that we actually initiate any muscular activity in our own vocal tract. This theory posits a level of representation of neural images without actually engaging the muscles. Older theories of this sort took the view that we actually make small articulatory motions while we are listening, but such views are not generally accepted nowadays.

ANALYSIS BY SYNTHESIS **Analysis by synthesis** is similar to motor theory but it does not focus on motor actions. This theory supposes that the hearer constructs a mental representation of how the vocal tract would be shaped (stage d) and how it would sound for specific segments or features and then compares that representation with the sounds heard. Note that there is no necessity for the unit of analysis to be limited to a single segment; the analysis by synthesis could be done syllable-by-syllable, for example.

DISCUSSION The active theories have been more widely received than have the passive ones. They explain problems of listening to various speakers and of segmenting the acoustic signal. Many problems of listening can be solved by an active theory since we can bring our knowledge of the language to bear on decoding the message. At the moment, speech perception is a poorly understood area where the theories seem to outnumber the facts that can be agreed on.

CONCLUSION

The chapter brings our examination of phonetics to an end. It is an extremely rich field of intellectual enquiry. We are constantly surrounded by speech. Whether looking at a spectrogram in the laboratory or overhearing a conversation on the streetcar, there is always something of interest.

TECHNICAL TERMS

active theories
analysis by synthesis
anvil
aphasia
arcuate fasciculus
auditory nerve
basilar membrane
binaural
bony shelf
Broca's aphasia
   Broca's area
cochlea
   cochlear duct
decoding
ear canal

eardrum
encoding
Eustachian tube
feature detector theory
hammer
helicotrema
hemisphere
inner ear
lateralisation
masking
mel scale
middle ear
motor theory
   of speech perception

organ of Corti
outer ear
oval window
passive theories
phonetic matrix theory
pinna
rate
round window
scala tympani
scala vestibuli
segmentation
stirrup
Wernicke's aphasia
   Wernicke's area

EXERCISES

BASIC

1. Practise the following nonsense forms:

pac	xɯnɛz̠	ðʀg̊d	ŋeɪcœ	ɔɦɲɑ
ʒim	teqaθ	z̥ɒŋʔ	saŋgu	ørby
ʀœɣ	ʋʀθʌj̊	kɛʔl	χøβɲi	ozʀœ
l̥eʂ	vuhaɾ	çɔɱv	tʋɸfo	aʒny
fɯj	ʒosiɰ	ʕuɬt	çɒɴðɯ	otβe

2. Practise the following voiceless sonorants:

m̥ɑ	n̥ɑ	ɲ̊ɑ	ŋ̊ɑ
m̥a̰	n̥a̰	ɲ̊a̰	ŋ̊a̰
m̥om	n̥on	ɲ̊o̥	ŋ̊o̥
lililili	mememememememe		
nononon̥on̥o	ɹɯɹɯɹɯɹɯɹɯ		
ɔl̥ma	ɛmɹ̥u	ynl̥ʌ	œɲʀɯ

3. Practise nasal vowels:

manɔ̃	nĭmɛ	ɑ̃ŋmɛ	ɑŋmɛ̃
mynodɛ̃	iẽɛ̃ã	ninẽnɛnã	ŋũŋõŋɔŋɑ

4. Say each row carefully; the following row changes one sound.

   so no de mu lɛ
   so nõ de mu lɛ
   so nõ de mu lɛ̃
   so nõ dẽ mu lɛ̃
   sõ nõ dẽ mu lɛ̃
   sõ no dẽ mu lɛ̃

5. Try the following build-up sequences. Say the first syllable, then add the second, then the third, etc. Don't hurry.

ˈɑpaˈfaβaˈmavaˈbaɸa
ˈekeˈgeɣeˈxeɲeˈɣexe
ˈsuluˈtunuˈθuzuˈðudu
ˈcɔɟɔˈjɔçɔˈʒɔɟɔˈʃɔɲɔ
ˈtɛnɛˈlɛdɛˈsɛzɛˈlɛnɛ

6. Nasal Release

Pronounce the following words first with a clear [ə], as in [ˈsadən]. Now try them with a syllabic nasal, e.g., [ˈsadn̩].

   sodden   sudden   hidden   laden   leaden   wooden

a. In words like *button*, we get a variety of pronunciations: [bʌtn̩bʌʔnbʌʔt̩n] where [ʔt] represents a simultaneous glottal stop and [t].

Transcribe your pronunciation of the following:

   button   kitten   rotten   batten

Try to pronounce each word in the row above with all the variations: e.g., [bʌtn̩ bʌʔn bʌʔt̩n].

A word like *bottom*, generally has a syllabic labial nasal which is not homorganic with the preceding sound. Some dialects have [baʔm]; more frequently we hear [bar̩m].

Listen closely and transcribe your pronunciation of the following:

   bottom   item   atom   datum

Do you have syllabic nasals in *prison, prism* ?

b. Labial and velar stops also have nasal plosion when followed by a homorganic nasal. Examples of these are sometimes only to be found in fairly colloquial speech.

Transcribe using syllabic nasal wherever possible:

e.g.: blacken   [ˈblækŋ̩]

   bacon   Fagan   Hogan   ship 'em   stab 'em   happen

7. Lateral release. Note the syllabic [l̩] in the following:

   ladle   [ˈlejdl̩]   marble   [ˈmaɹbl̩]

Transcribe the following:

   idle   ripple   trickle   dangle   nickel
   saddle   dabble   cuddle   hobble

8. Transcribe the following, paying careful attention to your own pronunciation:

   little   tattle   drizzle   hovel   victuals   throttle
   bristle   bible   nuzzle

9. Gbeya contrasts plain initial nasals with nasals preceded by glottal stops.

   mã   *to plant*   ʔma   *to open (fist)*
   mam   *to laugh*   ʔmam   *to get hold of*
   nun   *to smell*   ʔnum   *to enter (water)*

ADVANCED

10. Practise the following forms which include central vowels:

| bɨsi | kəlo | rɄnu | ɬɐφa | nəʃe | mɄxy | hɐga | jɨnɄ |
| ʋɛqə | ʌɔɹɄ | ʁɨfə | ʒɘχɄ | ɖ◌̥çɵ | ɲʌβɨ | ʋɒɟɐ | |

11. Try the following forms to practise creaky voice and murmur:

| ʃɨmi | zɄφu | səbo | ʔɔφe | tʃəfɨ | dzaɹə | gɄxɐ | ɣɐdʒɐ |
| lavʌ | pi◌̤Ʉ | nuɲi̤ | weɹə | jəso | cɐxɒ | kɄʑɨ | ɲa◌̤θu |

12. Practise the following ejectives, implosives, and clicks.

pʼa	tʼu	kʼo	papʼa	ʈʼutu	kɛkʼɛ
cʼeki	qutʼy	kʼøpʼɔ	sʼalu	ʈʼone	ʃʼɛmɒ
ɓe	ɗe	ɠe	ɗu	ɓɛ	ɠʌ
ɓiɗu	gaɗo	ɗɔga	⊙ ⊙ ⊙ ⊙	| | | |	! ! ! !	‖ ‖ ‖ ‖
⊙o	|a	!y	‖ɔ	ǀiǀi	ǁeǁe	⊙aⵔa	!ɛ!ɛ
ǀiǃeǃɛǃa	ǀaǀɔǀoǀu	‖yǁøǁœǁɶ	⊙ɒⵔʌⵔɣⵔɯ
paɳɛⵔuʋo	lɔǃequɯmy	jiɲʌǀafy	tɔǁasɒɣi

13. Try the tones in the following exercise ([´] is a high tone, [¯] is a mid tone, and [`] is a low tone):

bépʌ̀	zégèxò	ɳótɵ̀θá	ʃátɳ̀ì	ɹ̠àdʒíʒè	hìʋɔ̀lɛ́
mòkē	ʒɔ̄ɹǽφā	ɣɒ̀ɾǽnɔ̄	ɹ̠ḛ̀ʔ◌̄	d̠óðāɣɛ̀	n̠ɵ̄ʃáʔì
ðōd̠ó	móli̠lɵ̀	húɳóbɛ̀

14. Practise the following Dutch words which have some short and long diphthongs:

[mɛj]	mij	*me*	[mɛj]	Mei	*May*
[lɛj]	lei	*slate*	[bœj]	buj	*shower*
[hœɥs]	huis	*house*	[lœɥt]	luid	*loud*
[y:w]	uw	*your*	[ry:w]	ruw	*rough*
[dy:uə(n)]	duwen	*push*	[kɔwt]	kout	*cold*
[za:j]	zaai	*(I) sow*	[mo:j]	mooi	*beautiful*
[bu:j]	boei	*buoy*	[ni:w]	nieuw	*new*
[e:w]	eeuw	*century*			

15. Practise the long and short vowels and consonants in Estonian:

kɑlɑ	*fish*	kɑ:lu	*weight*
tore	*splendid*	to:res	*raw*
kɛru	*wheelbarrow*	kɛ:ru	*bend*
lømɑ	*mush*	lø:ma	*beat*
kynɑ	*trough*	ky:nɑl	*candle*
kɑpi	*hoof*	kɑppi	*wardrobe*
ti:p	*wing*	pi:pp	*pipe*
kolp	*piston*	kolpp	*skull*
sɑta	*hundred*	rɑttɑs	*wheel*
ko:t	*code*	ko:tt	*flail*

A PPENDIX A
ENGLISH CONSONANTAL ALLOPHONES

The following list of English allophones, although extensive, describes only the more common variations in Canadian English. Speakers of other accents will obviously have allophonic variations different from those shown here. As well, even within a single accent area, individuals often have personal variations.

For more details on the production and occurrence of the various allophones, consult the relevant section in Chapter 3.

/p/ voiceless bilabial stop

aspirated	[pʰ]	initially in stressed syllables;	*pay, appear*
		finally	*stop*
unaspirated	[p]	after syllable-initial /s/; initially in weakly stressed syllables;	*spy, spot* *upper, pyjamas*
		finally	*stop*
no release	[p˺]	before /b p/	*chipboard, rippoint*
inaudible release	[p˺]	finally; before other stop	*stop* *apt, ripcord*
nasal release	[pm]	before /m/	*topmast*
nasal onset	[mp]	after /m/	*ramp, lumpy*

/b/ voiced bilabial stop

partially voiceless	[#b̥b], [bb̥#]	at edge of word	*bun, bet, boat* *cob, ebb, robe*
voiced	[b]	medially	*lobby*
no release	[b˺]	before /b p/	*ribpoint, scrubboard*
inaudible release	[b˺]	before other stop	*rubbed, tubeguard*
nasal release	[bm]	before /m/	*submarine*
nasal onset	[mb]	after /m/	*lumber*

/t/ voiceless alveolar stop

aspirated	[tʰ]	initially in stressed syllables; finally	*toy, entire* / *write*
unaspirated	[t]	after syllable-initial /s/; syllable-initial in unstressed syllables, initially and after obstruents finally	sty / *tobacco, tomorrow* / *hefty, actor* / *write*
no release	[t˺]	before /t d/	*eight times, hot dog*
inaudible release	[t˺]	finally; before other stop	*write* / *Atkins, at best*
nasal release	[tn]	before non-syllabic /n/	*Bittner*
nasal onset	[nt]	after /n/	*went*
lateral release	[tl]	before /l/	*butler*
lateral onset	[lt]	after /l/	*belt, faulty*
tap	[ɾ]	at beginning of non-initial unstressed syllables after vowels and /ɹ/	*city, writer, dirty, barter*
tap with nasal release	[ɾm̩]	before syllabic [m̩]	*bottom*
nasal tap	[ɾ̃]	after /n/, at beginning of unstressed syllable	*winter, flinty*
tap with lateral release	[ɾl̩]	before syllabic [l̩]	*rattle, metal*
glottalised	[ʔt] or [ʔ]	before syllabic [n̩]	*button*
dental	[t̪]	before /θ ð/	*eighth, at three*
slightly retroflexed	[t̠]	after /ɹ/	*hurt, cart*
palato-alveolar affricate	[tʃ]	before /j/	*hit you*
rounded retroflexed palato-alveolar affricate	[tʃʷ]	before /ɹ/	*tree, sentry*

Speakers show a fair bit of variation in the allophones of /t/. In particular, many use glottalisation more frequently than this chart shows. Some replace taps with voiced stops.

/d/   voiced alveolar stop

partially voiceless	[#d̥d], [dd̥#]	at edge of word	*debt, dog, do* *add, odd, Ed*
voiced	[d]	medially	*ready*
no release	[d˺]	before /d t/	*Ed did, add two*
inaudible release	[d˺]	before other stops	*redcap, Edgar*
nasal release	[dn d̩n]	before /n/	*Sidney, sudden*
nasal onset	[nd]	after /n/	*bend*
lateral release	[dl d̩l]	before /l/	*bedlam, curdle*
lateral onset	[ld]	after /l/	*weld*
dental	[d̪]	before /θ ð/	*width, add them*
slightly retroflexed	[ḍ]	after /ɹ/	*bird, card*
palato-alveolar affricate	[dʒ]	before /j/	*feed you*
rounded retroflexed palato-alveolar affricate	[ḍʒ ʷ]	before /ɹ/	*dream, Andrew*

/k/   voiceless velar stop

aspirated		initially in stressed syllables	
...palatalised	[kʲʰ]	...before front vowels	*keep, kin, cane*
...non-palatalised	[kʰ]	...before other vowels; finally	*cook, cot, cone, cut* *lack, luck*
unaspirated		after /s/ in same syllable; medially, in weakly stressed syllables	
...palatalised	[kʲ]	...before front vowels	*skin, lucky*
...non-palatalised	[k]	...before back vowels; finally	*scan, luck*
no release	[k˺]	before /g k/	*sick girl, stoke coal*
inaudible release	[k˺]	finally; before other stops	*stack* *deck post, sock drawer*
nasal release	[kŋ]	before nasals, particularly in casual speech	*bacon*
nasal onset	[ŋk]	after /ŋ/	*drink*

/g/   voiced velar stop

partially voiceless		initially	
...palatalised	[#g̊ʲgʲ]	...before front vowels	*gear, geld, gale*
...non-palatalised	[#g̊g]	...before other vowels	*good, got, gum, go*
	[gg̊#]	finally	*egg, dog, rug*
voiced		medially	
...palatalised	[gʲ]	...before front vowels	*muggy*
...non-palatalised	[g]	...before other vowels	*rugger*
no release	[g˺]	before /g k/	*big game, eggcup*
inaudible release	[g˺]	before other stops	*nagged, bagpipes*

/f/ voiceless labio-dental fricative

	[f]	in all positions	*foul, suffer, enough*

/v/   voiced labio-dental fricative

partially voiceless	[#v̥v]	at edge of word	*van, vote, Vince*
	[vv̥#]		*love, sieve, salve*
voiced	[v]	medially	*having, grovel*

/θ/   voiceless dental fricative

	[θ]	in all positions	*thin, ether, smith*

/ð/   voiced dental fricative

partially voiceless	[#ð̥ð]	at edge of word	*then, that, those*
	[ð̥ð#]		*seethe, writhe*
voiced	[ð]	medially	*father, southern*

/s/   voiceless alveolar fricative

palato-alveolar	[ʃ]	before /j ʃ/	*miss you, this ship*
alveolar	[s]	in all other positions	*see, lesser, fuss*

/z/   voiced alveolar fricative

partially voiceless	[#z̥z]	at edge of word	*zeal, zip, zoo*
	[zz̥#]		*ease, close, raise*
voiced	[z]	medially	*gazing, easy*
palato-alveolar	[ʒ]	before /j ʃ/	*buzz you, has she?*

/ʃ/ voiceless palato-alveolar fricative

rounded	[ʃʷ]	in all positions	*shin, fissure, mesh*

/ʒ/   voiced palato-alveolar fricative

partially voiceless

...rounded	[#ʒʷʒʷ]	initially	*gigue, genre, Giles*
...not rounded	[ʒ̥ʒ#]	finally	*beige, rouge, garage*
voiced rounded	[ʒʷ]	medially	*vision, pleasure*

In initial and final position, some speakers replace /ʒ/ with /dʒ/.

/h/   voiceless vowel (glottal fricative)

voiceless vowel, same quality as following vowel	[h]	initially	*hello, hot, hip, hung*
murmured same quality as following vowel	[ɦ]	medially	*ahead, anyhow, ahoy*
voiceless palatal glide	[ç]	/hj/	*huge, Hugh*

/tʃ/   voiceless palato-alveolar affricate

rounded	[tʃʷ]	all positions	*chin, watch, nature*

/dʒ/   voiced palato-alveolar affricate

rounded	[dʒʷ]	in all positions	
partially voiceless	[#d̥ʒʷ] [dʒʷ#]	at edge of word	*gem, jug, Jones* *edge, age, gouge*
voiced	[dʒʷ]	medially	*logic, fragile*

/l/   alveolar lateral

Prevocalically, the phoneme /l/ has two major classes of allophones: clear [l] before front vowels, and dark [ɫ] before back vowels.

Clear [l]

voiceless	[l̥]	after aspirated stops	*play, clay, complain, incline*
partially voiceless	[l̥l]	after syllable-initial /s f θ ʃ/	*slip, athlete, Schlitz*
voiced	[l]	initially; medially, in weakly stressed syllables after a stop	*lie, litre, supplement, *settler, *circling, *fondling*

Dark [ɫ]

partially voiceless	[ɫ̥ɫ]	finally; before a voiceless consonant	*well, pile, fool* *milk, dealt, elf*
voiced	[ɫ]	after a vowel, before voiced consonant	*feels, twelve, weld*
syllabic	[ɫ̩]	finally, after a consonant	*table, chisel, fondle*
dental	[ɫ̪]	before /θ ð/	*filth, well then*

*Words such as *fondling, circling, settler* vary as to whether the /l/ is syllabic or not: [ˈfɑnd-lɪŋ] ~ [ˈfɑnd-ɫ̩-ɪŋ] ~ [ˈfɑnd-əɫ-ɪŋ].

/ɹ/ retroflex approximant

rounded voiced	[ɹʷ]	prevocalic, syllable-initial	*red, rotten*
voiced palato-alveolar with retroflexion	[ʒʷ]	after syllable-initial /d/	*dream, Andrew*
voiceless	[ɹ̥ʷ]	after aspirated /p k/	*pray, tray, crawl*
...palato-alveolar with retroflexion	[ʃʷ]	...after syllable-initial /t/	*tree, sentry*
unrounded voiced	[ɹ]	postvocalic	*car, purring*

/j/ palatal glide (semivowel)

voiceless	[j̥]	after aspirated /p k/	*pure, cute*
voiced	[j]	all other positions	*yes, beauty, bay*

See also /hj/ *under* /h/.

/w/ palatal glide (semivowel)

voiceless	[ʍ]	after aspirated /p k/	*quick*
voiced	[w]	all other positions	*wet, dwell, Gwen, know, now*

A PPENDIX B
GLOSSARY

Abdominal muscles /ˌæbˈdɑmɪnəl/ *n.* Muscles of the lower trunk used in expelling air from the lungs.

Accent *n.* (1) stress:*The accent is on the second syllable.* (2) A phonetic dialect: *an Australian accent.* (3) A diacritic, particularly a grave, acute, or circumflex accent [´ ` ^].

Acoustic /əˈkustɪk/*adj.* Referring to the physical nature of sound. —**Acoustics** *n.* The physical study of sound. —**Acoustic phonetics** *n.* The study of the physical properties of sounds used in human language. —**Acoustic feature** *n.* A feature in an acoustic record which distinguishes one sound from another.

Active theory *n.* A theory of hearing which holds that perception involves active participation of the hearer's brain and knowledge of the language.

Acute accent /əˌkjut/ *n.* The superscript diacritic [´], used to indicate a high tone or, sometimes, a primary stress.

Adam's apple *n.* The forward protrusion of the neck just below the chin, formed by the angle of the thyroid cartilage.

Affricate /ˈæfɹɪkət/ *n.* A sound consisting of a stop followed by a fricative, usually homorganic, often considered a single phonological unit; *e.g.,* [pf tʃ gɣ]. — **Affrication** /ˌæfɹɪˈkejʃən/ *n.* A process whereby a stop becomes an affricate, *e.g.,* t → ts. —**Affricated** *adj.*

Airstream *n.* A flow of air used to produce sounds. —**Airstream mechanism** *n.* The mechanism producing the airstream, *e.g.,* **pulmonic, glottalic, velaric.**

Allophone /ˈæləˌfon/ *n.* A variant of a phoneme. — **Allophonic** /ˌæləˈfɑnɪk/ *adj.*

Alveolar /ˌælˈviələr/ *adj.* Having an articulation with the tip or blade of the tongue at the alveolar ridge. —**Alveolar ridge** *n.* The bony ridge immediately behind the upper teeth. —**Alveolo-** *combining form.*

Alveolo-palatal /ˌæl̩viəˌlo'pælətəl/ *adj.* Having an articulation with the blade of the tongue at the very forward portion of the palate.

Alveolus /ˌæl'viələs/, pl. **alveoli** /ˌæl'viəli/. *n.* An airsac in the lungs.

Amplitude *n.* A property of a wave; in acoustics, normally measured as variation in the air pressure. Variations in amplitude are perceived as changes in loudness.

Analysis-by-synthesis *n.* A theory of speech perception which holds that listeners analyse speech by constructing an internal synthesis of what they hear.

Antepenultimate syllable /ˌæntipə'nʌltɪmət/ *n.* The third-last syllable of a word; same as **antepenult** [ˌænti'piˌnʌlt].

Anticipatory /ˌæn'tɪsɪpəˌtoɹi/ *adj.* Referring to changes in which a later element influences an earlier one; commonly applied to **assimilation** and **dissimilation**. Same as **regressive**. —**Anticipatory** (or **regressive**) **assimilation** /ˌæn'tɪsɪpəˌtoɹi/ *n.* The assimilation of an earlier sound to a later one; *e.g.,* in a sequence XY, X changes to become more like Y.

Anvil /'ænvɪl/ *n.* A bone in the middle ear.

Apex /'ejˌpɛks/ *n.* The tip of the tongue. —**Apical** /'æpɪkəl/ *adj.* —**Apico–** *combining form:* **apicodental**, **apicoalveolar**.

Aphasia /ə'fejʒə/ *n.* The loss or partial loss of normal speaking ability. —**Aphasic** /ə'fejzɪk/ *adj.*

Apico-alveolar /ˌæpɪˌkoˌæl'viələɹ/ *adj.* Having an articulation involving the tip of the tongue and the alveolar ridge.

Apico-dental /ˌæpɪˌko'dɛntəl/ *adj.* Having an articulation involving the tip of the tongue and the upper teeth.

Approximant /ə'pɹɑksɪmənt/ *n.* A manner of articulation with an opening less than that of a vowel and greater than that of a fricative. Approximants are made without a turbulent airstream; they include **liquids** and **glides**.

Arcuate fasciculus /ˌaɹˌkjuət fə'sɪkjələs/ *n.* An area of the brain connecting Broca's area and Wernicke's area.

Arrhotic /ə'ɹowtɪk ~ə'ɹɑtɪk/ *adj.* In English, referring to dialects, such as RP, which have lost codal /ɹ/. See **rhotic**.

Articulation /ˌɑɹˌtɪkjə'lejʃən/ *n.* The movement of the organs, especially of the upper vocal tract, so as to form different sounds. —**Articulate** /ɑɹ'tɪkjəˌlejt/ *v.* —**Articulator** *n.* An organ involved in articulation. The **upper articulators** are the upper lip, upper teeth, palate, velum, uvula, and posterior pharyngeal wall. The **lower articulators** are the lower lip and the various parts of the tongue. —**Articulatory** /ɑɹˈtɪkjuləˌtoɹi/ *adj.* —**Articulatory phonetics** *n.* The branch of phonetics dealing with how sounds are made. See **auditory** and **acoustic phonetics**.

Arytenoid cartilages /ˌɛɹɪˈtinɔjd~əˈɹɪtənɔjd/ *n.* Two pyramid-shaped cartilages of the larynx situated on the cricoid cartilage, and forming the rear point of attachment for the vocal cords.

Ascender *n.* A symbol extending above the x-height line.

Aspiration /ˌæspɪˈɹejʃən/ *n.* A period of voicelessness following a consonant, usually accompanied by a greater air pressure; written as [ʰ]: *e.g.*, [pʰ tʰ kʰ]. —**Aspirate** /ˈæspɪˌrejt/ *v.* —**Aspirated** *adj.* —**Aspirate** /ˈæspɪrət/ *n.* An aspirated consonant.

Assimilation /əˌsɪmɪˈlejʃən/ *n.* A process whereby one sound becomes more like another. See **anticipatory assimilation** and **progressive assimilation**. —**Assimilate** /əˈsɪməˌlet/ *v.* To become more like another sound.

Auditory /ˈɑdɪˌtoɹi/ *adj.* Referring to hearing. —**Auditory phonetics**. The branch of phonetics dealing with hearing and perception.

Auditory nerve *n.* The nerve leading from the inner ear to the brain.

Back *n.* The dorsum of the tongue; the rear portion of the horizontal surface of the tongue. —*adj.* (1) Referring to a sound made farther back in the vocal tract than another or than usual: *a back [k]*. (2) Referring to a vowel or glide made in the back portion of the vowel area: *e.g.*, [ɑ ʌ ɯ w]. See **front** and **central**.

Base line *n.* The imaginary line along the lower edge of symbols such as *x ε s t*.

Basilar membrane /ˈbæzɪləɹ/ *n.* A part of the cochlea in the inner ear.

Bernoulli principle /bəɹˈnuli/ *n.* An observation of physics that objects at the edge of a moving stream tend to move to the centre of the stream; the faster the flow of the stream, the faster the objects move to the centre. More precisely, the pressure perpendicular to the mid-line of a moving stream is inversely proportional to the velocity of the stream.

Bilabial /ˌbajˈlejbiəl/ *adj.* Having an articulation involving both lips, as in the sounds [p b m ɸ β].

Binary /ˈbajnəɹi/ *adj.* Referring to an **opposition** or **distinctive feature** having only two values: [+] and [−]. Each binary feature divides all sounds into two categories. See **unary** and **multivalued**.

Binaural /ˌbajˈnɑɹəl/ *adj.* Referring to hearing using both ears.

Blade *n.* The surface of the tongue just behind the tip, also called the **lamina**.

Bony shelf *n.* A spiral bony blade of the inner ear lying between the cochlear duct and the scala tympani.

Bounded *adj.* In metrical theory, referring to a foot having a constraint on the number of syllables allowed. Typically, a bounded foot has two syllables.

Boyle's law /bɔjlz/ *n.* A principle of physics that, in a closed container, the pressure of a gas varies inversely with the volume.

Breve /bɹiv/ *n.* The superscript diacritic [˘], occasionally used to mark (1) short vowels, (2) unstressed vowels , or (3) a falling-rising tone.

Broad transcription *n.* A transcription with little or no phonetic detail. A **phonemic transcription** is a broad transcription. See **narrow transcription**.

Broad-band spectrogram. *n.* A type of spectrogram, useful for seeing formants; also called a **wide-band spectrogram**.

Broca's aphasia /ˈbɹowkə/ *n.* An aphasia associated with damage to Broca's area, often resulting in poor articulation and loss of inflectional morphemes, but with meaning intact. —**Broca's area**. *n.* An area of the left hemisphere of the brain.

Bronchus /ˈbɹɑŋkəs/, pl. **bronchi** /ˈbɹɑŋki/ *n.* A tube leading from the trachea to the lungs.

C *n.* An abbreviation for **consonant**.

Canadian raising *n.* The occurrence of the diphthongs [ʌw] and [ʌj] before voiceless consonants, rather than [aw] or [aj]; typical of most Canadian dialects.

Cardinal vowel. *n.* An arbitrary reference point for describing vowel quality. —**Cardinal vowel theory** *n.* A theory of describing vowels by locating them in relation to the cardinal vowels.

Cartilage /ˈkɑɹtɪlɪdʒ/ *n.* A firm, flexible type of tissue such as that found in the larynx or earlobe. —**Cartilagenous glottis** /ˌkɑɹtɪˈlædʒɪnəs/ *n.* The portion of the glottis found between the arytenoid cartilages. See **ligamental glottis**.

Centisecond *n.* One one-hundredth of a second; 1 csec = 0.01 sec = 10 msec.

Central *adj.* (1) Referring to a vowel made in the central portion of the vowel area: *e.g.,* [ə ɨ ʉ]. (2) Referring to a vowel made more to the centre of the vowel area than another or than usual: *a central [e]*. See **front, back, and mid**. (3) Not **lateral**; referring to a manner of articulation with the air passing out through the centre of the vocal tract.

Chest pulse *n.* According to R. H. Stetson, a contraction of the rib cage expelling air from the lungs and responsible for the production of a syllable; Stetson's theory is not generally in favour today.

Chomsky-Halle features /ˈtʃɑmski ˈhæli/ *n.* A set of features belonging to a theory of phonological representation which holds that a segment is an unordered bundle of binary features. This theory was set out in *The Sound Pattern of English* (1968).

Circumflex accent /ˈsɜɹkəmˌflɛks/ *n.* The superscript diacritic [ˆ], sometimes used to mark a falling tone.

Class *n.* A group of sounds sharing one or more properties: *e.g.,* the class of bilabial fricatives.

Clear [l] *n.* A type of [l] with the quality of a front vowel. See **dark [l]**.

Click *n.* An ingressive glottalic stop; *e.g.,* [ʘ ǀ ǁ ǂ].

Closed syllable *n.* A syllable ending in a consonant.

Cluster *n.* A sequence of sounds, *e.g.,* [ks] is a consonant cluster.

Cochlea /ˈkowkliə~ˈkɑkliə/. *n.* A spiral-shaped part of the inner ear. —**Cochlear duct** *n.* The middle portion of the cochlea, lying between the **scala tympani** and the **scala vestibuli**.

Coda /ˈkowdə/ *n.* A part of a syllable, consisting of the consonants following the nucleus. —**Codal** *adj.*

Complementary distribution *n.* In phonological theory, two sounds are in complementary distribution if neither occurs in any environments in which the other occurs. See **contrastive distribution** and **free variation**.

Complex repetitive wave *n.* A wave with a repeating waveform and a more complex shape than that of a simple **sine wave.**

Consonant cluster simplification *n.* A process whereby a consonant cluster is simplified by the loss of one of its members.

Consonant *n.* A sound with an opening less than that of a vowel. Consonants include **obstruents**, **approximants**, and **nasals**; they typically function as the onset or coda of a syllable.

Contextual length *n.* Length which is dependent on the context. See **inherent length**.

Continuant /kənˈtɪnjuənt/ *adj.* A distinctive feature defining the class of sounds in which air flows out the oral cavity. **Vowels**, **approximants**, and **fricatives** are continuant sounds.

Contour tone language *n.* A language with a system of moving tones.

Contrastive distribution *n.* In phonological theory, two sounds are in contrastive distribution if they occur in the same environment, potentially forming a

difference of meaning. See **complementary distribution** and **free variation**.
—**Contrast** *v.* To be in contrastive distribution, to form a distinction of meaning.

Coronal /ˈkoɹənəl/ *adj.* A distinctive feature defining the class of sounds made with the tip or blade of the tongue.

Creaky voice *n.* An adjustment of the glottis, occasionally used in language.

Creole /ˈkɹiˌol/ *n.* A language which originated as a pidgin, but which has become a native language.

Cricoid cartilage /ˈkɹajˌkɔjd/ *n.* A ring-shaped cartilage at the bottom of the larynx, just above the trachea.

Cycle *n.* A single repetition of a wave pattern.

Dark [ɫ] *n.* A type of [l] with the quality of a back vowel. See **clear [l]**.

Decibel /ˈdɛsɪbəl ~ ˈdɛsɪˌbɛl/ *n.* A measurement comparing the power of two sounds. In common usage, the decibel level is a measure of the loudness of a sound. Abbreviated **dB**.

Decoding *n.* The process of using language to convert sound to meaning.

Degenerate foot /dɪˈdʒɛnəɹət/ *n.* In metrical theory, a foot having only one syllable. A degenerate foot results when a syllable is left over after dividing the form into bounded feet.

Deletion *n.* The loss of a sound.

Dental *adj.* Having an articulation involving the tip or blade of the tongue and the upper teeth. —**Denti-** *combining form.*

Descender *n.* A symbol extending below the base line.

Devoicing *n.* A process whereby a sound changes from voiced to voiceless.

Diacritic /ˌdajəˈkɹɪtɪk/ *n.* A mark which modifies the value of a symbol; for example a basic symbol [r] might be written with various diacritics: [r̃ r̥ rʷ r].

Dialect /ˈdajəˌlɛkt/ *n.* A variety of language, particularly a geographical one.

Diaphragm /ˈdajəˌfræm/ *n.* A large dome-shaped muscle below the lungs used in breathing.

Diphthong /ˈdɪfˌθɑŋ/ *n.* A vowel articulation with a noticeable change in quality, commonly analysed as a cluster of a vowel and a glide; *e.g.,* [aj] or [ju]. (Note especially the spelling and pronunciation of *diphthong.*) —**Diphthongal** /ˌdɪfˈθɑŋəl/ *adj.* —**Diphthongise** /ˈdɪfˌθɑŋˌajz/ *v.* See also **falling** and **rising diphthong**.

Discrete /dɪˈskɹit/ *adj.* Having definite boundaries with no overlapping.

Dissimilation /dɪˌsɪmɪˈlejʃən/ *n.* A process whereby one sound becomes less like another. —**Dissimilate** /dɪˈsɪmɪˌlet/ *v.*

Distinctive feature *n.* A unit smaller than a segment posited in phonology to account for contrastive differences in sounds; *e.g.,* [labial], [voiceless], [nasal].

Dorso-uvular /ˌdoɹˌsoˈjuvjələɹ/ *adj.* Having an articulation with the back of the tongue articulating with the uvula.

Dorso-velar /ˌdoɹˌsoˈviləɹ/ *adj.* Having an articulation with the back of the tongue articulating with the velum.

Dorsum /ˈdoɹsəm/ *n.* The back part of the tongue, which articulates with the velum and uvula. —**Dorsal** *adj.* —**Dorso-** *combining form:* **dorso-velar,** **dorso-uvular.**

Downdrift *n.* In tone languages, the gradual lowering of the pitch range.

Downstep *n.* In tone languages, the linguistically determined lowering of the pitch level used for high tone.

Ear canal *n.* The tubular part of the outer ear.

Eardrum *n.* A membrane separating the outer and inner ears.

Egressive /ˌiˈgɹɛsɪv/ *adj.* Referring to an airstream with the air flowing outwards.

Ejective /ˌiˈdʒɛktɪv/ *n.* A consonant, typically a stop, made with a glottalic airstream mechanism; *e.g.,* [pʼ, tʼ, kʼ, sʼ].

Encoding *n.* The process of using language to convert meaning to sound.

Environment *n.* The linguistic situation in which a sound occurs; *e.g.,* in *pin,* the environment of [ɪ] is [p—n].

Epenthesis /əˈpɛnθəsɪs/ *n.* The addition of a sound to a word. —**Epenthetic** /ˌɛpənˈθɛtɪk/ *adj.*

Epiglottis /ˌɛpɪˈglɑtɪs/ *n.* A cartilage of the larynx, rising up and back from the adam's apple, partially obscuring the vocal cords from above. —**Epiglottal** /ˌɛpɪˈglɑtəl/ *adj.*

Eustachian tube /juˈstejʃən/ *n.* A tube leading from the middle ear to the pharynx.

Expanded *adj.* A distinctive feature defining the class of vowels made with the tongue root advanced and with the larynx lowered.

External intercostals /ˌɪntəɹˈkɑstəlz/ *n.* Muscles located between the ribs, used in breathing.

Extrametrical /ˌɛkstɹə'metɹɪkəl/ *adj.* In metrical theory, referring to a syllable which is overlooked in establishing the metrical structure of a word. — **Extrametricality** /ˌɛkstɹəˌmetɹɪ'kælɪti/ *n.*

Falling diphthong *n.* A diphthong with a falling prominence, with the vowel preceding the glide; *e.g.,* [aj, ow, ɛɥ].

False vocal cords *n.* Bands of tissue located above the vocal cords, not ordinarily used in speech.

Falsetto *n.* An adjustment of the glottis with a portion of the vocal cords vibrating; not ordinarily used in speech, but found in singing, especially yodelling.

Faucial pillars /'faʃəl/ *n.* Two pairs of muscular arches at the rear of the mouth; also called **faucal** /'fakəl/.

Feature detector theory *n.* A theory of perception which holds that humans have detectors sensitive to certain phonetic features.

Feature *n.* A unit of speech, smaller than a segment describing an aspect of articulation; *e.g.,* [nasal], [high], [round]. —**Feature geometry** *n.* A theory of phonological representation which holds that the features of a segment are hierarchically arranged. See **Chomsky-Halle features**.

Final *adj.* At the end of a unit; typically, of a word.

Flap *n.* A manner of articulation in which the lower articulator strikes the upper articulator in passing. See also **tap**.

Foot *n.* In phonological theory, an organisational unit comprising one or more syllables; used especially in describing the stress pattern. —**Foot line** *n.* The line in a metrical description describing the placement of stress in the feet.

Formant /'fɔɹmənt/ *n.* In acoustic phonetics, a concentration of energy at specific frequencies. Formants are apparent in broad-band spectrograms.

Fourier analysis /'fuɹiˌe/ *n.* A mathematical analysis of a complex repetitive wave as a sequence of sine waves.

Free variation *n.* In phonological theory, two sounds are in free variation if they occur in the same environment without forming a difference of meaning; *e.g.,* [t tʰ t˺] are in free variation word-finally in English, in that any of the three may occur with no difference in meaning. See **complementary distribution** and **contrastive distribution**.

Frequency *n.* An acoustic property of a wave, corresponding to the number of cycles per second; measured in Hertz (Hz). Variations in frequency are perceived as changes in pitch.

Frication /fɹi'kejʃən/ *n.* The noise of a turbulent airstream, typical of fricatives.

Fricative /ˈfɹɪkətɪv/ *n.* A manner of articulation in which the opening is sufficiently narrow to cause a turbulent airstream; also called **spirant**.

Front *n.* The part of the tongue between the blade and the back, articulating with the palate. —*adj.* (1) Referring to a sound made farther to the front of the vocal tract than another or than usual: *a front* [g]. (2) Referring to a vowel or glide made in the forward part of the vowel area: *e.g.* [i y j]. See **back** and **central**.

Fundamental (harmonic) *n.* The lowest harmonic; abbreviated F_0. The fundamental frequency determines the pitch of a sound.

Gap *n.* (1) A non-occurring sequence of sounds. An **accidental gap** is potentially a word, but does not actually occur: *e.g.,* Eng. /glɪg/. A **systematic gap** is a sequence of sounds not allowed in a language: *e.g.,* Eng. initial /tl–/. (2) The absence of energy in a spectrogram, typically indicating a stop.

Geminate /ˈdʒɛmɪnət/ *n.* One of two identical, adjacent sounds: *e.g.,* [p] in [appu].

Glide *n.* A short, rapidly moving vowel sound. In the diphthong [aj], the vowel sound [a] is relatively steady, but the tongue moves rapidly during the [j] glide. Same as **semivowel**.

Glottis /ˈglɑtɪs/ *n.* The space between the vocal cords. —**Glottal** *adj.* —**Glottal stop** *n.* A stop formed by a complete closure of the vocal cords, written [ʔ]. — **Glottalic** /ˌglɑˈtælɪk/ *adj.* Referring to an airstream mechanism having the closed glottis as initiator.

Grave accent /gɹɑv~gɹejv/ *n.* The superscript diacritic [`], used to indicate a low tone or a secondary stress.

Haček /ˈhɑˌtʃɛk/ *n.* (1) The superscript diacritic [ˇ], used to indicate a rising tone. (2) In non-IPA transcriptions, a haček is sometimes used to modify certain consonantal symbols:

$$\check{s} = \int \qquad \check{c} = t\int \qquad \check{z} = ʒ \qquad \check{j} = dʒ.$$

H-aspiré /aʃaspiˈre/ *n.* A boundary in French which prevents liaison, written *h*.

Hammer *n.* A bone of the middle ear.

Haplology /ˌhæpˈlɑlədʒi/ *n.* The process whereby similar sounds are lost, *e.g., morphophonemic* becoming *morphonemic,* or *alveopalatal* from *alveolopalatal*.

Harmonic /ˌhɑɹˈmɑnɪk/ *n.* A component of a complex wave having the form of a sine wave.

Head *n.* (1) The central or crucial part of an element. (2) In metrical theory, the stressed syllable of a foot.

Heavy syllable. *n.* A syllable typically with a coda or with a long vowel in the nucleus.

Helicotrema /ˌhɛliˌkoˈtrimə/ *n.* The end of the cochlea in the inner ear, joining the scala tympani with the scala vestibuli.

Hemisphere *n.* A lateral half of the brain.

Hertz /hɜɹts/ *n.* A unit of frequency equal to one cycle per second, abbreviated **Hz**.

High *adj.* (1) Referring to a vowel or glide made in the high portion of the vowel area: *e.g.,* [i, j]. (2) Referring to a vowel or glide made higher than another or than usual: *e.g., a high [e]*. (3) Referring to a tone with a greater frequency than another or than usual. See **low** and **mid**. —**Height** *n.* (1) The vertical position of the tongue, used in describing vowels. (2) A distinctive feature describing vowel height. (3) The pitch level of a tone.

Homorganic /ˌhomoɹˈgænɪk/ *adj.* Having the same place of articulation; *e.g.,* in [mp nt ŋk], the nasal is homorganic with the following stop.

Hyoid bone /ˈhajˌɔjd/ *n.* A horseshoe-shaped bone located behind the chin.

Implosive /ˌɪmˈplowsɪv/ *n.* (1) A stop made with the vocal cords vibrating as the larynx is lowered. (2) A stop made with an ingressive glottalic airstream mechanism.

Inaudible *adj.* Not capable of being heard; as in the release of the [p] in English *apt*.

Ingressive /ˌɪŋˈgɹɛsɪv/ *adj.* Referring to an airstream with air flowing inwards. See **egressive**.

Inherent length *n.* Length which is independent of the context. See **contextual length**.

Initial *adj.* At the beginning of a unit; typically, of a word.

Initiator *n.* The vocal organ which sets the airstream in motion.

Inner ear *n.* The inmost section of the ear, containing the cochlea.

Insertion *n.* The introduction of a sound into a sequence.

Intensity *n.* An acoustic property of a sound related to amplitude. Variations in intensity are perceived as changes in loudness.

Interdental *adj.* Having an articulation in which the tip or blade of the tongue is between the teeth.

Internal intercostals /ˌɪntəɹˈkɑstəl/ *n.* Muscles located between the ribs, used in breathing.

International Phonetic Alphabet *n.* The official phonetic transcription system of the **International Phonetic Association** and the one used in this book. Both the alphabet and the Association are abbreviated **IPA** /ˌaj ˌˌpi ˈej/.

Intervocalic /ˌɪntəˌɹˌvoˈkælɪk/*adj.* Between vowels; *e.g.,* the [n] in *any.*

Intonation *n.* A distinctive pattern of pitch. —**Intonation contour** *n.* A pattern of intonation.

IPA See **International Phonetic Alphabet** and **International Phonetic Association.**

Joual /ʒwɑl/ *n.* A dialect of Canadian French, often stigmatised and considered typical of lower-class speech in Montréal.

Kinæsthesia /ˌkɪnəsˈθiʒə/ *n.* The sensations associated with physical movement. —**Kinæsthetic** /ˌkɪnəsˈθɛtɪk/, *adj.*

Labial /ˈlejbiəl/ *adj.* Referring to the lips; a general term for either bilabial or labio-dental. *n.* **Labialisation** /ˌlebiəliˈzejʃən/ *n.* A secondary articulation involving lip-rounding. —**Labialised** /ˈlejbiəlˌajzd/ *adj.* —**Labio-** *combining form:* **labio-dental.**

Labial velar *adj.* Having a double articulation which is simultaneously labial and velar.

Labio-dental /ˌlebiˌˌoˈdɛntəl/ *adj.* Having an articulation involving the lower lip and the upper teeth.

Lallans /ˈlælənz/ *n.* A traditional dialect of English spoken in the lowlands of Scotland.

Lamina /ˈlæminə/ *n.* The surface of the tongue between the apex and the front. Same as **blade.** —**Laminal** /ˈlæmɪnəl/*adj.* —**Lamino-** *combining form:* **lamino-alveolar, lamino-dental.**

Lamino-alveolar /ˌlæmɪˌˌnoˌælˈviəlɹ/ *adj.* Having an articulation involving the blade of the tongue and the alveolar ridge.

Lamino-dental /ˌlæmɪˌˌnoˈdɛntəl/ *adj.* Having an articulation involving the blade of the tongue and the upper teeth.

Laryngeal pharynx *n.* The lower portion of the pharynx, just above the larynx.

Larynx /ˈlɛɹɪŋks/, pl. **larynges** /ləˈɹɪndʒiz/ *n.* The voice box, a structure of cartilage and muscle above the windpipe and below the throat, containing the vocal cords. —**Laryngeal** /ləˈɹɪndʒəl/ *adj.*

Lateral *adj.* Referring to a manner of articulation in which the centre of the vocal tract is closed but the sides are open allowing air to escape; the opposite of

central. —*n.* A sound made with a lateral articulation: *e.g.,* [l ʎ ɬ]. —**Lateral onset** *n.* A lateral followed by a homorganic stop, with a transition consisting only of raising the sides of the tongue: *e.g.,* [ld]. —**Lateral release** *n.* A stop followed by a homorganic lateral, with a transition consisting only of lowering the sides of the tongue: *e.g.,* [dl].

Lateralisation *n.* The location of certain functions, such as speech, in one hemisphere of the brain.

Lax *adj.* The opposite of **tense**.

Length *n.* The duration of a segment.

Level *n.* (1) The pitch height of a sound; *e.g., The pitch falls from a high level to a lower level.* (2) A type of representation: *e.g.,* **broad**, **narrow**, **phonemic**, **phonetic**. —*adj.* Not moving; *e.g., a level tone.*

Liaison /ˈlieˌzɑn~ljeˈzɔ̃/ *n.* A phenomenon of French involving allomorphic variation in a word-final consonant, conditioned by the following environment.

Ligamental glottis /ˌlɪɡəˈmɛntəl/ *n.* The portion of the glottis lying between the vocal cords.

Light syllable *n.* A syllable with neither a long vowel in the nucleus nor a coda.

Linguistics /ˌlɪŋˈgwɪstɪks/ *n.* The study of language.

Liquid *n.* A term referring to the class of **laterals** and **rhotics**.

Lisp *n.* A speech problem, involving the substitution of [θ ð] for [s z].

Locus /ˈlowkəs/, pl. **loci** /ˈlowˌsaj/ *n.* On a spectrogram, the point to which the transition of the second formant appears to be pointing.

Long *adj.* Referring to a segment of greater duration than another or than usual. Length is usually marked with a colon or a raised dot: [ɑː eˑ].

Loudness *n.* A perceptual quality of a sound, corresponding generally to its intensity.

Low *adj.* (1) Referring to a vowel made in the lower portion of the vowel area: *e.g.,* [a ɑ ɒ]. (2) Referring to a vowel made lower than another or than usual: *e.g., a low* [i]. (3) Referring to a tone with a lower frequency than another or than usual. See **high** and **mid**. —**Lowering** *n.* The process whereby a vowel moves to a lower position: *e.g.,* [u] → [o].

Lower articulator *n.* The articulators of the lower jaw and tongue: *i.e.,* lower lip, lower teeth, apex, lamina, front, dorsum, root.

Macron /ˈmejkɹən/ *n.* The superscript diacritic [¯] used to indicate (1) a mid tone or (2) sometimes a long vowel.

Major class feature *n.* The features [sonorant] and [consonantal], which divide sounds into the major categories, of consonant, vowel, approximant, etc.

Manner of articulation *n.* The kind of articulation, particularly the degree of opening, nasality, and laterality.

Masking *n.* The phenomenon whereby the presence of one sound makes another simultaneous sound harder to hear.

Medial *adj.* In the middle of a unit; typically, of a word.

Mel /mɛl/ *n.* A unit of pitch. —**Mel scale** /mɛl/ *n.* A scale for measuing pitch, as opposed to frequency.

Mid *adj.* Between **high** and **low**; used with vowels and tones. See **central**.

Middle ear *n.* The middle section of the ear, transmitting sound from the eardrum to the inner ear.

Millisecond /ˈmɪlɪˌsɛkənd/ *n.* One one-thousandth of a second; 1 msec = 0.1 csec = 0.001 sec.

Minimal pair *n.* Two forms which differ only by one sound, as *pair, care.*

Monophthong /ˈmɑnəfˌθɑŋ/ *n.* A steady vowel; see **diphthong**.

Mora /ˈmoɹə/, pl. **moræ** /ˈmoɹi/ *n.* A unit of time, used in describing certain languages, such as Japanese.

Morpheme /ˈmoɹˌfim/ *n.* The smallest meaningful unit of a word. —**Morphology** /ˌmorˈfalədʒi/ *n.* The study of **morphemes**.

Motor theory of speech perception *n.* A theory of perception which holds that the listener constructs a model of the articulatory movements necessary to produce the sounds being heard.

Moving tone *adj.* Referring to non-level tones.

Multivalued *adj.* Referring to an **opposition** or **distinctive feature** having more than two values. See **unary** and **binary**.

Murmur /ˈməɹməɹ/ *n.* An adjustment of the glottis, occasionally used in language, made with the vocal cords vibrating, but with considerable escape of air.

Narrow transcription *n.* A transcription showing phonetic detail. An **allophonic transcription** is an example of a narrow transcription. See **broad transcription**.

Narrow-band spectrogram *n.* A type of spectrogram, useful for seeing harmonics.

Nasal *adj.* Referring to sounds, both consonants and vowels, with velic opening and air flowing out through the nasal passage. —*n.* A nasal stop: *Scots Gaelic has four nasals.* —**Nasal cavity** *n.* The air cavity leading from the top of the pharynx to the nostrils. —**Nasal onset** *n.* A nasal followed by a homorganic stop, with a transition consisting only of raising the velic: *e.g.,* [nd]. —**Nasal pharynx** *n.* The upper portion of the pharynx, opening into the nasal cavity. —**Nasal release** *n.* A stop followed by a homorganic nasal, with a transition consisting only of lowering the velic, *e.g.,* [dn]. —**Nasalisation** *n.* The process whereby a sound becomes **nasalised**. —**Nasalised** *adj.* Same as **nasal**.

Natural *adj.* Referring to what is universal or common in language and can be described simply and plausibly. —**Natural class** *n.* A class of sounds that can be described with few features and that recurs in the description of many languages. —**Natural process** *n.* A process that recurs in the description of many languages and that is phonetically plausible.

Node *n.* A branching point on a tree diagram.

Noise *n.* Sound resulting from vibration without a regular repeated cycle, typical of fricatives.

Nonsense *n.* A form in a language which is phonologically possible, but which does not happen actually to occur in that language; *e.g.,* in English /ˈbɹɪlig, ˈslajˑði, towvz, ˌʌwtˈgɹejb/.

Nucleus /ˈnukliəs/ *n.* The part of the syllable with the greatest sonority; typically, the vowel of a syllable.

Obstruent /ˈɑbstɹuənt/ *n.* A class of sounds which includes stops, fricatives, and affricates.

Œsophagus /əˈsɑfəgəs/ *n.* The tube which carries food from the throat to the stomach. —**Œsophagic** /ˌɛsəˈfejdʒɪk/ *adj.* Referring to an airstream mechanism with the œsophagus as initiator, using **œsophageal** /əˌsɑfəˈdʒiəl/ air. [All of these are sometimes spelled *eso-*.]

Onset *n.* The elements in a syllable preceding the nucleus. See also **lateral onset** and **nasal onset**; see **release**.

Open syllable *n.* A syllable with no final consonant. See **closed syllable**.

Open vowel *n.* A low vowel.

Opposition *n.* A type of contrast: **unary, binary, multivalued**.

Oral *adj.* (1) Referring to the mouth. (2) Not nasal: *e.g., an oral stop.* —**Oral cavity** *n.* The air cavity leading from the throat to the lips; the mouth. —**Oral pharynx** *n.* The mid portion of the pharynx, opening directly to the oral cavity; the throat.

Organ of Corti /ˈkoɹti/ *n.* A part of the inner ear, containing the auditory nerve endings.

Orthography /ˌɔɹˈθɑɡɹəfi/ *n.* The ordinary way of writing a language, as opposed to a phonological or phonetic transcription.

Oscillation /ˌɑsɪˈlejʃən/ *n.* A repeated alternation.

Outer ear *n.* The outermost section of the ear.

Oval window *n.* A membrane through which sound passes from the middle ear to the inner ear.

Overlapping *n.* A situation in which the articulations of two adjacent segments are not simultaneously sequential; *e.g.,* the articulations of [p] and [t] in English *apt* overlap.

Overtone *n.* Harmonic.

Palatal /ˈpælətəl/ *adj.* Having an articulation involving the front of the tongue and the hard palate. —**Palate** /ˈpælɪt/ *n.* The hard palate. —**Palatalisation** /ˌpælɪtəlɪˈzejʃən/ *n.* (1) The process whereby an articulation moves more towards the palate. (2) A secondary articulation with the quality of a high front unrounded vowel. —**Palatalised** /ˈpælɪtəˈlajzd/ *adj.*

Palato-alveolar /ˌpælətoælˈviələɹ/ *adj.* Having an articulation involving the tip or blade of the tongue and the area bordering the alveolar ridge and the palate.

Passive theory *n.* A theory of hearing which holds that perception occurs without using knowledge of the language or of speech production.

Penultimate syllable /pənˈʌltɪmət/ *n.* The second-last syllable of a word; same as **penult** /ˈpinˌʌlt/ *n.*

Pharynx /ˈfeɹɪŋks/ (pl. **pharynges** /fəˈɹɪndʒiz/) *n.* The vertical tube leading from the larynx past the oral cavity to the nasal cavity. —**Pharyngeal** /ˈfəˈɹɪndʒəl/*adj.* Having an articulation involving the root of the tongue and the **pharyngeal wall,** the rear wall of the pharynx. Same as radico-pharyngeal. —**Pharyngealisation** /fəˌɹɪndʒəlɪˈzejʃən/ *n.* A secondary articulation involving the quality of a pharyngeal constriction. —**Pharyngealised** /fəˈɹɪndʒəˌlajzd/ *adj.*

Phonation /ˌfoˈnejʃən/ *n.* The phonetic activities of the vocal cords.

Phoneme /ˈfowˌnim/ *n.* A contrastive segment in a language. —**Phonemic** /fəˈnimɪk/, *adj.*

Phonetic /fəˈnɛtɪk/ *adj.* (1) Referring to phonetics. (2) Emphasising detail and variation in speech; **allophonic.**

Phonetic matrix theory /ˈmejtɹɪks/*n.* A theory of perception which holds that the analysed acoustic signal is compared to a stored set of phonetic matrices to determine which sound occurred.

Phonetic phrase *n.* A stretch of speech spoken without a break.

Phonetic word *n.* The smallest stretch of speech which is normally spoken without a break.

Phonetics /fə'nɛtɪks/ *n.* The study of the sounds of human language. — **Articulatory phonetics** *n.* The branch of phonetics having to do with the production of sounds. —**Acoustic phonetics** *n.* The branch of phonetics having to do with the physical properties of sound. —**Auditory phonetics** *n.* The branch of phonetics having to do with hearing and perception. —**Phonetician** /ˌfonə'tɪʃən/ *n.* A specialist in phonetics; a nice sort of person.

Phonology /fə'nɑlədʒi/ *n.* The study of the sound systems of human language. — **Phonological** *adj.* Emphasising the internal structure of a sound system as opposed to **phonetic** detail.

Phonotactics /ˌfoˌˌno'tæktɪks/ *n.* The description of the arrangement of sounds in a language with respect to each other; *e.g.,* in English, initial clusters of stop–approximant occur, except /tl/ and /dl/.

Pinna /'pɪnə/ *n.* The ear lobe.

Pitch accent *n.* A type of tone system in which a lexically determined syllable alters the otherwise predictable tone pattern of an utterance.

Pitch *n.* The perceptual property of sound which distinguishes, for example, notes on a piano; pitch corresponds generally to the physical property of frequency.

Place of articulation *n.* For a particular sound, the place of greatest closure in the vocal tract.

Plosive /'plowsɪv/ *n.* An egressive pulmonic stop.

Point of articulation *n.* Same as **place of articulation**.

Post- A prefix modifying a term to indicate a place of articulation farther to the back, *e.g.,* post-alveolar.

Posterior /ˌpɑs'tiɹɪəɹ/ *adj.* (1) Rear. (2) A distinctive feature defining the class of palato-alveolar sounds as opposed to alveolar ones.

Postvocalic /ˌpostˌˌvo'kælɪk/ *adj.* After a vowel.

Pre- A prefix modifying a term to indicate a place of articulation farther to the front, *e.g.,* pre-alveolar.

Primary articulation *n.* The part of an articulation having the greatest stricture. See **secondary articulation**.

Primary cardinal vowel. *n.* In the cardinal vowel system, one of the vowels [i e ɛ a u o ɔ ɑ].

Primary stress *n.* The strongest degree of stress.

Process *n.* A phonetic change, such as **assimilation, metathesis.**

Progressive *adj.* Referring to changes in which a later element is influenced by an earlier one. See **anticipatory**, and also **assimilation, dissimilation. —Progressive assimilation** *n.* The assimilation of a later sound to an earlier one; *e.g.,* in a sequence XY, Y changes to become more like X.

Prominence *n.* The degree to which a sound or group of sounds stands out from its neighbours in length, loudness, stress, or pitch.

Propagation *n.* The method by which a sound wave is propelled through the air.

Pulmonic /ˌpʊlˈmɑnɪk/ *adj.* Referring to an airstream mechanism having the lungs as initiator.

Radix /ˈɹejdɪks/ *n.* The root of the tongue. —**Radical** *adj.* —**Radico-** *combining form:* **radico-pharyngeal** /ˌɹædɪˌkofəˈɹɪndʒəl/ *adj.* Having an articulation involving the root of the tongue and the pharyngeal wall.

Raising *n.* The process whereby a vowel moves to a higher position: *e.g.,* [ɛ] → [i].

Rate *n.* The production speed of segments.

Received Pronunciation *n.* The standard English accent in England, abbreviated **RP**.

Reduced vowel *n.* In English, a vowel which has undergone reduction, changing it to a [ə] or [ɪ].

Register tone language *n.* A language with a system of level tones.

Regressive. See **anticipatory**.

Release *n.* (1) The point at which the closure of a stop opens. (2) The manner in which the closure of a stop opens; see **lateral release** and **nasal release**.

Resonance *n.* The property of an object allowing it to vibrate in response to outside vibrations. In speech, the vocal tract resonates selectively to the vibrations of the vocal cords, altering the spectrum of the original wave. — **Resonance curve** *n.* A curve showing the natural vibrating tendency of an object.

Retracted *adj.* Farther back than usual.

Retroflex(ed) /ˈɹɛtɹoˌflɛks(t)/ *adj.* (1) Having an articulation with the tip or blade of the tongue curled back and articulating with the back of the alveolar ridge. (2) Referring to a vowel with the tongue curled back towards the retroflexed position, producing an [ɹ]-quality; see **rhotic**.

Rhotic /ˈɹowtɪk ˈɹɑtɪk/ *n.* An r-like sound: *e.g.,* [r ɹ ʀ ʁ ɾ ɻ]. —*adj.* (1) Referring to a vowel with a retroflexed articulation. (2) In English, referring to a dialect such as Canadian English, which has retained historic codal /ɹ/, as in *car, father.*

Rhyme /ɹajm/ *n.* The portion of the syllable after the onset, containing the nucleus and coda, *i.e.,* the vowel and any following consonants.

Rhythm *n.* The metrical cadence of a language; the pattern of prominent elements.

Rising diphthong *n.* A diphthong with a rising prominence; *i.e.,* with the vowel following the glide: *e.g.,* [ju wɔ].

Root *n.* The rear vertical surface of the tongue; see **radix**.

Root node *n.* The highest node in a linguistic tree; in feature geometry, including the features [consonantal] and [sonorant].

Root tier *n.* The root nodes of a word, taken together.

Round window *n.* A membrane between the end of the cochlea and the middle ear.

Round(ed) *adj.* Made with rounded lips; **labialised**: *e.g.,* [o u tʷ]. —**Rounding** *n.* (1) The quality of being rounded. (2) The process whereby a sound becomes rounded. See **labialisation**.

RP /ˌɑɹ ˈpi/ *n.* See **Received Pronunciation**.

Rule *n.* A formal statement of a linguistic relationship. **Phonological rules** state the relationship between **phonemes** and **allophones**.

Scala tympani /ˈskɑlə ˌtɪmˈpɑni/ *n.* A chamber of the cochlea, joined to the **scala vestibuli** by the **helicotrema**.

Scala vestibuli /ˈskɑlə ˌvɛsˈtibjuli/ *n.* A chamber of the cochlea, joined to the **scala tympani** by the **helicotrema**.

Schwa /ʃwɑ/ *n.* A mid-central vowel, symbolised [ə].

Scots *n.* The dialects of English historically spoken in the lowlands of Scotland. See **Lallans**.

Secondary articulation *n.* The part of an articulation having the second greatest stricture: **labialisation, palatalisation, velarisation, pharyngealisation.**

Secondary cardinal vowel. *n.* In the cardinal vowel system, one of the vowels [y ø œ ɶ ɯ ɤ ʌ ɒ].

Secondary stress *n.* A stress weaker than a primary stress, as in the first syllable of *photographic* /ˌforəˈgɹæfɪk/.

Segment *n.* A consonant or a vowel. —**Segmentation** *n.* The division of a stream of speech into segments.

Semivowel *n.* A glide.

Serif /ˈsɛɹɪf/ *n.* A short horizontal stroke at the top or bottom of a symbol.

Sibilant /ˈsɪbɪlənt/ *n.* The sounds [s] or [z], and sometimes [ʃ] or [ʒ].

Sine wave /sajn/ *n.* A specific type of simple repetitive wave; same as **sinusoidal wave** /ˌsajnjəˈsɔjdəl/.

Slant lines *n.* See **solidi**.

Solidi /ˈsɑlɪdi/ (sg. **solidus** /ˈsɑlɪdəs/) *n.* The symbols / /, used to enclose phonemic transcriptions; also known as **virgules** /ˈvəɹˌgjulz/ or **slant lines**. See **square brackets**.

Sonorant /ˈsownəɹənt ~ˈsɑnəɹənt/ *n.* (1) A class of sounds including **nasals, liquids, glides,** and **vowels**; the sounds which are not **obstruents**. —*adj.* A distinctive feature.

Sonority /səˈnoɹɪti/ *n.* The overall loudness of a sound in comparison to others of same length, stress, and pitch.—**Sonority curve** *n.* A curve showing the sonority for each segment of a word.

Sound system *n.* The inventory and interrelationships of the sounds of a language.

Spectrogram /ˈspɛktɹəˌgɹæm/ *n.* A representation of the sound spectrum of a stretch of speech. **Spectrograph** /ˈspɛktɹəˌgɹæf/ *n.* A machine which produces spectrograms.

Spectrum /ˈspɛktɹəm/, pl. **spectra** /ˈspɛktɹə/ *n.* A representation of the harmonic components of a sound, showing their frequency and amplitude (or intensity).

Spike *n.* In a spectrogram, a vertical stroke, typically showing the release of a stop.

Spirant /ˈspajɹənt/ *n.* A **fricative**.

Square brackets *n.* The brackets [ ], used to enclose phonetic transcriptions and features: *e.g.,* [fəˈnɛtɪk], [coronal]. See **solidi**.

Standard French *n.* A dialect of French typically used by educated people.

Stirrup /ˈstəɹəp/ *n.* A bone of the middle ear.

Stop *n.* A manner of articulation involving a complete closure so that no air exits through the mouth. The use of *stop* alone implies an **oral stop**, as opposed to a **nasal stop**.

Stress *n.* A property of a syllable, generally related to the syllable's prominence in relation to its neighbours.

Stress language *n.* A language which uses stress to contrast different lexical items; *e.g.,* English: [ˈsəɹˌvej – ˌsəɹˈvej].

Stress parameter *n.* A constraint governing the placement of stress in a language.

Stress-timed *adj.* Referring to languages in which major stresses tend to occur at even intervals of time. See **syllable-timed**.

Stricture /ˈstɹɪktjəɹ/ *n.* A closure, complete or partial, involved in an articulation.

Strong form *n.* In English, the form of certain words (*e.g.,* /ˈhæv/) occurring in a stressed position, as opposed to a **weak** form (*e.g.,* /əv/) occurring without stress.

Subglottal /ˌsʌbˈɡlɑtəl/ *n.* Below the glottis. Subglottal air-pressure refers to pressure in the lungs.

Supraglottal /ˌsupɹəˈɡlɑtəl/ *adj.* Above the glottis. Same as **supralaryngeal**.

Supralaryngeal /ˌsupɹələˈɹɪndʒəl/ *adj.* Above the glottis; *i.e.,* including the pharyngeal, oral, and nasal portions of the vocal tract.

Suprasegmental /ˌsupɹəˌsɛɡˈmɛntəl/ *adj.* Referring to various phenomena which may extend over more than one segment: *i.e.,* tone, stress, length, rhythm.

Syllable /ˈsɪləbəl/ *n.* A unit of phonological organisation, typically larger than a segment and smaller than a word. Every syllable has a nucleus, consisting of a vowel or syllabic consonant. —**Syllabic** /sɪˈlæbɪk/ *adj.* (1) Referring to syllables. (2) Referring to the element of a syllable forming the nucleus. — **Syllabic consonant** *n.* A consonant which forms the nucleus of a syllable. — **Syllabicity** /ˌsɪləˈbɪsɪti/ *n.* The property of forming, or potentially forming, a syllable. —**Syllabification** /sɪˌlæbɪfɪˈkejʃən/ *n.* The division of a form into syllables. —**Syllabified** *adj.* Divided into syllables.

Syllable-timed *adj.* Referring to languages in which each syllable of an utterance takes about the same amount of time. See **stress-timed**.

Symbol *n.* A graphic mark representing a phonetic element, particularly a segment.

Tap *n.* A manner of articulation in which the lower articulator strikes the upper articulator in a brief, ballistic fashion. The [ɾ] of Canadian English is a tap.

Tense *adj.* In English, *tense* is used to refer to the diphthongs and the vowels [i u ɑ]. *Tense* refers to a classification of English sounds, rather than to a measurable phonetic property. See **lax**.

Tertiary stress *n.* A level of stress weaker than **secondary stress**, but stronger than that of unstressed syllables.

Thyroid cartilage *n*. The plough-shaped cartilage at the front of the larynx.

Tilde /'tɪldə/ *n*. A diacritic [˜] written (1) above a symbol [ẽ] to indicate nasalisation, (2) below a symbol [ḛ] to indicate creaky voice. or (3) through a symbol [ɬ ɖ] to indicate velarisation or pharyngealisation.

Tip *n*. The foremost point of the tongue; same as **apex**.

Tone *n*. The phonological use of **pitch**. —**Tone language** *n*. A language which distinguishes words using pitch.

Tonic syllable /'tɑnɪk/ *n*. In English, the syllable of a phrase with the major pitch change.

Trachea /'tɹejkiə/ *n*. The tube leading from the **bronchi** to the **larynx**.

Transcription *n*. The written representation of speech sounds. A very abstract transcription of an utterance is a **broad** or **phonemic transcription**; a **narrow** or **phonetic transcription** shows a great deal of detail. —**Transcribe** *v*.

Transition *n*. A change; particularly, the change in shape of a formant at the edge of a segment.

Tree *n*. A diagram showing the internal, hierarchical structure of a linguistic unit, such as a segment.

Trill *n*. A manner of articulation in which one organ vibrates against another in a rapid series of articulations.

Ultima /'ʌltɪmə/ *n*. The last syllable of an utterance.

Umlaut /'um‚lawt/ *n*. (1) The process whereby a back vowel becomes a front vowel. (2) The diacritic [¨].

Unary *adj*. Referring to a **distinctive feature** having only one value. See **binary** and **multivalued**.

Unbounded *adj*. In metrical theory, referring to a foot with no upper limit on the number of syllables it may contain.

Unstressed *adj*. Having the weakest level of stress.

Upper articulator *n*. The articulators of the upper jaw: *i.e*, upper lip, upper teeth, alveolar ridge, palate, velum, uvula, pharyngeal wall.

Upper vocal tract *n*. The **supralaryngeal vocal tract**; *i.e.,* the vocal tract above the larynx, consisting of the mouth, the nasal passage, and the pharynx.

Upstep *n*. In tone languages, the linguistically determined raising of the pitch level used for high tone.

Utterance. *n*. A stretch of speech.

Uvula /ˈjuvjələ/ *n.* The small appendage hanging down at the back of the velum. —**Uvular** /ˈjuvjələɹ/ *adj.* Having an articulation with the dorsum of the tongue articulating with the uvula.

V *n.* An abbreviation for **vowel**.

Velaric /vəˈleɹɪk/ *adj.* Referring to an airstream mechanism having the velum as initiator.

Velic /ˈvilɪk/ *adj.* Referring to the upper surface of the velum. With a **velic closure**, airflow through the nose is cut off, producing an oral sound; with a **velic opening**, nasal sounds are produced.

Velum /ˈviləm/ *n.* The soft palate. —**Velar** /ˈviləɹ/ *adj.* Having an articulation with the dorsum of the tongue articulating with the velum. —**Velarisation** [ˌviləɹɪˈzejʃən] *n.* A secondary articulation with the quality of a high back unrounded vowel. —**Velarised** /ˈviləˌɹajzd/ *adj.*

Ventricle of Morgagni /ˌvɛntɹɪkəl əv ˌmoɹˈɡɑnji/ *n.* The cavity between the false and true vocal cords. **Ventricular** /ˌvɛnˈtɹɪkjələɹ/.

Vertical striation *n.* A vertical line in a broadband spectrogram, corresponding to a vocal cord vibration.

Vibration *n.* A rapid movement back and forth.

Virgules *n.* See **solidi**.

Vocal cords *n.* Two bands of muscle and other tissue extending from a single point at the **thyroid cartilage** back to each of the **arytenoid cartilages**. The space between the vocal cords is known as the **glottis**.

Vocal organs *n.* The parts of the body used in speech.

Vocal tract *n.* Generally, the air passages used in speech production; especially, the supralaryngeal vocal tract; *i.e.,* the pharynx and the oral and nasal cavities.

Vocalic /ˌvoˈkælɪk/ *adj.* Referring to vowels.

Voice bar *n.* A dark bar sometimes found at low frequencies in a spectrogram, indicating voice.

Voice onset time *n.* In a consonant–vowel sequence, the time between the release of the closure and the beginning of voicing.

Voice, voicing *n.* A glottal adjustment involving vibration of the vocal cords. —**Voiced** *adj.* Referring to a sound made with voicing. —**Voiceless** *adj.* Referring to an adjustment of the glottis with the vocal cords not vibrating. —**Devoice** *v.* To change from voiced to voiceless.

Vowel /ˈvawəl/ *n.* A sound made with the vocal tract quite open; vowels typically function as the nucleus of a syllable. —**Vowel colour** *n*. Vowel quality; *i.e.*, [i] not [e].

Wave *n*. In phonetics, the alternations of air-pressure which convey sound. —**Waveform** *n*. The graphic representation of a sound wave, showing the variation in amplitude (or intensity) over time.

Weak form *n*. In English, the form of certain words (*e.g.*, /əv/) occurring in an unstressed position, as opposed to a **strong** form (*e.g.*, /ˈhæv/) occurring with stress.

Wernicke's aphasia /ˈveɹnɪkə/ *n*. An aphasia associated with Wernicke's area, characterised by fluent, but nonsensical speech. —**Wernicke's area** *n*. An area of the left hemisphere of the brain.

Wh-question /ˌdʌbəlˌjuˈejtʃ ˌkwɛstʃən/ *n*. A question which asks for information other than 'yes' or 'no'; in English, typically beginning with *wh–: who, what, when where, how.*

Whisper *n*. An adjustment of the vocal cords used in whispering. —**Whispering** *n*. A quiet way of speaking using **voicelessness** and **whisper**.

Wide-band spectrogram *n*. See **broad-band spectrogram**.

Word line *n*. The line in a metrical description describing the placement of stress in the word.

X-height line *n.* The imaginary line along the upper edge of symbols such as *x e s a.*

A PPENDIX C
CALLIGRAPHY

Writing transcriptions clearly and legibly is important. Most transcriptions have very little redundancy. If you make a mistake, there is little to indicate that you did so. This appendix shows you how to write the symbols introduced in this book. If you write your transcriptions carefully according to the examples in this appendix, you (and others) will be able to read them in years to come. If you are handing in assignments in a course, clear writing will keep your work from being marked down for unintelligibility.

- Keep punctuation to an absolute minimum. Periods are easily confused with diacritics.
- Ordinary capital letters are not used, although some 'small capitals' are used. Small capitals look like capital letters, but are the same height as ordinary lower-case letters: [ʀ ɴ a e]. Do NOT use lower-case letters where small capitals are required, or vice versa.
- Do not capitalise proper nouns or adjectives: e.g., ['kænədə], ['suzən]. The only capital letters used are the small capitals, which are special phonetic symbols.
- Phonetic writing is usually clearer if each symbol is written separately and not joined together cursively.

Look at the word *drop* in Figure C-1. Notice the **base line**. The letters *d, r,* and *o* sit on the base line, and the bowl of the *p* rests on the base line. Almost all phonetic symbols either sit or hang from the base line.

The line at the top of the *r* and the *o* is called the **x-height line**. It shows the height of many lower-case letters, such as *x.* Many symbols are written totally between the x-height line and the base line.

x-HEIGHT LINE

BASE LINE

Figure C-1

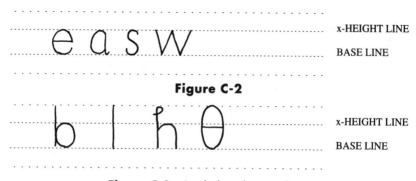

x-HEIGHT LINE

BASE LINE

Figure C-2

x-HEIGHT LINE

BASE LINE

Figure C-3   Symbols with ascenders

Some symbols, such as *d,* are written partially above the x-height line. Such symbols are said to have **ascenders**:

Similarly, some symbols, such as *p,* are written partially below the base line; such symbols are said to have **descenders**.

A few symbols have both ascenders and descenders:

In looking at the examples, notice the height of the symbol, paying particular attention to any ascenders and descenders. Many symbols are somewhat similar to each other. Often small matters, such as ascenders and descenders are crucial.

Many symbols have **serifs** /ˈseɹɪf/; these are the small lines often found at the tops and bottoms of strokes in printed type. In handwriting, serifs are generally absent. In handwritten phonetic transcriptions, serifs are occasionally important in distinguishing similar symbols: *e.g.,* [ɤ ɣ], [y ɥ].

Many people have made serious efforts to develop an interesting writing style for themselves and find the conventions of phonetic transcription confining. Phonetic calligraphy does not exclude individuality, but its main purpose is conveying information clearly, not looking interesting or impressive. You are certainly free to develop your own style, provided your writing is legible. Perhaps you will become one of the great calligraphic masters of phonetics that future generations will strive to emulate.

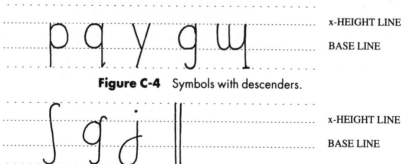

x-HEIGHT LINE

BASE LINE

Figure C-4   Symbols with descenders.

x-HEIGHT LINE

BASE LINE

Figure C-5   Symbols with both descenders and ascenders.

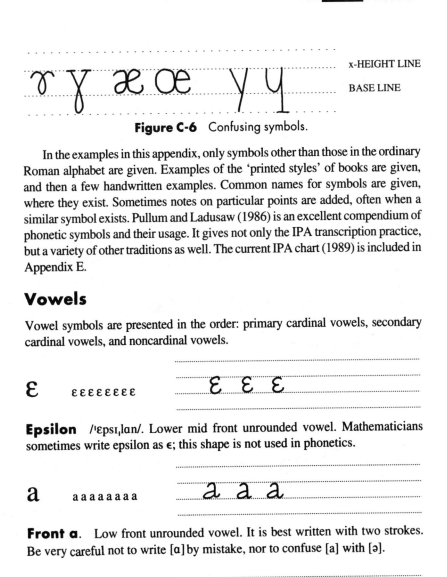

x-HEIGHT LINE

BASE LINE

Figure C-6 Confusing symbols.

In the examples in this appendix, only symbols other than those in the ordinary Roman alphabet are given. Examples of the 'printed styles' of books are given, and then a few handwritten examples. Common names for symbols are given, where they exist. Sometimes notes on particular points are added, often when a similar symbol exists. Pullum and Ladusaw (1986) is an excellent compendium of phonetic symbols and their usage. It gives not only the IPA transcription practice, but a variety of other traditions as well. The current IPA chart (1989) is included in Appendix E.

Vowels

Vowel symbols are presented in the order: primary cardinal vowels, secondary cardinal vowels, and noncardinal vowels.

Epsilon /ˈɛpsɪˌlɑn/. Lower mid front unrounded vowel. Mathematicians sometimes write epsilon as ϵ; this shape is not used in phonetics.

Front a. Low front unrounded vowel. It is best written with two strokes. Be very careful not to write [ɑ] by mistake, nor to confuse [a] with [ə].

Open o. Lower mid back rounded vowel.

ɑ   ɑ ɑ ɑ ɑ ɑ ɑ ɑ ɑ   *a a a*

Back a.   Low back unrounded vowel. This must be kept distinct from [a]. Be careful not to write one when you mean the other.

ø   ø ø ø ø ø ø ø ø   *ø ø ø* c.f. *φ ø*

Slashed o.   Higher mid front rounded vowel. It is important to keep this vowel symbol distinct from the symbol for null — Ø, and from phi [φ]. In handwriting, I usually write the null symbol with a backwards slash.

œ   œ œ œ œ œ œ œ   *œ œ œ*

O-E digraph.   Lower mid front rounded vowel. This symbol must be kept distinct from capital o–e digraph [Œ] and from ash [æ].

Œ   Œ Œ Œ Œ Œ Œ   *Œ Œ Œ*

Capital O-E digraph.   Low front rounded vowel. This symbol must be kept distinct from o–e digraph [œ], and from ash [æ].

ɯ   ɯ ɯ ɯ ɯ ɯ ɯ   *ɯ ɯ ɯ*

Turned m.   A high back unrounded vowel. Keep distinct from [w] and [ɥ].

ɤ   ɤ ɤ ɤ ɤ ɤ ɤ ɤ   *ɤ ɤ ɤ* c.f. *ɣ*

Ram's horns.   A higher mid back unrounded vowel. Keep distinct from gamma [ɣ] (a velar fricative). Ram's horns is the same height as [e]; gamma goes below the base line. The IPA recommends sloping shoulders to help distinguish it from gamma.

Λ   ΛΛΛΛΛΛΛ

Caret. /ˈkeɹət/ or /kəˈɹej/. A lower mid back unrounded vowel. A turned [v].

ɒ   ɒɒɒɒɒɒɒ

Turned back a. A low back rounded vowel. A rounded [ɑ].

I   ɪɪɪɪɪɪɪɪɪ

Small capital I. Extra symbol for a vowel in the high front unrounded region. Make sure that it is the same height as [e].

Y   ʏʏʏʏʏʏʏ

Small capital y. Extra symbol for a vowel in the high front rounded region. Be sure to make all small capital letters no higher than a lower-case [e]. Serifs help to distinguish this symbol from the ordinary [y].

æ   æææææææ

Ash /æʃ/. Extra symbol for a vowel in the low front unrounded region. Take special care in writing this symbol. It is made with one stroke. The backs of each half should touch. Make sure that it is distinct from [œ].

ɨ   ɨɨɨɨɨɨɨɨɨ

Barred i. High central unrounded vowel. An ordinary [i] with a short stroke through the middle. It must be distinct from [i] and [ɪ].

ʉ   ʉʉʉʉʉʉ   ʉ   ʉ   ʉ

Barred u. High central rounded vowel. An ordinary [u] with a short stroke through the middle.

ə   əəəəəəə   ə   ə   ə   ə

Schwa /ʃwɑ/. A mid central unrounded vowel. A turned [e]. Be careful to keep this symbol distinct from [a].

ɚ   ɚɚɚɚɚɚɚ   ɚ   ɚ   ɚ   ɚ

Rhotic schwa, r-coloured schwa. A mid central unrounded vowel with retroflexion. Essentially the vowel [ə] combined with the rhotic diacritic [˞]. Must be distinct from [ə].

θ   θθθθθθθ   θ   θ   θ

Barred o. Extra symbol for a vowel in the mid central rounded region. Must be distinct from [θ]. Barred o [ɵ] does not rise above the x-height line; [θ] does.

ɜ   ɜɜɜɜɜɜɜɜ   ɜ   ɜ   ɜ

Reversed epsilon. Extra symbol for a vowel in the mid central unrounded region. Be sure not to confuse this with [ɛ].

ɐ   ɐɐɐɐɐɐɐ   ɐ   ɐ   ɐ

Turned a. Extra symbol for a vowel in the low central unrounded region.

ʊ   ʊʊʊʊʊʊʊ   ʊ   ʊ   ʊ

Small capital U. Extra symbol for a vowel in the high back rounded region. Make sure that it is the same height as [e].

Consonants

Consonant symbols are presented in the order: stops, fricatives, nasals, laterals, rhotics, other approximants, other consonants. Within each of these categories, the consonants are ordered by place of articulation, moving from front to back.

ɟ   ɟɟɟɟɟɟɟɟ

Barred dotless ɟ. A voiced palatal stop. This symbol can be made as a turned [f]. Note that the curled tail is a descender; The top serif is usual.

ɡ   ɡɡɡɡɡɡɡɡ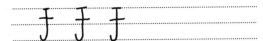

G /dʒi/. A voiced velar stop. The cursive form [ɡ] is much commoner in phonetic transcription than the printed form [g].

ɢ   ɢɢɢɢɢɢɢɢ

Small capital g. A voiced uvular stop. Make sure that this small capital symbol is the same height as [e]. Keep it clearly distinct from [c].

ʔ   ʔʔʔʔʔʔʔʔ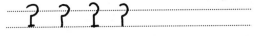

Glottal stop. A dotless question mark. This symbol MUST NOT have a dot. The bottom horizontal serif is optional.

ɸ   ɸɸɸɸɸɸɸɸ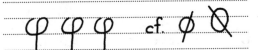

Phi /faj/. A voiceless bilabial fricative. This symbol must be kept distinct from the vowel [ø] and from the null sign ∅. An alternative version of phi exists—[ɸ], which in handwriting, is easily confused with [ø] or ∅.

β   β β β β β β β

Beta /ˈbejtə/. A voiced bilabial fricative. Note that the upper bowl is above the x-height line, and the lower stem extends below the base line.

θ   θ θ θ θ θ θ θ

Theta /ˈθejtə/. A voiceless dental fricative. This symbol extends above the x-height line. It must be kept distinct from the vowel [ə], which is the same height as *ə*.

ð   ð ð ð ð ð ð ð

Eth /ɛð/. A voiced dental fricative. The stem leans to the left. A mathematician's delta δ is not correct. The curls on the crossbar are optional.

ʃ   ʃ ʃ ʃ ʃ ʃ ʃ ʃ

Esh /ɛʃ/. A voiceless palato-alveolar fricative. It has both an ascender and a descender.

ʒ   ʒ ʒ ʒ ʒ ʒ ʒ ʒ

Ezh /ɛʒ/. A voiced palato-alveolar fricative. A [z] with a lower tail.

ɕ   ɕ ɕ ɕ ɕ ɕ ɕ ɕ

Curly tailed c. A voiceless alveolo-palatal fricative. The tail extends slightly below the base line. This symbol must be kept distinct from [ç].

ʑ   ʑ ʑ ʑ ʑ ʑ ʑ ʑ

Curly tailed z. A voiced alveolo-palatal fricative. The tail extends slightly below the base line.

ç   ç ç ç ç ç ç ç   ç ç ç

C-cedilla /ˌsi səˈdɪlə/. A voiceless palatal fricative. A [c] with a small hook underneath, as used in French. This symbol must be kept distinct from [ɕ].

ʝ   ʝ ʝ ʝ ʝ ʝ ʝ ʝ   ʝ ʝ ʝ

Curly ʝ . A voiced palatal fricative. Take care to keep this symbol distinct from an ordinary [j].

ɣ   ɣ ɣ ɣ ɣ ɣ ɣ ɣ   ɣ ɣ ɣ cf. ɤ

Gamma /ˈgæmə/. A voiced velar fricative. The bowl is made below the base line. This symbol must be kept distinct from the vowel [ɤ] (ram's horns). The IPA reccommends flat serifs for gamma and sloping shoulders for ram's horns.

χ   χ χ χ χ χ χ χ   χ χ χ cf. x

Chi /kaj/. A voiceless uvular fricative. This symbol must be kept distinct from the velar fricative [x]; a lengthened stroke from top left to bottom right helps. Curling the ends of this stroke adds distinctiveness as well.

ʁ   ʁ ʁ ʁ ʁ ʁ ʁ ʁ   ʁ ʁ ʁ

Inverted small capital r. A uvular approximant. Make sure that this symbol is the same height as *e*. Make sure not to reverse this symbol; keep the straight vertical line on the left.

ħ   ħ ħ ħ ħ ħ ħ ħ   ħ ħ ħ

Crossed h. A voiceless pharyngeal fricative.

ʕ   ʕʕʕʕʕʕʕ

Reversed glottal stop. A voiced pharyngeal fricative. Be careful not to write an ordinary glottal stop [ʔ] by mistake.

ɦ   ɦɦɦɦɦɦɦ

Hooktop h with tail. A voiceless alveolo-palatal velar fricative. Keep distinct from [ɦ] and from [ŋ].

ɱ   ɱɱɱɱɱɱɱ

Labio-dental nasal. An m with a long tail.

ɲ   ɲɲɲɲɲɲ

Palatal n. A palatal nasal. Be sure that the tail is on the left side, pointing to the left.

ŋ   ŋŋŋŋŋŋŋ

Ing /ɪŋ/. A velar nasal. Make sure that the tail is on the right side, pointing to the left.

N   NNNNNNNN

Small capital n. A uvular nasal. Make sure that this small capital symbol is the same height as *e*.

ɬ   ɬɬɬɬɬɬɬ

Belted l. A voiceless alveolar lateral fricative. The crossbar has a loop on the left side; this symbol must be kept distinct from dark [ɫ], with a curled crossbar without the loop.

ꞎ   ꞎ ꞎ ꞎ ꞎ ꞎ ꞎ ꞎ

L-ezh ligature. A voiced alveolar lateral fricative. The [l] and [ʒ] are written together as one symbol

ʎ   ʎ ʎ ʎ ʎ ʎ ʎ ʎ

Turned y. A palatal lateral approximant. Note that this is a *y*, turned upside-down, not a Greek lambda λ.

ʟ   ʟ ʟ ʟ ʟ ʟ ʟ ʟ ʟ

Small capital L. A velar lateral approximant. Make sure that it is the same height as an [e].

ʀ   ʀ ʀ ʀ ʀ ʀ ʀ ʀ ʀ

Small capital r. A uvular trill. Make sure that this symbol is the same height as [e].

ɾ   ɾ ɾ ɾ ɾ ɾ ɾ ɾ ɾ

Fish-hook r. An alveolar flap. This symbol is an [r] with the upper left serif missing. The lower horizontal is usually present.

ɽ   ɽ ɽ ɽ ɽ ɽ ɽ ɽ

R with right tail. A retroflex flap.

ɺ   ɺ ɺ ɺ ɺ ɺ ɺ ɺ ɺ

Turned long-legged r. An alveolar lateral flap.

ɻ   ɻɻɻɻɻɻɻɻ   ɻ ɻ ɻ

Turned r.   A retroflex approximant. Keep the stem vertical; if the legs get too splayed, it looks like a [ʌ].

ʋ   ʋ ʋ ʋ ʋ ʋ ʋ ʋ   ʋ ʋ ʋ ʋ

Curly v.   A labio-dental approximant. Keep distinct from [v] and [u]; a loop on the right stem helps maintain the distinction.

ɰ   ɰ ɰ ɰ ɰ ɰ ɰ   ɰ ɰ ɰ

Turned m with long right leg.   A high back unrounded semivowel; a velar approximant. Keep distinct from [ɯ].

ɥ   ɥɥɥɥɥɥɥɥ   ɥ ɥ ɥ   cf. y

Turned h.   A high front rounded semivowel; a labial-palatal approximant. Keep this symbol clearly distinct from [y]. The lower horizontal serif is helpful in maintaining the distinction.

ʍ   ʍ ʍ ʍ ʍ ʍ ʍ   ʍ ʍ

Inverted w.   A voiceless high back rounded semivowel; a voiceless labial-velar approximant. Keep this symbol clearly distinct from [m].

ɦ   ɦ ɦ ɦ ɦ ɦ ɦ ɦ   ɦ ɦ ɦ

Hooktop h.   A murmured vowel. A curl on the top helps keep it distinct from ordinary [h].

ɓ   ɓɓɓɓɓɓɓ

Hooktop b. An implosive bilabial stop. A curl on the top helps keep it distinct form ordinary *b*.

ɗ   ɗɗɗɗɗɗɗ

Hooktop d. An implosive alveolar stop. A curl on the top helps keep it distinct form ordinary *d*.

ɠ   ɠɠɠɠɠɠɠ

Hooktop g . An implosive velar stop. A curl on the top helps keep it distinct form ordinary [g].

⊙   ⊙⊙⊙⊙⊙⊙⊙

Bullseye. A bilabial click.

| |||||||||

Pipe. A dental click. Making this symbol with a descnder keeps it distinct from a lower case [l]. Be sure not to slant it and confuse it with a virgule, used to enclose phonemic transriptions.

ǃ   ǃǃǃǃǃǃǃǃ

Exclamation point. A palatal click.

‖   ‖‖‖‖‖‖‖‖‖

Double pipe. An alveolar lateral click.

Diacritics

Diacritics are marks added to the main symbol to alter its value. Their placement in relation to the main symbol is important. Most are placed above, below, or after the main symbol. In the following presentation, a dotted box is used to show the position of the main symbol in relation to the diacritic. Examples show symbols typically used with the diacritic. The diacritics are presented in the order superscript, subscript, postposed, other.

$$\tilde{e} \quad \tilde{\imath} \quad \tilde{w}$$

Tilde /'tɪldə/. Nasalisation. Note that the left side is low, and the right side is high.

$$\grave{e} \quad \grave{\imath} \quad \grave{y}$$

Grave /gɹɑv/ or /gɹejv/. A low tone; a secondary stress.

$$\bar{o} \quad \bar{æ} \quad \bar{a}$$

Macron /'majkɹən/. A level tone; occasionally used for a long vowel.

$$\acute{ε} \quad \acute{ʌ} \quad \acute{ɤ}$$

Acute /ə'kjut/. A high tone; a strong stress.

$$\hat{u} \quad \hat{w} \quad \hat{ø}$$

Circumflex /'sɔɹkəmˌflɛks/. A falling tone. Note that this diacritic has a pointed top; do not use a rounded top.

$$\check{a} \quad \check{+} \quad \check{œ}$$

Haček /'hatʃɛk/. A rising tone. This diacritic must have a pointed bottom. Keep it distinct from a breve [˘] with a rounded bottom.

$$\breve{a} \quad \breve{\mathfrak{z}} \quad \breve{e}$$

Breve /bɹiv ~ bɹɛv/. A syllable with weak stress; in Pinyin transcription of Chinese used for falling-rising tone. Note that this diacritic has a rounded bottom. Keep it distinct from a haček with a pointed posterior.

$$\underset{\sqcap}{t} \quad \underset{\sqcap}{d} \quad \underset{\sqcap}{n} \quad \underset{\sqcap}{l}$$

Subscript bridge . Dental. This diacritic converts an alveolar symbol to a dental one.

$$\underset{.}{t} \quad \underset{.}{d} \quad \underset{.}{n}$$

Subscript dot. Retroflex. This diacritic converts an alveolar symbol to a retroflex one.

$$\underset{\circ}{m} \quad \underset{\circ}{e} \quad \underset{\circ}{l}$$

Under-ring. Voiceless. A subscript ring; keep distinct from subscript dot.

$$\underset{..}{b} \quad \underset{..}{J} \quad \underset{..}{a}$$

Subscript umlaut /ˈumˌlawt/. Murmur.

$$\underset{\sim}{a} \quad \underset{\sim}{u} \quad \underset{\sim}{m}$$

Subscript tilde /ˈtɪldə/. Creaky voice.

$$\underset{...}{i} \quad \underset{...}{d} \quad \underset{...}{w}$$

Three subscript dots. Whisper. Make sure that the individual dots are clear; keep distinct from subscript umlaut [. .].

n̩ | l̩ | m̩

Syllabic mark. Used to make a consonant syllabic. A vertical subscript stroke. Keep distinct from a subscript dot and from the mark for secondary stress, which precedes a symbol.

e̯ y̯ u̯

Subscript arch. Non-syllabic. Converts a vowel to the corresponding semivowel.

pʰ cʰ qʰ

Raised h. Aspiration.

tʷ sʷ kʷ

Raised w. Labialisation.

dʲ zʲ nʲ

Raised j. Palatalisation.

dˠ sˠ nˠ

Raised ram's horns. Velarisation. See also mid tilde.

nˤ dˤ lˤ

Raised reversed glottal stop. Pharyngealisation. See also mid tilde.

ʔ   ʔ ʔ ʔ ʔ ʔ ʔ   pʼ cʼ qʼ

Ejective mark.   This symbol must be curved to the left and not straight.

˞   ˞ ˞ ˞ ˞ ˞ ˞   ɚ ɚ ʊɹ

Rhotic hook.   A raised hook attached to the right side of the main symbol.

˺   ˺ ˺ ˺ ˺ ˺ ˺   p˺ t˺ ɡ˺

Corner.   Inaudible release or unreleased.

ː   ː ː ː ː ː ː ː   ɛː aː nː

Length.   In handwriting, this symbol is normally a colon; in careful transcription it is made of two triangles.

ˑ   ˑ ˑ ˑ ˑ ˑ ˑ   ɔˑ lˑ sˑ

Half length.   In handwriting, this symbol is normally a raised dot; in careful transcription it is made of a triangle.

˕   ˕ ˕ ˕ ˕ ˕ ˕   e˕ j˕ o˕

Down arrow.   Shows a pronunciation lower or more open than usual.

˔   ˔ ˔ ˔ ˔ ˔ ˔   ə˔ ɔ˔ e˔

Up arrow.   Shows a pronunciation higher or more closed than usual.

k꜌ t꜌ ʌ꜌

Right arrow. Shows a pronunciation more retracted (towards that back of the vocal tract) than usual.

g˖ l˖ ɨ˖

Left arrow. Shows a pronunciation more advanced (towards the lips) than usual.

ꜛba ꜛni

Upstep. A superscript shafted arrow pointing up.

ꜜdo ꜜsu

Downstep. A superscript shafted arrow pointing down.

ɣ ƚ ᴀ

Mid tilde. A diacritic indicating either velarisation or pharyngealisation. Drawn horizontally through the middle of a symbol. Care must be taken that the basic symbol is clear. See superscript ram's horns and superscript reversed glottal stop.

ˈga ˈɛ

Primary stress. Precedes a syllable with primary stress.

ˌku ˌðo

Secondary stress. Precedes a syllable with secondary stress.

ˌˌfa ˌˌle

Tertiary stress. Precedes a syllable with tertiary stress.

Miscellaneous symbols

*blɛx *sʌ

Asterisk /ˈæstəɹɪsk/. Often used to indicate a form which is ungrammatical or nonexistent. Sometimes used to indicate a proper name: *e.g.*, [*ˌælˈbəɹtə].

g͡b k͡p p͡t

Top ligature. Written above two symbols to indicate that they are pronounced simultaneously (*e.g.*, [k͡p]) or that they form a single phonological unit (*e.g.*, an affricate [t͡ʃ]).

[opsk]

Square brackets. Used in pairs to enclose phonetic transcriptions.

/ mudʒ /

Solidus /ˈsɑlɪdəs/ (pl. **solidi** /ˈsɑlɪˌdi/). Also known as **virgule** /ˈvəɹgjul/ and **slant line**. Used in pairs to enclose phonemic transcriptions.

APPENDIX D
CHOMSKY-HALLE FEATURES

The features proposed by Chomsky and Halle /ˈtʃɑmski ˈhæli/ in *The Sound Pattern of English* (1968) have had an enormous influence in phonetics and phonology. The majority of phonological literature during the past twenty years refers to this system. This appendix includes the features necessary for a description of English to help you understand how this system works.

MAJOR CLASS FEATURES

The features [consonantal], [syllabic], and [sonorant] divide sounds into large, basic classes.

[consonantal]: The feature [consonantal] divides sounds into consonants and vowels. The criterion is the degree of opening in the vocal tract. The dividing line between [+cons] and [–cons] sounds lies in the degree of closure. Sounds with a closure as great or greater than an approximant are [+cons].

    [+cons] : obstruents, nasals, approximants
    [–cons] : glides, vowels

[syllabic]: The feature [syllabic] distinguishes the sounds which form the nucleus of a syllable from those which form the onset or coda. Any sound which forms the nucleus of a syllable is [+syll].

    [+syll] : vowels, syllabic consonants
    [–syll] : glides, non–syllabic consonants

[sonorant]: The feature [sonorant] divides consonants into two groups: those made with a fairly open vocal tract and those with the vocal tract closed or only sightly open. The [+son] sounds have considerable acoustic energy. They are usually voiced.

    [+son] : nasals, liquids, glides, vowels
    [–son] : obstruents

VOICING

[voiced]: Voiced sounds are [+vce], and voiceless ones are [–vce].

    [+vce] : [b d g dʒ v ð z ʒ m n ŋ l ɹ]; glides, vowels
    [–vce] : [p t k tʃ f θ s ʃ h]

PLACE OF ARTICULATION

The features [anterior] and [coronal] are the primary ones for place of articulation. The features [high], [back], and [low] are used to refine the primary classification. The table shows how [anterior] and [coronal] combine to divide the places of articulation into four categories:

	labial, labio-dental	dental, alveolar	palato-alveolar	palatal, retroflex, velar
anterior	+	+	−	−
coronal	−	+	+	−

[**anterior**]: The feature [anterior] distinguishes the front places of articulation from the back ones. The [+ant] sounds are made from the alveolar region forward; [−ant] describes those made further back.

    [+ant]   :   bilabial, labio-dental, dental, alveolar

    [−ant]   :   palato-alveolar, retroflex, palatal, velar; glides, vowels

[**coronal**]: The feature [coronal] /ˈkoɹənəl/ distinguishes the middle places of articulation from the ones at the far front and far back. The [+cor] sounds are made from the teeth back to the post-alveolar region. The specification [−cor] defines a discontinuous class of sounds consisting of those made with the lips and those made in the palatal region and farther back.

    [+cor]   :   dental, alveolar, palato-alveolar, retroflex

    [−cor]   :   bilabial, labio-dental, palatal, velar; glides, vowels

The features [anterior] and [coronal] are not sufficient to describe all places of articulation. We need in addition the features [high], [low], and [back] which are used to refine these categories.

[**high**]: The feature [high] is used to distinguish sounds made with the body (front and back) of the tongue raised. The [+high] sounds include those from the palato-alveolar through the velar region, and also high vowels.

    [+high]   :   palato-alveolar, retroflex, palatal, velar; high vowels, glides

    [−high]   :   bilabial, labio-dental, dental, alveolar; mid and low vowels

[**low**]: The feature [low] is used to distinguish sounds made with the body of the tongue lowered. All low vowels are [+low]. Note that mid vowels are [−high, -low]. For the purposes of feature specification, the consonant [h] is considered to be a glottal fricative, and thus [h] is [+low].

    [+low]   :   [h]; low vowels

    [−low]   :   all consonants except [h]; mid and high vowels, glides

[**back**]: The feature [back] is used to distinguish sounds with the tongue body retracted; [+back] consonants include all those from the velars back. Central and back vowels are [+back]. As mentioned above, [h] is considered a glottal fricative, and thus is [−back]. Note that there is no feature [front].

    [+back]   :   velars and [h]; central and back vowels; [w]

    [−back]   :   consonants other than [h] and the velars; front vowels, [j]

MANNER OF ARTICULATION

[**continuant**]: With [–cont] sounds, the air is blocked from passing through the oral cavity. Note particularly that with nasal stops, no air passes out the mouth, only out the nose; nasals therefore are [–cont].

[+cont]	:	fricatives, approximants, glides, vowels
[–cont]	:	stops, nasal stops, affricates

[**nasal**]: The [+nasal] sounds have air passing through the nasal cavity. With [–nasal] sounds, there is a velic closure, preventing air from entering the nasal passage.

[+nasal]	:	nasal consonants; nasal vowels
[–nasal]	:	all other sounds

[**strident**]: The feature [strident] is primarily used to distinguish [s z ʃ ʒ] from [θ ð]. The [+strid] sounds are characterised by a strong fricative noise in the higher frequencies. Affricates are [+strid] or [–strid] according to their fricative element.

[+strid]	:	[f v s z ʃ ʒ tʃ dʒ]
[–strid]	:	all other sounds

[**delayed release**]: The feature [+DR] is used to specify affricates.

[+DR]	:	[tʃ dʒ]
[–DR]	:	all other sounds

[**lateral**]: In [+lat] sounds air passes out the sides of the articulatory channel; the only [+lat] sound in English is [l].

[+lat]	:	[l]
[–lat]	:	all other sounds

VOWELS AND SEMIVOWELS

The features [high] and [low] describe height. Note that mid vowels are

$$\begin{bmatrix} \text{–high} \\ \text{–low} \end{bmatrix}$$

The specification

$$\begin{bmatrix} \text{+high} \\ \text{+low} \end{bmatrix}$$

is not possible. The feature [back] divides the vowels according to backness; central vowels are [+back]. There is no feature [front].

[**high**]: [+high] describes only the high vowels and semivowels; mid and low vowels are [–high]. See above for the use of [high] with consonants.

[+high]	:	[i ɪ u ʊ]; [w j]
[–high]	:	[e ɛ æ a ɑ o ɔ ʌ ə]

[**low**]: [+low] describes only the lowest vowels; mid and high vowels and semivowels are [–low]. For the use of [low] with consonants, see above.

[+low]	:	[æ a ɑ ɔ ʌ]
[–low]	:	[i ɪ u ʊ e ɛ o ə]; [w j]

[**back**]: [+back] includes the central and back vowels

    [+back] :   [u ʊ o ɔ ɑ ʌ ə]; [w]

    [–back] :   [i ɪ e ɛ æ a]; [j]

[**round**]: The vowels with lip rounding are [+rnd]; all others are [–rnd]. All English consonants are [–round].

    [+rnd] :   [u ʊ o ɔ]; [w]

    [–rnd] :   [i ɪ e ɛ æ a ɑ ʌ ə]; [j]

[**tense**]: The problems involving the feature [tense] are discussed in Chapter 4. Here, it is used to distinguish certain vowels on the basis of their phonotactic distribution. The feature [tense] is not necessary for English consonants, although [+tense] consonants could be considered equivalent to those that are [–vce], and [–tense] equivalent to [+vce] consonants. The vowels involved in diphthongs: [e a o ɔ] are considered [+tense], since the diphthongs pattern with the tense vowels.

    [+tns]:   [i e a ɑ u o ɔ]

    [–tns]:   [ɪ ɛ æ ʊ ʌ ə]

CHARTS
CONSONANTS

All consonants are [+cons]. Syllabic consonants are [+syll]; others are [–syll].

Place of Articulation

		ant	cor	high	low	back
labial	p b m	+	–	–	–	–
labio-dental	f v	+	–	–	–	–
dental	θ ð	+	+	–	–	–
alveolar	t d s z n	+	+	–	–	–
palato–alveolar	ʃ ʒ tʃ dʒ	–	+	+	–	–
retroflex	ɹ	–	+	+	–	–
palatal	j	–	–	+	–	–
velar	k g	–	–	+	–	+
glottal	h	–	–	–	+	+

Manner of articulation

	cons	son	syl	nas	lat
stops	+	–	–	–	–
fricatives	+	–	–	–	–
affricates	+	–	–	–	–
nasals	+	+	±	+	–
l	+	+	±	–	+
ɹ	+	+	±	–	–

The consonants [l ɹ m n ŋ] are [+syll] if they form the nucleus of a syllable as described in Chapter 3 under syllabic consonants; otherwise, they are [-syll].

Vowels

All vowels in English are [−cons, +son, +syll, −ant, −cor, −strid, −nas, −lat].

	high	low	back	round	tense
i	+	−	−	−	+
ɪ	+	−	−	−	−
e	−	−	−	−	+
ɛ	−	−	−	−	−
æ	−	+	−	−	−
a	−	+	−	−	+
ɑ	−	+	+	−	+
ʌ	−	+	+	−	−
ɔ	−	+	+	+	+
o	−	−	+	+	+
ʊ	+	−	+	+	−
u	+	−	+	+	+
ə	−	−	+	−	−

Semivowels

All semivowels in English are [−cons, +son, −syll, −ant, −cor, −strid, −nas, −lat].

	high	low	back	round
j	+	−	−	−
w	+	−	+	+

A PPENDIX E
PHONETIC CHARTS

THE INTERNATIONAL PHONETIC ALPHABET

The **International Phonetic Association (IPA)** was founded in 1886 and for the past century has recommended an alphabet of phonetic symbols suitable for the transcription of any language. The **International Phonetic Alphabet (IPA)** has been repeatedly revised over the decades, the last time being in the summer of 1989. The chart of the 1989 version of the Alphabet forms Figure E-1.

Although phonetic transcription in practice has steadily moved towards the official IPA, phoneticians and linguists have often introduced their own symbols and usages. In particular, linguists and, less often, phoneticians trained or practising in the United States have followed a slightly different tradition. *Phonetic Symbol Guide* (Pullum and Ladusaw, 1986) provides an excellent survey of transcription practice, although, of course, it does not include the revisions of the IPA of 1989.

THE INTERNATIONAL PHONETIC ALPHABET
(revised to 1989)

CONSONANTS

	Bilabial	Labiodental	Dental	Alveolar	Postalveolar	Retroflex	Palatal	Velar	Uvular	Pharyngeal	Glottal
Plosive	p b			t d		ʈ ɖ	c ɟ	k g	q ɢ		ʔ
Nasal	m	ɱ		n		ɳ	ɲ	ŋ	ɴ		
Trill	ʙ			r					ʀ		
Tap or Flap				ɾ		ɽ					
Fricative	ɸ β	f v	θ ð	s z	ʃ ʒ	ʂ ʐ	ç ʝ	x ɣ	χ ʁ	ħ ʕ	h ɦ
Lateral fricative				ɬ ɮ							
Approximant		ʋ		ɹ		ɻ	j	ɰ			
Lateral approximant				l		ɭ	ʎ	ʟ			
Ejective stop	p'			t'		ʈ'	c'	k'	q'		
Implosive	ɓ ɓ			ɗ ɗ			ʄ	ɠ	ʛ		

Where symbols appear in pairs, the one to the right represents a voiced consonant. Shaded areas denote articulations judged impossible.

Figure E-1 The International Phonetic Alphabet.

DIACRITICS

̥ Voiceless	n̥ d̥	̹ More rounded	ɔ̹	ʷ Labialized	tʷ dʷ	̃ Nasalized	ẽ
̬ Voiced	s̬ t̬	̜ Less rounded	ɔ̜	ʲ Palatalized	tʲ dʲ	ⁿ Nasal release	dⁿ
ʰ Aspirated	tʰ dʰ	̟ Advanced	u̟	ˠ Velarized	tˠ dˠ	ˡ Lateral release	dˡ
̤ Breathy voiced	b̤ a̤	̠ Retracted	i̠	ˤ Pharyngealized	tˤ dˤ	̚ No audible release	d̚
̰ Creaky voiced	b̰ a̰	̈ Centralized	ë	̴ Velarized or pharyngealized	ɫ		
̼ Linguolabial	t̼ d̼	̽ Mid centralized	e̽	̝ Raised	e̝ ɹ̝ (ɹ̝ = voiced alveolar fricative)		
̪ Dental	t̪ d̪	̘ Advanced Tongue root	e̘	̞ Lowered	e̞ β̞ (β̞ = voiced bilabial approximant)		
̺ Apical	t̺ d̺	̙ Retracted Tongue Root	e̙	̩ Syllabic	ɹ̩	̯ Non-syllabic	e̯
̻ Laminal	t̻ d̻	˞ Rhoticity	ə˞				

VOWELS

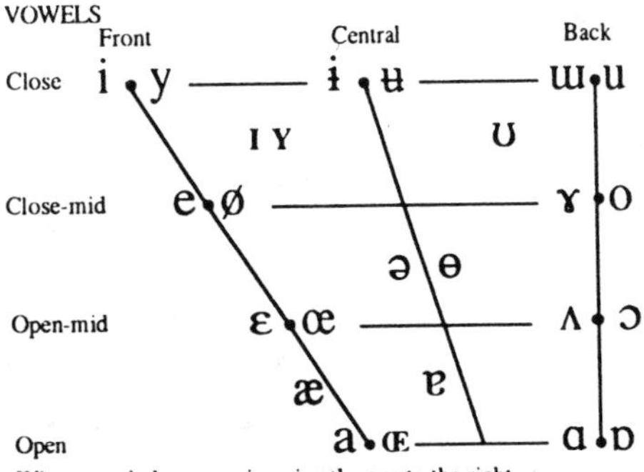

Where symbols appear in pairs, the one to the right represents a rounded vowel.

OTHER SYMBOLS

ʍ Voiceless labial-velar fricative

w Voiced labial-velar approximant

ɥ Voiced labial-palatal approximant

ʜ Voiceless epiglottal fricative

ʡ Voiced epiglottal plosive

ʢ Voiced epiglottal fricative

ɧ Simultaneous ʃ and x

ɜ Additional mid central vowel

Affricates and double articulations can be represented by two symbols joined by a tie bar if necessary. k͡p t͡s

ʘ Bilabial click

ǀ Dental click

ǃ (Post)alveolar click

ǂ Palatoalveolar click

ǁ Alveolar lateral click

ɺ Alveolar lateral flap

ɕ ʑ Alveolo-palatal fricatives

SUPRASEGMENTALS

ˈ Primary stress ˌfoʊnəˈtɪʃən

ˌ Secondary stress

ː Long eː

ˑ Half-long eˑ

̆ Extra-short ĕ

. Syllable break ɹi.ækt

| Minor (foot) group

‖ Major (intonation) group

‿ Linking (absence of a break)

↗ Global rise

↘ Global fall

LEVEL TONES

̋ or ˥	Extra-high	
́ ˦	High	
̄ ˧	Mid	
̀ ˨	Low	
̏ ˩	Extra-low	
↓	Downstep	
↑	Upstep	

CONTOUR TONES

̌	or ˩˥	rise
̂	˥˩	fall
᷄	˦˥	high rise
᷅	˩˨	low rise
᷈	˧˦˧	rise fall
		etc.

Figure E-1 The International Phonetic Alphabet. *(continued)*

SYMBOLS USED IN THIS BOOK

This book follows the IPA usage quite closely. One small variation is that retroflex consonants are transcribed with a diacritic, a subscript dot; compare the special IPA symbols in Figure E-1. The reason for this choice comes partly from my own teaching experience that students confuse the IPA symbols for retroflex consonants easily; further, phoneticians of every stripe use the subscript dot, probably more often than they use the special IPA symbols. A second variation is the use of arrowheads to indicate slight variations from the norm: [˘ ˄ ‹ ›]. The iconic simplicity of this system seems preferable to the more complex IPA recommendations.

The following charts show the symbols as they have been presented in this book:

VOWELS
Cardinal Vowels

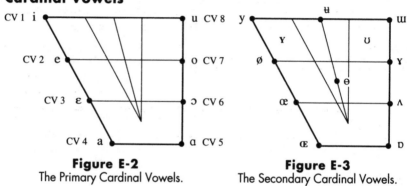

Figure E-2
The Primary Cardinal Vowels.

Figure E-3
The Secondary Cardinal Vowels.

Unrounded and Rounded Vowels

These charts show the additional vowel symbols together with the cardinal vowel symbols.

The symbol [ɜ] is available for a mid central vowel in addition to [ə].

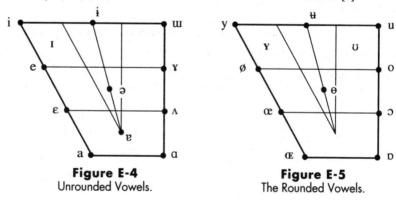

Figure E-4
Unrounded Vowels.

Figure E-5
The Rounded Vowels.

CONSONANTS

Where two symbols are included in the same cell of a chart, the one on the left is voiceless, and the one on the right is voiced.

Stops

	bilabial	dental	alveolar	retroflex	palatal
stop	p b	t̪ d̪	t d	ʈ ɖ	c ɟ

	velar	uvular	glottal	labial-alveolar	labial-palatal	labial-velar
stop	k g	q ɢ	ʔ	p͡t b͡d	p͡c b͡ɟ	k͡p g͡b

Fricatives

	bi-labial	labio-dental	dental	alveo-lar	alveolo-palatal	palato-alveolar	retro-flex
fricative	φ β	f v	θ ð	s z	ɕ ʑ	ʃ ʒ	ʂ ʐ

	palatal	velar	uvular	pharyn-geal	labial-palatal	labial-velar	velar palato-alveolar-
fricative	ç ʝ	x ɣ	χ ʁ	ħ ʕ	ɥ̊ ɥ	ʍ w	ɧ

[h] is a voiceless vowel, and [ɦ] is a murmured vowel.

Nasals

	bilabial	labio-dental	dental	alveolar	retro-flex	palatal	velar	uvular
nasal	m	ɱ	n̪	n	ɳ	ɲ	ŋ	N

Laterals

	dental	alveolar	retroflex	palatal	velar
fricatives	ɬ̪ ɮ̪	ɬ ɮ	ɭ̥ ɭ	ʎ̥ ʎ	ʟ̥ ʟ
approximants	l̥ l̪	l̥ l	l̥ ɭ	ʎ̥ ʎ	l̥ ʟ

Rhotics

bilabial trill	ʙ
dental trill	r̪
alveolar trill	r
alveolar fricative trill	r˄
uvular trill	ʀ
alveolar tap	ɾ
retroflex flap	ɽ
lateral flap	ɺ

Other approximants, including glides

	labio-dental	retro-flex	palatal	velar	uvular	labial–palatal	labial–velar
approximant	ʋ	ɻ, ɹ̩	j	ɰ	ʁ	ɥ	ʍ w

Airstream mechanisms

	pulmonic	glottalic	velaric
egressive	plosives p t k	ejectives pʼ tʼ kʼ	———
ingressive	———	*implosives ɓ ɗ ɠ	clicks ʘ ǀ ! ǁ ǂ

*As described in the text, implosives are not made with a glottalic ingressive mechanism; it is convenient and traditional, however, to show them on a chart in this slot.

Diacritics

The placement of the diacritic is shown in relation to an empty box ▢ representing the position of the main symbol.

▢̪	dental	▢ː	long
▢̣	retroflex	▢ˑ	half long
▢̃	nasal	▢ˆ	raised
▢˞	rhotic	▢˅	lowered
▢̥	voiceless	▢˂	fronted
▢̈	murmur	▢˃	backed
▢̰	creaky voice	ˈ▢	primary stress
▢̬	whisper	ˌ▢	secondary stress
▢̩	syllabic	ˌˌ▢	tertiary stress
▢̯	non-syllabic	▢́	high tone (primary stress)
▢˺	unreleased	▢̄	mid tone
▢ʰ	aspirated	▢̀	low tone (secondary stress)
▢ʷ	labialised	▢̂	falling tone
▢ʲ	palatalised	▢̌	rising tone
▢ˠ	velarised	▢↑	upstep
▢ˤ	pharyngealised	▢↓	downstep
▢̴	velarised or pharyngealised	◌͡◌	simultaneous articulation
▢ʔ	ejective		

Bouhuys, A. *Breathing.* Grune & Stratton, New York, 1974.

Browman, Catherine P. and Louis M. Goldstein. 'Dynamic modelling of phonetic structure'. In Fromkin, 1985.

Browman, Catherine P. and Louis M. Goldstein. 'Towards an articulatory phonology'. Phonology Yearbook 3.219–252, 1986.

Browman, Catherine P. and Louis Goldstein. 'Articulatory gestures as phonological units', in Phonology 6.201-252, 1989.

Butcher, Andrew and Kusay Ahmad. 'Some acoustic and aerodynamic characteristics of pharyneal consonants in Iraqi Arabic'. Phonetica 44.156-72, 1987.

Carnochan, J. 'A Study in the Phonology of an Igbo Speaker'. Bulletin of the School of Oriental and African Studies 12.415–30, 1948.

Catford, J. C. *Fundamental Problems in Phonetics.* Indiana University Press, Bloomington, 1977.

Catford, J. C. *A Practical Introduction to Phonetics.* Oxford University Press, Oxford, 1988.

Catford, J.C. and David B. Pisoni. 'Auditory vs. articulatory training in exotic sounds'. Modern Language Journal 54.477–81, 1970.

Chao, Yuen Ren. *Cantonese Primer.* Greenwood Press, New York, 1969 (1947).

Chatterji, Suniti Kumar. *Brief Sketch of Bengali Phonetics.* London and Paris, 1921. = 'Bengali phonetics', BSOS 2.1–25, 1921.

Chayen, M. J. *The Phonetics of Hebrew.* Mouton, The Hague, 1973.

Cho, Seung-Bog. *A Phonological Study of Korean.* Uppsala, 1967.

Chomsky, Noam and Morris Halle. *The Sound Pattern of English.* Harper and Row, New York, 1968.

Clark, John and Colin Yallop. *An Introduction to Phonetics and Phonology.* Basil Blackwell, 1990.

Clements, G. N. 'The geometry of phonological features'. Phonology Yearbook 2.223–50, 1985.

Cruttenden, Alan. *Intonation.* Cambridge University Press, Cambridge, 1986.

Crystal, Thomas H. and Arthur S. House. 'The duration of American–English stop consonants'. Journal of Phonetics 16.285–94, 1988a.

Crystal, Thomas H. and Arthur S. House. 'The duration of American–English vowels: an overview'. Journal of Phonetics 16.263–84, 1988b.

Delattre, Pierre and Donald C. Freeman. 'A dialect study of American *r*'s by X-ray motion picture'. Linguistics 44.29-68 1968.

Dickson, David Ross and Wilma Maue-Dickson. *Anatomical and Physiological Bases of Speech.* Little, Brown, Boston, 1982.

Dieth, Eugen. *Vademecum der Phonetik.* Francke, Berne, 1950.

Doke, Clement. *Phonetics of the Zulu Language.* Special number *Bantu Studies,* 1926.

Doke, Clement. *Textbook of Zulu Grammar.* Longmans Southern Africa, Capetown, 1927.

Dow, Francis D. M. *An outline of Mandarin Phonetics.* Faculty of Asian Studies in association with the Australian National University Press, Canberra, 1972.

Draper, M. H., P. Ladefoged, and D. Whitteridge. 'Expiratory muscles involved in speech', J. Physiol. 138.17–18P, 1957.

Draper, M. H., P. Ladefoged, and D. Whitteridge. 'Respiratory muscles in speech', J. Speech & Hearing Res. 2.16–27, 1958.

Draper, M. H., P. Ladefoged, and D. Whitteridge. 'Expiratory muscles and airflow during speech', British Medical Journal 18 June, 1837–43, 1960.

Dulong, G. and G. Bergeron. 'Le parler populaire du Québec et ses régions voisines'. *Atlas linguistique de l'est du Canada.* L'Éditeur officiel du Québec, Québec, 1980.

Essen, Otto von. *Grundzüge der hochdeutschen Satzintonation.* A. Henn, Ratingen, 1964.

Fennell, Trevor G. and Henry Gelsen. *A Grammar of Modern Latvian.* Mouton, The Hague, 1980.

Ferguson, Charles, A. and Munier Chowdhury. 'The phonemes of Bengali'. Lg. 36.22–59, 1960.

Fink, B. Raymond and Robert J. Demarest. *Laryngeal Biomechanics.* Harvard University Press, Cambridge, Mass., 1978.

Fok Chan Yuen-Yuen. *A Perceptual Study of Tones in Cantonese.* University of Hong Kong, 1974.

Fox, Anthony. *German Intonation: An Outline.* Oxford University Press, Oxford, 1984.

Friðjónsson, Jón. *Phonetics of Modern Icelandic.* Reykjavik, 1981.

Fromkin, Victoria A. *Phonetic Linguistics: Essays in Honor of Peter Ladefoged.* Academic Press, Orlando, 1985.

Fry, D. B., ed. *Acoustic Phonetics.* Cambridge University Press, Cambridge, 1976.

Fry, D. B. *The Physics of Speech.* Cambridge Univeristy Press, Cambridge, 1979.

Gairdner, W. H. T. *The Phonetics of Arabic.* Humphrey Milford, London, 1925.

Gendron, Jean-Denis. *Tendances phonétiques du français parlé au Canada.* Klincksieck, Paris, 1966.

Gimson, A. C. *A Introduction to the Pronunciation of English.* Edward Arnold, London, 1980.

Grant, William. *The Pronunciation of English in Scotland.* Cambridge University Press, Cambridge, 1913.

Gregg, Robert J. *A Student's Manual of French Pronunciation.* Macmillan, Toronto, 1960.

Halle, Morris and Jean-Roger Vergnaud. *An Essay on Stress.* MIT, 1987.

Halle, Morris and K. N. Stevens. 'On the feature "Advanced tongue root"'. Quarterly Progress Report, MIT Research Laboratory of Electronics 94.209–15, 1969.

Halle, Morris and K. N. Stevens. 'Some reflections on the theoretical bases of phonetics'. In Lindblom and Ohman 1979, 335–49.

Halle, Morris. 'On distinctive features and their articulatory implementation'. Natural Language and Linguistic Theory 1.91–105, 1983.

Handel, Stephen. *Listening : An Introduction to the Perception of Auditory Events.* MIT Press, Cambridge, 1989.

Hanna, Sami A. and Naguib Greis. *Writing Arabic.* E.J. Brill, Leiden, 1972.

Hardcastle, W.J. *Physiology of Speech Production: An Introduction for Speech Scientists.* Academic Press, London, 1976.

Henderson, Janette B. and Bruno H. Repp. 'Is a stop consonant released when followed by another stop consonant?' Phonetica 39.71–82, 1982.

Hillien, Harry and Patricia Hillien. *Current Issues in the Phonetic Sciences.* John Benjamins, Amsterdam, 1979.

Hoffman, C. F. *A Grammar of the Margi Language.* Oxford University Press, Oxford, 1963.

Howie, John Marshall. *Acoustical Studies of Mandarin Vowels and Tones.* Cambridge University Press, 1976.

Howren, Robert. 'The phonology of Rae Dogrib'. In National Museum of Man, 1 – 6, 1979.

Hulst, Harry van der and Norval Smith, eds. *Autosegmental Studies on Pitch Accent.* Foris, Dordrecht, 1988.

Hulst, Harry van der and Norval Smith. 'The variety of pitch accent systems: Introduction'. In Hulst, Harry van der and Norval Smith, pp. ix-xxiv, 1988.

Hyman, Larry M. *Phonology: Theory and Analysis.* Holt, Rinehart and Winston, New York, 1975.

Jakobson, Roman, Gunnar Fant, and Morris Halle. *Preliminaries to Speech Analysis.* MIT Press, Cambridge, Mass., 1952.

Jassem, Wiktor. 'The acoustics of consonants'. In Fry, 1976, 124–31.

Jones, Daniel. *An Outline of English Phonetics.* 9th ed. Cambridge University Press, Cambridge, 1975.

Jones, Daniel and Dennis Ward. *The Phonetics of Russian.* Cambridge University Press, Cambridge, 1969.

Kálmán, Béla. 'Hungarian Historical Phonology'. In Benkő and Imre, 49 – 84, 1972.

Kahane, Joel C. and John W. Folkins. *Atlas of Speech and Hearing Anatomy.* Charles E. Merrill, Columbus, 1984.

Kao, Diana L. *Structure of the Syllable in Cantonese.* Mouton, The Hague, 1971.

Keating, Patricia. 'A survey of phonological features'. UCLA Working Papers in Phonetics 66.124–50, 1987.

Killingley, Siew–Yue. *A new look at Cantonese Tones: Five or Six.* Newcastle upon Tyne, 1985.

Kim, C. W. 'A theory of aspiration'. Phonetica 21.107–16, 1970.

Kim, C. W. 'On the autonomy of the tensity features in stop classification (with special reference to Korean stops)'. Word 21.339–59, 1965.

King, Quindel. 'Chilcotin phonology and vocabulary'. In National Museum of Man, 7 – 41, 1979.

Kökeritz, Helge. *A Guide to Chaucer's Pronunciation.* University of Toronto Press, Toronto, 1978.

Kökeritz, Helge. *Shakespeare's Pronunciation.* Yale University Press, Toronto, 1953.

Kostić, Djordje and Rhea S. Das. *A Short Outline of Bengali Phonetics.* Statistical Publishing society, Calcutta, 1972

Kreidler, Charles W. *The Pronunciation of English.* Basil Blackwell, Oxford, 1989.

Ladefoged, Peter. 'Cross-linguistics studies of speech production'. Pp. 177–88 in MacNeilage 1983.

Ladefoged, Peter. *A Course in Phonetics.* Harcourt Brace Jovanovich, San Diego, 1982

Ladefoged, Peter. *A Phonetic Study of West African Languages.* Cambridge University Press, Cambridge, 1964.

Ladefoged, Peter. *Three Areas of Experimental Phonetics.* Oxford University Press, London, 1967

Ladefoged, Peter. *Preliminaries to Linguistic Phonetics.* University of Chicago Press, 1971.

Ladefoged, Peter, A. Cochran, and S. Disner. 'Laterals and trills'. Journal of the International Phonetic Association 7.46–54, 1977.

Ladefoged, Peter and Morris Halle. 'Some major features of the International Phonetic Alphabet'. Lg. 64.577–82, 1988.

Ladefoged, Peter and Peri Bhaskararao. 'Non-quantal aspects of consonant production: a study of retroflex consonants'. Journal of Phonetics 11.291–302, 1983.

Ladefoged, Peter and Ian Maddieson. *Some of the sounds of the World's Languages: (Preliminary version).* UCLA Working Papers in Phonetics, 64, 1986.

Ladefoged, Peter and Anthony Traill. 'Linguistic phonetic description of clicks'. Lg. 60.1–20, 1984.

Laufer, Asher and I. D. Condax 'The epiglottis as an articulator'. JIPA 9.50–6, 1979.

Léon, Pierre R. *Prononciation du français standard.* Didier, Montréal, 1966.

Léon, Pierre R., ed. *Recherches sur la structure phonique du français canadien.* Didier, Montréal, 1968.

Lieberman, Philip and Sheila E. Blumstein. *Speech Physiology, Speech Perception, and Acoustic Phonetics.* Cambridge University Press, Cambridge, 1988.

Lindau, Mona. 'The feature Advanced tongue root'. In Voeltz 1974, 127–34.

Lindau, Mona. 'The feature expanded'. Journal of Phonetics 7.163–176, 1979.

Lindau, Mona. 'Vowel features' Lg. 54.541–63, 1978.

Lindau, Mona. 'The story of /r/'. In Fromkin 1985, 157–68.

Lindblom, B. and S. Ohman. *Frontiers of Speech Communication.* Academic Press, London, 1979.

Lisker, L. and A. S. Abramson. 'Linguistic segments, acoustic segments, and synthetic speech'. Lg. 33, 1957.

Lisker, L. and A. S. Abramson. 'Distinctive features and laryngeal control'. Lg. 47. 767–85, 1971.

Lowery, Brenda Marion. 'The phonological system of Blackfoot'. In National Museum of Man, 41 – 66, 1979.

McAlpin, David W. 'The morphophonology of the Dravidian Noun'. In Schiffman and Eastman, 206 – 223, 1975.

McCarthy, John J. 'Feature geometry and dependency: A review'. Phonetica 43.84–108, 1988.

McCawley, James D. *The Phonological Component of a Grammar of Japanese.* Mouton, The Hague,1968.

MacNeilage, Peter F. 'Neural mechanisms in speech production'. In Hillien and Hillien 1979.

MacNeilage, Peter F. *The Production of Speech.* Springer-Verlag, New York, 1983.

Maddieson, Ian and Karen Emmorey. 'Is there a valid distinction between voiceless lateral approximants and fricatives?' Phonetica 41.181–90, 1984.

Maddieson, Ian. *Patterns of Sounds.* Cambridge University Press, 1984.

Maddieson, Ian. 'Phonetic cues to syllabification'. In Fromkin 1985, 203–22.

Malmberg, Bertil. *Svensk Fonetik.* Gleerups, Lund, 1970.

Merrifield, William R. 'Palantla Chinantec syllable types'. Anthropological Linguistics 5.1–16, 1963.

Minifie, Fred, Thomas J. Hixon, and Frederick Williams. *Normal Aspects of Speech, Hearing, and Language.* Prentice-Hall, Englewood Cliffs, N.J., 1973.

Mitchell, A. G., and A. Delbridge. *The Speech of Australian Adolescents: A survey.* Angus Robertson, Sydney, 1965.

Mougeon, Raymond and Édouard Beniak. *Le français canadien parlé hors Québec.* Presses de l'Université Laval, Québec, 1989.

National Museum of Man *Contributions to Canadian Linguistics.* Mercury Series, Canadian Ethnology Service Paper No. 50., National Museums of Canada, Ottawa, 1979.

Newmeyer, Frederick J. *Linguistics: The Cambridge Survey.* Cambridge University Press, Cambridge, 1988.

Norlin, Kjell. *A Phonetic Study of Emphasis and Vowels in Egyptian Arabic.* Working Papers No. 30, Lund University, Department of Linguistics, 1987.

Obrecht, Dean H. *Effects of the Second Formant on the Perception of Velarization Consonants in Arabic.* Mouton, the Hague, 1968.

O'Grady, William and Michael Dobrovolsky. *Contemporary Linguistic Analysis: An Introduction.* Copp Clark Pitman, Toronto, 1987.

Okell, John. *A Reference Grammar of Colloquial Burmese.* Oxford, London, 1969.

Ostiguy, Luc and Robert Sarrasin. *Phonétique comparée du français et de l'anglais nord-américans.* Trois Rivières, Réseau 1985.

Paddock, Harold. 'Some variations in the phonology and grammar of Newfoundland English'. ms., 1974.

Painter, Colin. 'Cineradiographic data on the feature "covered" in Twi vowel harmony'. Phonetica 28.97–120, 1973.

Perkell, J. 'Physiology of speech production: A preliminary study of two suggested revisions of the features specifying vowels'. Quarterly Progress Report, MIT Research Laboratory of Electronics 102.123–139, 1971.

Picard, Marc. *An Introduction to the Comparative Phonetics of English and French in North America.* Amsterdam: John Benjamins, 1987.

Pierrehumbert, Janet and Mary Beckman. *Japanese Tone Structure.* MIT, 1988.

Pike, Kenneth. *Phonetics.* University of Michigan, Ann Arbor, 1963.) reports

Pike, Kenneth. 'Tongue-root position in practical phonetics'. Phonetica 17, 129–40, 1967.

Pullum, Geoffrey K. and William A. Ladusaw. *Phonetic Symbol Guide.* University of Chicago Press, Chicago, 1986.

Ramos, Teresita V. *Tagalog Structures.* University of Hawaii Press, Honolulu, 1971.

Roberts, Peter A. *West Indians and their Language.* Cambridge University Press, Cambridge, 1988.

Samarin, William J. *The Gbeya Language: Grammar, Texts, and Vocabularies.* University of California Publications in Linguistics, 44. 1966.

Santerre, L. 'Les (r) montréalais en regression rapide', in Lavoie *Les français régionaux du Québec.* Protée vii.2, 1979.

Santerre, L. 'Des r montréalais imprévisibles et inouïs'. Revue québécoise de linguistique 12.77–96, 1982.

Schiffman, Harold F. and Carol M. Eastman. *Dravidian Phonological Systems.* University of Washington, Seattle, 1975.

Schuh, W. R. 'The phonology of intonation in Hausa'. NELS 17,327–41, 1986.

Selkirk, Elisabeth. 'On the major class features and syllable theory'. In *Language Sound Structure,* eds. Mark Aronoff and Richard T. Oehrle, MIT, 1984.

Shearer, William M. *Illustrated Speech Anatomy.* Charles C. Thomas, Springfield, Ill, 1979.

Solá, Donald F. *Spoken Cuzco Quechua.* Yachay-Wasi Academy of Quechua, Lima, 1972.

Stetson, R. H. *Motor Phonetics.* North Holland Publ. Co., Amsterdam, 1928, 1951.

Stewart, J. M. 'Tongue root position in Akan vowel harmony'. Phonetica 16. 185–204, 1967.

Strevens, Peter. 'Spectra of Fricative noise in human speech'. In Fry 1976, 132–50.

Suárez, Jorge A. *The Mesoamerican Indian Languages.* Cambridge University Press, Cambridge, 1983.

Syamala Kumari, B. *Malayalam Phonetic Reader.* Central Institute of Indian Languages, Mysore.

Thomas, A. *La variation phonétique cas du franco-ontarien.* Didier, Montreal, 1987.

Thompson, Laurence C. *A Vietnamese Grammar.* University of Washington Press, Seattle, 1965.

Tranel, Bernard. *The Sounds of French.* Cambridge UP, Cambridge, 1987.

Trubetzkoy, N. S. *Grundzüge der Phonologie.* Vandenhoeck & Ruprecht, Göttingen, 1939.

Tyler, Stephen A. *Koya: An Outline Grammar.* University of California Publications in Linguistics 54, Berkeley, 1969.

Vance, Timothy J. *An Introduction to Japanese Phonology.* State University of New York Press, Albany, 1987.

Vinay, J.-P. 'Bout de la langue ou fond de la gorge'. French Review 23.489–98, 1950.

Voeltz, E. *Third Annual Conference on African Languages.* Indiana University Press, Bloomington, 1974.

Walker, Douglas C. *The Pronunciation of Canadian French.* University of Ottawa Press, Ottawa, 1984.

Walker, Richard. 'Central Carrier phonemics'. In National Museum of Man, 93 – 118, 1979.

Wardhaugh, Ronald. *An Introduction to Sociolinguistics.* Basil Blackwell, Oxford, 1986.

Westerman, D. and Ida Ward, *Practical Phonetics for Students of African Languages.* Oxford University Press, Oxford, 1957.

Witting, Claes. *Studies in Swedish Generative Phonology.* Uppsala, 1977.

Zemlin, Willard R. *Speech and Hearing Science.* Prentice-Hall, Englewoods Cliffs, N.J., 1981.

INDEX

A

Abi Dabi 255
abdominal muscles 259
acoustic phonetics 124–135
adam's apple 4, **5**, 11
advanced tongue root, see *expanded*.
affricates 20, 39, 173, 223, 233
air pressure 256, 260
airstream mechanisms 256–264
    glottalic 258, **261**, 262
    œsophagic **264**
    pulmonic 258, **261**
    simultaneous 263
    velaric 258, 262–264
allophones 33–34
    English 306–311
alveolar ridge 5, 6, 12
alveolars **6**, 18, 204
    English 37
alveolo-palatals 204, **206**, 255
Amharic 268
amplitude 126
American English 94–96
analysis by synthesis 302
antepenultimate syllable 272
apex 8, **12**
aphasia 299
apical 8, 201–203
approximants 20, 222, 224

---

† Page numbers in bold-faced type refer
to illustrations

    English 45, 47
    French 109
    Arabic 210, 221
articulation, see also *place* and *manner*.
    double **211**
    secondary 212, **213**
articulators 5, 199
arytenoid cartilages 239, **240–242**
assimilation 37, 40
aspiration 33, 39, 68, 250
Australian English 99–100

B

back, see *dorsum, vowels–backness*.
Bearlake Slave 266
Bengali 217, 254, 255, 292
Bernoulli principle 226, 244
Bhojpuri 254
bilabials 6, 17, 200
binaural 298
blade, see *lamina*.
bounded foot 284
Boyle's Law 256
branching nuclei 272
breathing 245, **246**
broad transcription 35
broad-band spectrogram 140
Broca's aphasia 300
bronchi 4, **5**, 258
Bura 212
Burmese 243

C

calligraphy 335–353
Canadian English 21–22, 90
Canadian French 107–119, 196
Canadian raising 59, **60**, 66
Cantonese 291
cardinal vowels 179–183, 192–193, 362
cartilagenous glottis 240, **241**, **242**
categorical perception 298
central 20, see also *vowels–backness.*
Central Carrier 292
Chaucer, Geoffrey 137
chest pulse 273
Chilcotin 268
Chinese 261, 278, 279, 291
Chomsky, Noam 171
Chomsky-Halle features 171
clicks **262**, 266
closed syllable 56, 271
cochlea 295, **296**
coda 271
connected speech 72
consonants 14, 222, 363–364
 English 16–21, 33–47, 73, 150–157,
  306–311
 French 108, 112–113
 manner of articulation 20, 153, 168,
  199, 222–230
 place of articulation 17, 37–39, 152,
  167, 199–214
 syllabic 46, 271–272
contextual length 58
continuants 20, 168
contour tones 279
contrast 34, 164
coronal 167
creaky voice **247**, 254
creoles 97
cricoid cartilage 238, **239**, **240**, **241**
cycle 127

D

degenerate syllable 283
decibel 126

dentals **6**, 17, 120, 216, 219
 English 37
 French 110
diacritics 33, 348–353, 365
diaphragm 259
diphthongs 123, 189, 194
 English 26–27, 56, 144
 French 117
distributional restrictions 55
dorsal 167
dorso-velars, see *velars.*
dorsum 8, **12**
double articulations 19, **211**, 219, 268
downdrift 279, 280
downstep 280
drift 279–280
Dutch 305

E

ear 294–296
ejectives **261**, 265
elision 118
English
 acoustics 139–157
 American 94–96
 Australian 99–100
 Canadian 21–22, 89–90
 consonants 16–21, 33–47, 73,
  150–157, 306–311
 as used in this book 21
 dialects 88–100
 history 88
 RP 90–94
 Scottish 98–99
 stress 28–29, 59, 77, 147
 vowels 21–28, 141–150
 West Indian 97–98
environment 34
epiglottis **5**, 9, 210, **239**, **241**
Eskimo, see *Inuktitut.*
Estonian 305
Ewe 86, 200, 217, 233, 277
expanded vowels 187
external intercostals 259, 273
extrametrical syllable 285

F

F₀, see *fundamental.*

F_0, see *fundamental.*
falling diphthongs 189
false vocal cords 241
falsetto 247
Fant, Gunnar 170
faucial pillars **12**
feature detector theory 301
feature geometry 170–176
features 164–176, 354–358
flaps 228, 237
foot, metrical 283
formants 134, 140, 150
   English vowels 141
Fourier analysis 129, 139
free variation 34
French 107–119, 248, 283
   approximants 109
   consonants 108, 112–113
   dentals 110
   diphthongs 117
   elision 118
   laxing 116
   nasals 109, 113
   nasal vowels 114, 115
   /r/ 111
   rhythm 119
   schwa 114
   stops 108
   stress 119
   suprasegmentals 118–119
   syllable 118
   voicing 109
   vowels 113–118
frequency 127
   fundamental 130
   perception 296, 297
frication 222
fricatives 20, 153, 222–223
   English 42
   French 108
front 8, **12**, 169, 207 see also *vowels–backness.*
fundamental 130

G

Gã 195, 218, 219
gap 74
Gbeya 262, 292, 304
geminates 271
Georgian 105, 217
German 208, 217, 233, 234, 277, 287
glides 20, 25, 116, 189, 225
glottal 19, 210
glottal stop 4, 19, 45, 69, 210, 242
glottal wave 140
glottalic airstream mechanisms 261–262
glottis 4, 238–252
Greek 218
Gujarati 254

H

h-aspiré 118
Halle, Morris 170–171, 188
harmonics 130
Hausa 228, 280
head, metrical 283
hearing 294–296
heavy syllables 271, 27**2**
Hertz 127
high, see *vowels–height.*
Hindi 247
homorganic 38
Hungarian 219
hyoid bone 239

I

Icelandic 195
Igbo 279
Ijo 195
implosives **262**, 266, 268
inaudible release 51
inherent length 57
intensity 126, **297**
interdentals 18, 201
internal intercostals 258

International Phonetic Alphabet 359
International Phonetic Association 15, 179, 237, 359
initiator 256
intonation 286–288
   English 79
   Swedish 281
intonation contours 79
Inuktitut 237
IPA, see *International Phonetic Alphabet / Association.*
Italian 277

J

Jakobson, Roman 170
Japanese 228, 243, 255, 275, 282

K

kinæsthetic 19
Korean 251
Koya 286

L

labial 167
labial-velars 19, 211, 219
labialisation 212, 217
labio-dental 6, 17
lamina 9, **12**
laminal 18, 168
Lango 254
Lardil 260
laryngeal 210
larynx 4, 5, 11, 238, **239, 240, 241**
lateral onset and release 45
lateralisation 299
laterals 20, 45, 157, 169, 229, 253
lax, see *tense.*
length 36, 57–59, 147, 188, 276, 290
levels of representation 34
liaison, French 117

ligamental glottis 240, **241**, 242
light syllables 271, **272**
Lindau, Mona 188
lips **5**, 6
liquids 21, 225
loudness 127
low, see *vowels–height.*
lower articulators 199
lungs 3, **5, 259**

M

Malayalam 202
manner of articulation 20, 39–47, 153, 168, 199, 222–230
Maranungku 284
Margi 247
masking 297
mel 296, **297**
mid, see *vowels–height.*
minimal pair 34
monophthongs 55
   English 56
moræ 275–276
morpheme 35
motor theory 302
multivalued oppositions 166
murmur 246, 252, 254
   English 43

N

Nama 263
narrow transcription 35, 63
narrow-band spectrogram 140
nasal 21, 168
   cavity 5
   onset and release 45
   vowels 62, 69, 121, 122, 186
nasals 9, 21, 155, 223, 230
   French 109, 114–115
   homorganic 38
naturalness 164
Newfoundland English 96, 261
Ngwe 184
node 172

noise 151
nucleus 74, 271
Nupe 279

O

obstruents 21, 223
œsophagus **5**, 258, 264
Ohm, Georg 139
onset 74, 271
　lateral 45
　nasal 44
open syllables 56, 271
opposition 165
oral 9, 21, 223
　cavity 5, 12
orthography 14
overlapping 52
　English 41, **42**

P

palatalisation 212, 213, 218
palatals 7, 8, 19, 207, 216
palate **5**, 7, 12
palato-alveolars 6, **7**, 18, 204, 206, 255
penultimate syllable 272
perception 296–302
pharyngealisation 212, 214, 220
pharyngeals 210, 236
pharynx **5**, 12
phonation 238–252
phoneme 34
phonetic matrix theory 301
phonology 34
phonotactics 55
　English 57, 73
phrase
　phonetic 72
Pig Latin 234, 255
Pinyin 278
pitch 127, 278, see also *tone* and
　intonation.
pitch accent 281
place of articulation 17, 152, 167,
　199–214

English 37–39
plosives 260
point of articulation, see *place of
　articulation.*
Polish 204, 285
posterior 168
pulmonic airstream mechanisms
　258–261

Q

Quechua 209, 261

R

radical 9, 187, 210
Rae Dogrib 269
rate of speech 299
Received Pronunciation 90–94
register tones 279
release 40–41, 45
resonance 133–135
retroflex 7, 18, 37, 206, **207**, 219, 255
rhotacisation, see *rhotic.*
rhotic 47, 91, 186, 224
rhyme 271
rhythm 82, 119
rising diphthongs 189
root 9, 187, 210
root node 172, 175
root tier 175
rounding 24, 179
RP, see *Received Pronunciation.*

S

schwa 27, **28**, 114
Scots Gaelic 188, 208, 214, 248, 250,
　283
Scott, Sir Walter 197
Scottish English 98–99
secondary articulation 212, **213**
segments 14, 15, 164, 270, 298

semivowels 20, 25, 116, 189, 225
Shakespeare, William 87, 106, 163
Sherbro 202, 211, 279
shibilants 21, 223
Shona 229
sibilants 21, 223
sine wave 125
sinusoidal wave, see *sine wave.*
sonorants 21, 53, 167, 223
sonority 273–275
   curve 274
   hierarchy 273
Sound Pattern of English 171
sound waves 124–131
Spanish 215, 226
spectrogram 131, 140–141, 157
spectrum 131–133
spike 153
spirants, see *fricatives.*
step 279–280
Stevens, Kenneth 188
stops 20, 222, 223
   English 39–42
   French 108
stress 282, 284
   English 28–29, 59, 77, 147
   French 119
stressed-timed 83
stricture 222–223
strong form 78
subglottal 4
supralaryngeal 4
suprasegmentals 14, 270
   English 72–83
   French 118–119
Swahili 68
Swedish 212, 261, 282-283
syllabic consonants 46, 271, 272
syllable-timed 83, 119
syllables 270–276
   closed 56
   English 73–74
   extrametrical 285
   French 118
   heavy 272
   light **272**
   open 56
   perception 273–275
   production 272–273
   prominence 274
   structure 73–74, 270, **271**–272
   tonic 80

symbols 14, 33, 335–353, 359–365
   consonants 341–347, 363–364
   diacritics 33, 348–353, 365
   vowels 337–340, 362

T

Tagalog 211, 217
taps 157, 226
   English 41, 51, 54
   RP 91
teeth **5**, 6
Temne 202
tense 55–57, 169, 189
Thai 292
thyroid cartilage 238, **239–242**
tip, see *apex.*
Tojolabal 261
tone 289–290
   Swedish 281
tone languages 79, 277–283
tongue **5**, 8–9, 12
tonic syllable 80
trachea 4, **5**, 238, **239**, 258
transcription 14, 35, 63
transition 152
tree 172
trills 226, 235–236
Twi 207, 213, 220

U

Ukrainian 214
ultima 272
unary oppositions 165
unstressed 28
upper articulators 199
upstep 280, 281
utterance 14
uvula **5**, 8, **12**
uvulars **8, 111,** 209, 234, 235

V

velaric airstream mechanisms 262–264
velarisation 212, 214, 218
velars 7, 19, 37, 104, 207–209
velic 9, 10
velum 5, 7, 12
Ventricle of Morgagni **241**
vertical striations 147
vibrations 124
Vietnamese 268, 279
vocal cords 4, **5**, 11, 238, **240**, **241**
    false **241**
vocal tract 2, **5**, 139, 199, **259**
voice bar 154
voice onset time 39, 40, 248
voicing 4, 36, 109, 147, 151, 169,
    243–244, 253
VOT, see *voice onset time.*
vowel systems 190
vowels 14, 16, 178, 186–191, 220, 222,
    236
    acoustic properties 183
    allophonic variation in English 57
    and stress in English 59
    backness 23, 24, 178
    before /l/ in English 62
    before /ɹ/ in English 60
    cardinal 179
    central 27, 178
    English 21–28, 55–63, 89, 141

    expanded 187
    formants 141–150
    French 113–118
    front 24, 178
    height 23, 169, 178
    length 147, 188
    nasal 62, 114, 115, 186
    rhotacised 186
    rounding 23, 24, 178

W

waveform 125
waves, see *sound waves.*
weak form 78
Weri 283
Wernicke's aphasia 300
West Indian English 97–98
wh-questions 81
whisper 247, 255
wide-band, see *broad–band.*
word line, metrical 284

Y

yes-no questions 81
Yoruba 290